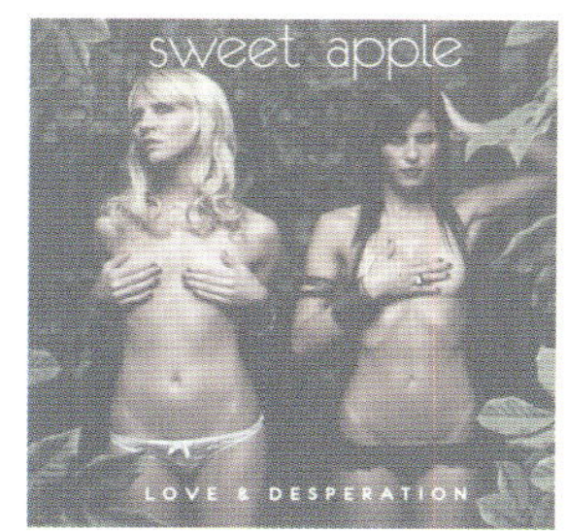

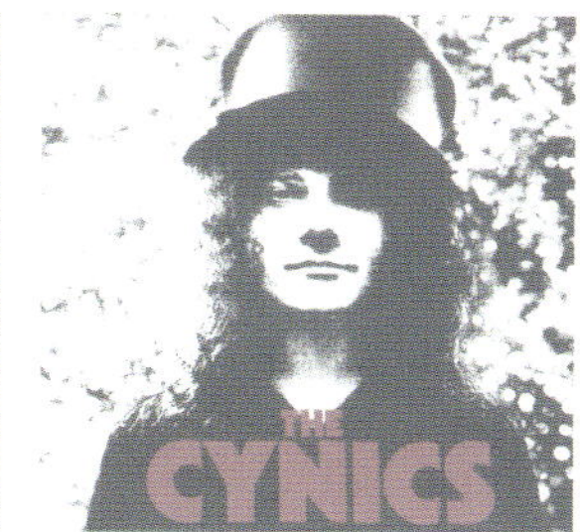

COVERED *CLASSIC SLEEVES AND THEIR IMITATORS*

COMPILED BY JAN BELLEKENS

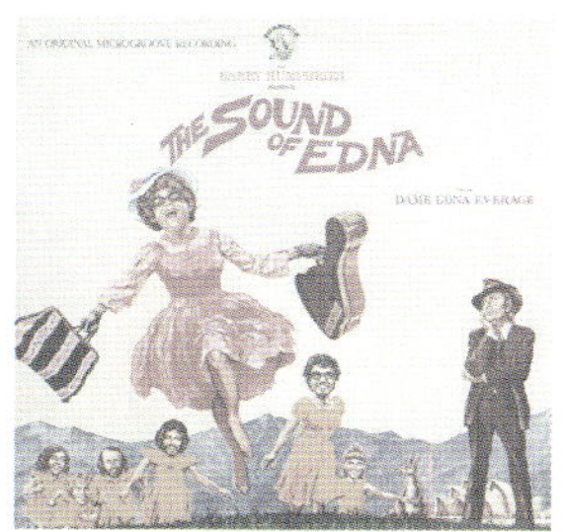

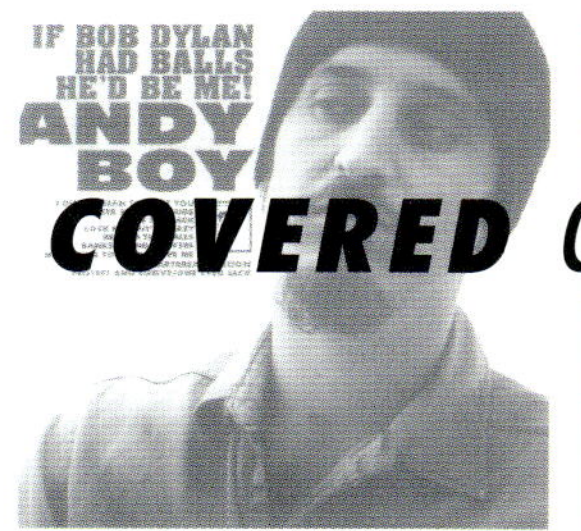

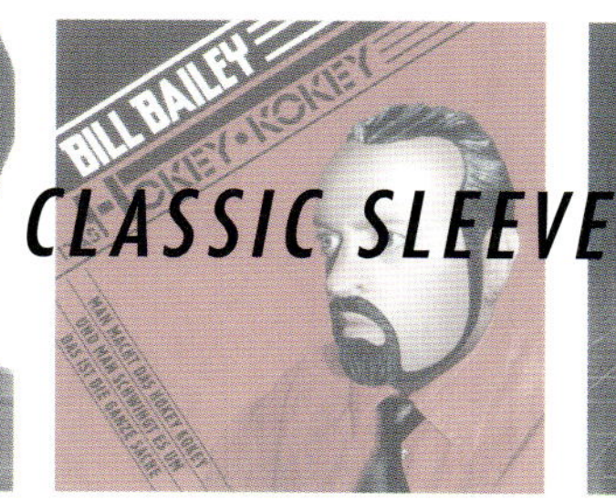

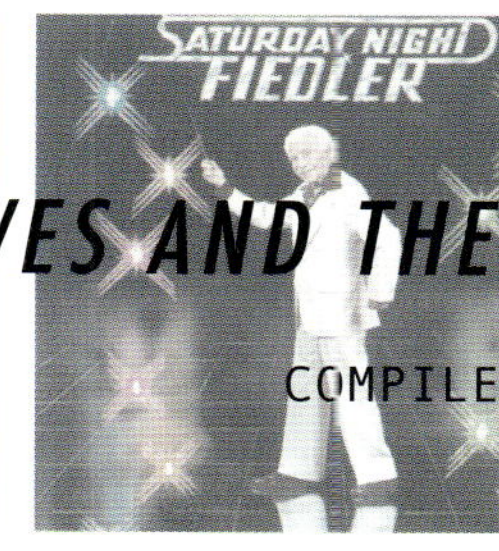

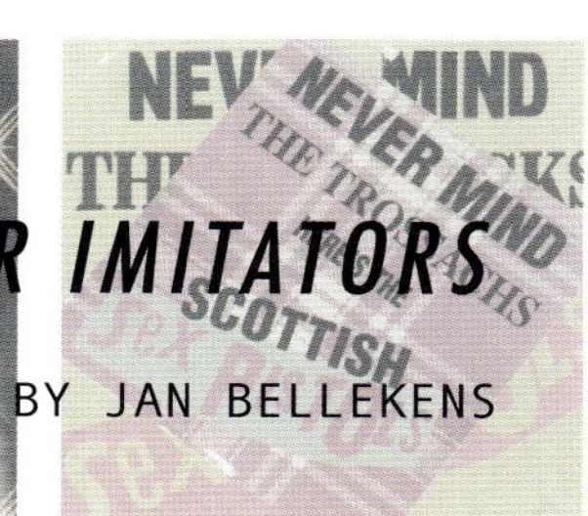

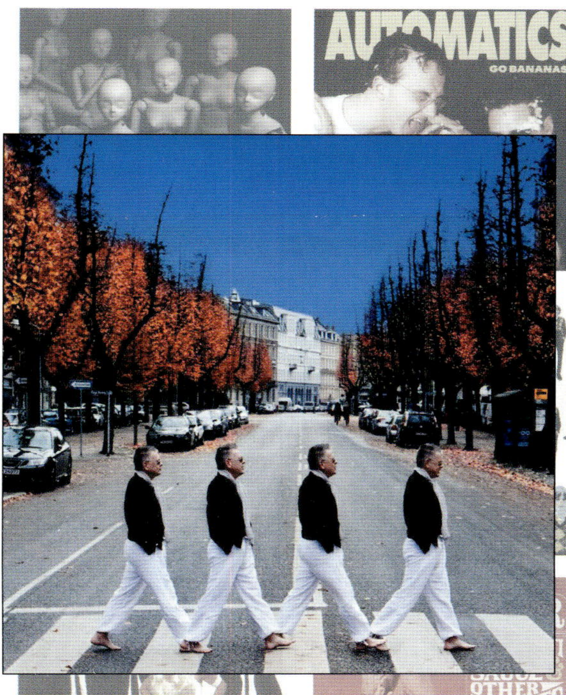

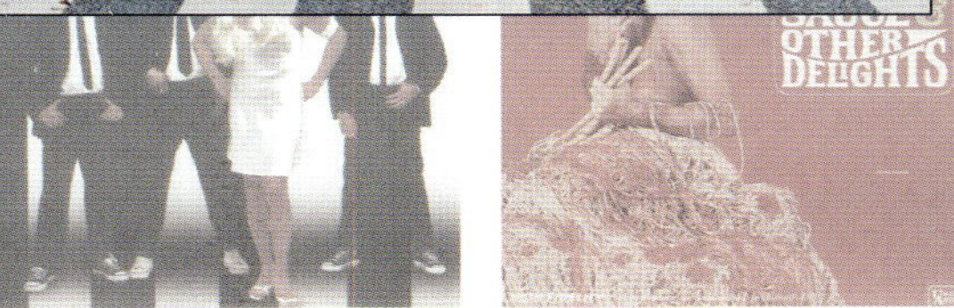

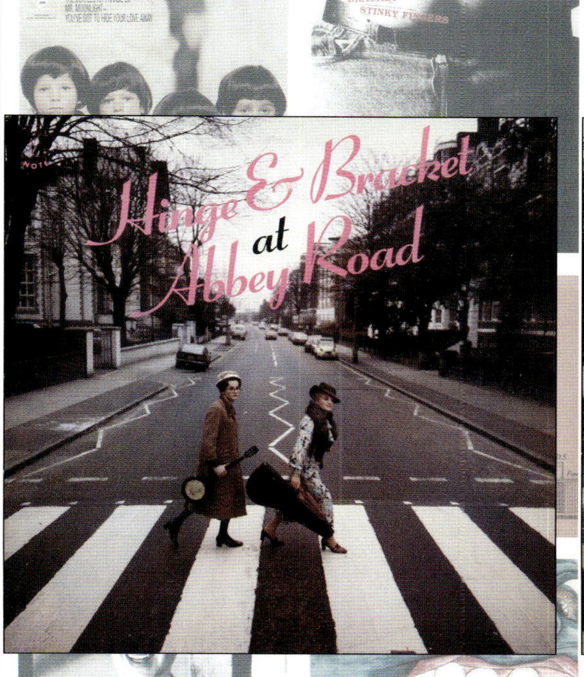

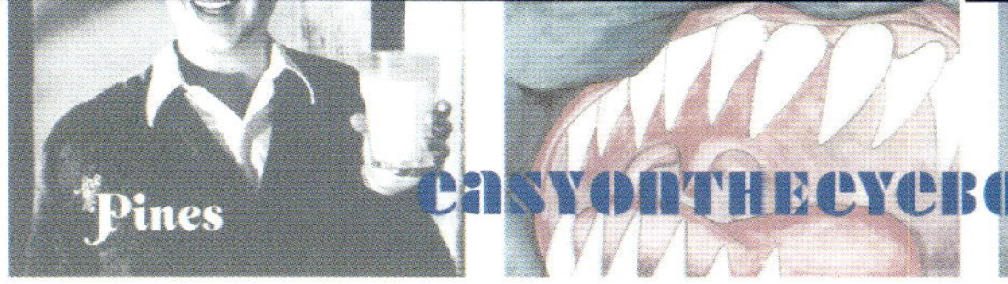

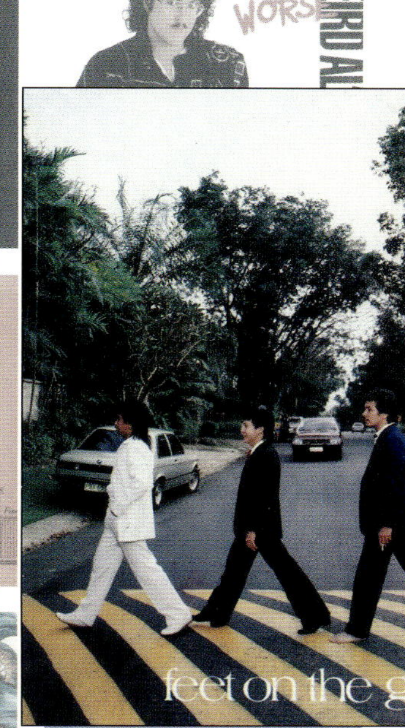

Below row images (top mid): AUTOMATICS GO BANANAS! ; BRACKET STINKY FINGERS ; EVEN WORSE "WEIRD AL"

easy on the eye books
74 Nethergate
Sheffield S6 6DJ

www.easyontheeye.net
www.easyontheeyebooks.wordpress.com

First edition 2011

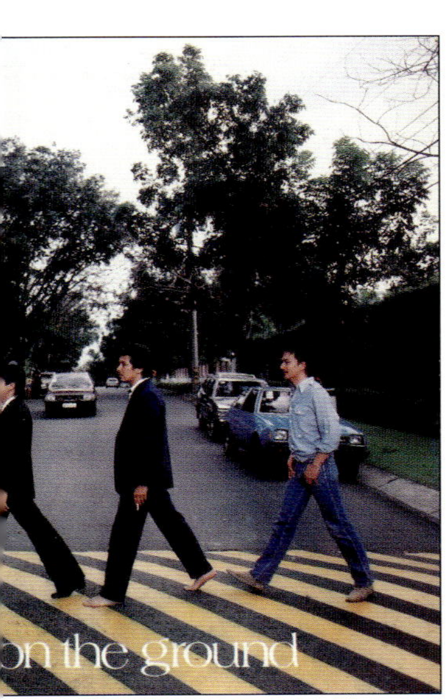

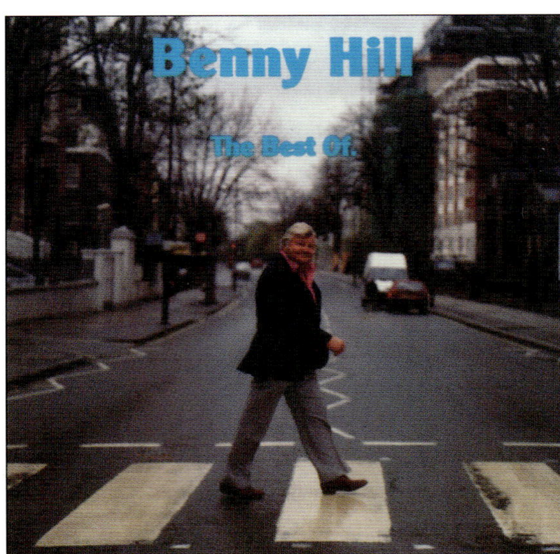

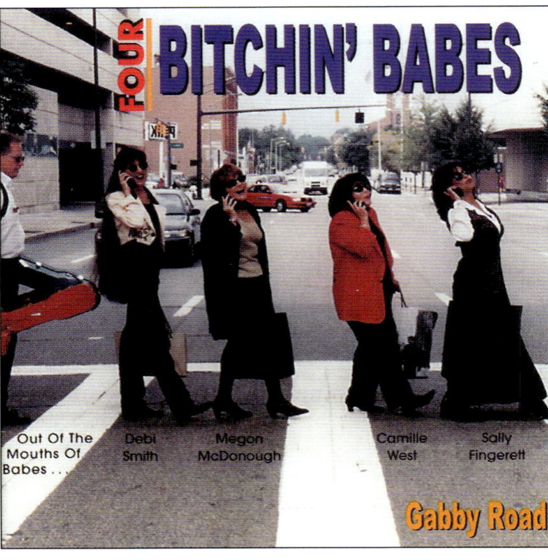

*You don't need us to tell you which famous sleeve these bands are working from. Those responsible are (from inside front cover to page
2): Anders Danman : All You Need [2010, King International. Artwork : Torbjörn Lagerwall. Photo : Leif Johansson, Anita Schulin] / Hinge
& Bracket : At Abbey Road [1980, EMI. Artwork photo : Iain MacMillan] / Apo Hiking Society : Feet On The Ground [1984, WEA. Artwork :
Reygob. Photo : Victor Ang] / Benny Hill : The Best Of Benny Hill [1992, Continuum Records. Artwork : Kimon Katafigiotis. Photo : Barry
Breckon] / Four Bitchin' Babes : Gabby Road [1997, Shanachie. Artwork : Joan Pelosim, Sally Fingerett. Photo : Ken Van Dyne]*

introduction

As someone who has been nosing around vinyl racks for 40 years now, fascinated by sleeve design (and to some extent collecting same), I liked to think I was familiar with a lot of album covers and many of the better known designers. Over that time I've often noticed covers which were obviously inspired by earlier works and even picked up a few out of interest, but never really considered just how much of this had gone on. So when I first saw the extent of Jan's collection I was astonished, and urged him to put a book together. "I have," was his reply, "but I can't find a publisher who is interested..."

So here we are. Jan had reached that stage in the project where he wasn't sure quite where to go, so I suggested if he throw the whole lot over to me, I would bring fresh eyes to the collection. In the end it was the postal service which actually threw the stuff, but once we'd hacked into the remains of the hard drive to rescue the files and gone through the images, I was fascinated both by just how many and how often covers drew on what had gone before. I was also taken aback at seeing so many sleeves which were completely new to me, and had more than a few laughs at some of the stranger parodies.

It was immediately apparent that just as popular music continues to rifle (often unapologetically) through the music and bands of earlier generations, both reassembling and reinventing, many designers had had been equally busy doing just the same - either drawing on their own interest in (and knowledge of) what had gone before, or working to the suggestions of bands themselves. It should not be surprising that when musicians come to release a record, and have admired or even idolised a particular band so much, they might also want to release their offering in a cover which owes something to that of one of their faves. It's as much a way of owning up if nothing else, either for the inspiration or the riffs, or both. Their immediate fans might not always be aware of what has gone on, but it can be a neat in-house reference for those with a more detailed knowledge of popular music culture. In wanting to pay homage to their influences, styling a cover after one of the past greats does the job.

So it is that bands caught up in the music of the sixties often choose to style covers after those from the period. It may be they've seen a sleeve idea which they like so much they want to borrow it, and it has to be said in some cases the attention to detail in the recreations is extreme, both in getting the band photograph just right, as well as tracking down the correct typeface and even making sure the retro record company logos are

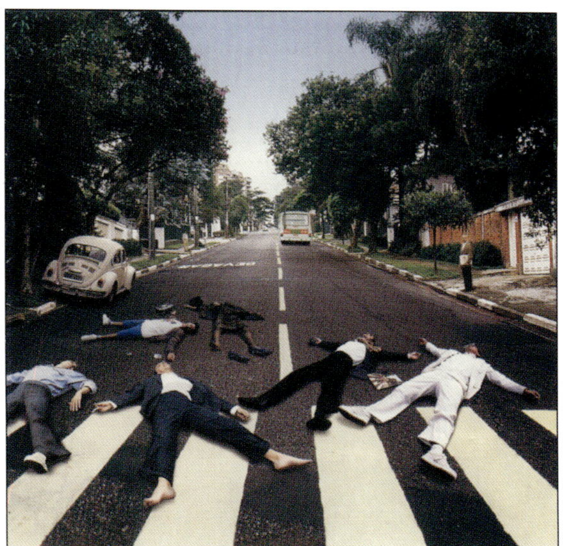
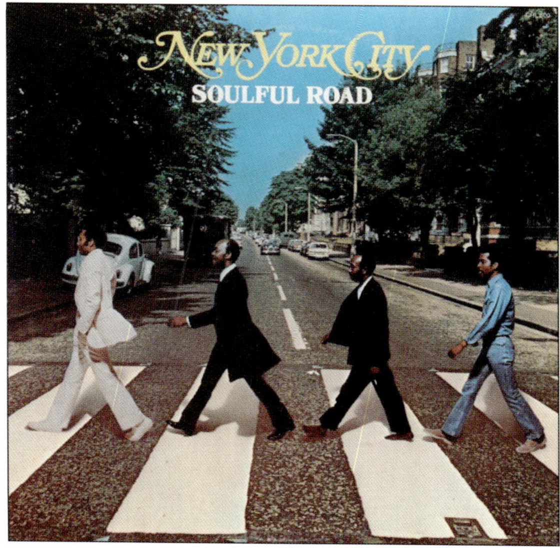

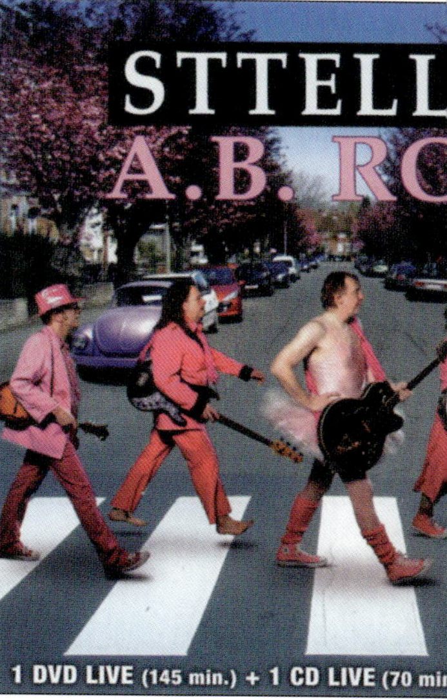

This page : Lingua De Trapo : Vinte E Um Anos Na Estrada [2000, Sonopresso. Artwork : César Pinamori. Photo : Antonio Rodrigues] / New York City : Soulful Road [1974, Chelsea. Artwork : Big Cigar. Photo : Ian Macmillian] / Sttellla : A.B. Rose [2008, Team4Action. Artwork : Jean-Luc Fonck, Bruno Marcandella. Photo : Fabian Dedave, Arthur]

closely echoed.

On top of that I'm sure there are examples in this book where the designer, pushed for time, short of budget (or both), has just relied on the youth or ignorance of his clients not to recognise where a cover idea has come from.

Having worked on a number of CD and vinyl reissues, trying to package rare and archive material with respect for the original context and period, there are clearly times when looking back helps to provide inspiration - the borrow of an old logo or vintage advert can give a feeling of history. A recent 7" cover for a limited edition Deep Purple single (opposite) serves as a good example of a less than subtle backwards nod. In this case, it was a vintage Dutch cover for the group which provided a template for the new design, which was then adapted as necessary. At least one buyer saw it on a web site and thought it was a rare original they'd never seen before, so job done.

Leaving aside borrowings for context and youthful homage, similarities on covers can be less well intentioned, taking an irreverant attitude to the originals, the new covers designed to mimic or poke fun at older designs and bands (many of whom were often referred to in the Punk years as Boring Old Farts). Sometimes these covers are a deliberate spoof of a well-known piece of artwork, done for subversive or mischievous reasons.

Again this often relies on some knowledge of pop history, both on the part of the band, designer and/or audience. It is interesting just how many covers along these lines simply reproduce older designs, perhaps slapping new heads over the old. Some just start vandalising existing covers, scribbling over the old titles and adding in new, or pasting photos over the originals. This anarchic cut and paste approach continues to thrive, despite the potential copyright issues which must give label owners sleepless nights on some occasions (having been on the receiving end of letters threatening action for simply using a redundant sixties Radio One Club logo on a reissue I can readily sympathise).

There are also the purveyors of contemporary parody; several bands seem to have spent their entire careers issuing albums which mocked the superstars of the day. We've refrained from filling the book with examples of all their efforts, instead using a sample cover or two from those who have done it best. And at their best they are often very funny indeed.

Of course at the more transient edges of rock and pop, some of these cover jokes are wasted on subsequent generations. A guy in glasses and little else, covered in spaghetti? It just looks weird today. Unless you know the fabulous Whipped Cream & Other Delights sleeve which he was aiming to parody (though in this case if he was hoping for similar notoriety he was going to be

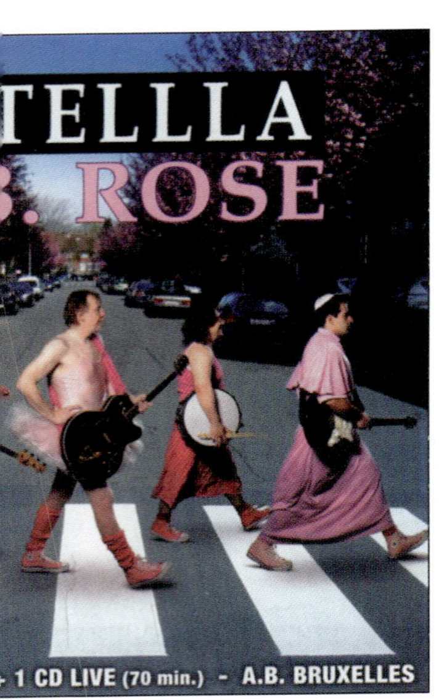

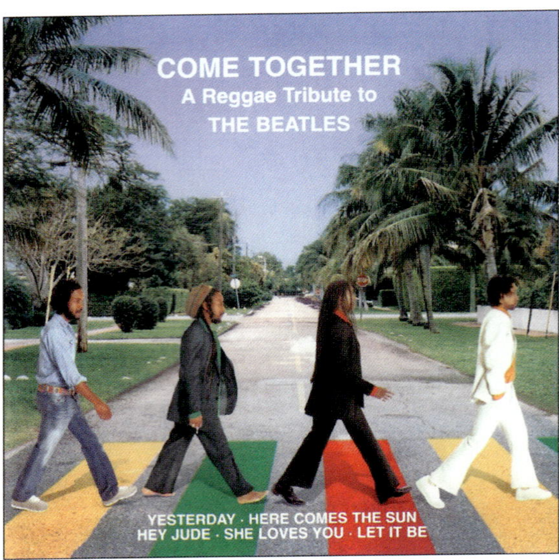

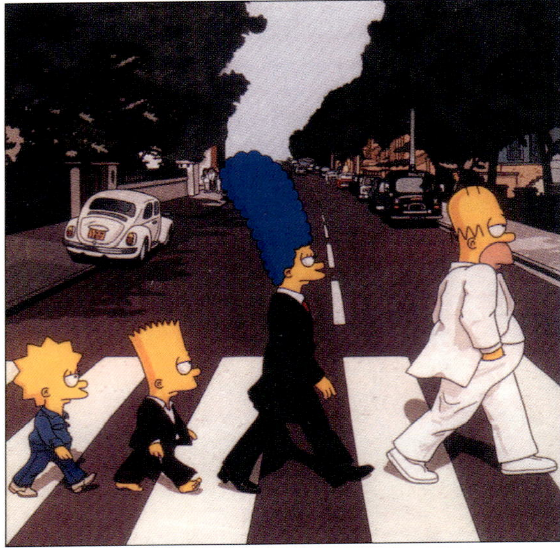

This page : V/Artists : Come Together, A Reggae Tribute To The Beatles [2002, Eurotrend. Artwork : Ria Paterson] / The Simpsons : promotional postcard (couldn't resist sneaking this in!).

disappointed). Similarly a lot of the bands doing the copying are themselves often less well known, even downright obscure in some cases; groups which burst on a local scene full of enthusiasm, created a buzz and then fizzled out for any number of reasons.

Today the opportunities for album cover artwork are reducing as more contemporary releases move to the download arena, with the once mighty album sleeve reduced to a few hundred pixels on an LCD display. Despite that, vinyl continues to fascinate musicians who weren't born when the CD arrived on the scene (and is still thriving in a niche way both for new titles and classic reissues), so there should still be plenty of scope for Jan to grow his collection in years to come.

Reproduction notes: The majority of sleeves in this book were photographed from Jan's own collection and some show their age . CD covers are often printed with a coarse dot screen which is hard to eliminate, and we apologise for moiré patterns on some of these. In a few cases Jan had to rely on scans (and even a couple of colour photocopies) from other sources.

Artist, title, year of release, format and label information is included for the majority of covers. A lot of sleeves failed to acknowledge their designers, but where we have been able to glean this information it is of course included. We'd be happy to hear from any designers not named.

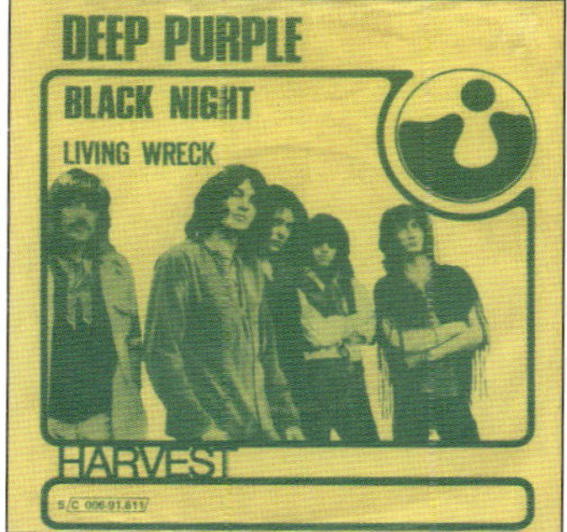
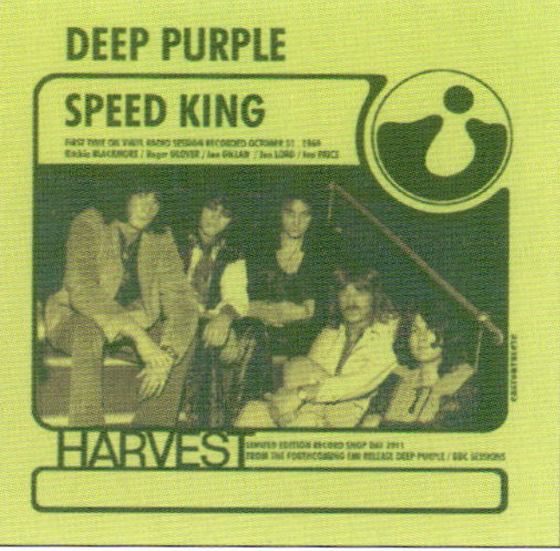

Here's the cover mentioned on page 4, a limited edition 7" single issued by EMI for Record Store Day, April 2011. The two Deep Purple recordings were unissued sessions from 1968/69, so I wanted a cover which had a bit of an underground rock feel, paid homage to the hundreds of now collectable old single covers, as well as reflecting the heritage of the Harvest label (and Roger Dean's neat logo design).

Scanning an original Harvest bag produced mixed results; under the scrutiny of a digital scanner all the flaws of the original hand-drawn art could be seen, so I recreated this digitally. Using the pattern of the 1970 Dutch cover shown left, I brought in an old EMI publicity photograph and upped the contrast. The last move was to sample the original sleeve colours and bring these into the new design. It was tempting to go further and add some aging and creases to give it a vintage look but sometimes less is more.

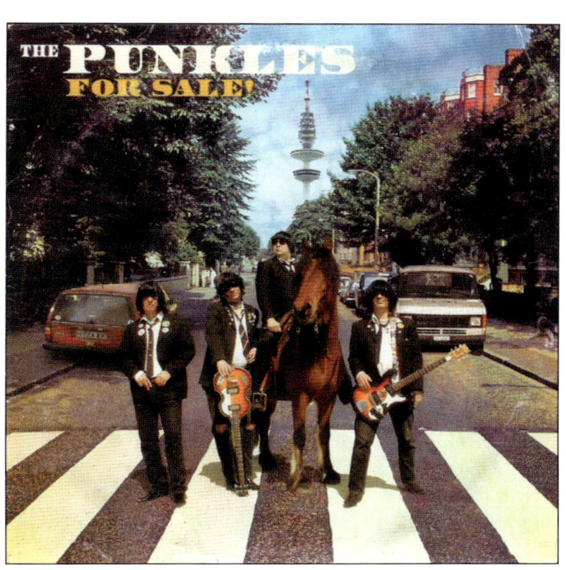
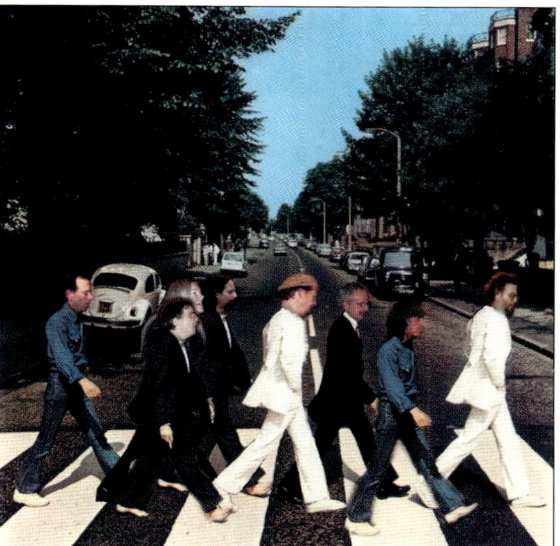
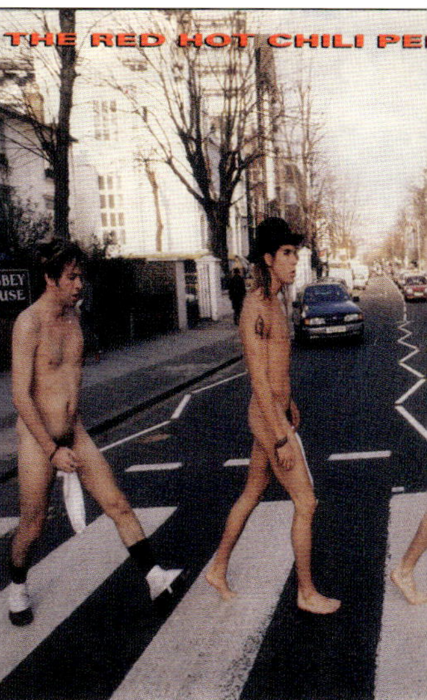

This page : The Punkles : For Sale! [2006, Punkles Records. Photo : Maya Demmerle] / The Flying Other Brothers Band : Abbey Road [2001. Artwork : Unknown] / Red Hot Chili Peppers : The Abbey Road E.P. [1988, EMI Manhattan. Artwork : Abrahams Pants. Photo : Chris Clunn] / *continued page 154*

With such a seminal album, it's not surprising that the cover for The Psychedelic Sounds Of The 13th Floor Elevators [1966 : International Artists. Artwork : John Cleveland] has been borrowed such a lot, often by psych upstarts (also leaning on the music) and CD compliers wanting some of the early sixties garage ambience to rub off on them. The result is a great display of primary colours.

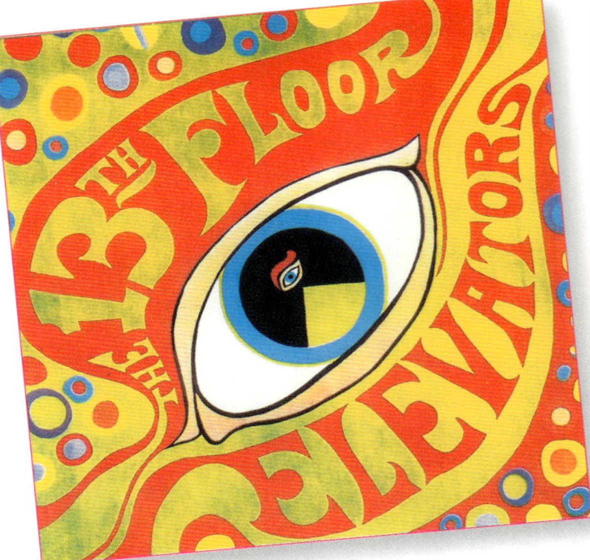

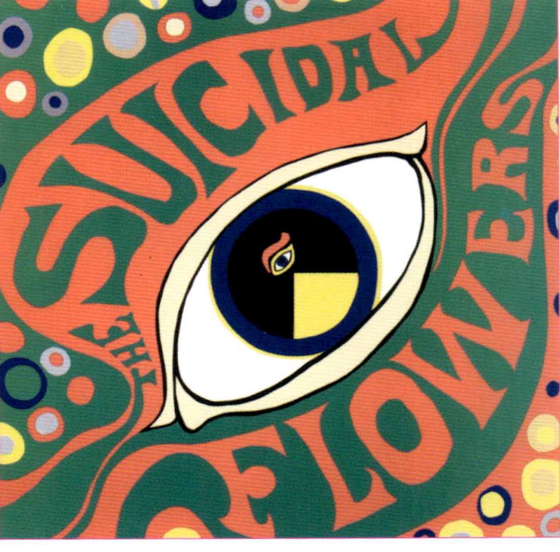

Artist : The Suicidal Flowers
Title : The Psychedevilic Sounds Of The Suicidal Flowers / 1997
Album / Suicidal Flowers
Artwork : Unknown

Artist : Various Artists
Title : The Pseudoteutonic Sounds Of The Prae-Kraut Pandaemonium # 14 / 2003
Album / Lost Continence
Artwork / Reinhard Gehlen - Andrea Duwa - Splash 1

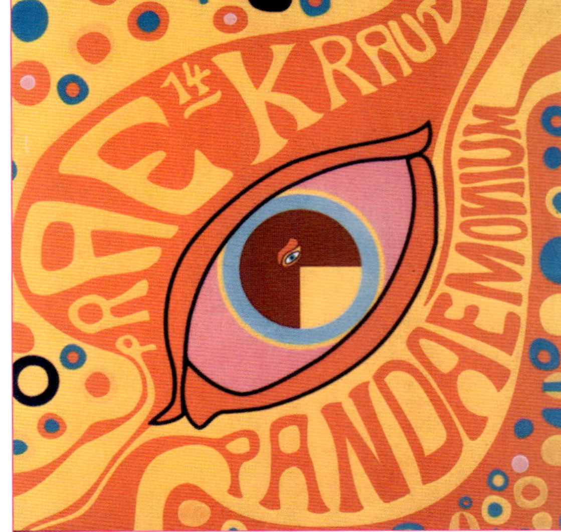

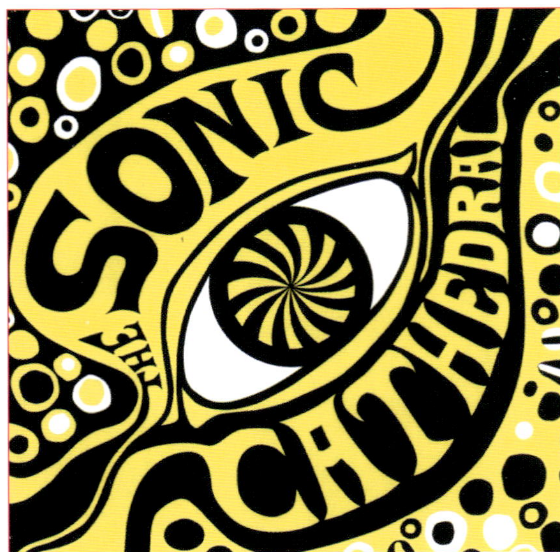

Artist : Various Artists
Title : The Psychedelic Sounds Of The Sonic Cathedral / 2010
Album / Sonic Cathedral Recordings
Artwork : Jimmy Young

This cover faithfully copies New Romantic outift Adam and The Ant's 1981 debut album Prince Charming, but confusingly the band's name is based on the Southern boogie outfit Lynyrd Skynyrd (a second band - The Wynona Riders (!) - claimed the back cover).

As we'll see, Japanese musicians seem keener than many to recreate classic covers, here it is Ash Ra Tempel's New Age Of Earth [1972 : Virgin. Artwork + photo : Christian Remer / Peter Butschkow] which has been faithfully copied.

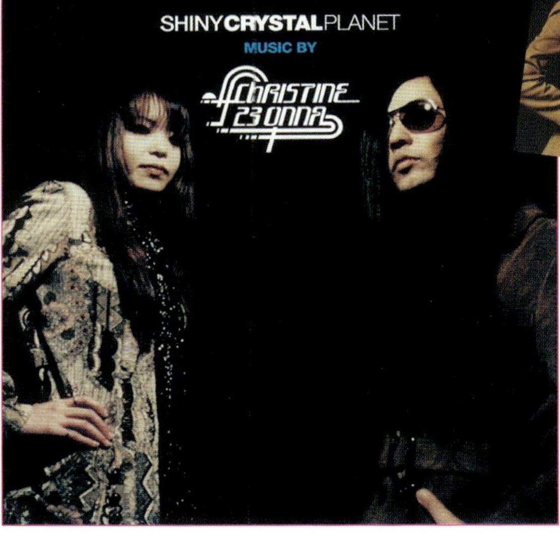

Artist : Lynyrd's Innards / The Wynona Riders
Title : Split 10" / 1996
10" / What Else? Records
Artwork : Unknown

Artist : Christine 23 Onna
Title : Shiny Crystal Planet / 2000
Album / Alchemy Records
Artwork : Christine 23 Onna / Masahiko Ohno Photo : Tadashi Fukumoto

Artist : The Hippos
Title : Heads Are Gonna Roll / 1999
Album / Interscope Records
Artwork : Francesca Restrepo for Design Palace (Photo : Rocky Schenck)

Artist : Whipping Post
Title : Live At Norwegian Wood / 2000
Album/ Glitterhouse Records
Artwork : Björn Kulseth at Union Design (Photo : Raymond Mosken)

There's no real logic to the way the titles were done on the U.S. edition of the 1964 Animals album [MGM], though labels there did their own thing with a lot of the British acts. Idiosyncratic enough for someone looking for a sixties feel to want to copy it.

The Allman Brothers Band At Fillmore East from 1971, with a grainy cover shot by Jim Marshall, has clearly inspired this CD from 2000.

Two from AC/DC, both from 1978 (on Atlantic) and both with art by Bob Defrin and photos by Jim Houghton. If You Want Blood, You've Got It and Powerage are not design masterpieces but certainly of their time, and have served as inspiration for discs as diverse as The Shitheads (a lousy copy, sorry), American Dog (if you can't make it out, that's a bottle of Bud plunging into the guy) and a Simpsons image which at a guess might not have been 100% approved...

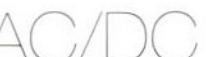

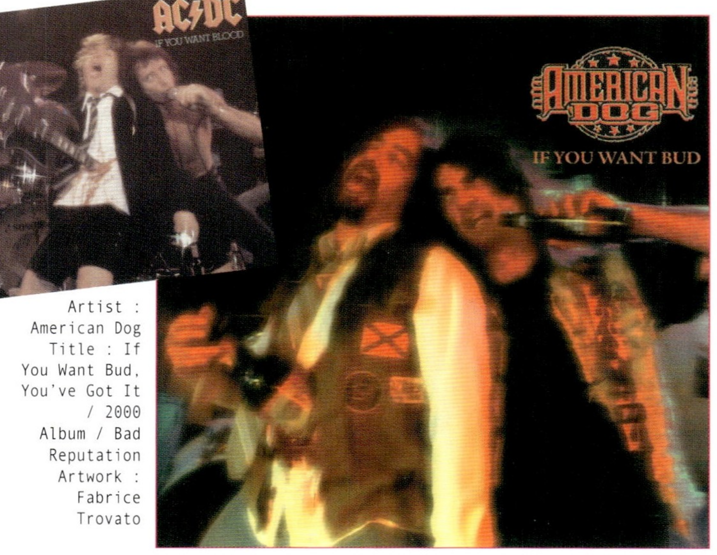

Artist :
American Dog
Title : If
You Want Bud,
You've Got It
/ 2000
Album / Bad
Reputation
Artwork :
Fabrice
Trovato

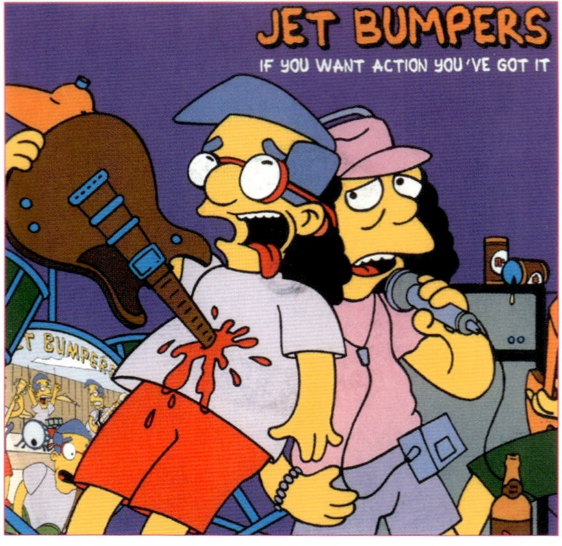

Artist : Jet
Bumpers
Title : If You
Want Action ,
You've Got It
/ 1999
3 track EP /
Radio Blast
Recordings
Artwork :
Unknown

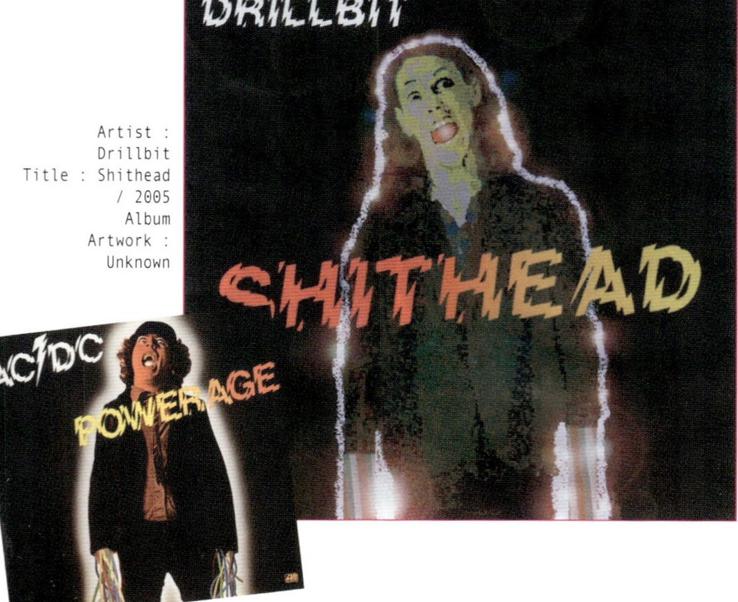

Artist :
Drillbit
Title : Shithead
/ 2005
Album
Artwork :
Unknown

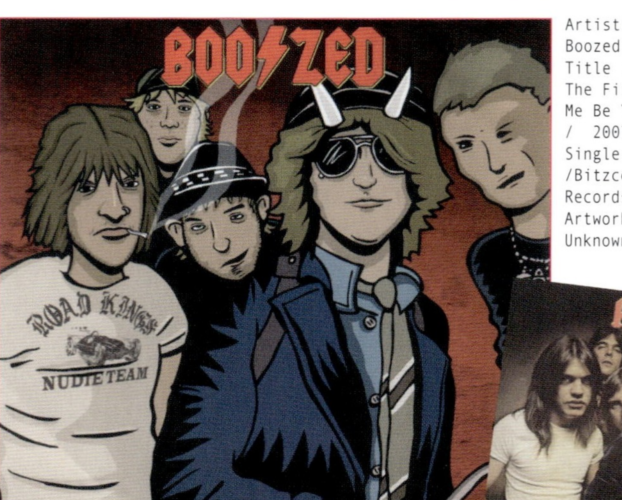

Artist :
Boozed
Title : Gimme
The Fire - Let
Me Be Your Dog
/ 2007
Single
/Bitzcore
Records
Artwork :
Unknown

AC/DC's 1979 Highway To Hell album and Jim Houghton's cover photo provide the basis for Boo/Zed's graphic illustration, the 2007 effort also using a variation of the band's well-known lightning logo.

Leona Anderson's 1958 long-player Music To Suffer By (Unique Records) is a gem, though I must admit I've never been able to get vinyl albums to shatter quite like that (or the old Buzzcocks TV show intro). The Makers have actually copied the original image for their EP and then just added a new label design.

Artist : The Makers
Title : Music To Suffer By / 1995
3 track EP / Estrus Wreckers
Artwork : Art Chantry

This copy of Ash Ra Tempel's 1973 album Starring Rosi lovingly recreates Peter Geitner's original [Photo : Claus Kranz].

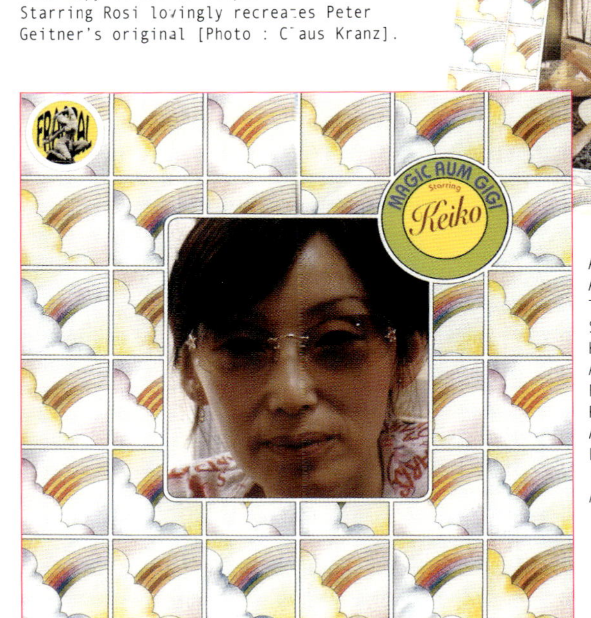

Artist : Magic Aum Gigi
Title : Starring Keiko/ 2000?
Album / Fractal Records
Artwork : Peter Geitner (Photo : Magic Aum Gigi)

Artist : Smiff-N-Wessum
Title : Dah Shinin' / 1995
Album / Wreck Records
Artwork : C.M.O.N. (Photo : Gary Spector)

Groups looking down at a fish-eye lens was popular in the late 60s, here on Roy Ayers' '71 Polydor LP He's Coming [Artwork : Kinji Nakamura, Kats Ahe. Photo : Minoru Aoki], but with the eye peering through, it's clear this cover was Smiff-N-Wessum's inspiration.

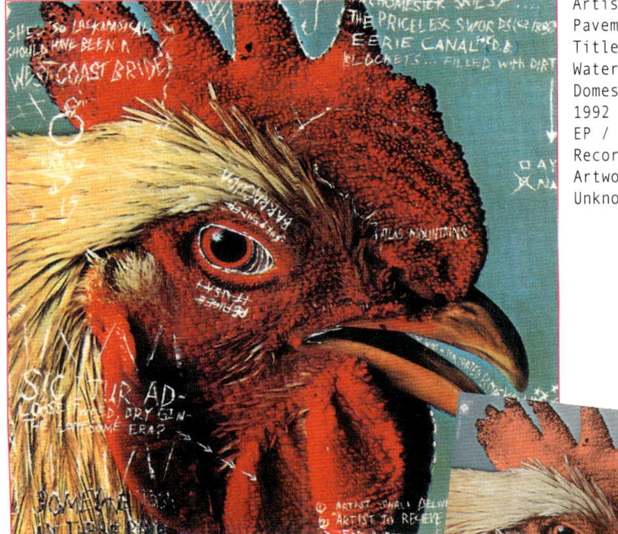

Artist : Pavement
Title : Watery, Domestic / 1992
EP / Matador Records
Artwork : Unknown

Ambergris' eponymous 1970 album on Paramount featured artwork by Thom Williams (and a rooster called "Jin"!) and forms the basis for a 7" 1992 reworking by designers unknown.

Artist : Jay Geils
Title : Plays Jazz / 2004
Album / Stony Plain Records
Artwork : Rebecca Fagan

Artist : Radio Caroline
Title : Dead Groovy Action / 2004
Album / Triad - Columbia
Artwork : Spector Limited

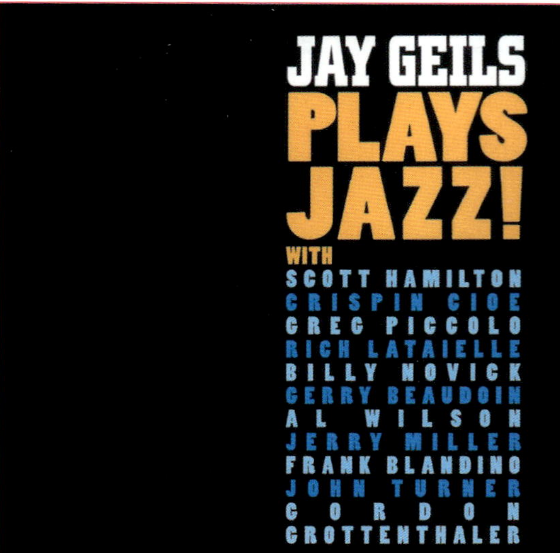

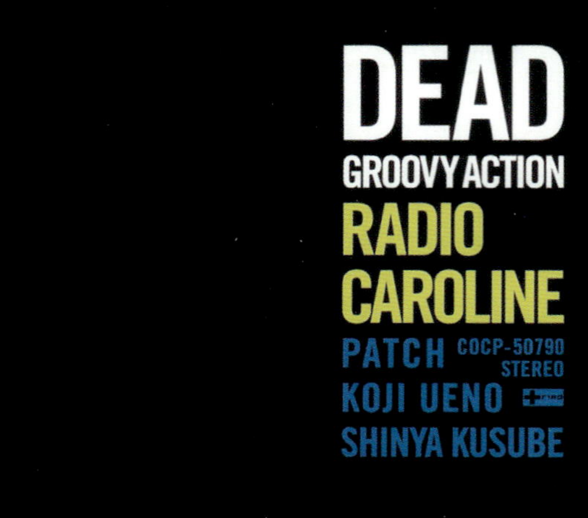

Blue Note's contributions to album sleeve art remain a benchmark and have inspired no end of designers and bands over the years, so it's quite nice to see one of their early cover designs come full circle for once, with this deceptively simple classic piece of typography by Reid Miles for Blue Note in 1958 reused a number of time before Blue Note themselves reworked it for a CD collection in 2007 (the hard edged type on the CD cover compared to the softer letter forms on the old vinyl are hard to ignore, and I know which I prefer).

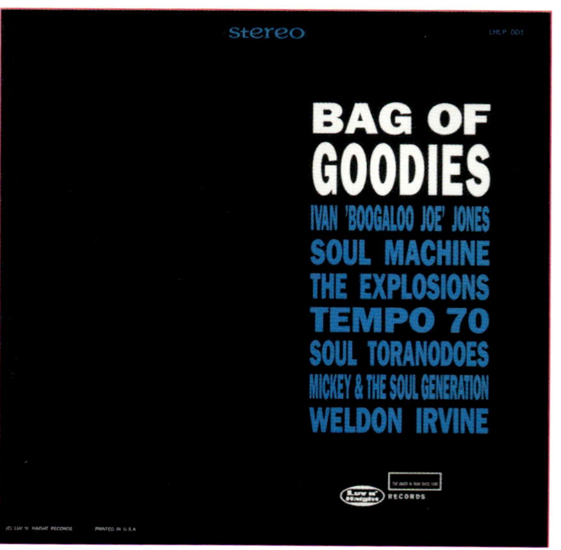

Artist : Various Artists
Title : Bag Of Goodies / 1991
Album / Luv N' Haight Records
Artwork : Dan Prothero for Fog City Graphics

Artist : Various Artists
Title : Somethin' New - Jazz Sampler 2007 / 2007
Album / Blue Note
Artwork : Unknown

As Herb Alpert founded A&M Records in the early sixties, he was able to push for cover budgets which many labels might have quickly over-ruled. Alpert (who originally was the Tijuana Brass, just overdubing his own trumpet playing) found himself with hits and quickly recruited a real backing band for tours and TV. For his fourth album he went for a design by Peter Whorf Graphics. Back in 1965 this was seriously saucy stuff for a mainstream album cover and Whipped Cream & Other Delights has rightly become a favourite of sleeve collectors the world over. There is even a Stateside collector who buys every second-hand copy of the original he found and decorating his apartment with them... The album sold by the truck load, 6 million copies according to some sources (that guy will need a big apartment), and the sleeve has perhaps not surprisingly inspired a lot of tributes (and even a band called Whipped Cream, their 1991 album - above - on Radium Records redrew the original title block), some recreating their own version of the cover, others picking up on the decorated type (which has echoes of Victorian decorated fonts as well as the emerging organic contemporary West Coast look), and many doing both. *More overleaf.*

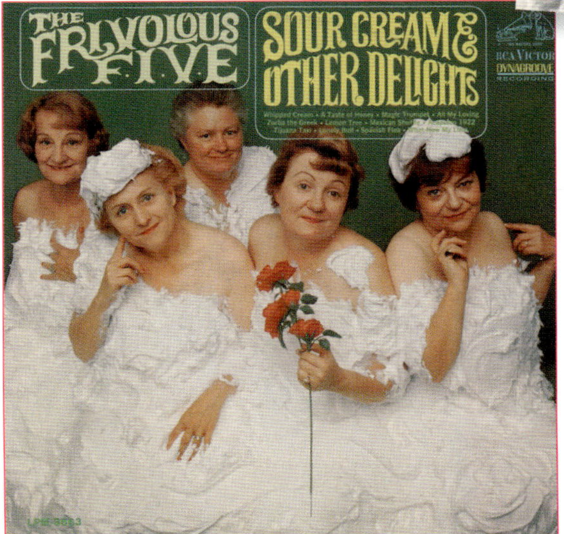

Artist : The Frivolous Five
Title : Sour Cream & Other Delights / 1966
Album / RCA Victor
Artwork : Unknown

Artist : Cherry Capri & The Martini Kings
Title : Creamy Cocktails & Other Delights / 2007
Album / SwingOmatic Records
Artwork : M-M Straton (Photo : Toso Papadakis)

Artist : Various Artists
Title : Right To Chews - Bubblegum Classics Revisited / 2002
Album / Not Lame
Artwork : Mike Simmons (Photo : Peter Kuehl)

Artist : Various Artists
Title : Surfin' Senorita / 1999
Album / Wildebeest Records
Artwork : Steve Bracamontez & Doug Kaiser (Photo : Mark Stultz)

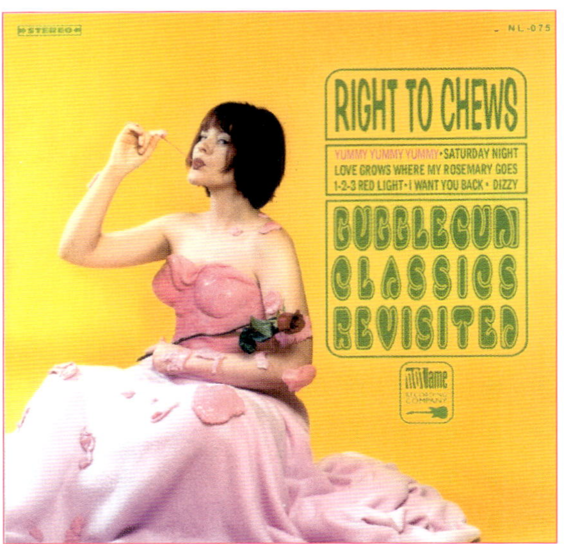

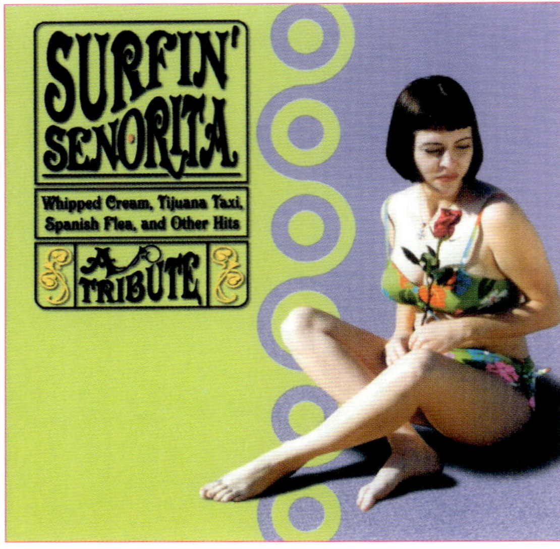

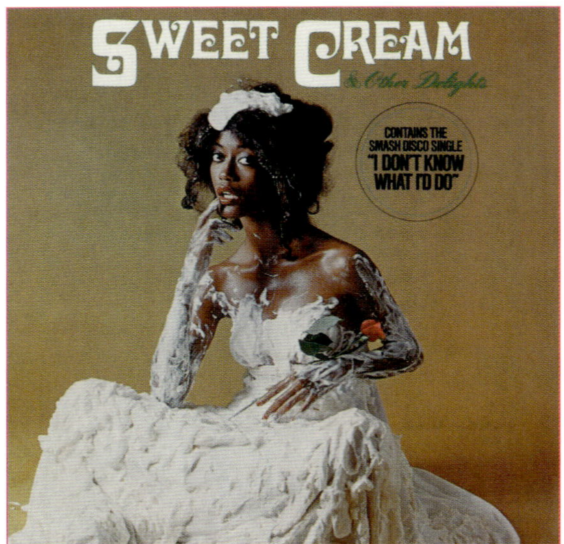

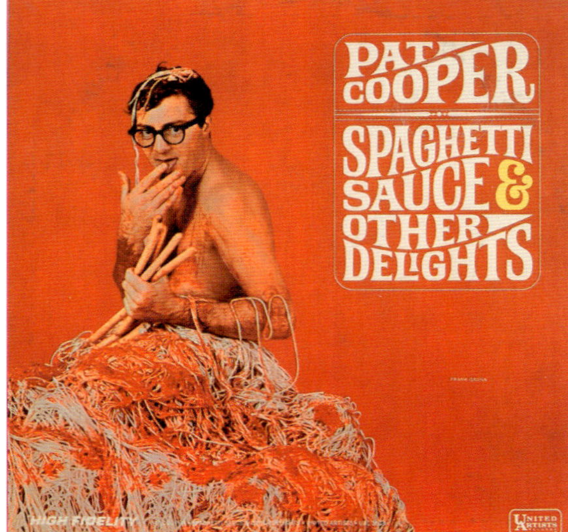

Artist : Sweet Cream
Title : Sweet Cream & Other Delights / 1978
Album / Shadybrook Records
Artwork + photo : Dirk Bakker

Artist : Pat Cooper
Title : Spaghetti Sauce & Other Delights / 1967
Album / United Artists
Artwork : Frank Gauna

Artist : The Hellacopters
Title : Disappointment Blues / 1998
Album / Au-Go-Go Records
Artwork : Mr. N. Royale & Guerilla Art (Photo : Stefan Mattsson)

Artist : Soul Asylum
Title : Clam Dip & Other Delights / 1988
Album / Twin Tone Records
Artwork : Swiped Graphics by Dan Kalal

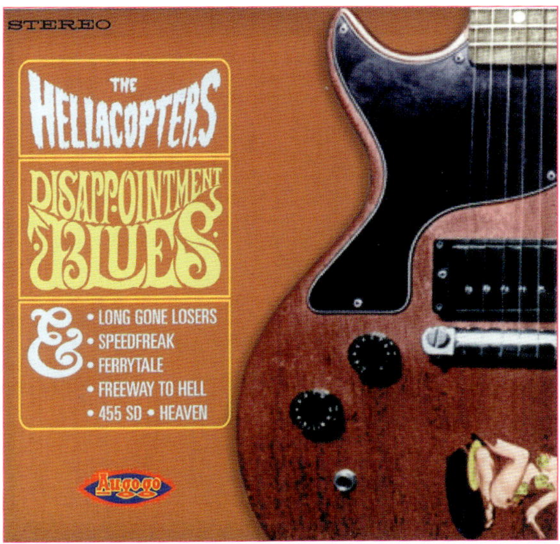

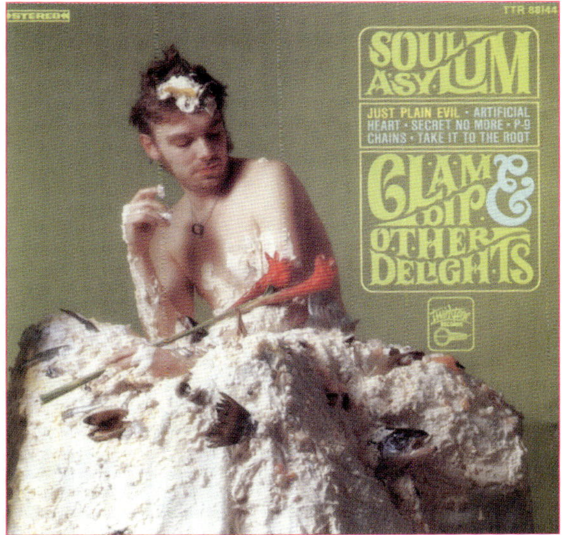

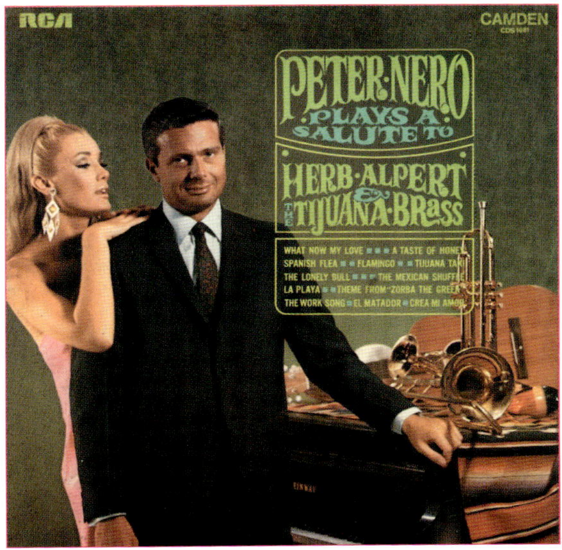

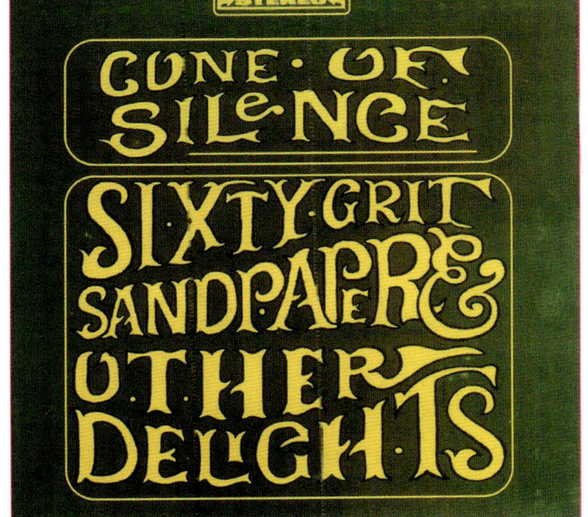

Artist : Peter Nero
Title : Plays A Salute To Herb Alpert & The Tijuana Brass / 1971
Album / RCA
Artwork : Unknown

Artist : Cone Of Silence
Title : Sixtie-Grit Sandpaper & Other Delights / 2004
Album / Melograph Records
Artwork : Unknown

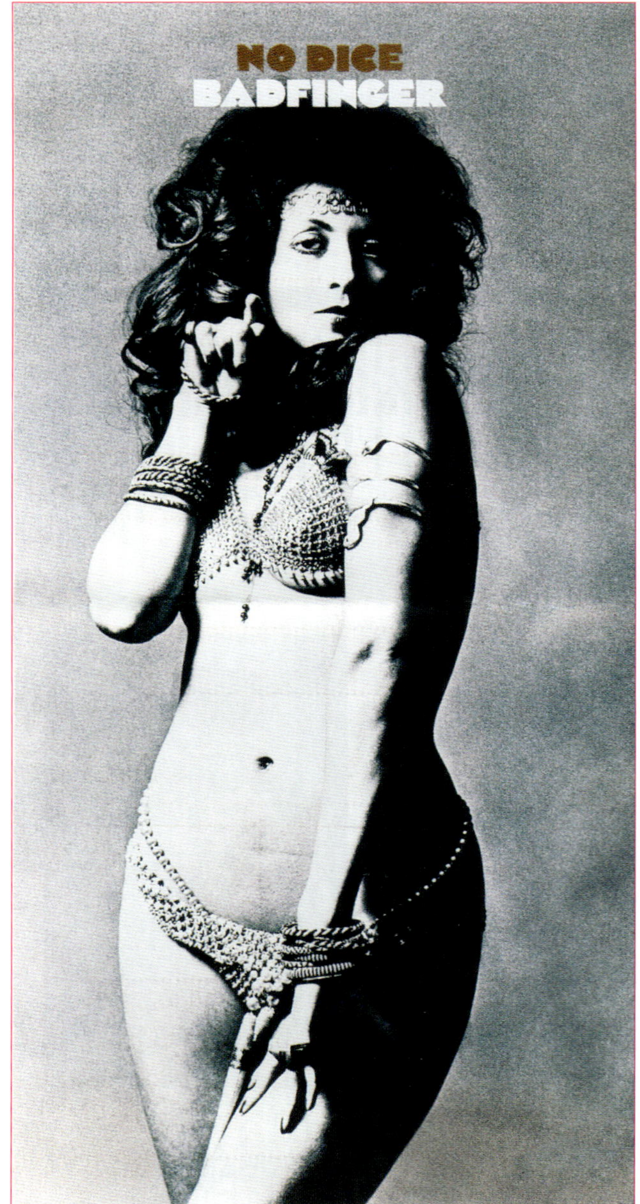

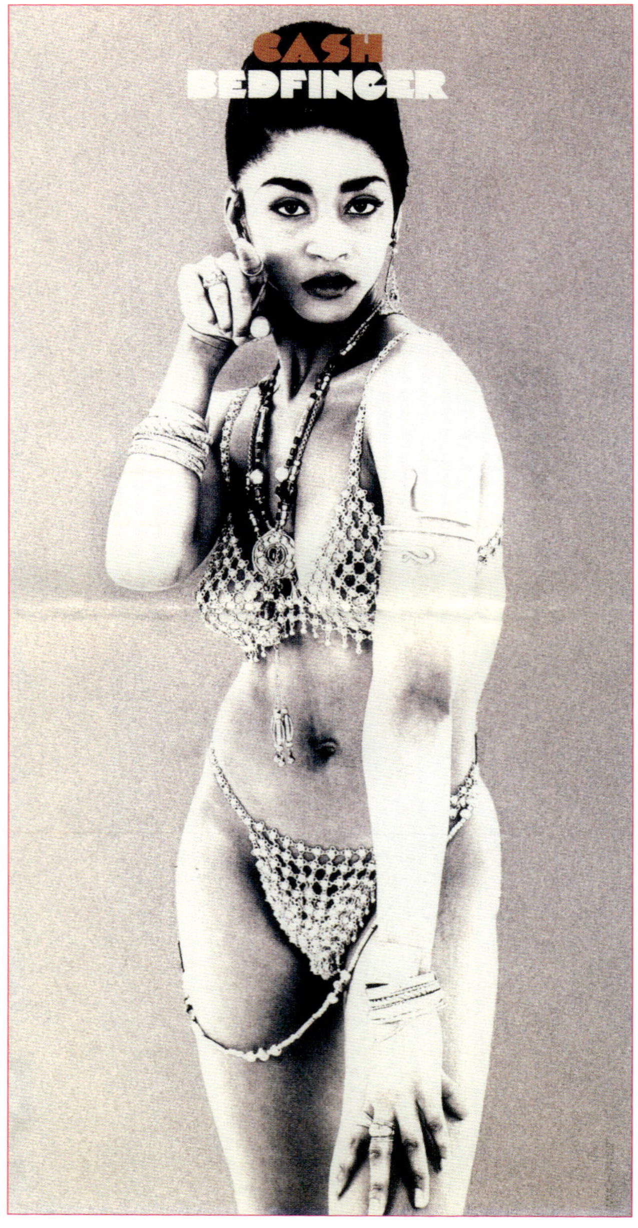

Badfinger's 1970 LP No Dice managed to cleverly echo the risque New York dancers of the 1920s through Richard Dilello's photo [Artwork : Gene Matton]. It provided the template for Cash's sleeve which substitued a Asian girl but is otherwise very close, right down to the typography.

Artist : Cash
Title : Bedfinger / 1992
Album / Yoroshita Music
Artwork : Kodahman / Shingo "Tokutaisei"
Yamagami (Photo : Chukyo Ozawa)

Bad Religion as a band passed me by but clearly their work was influential enough to find the covers from 1982's How Could Hell Be Any Worse? [Artwork : Brett Gurewitz / Ed Colver] and Suffer from 1988 [Artwork : Jerry Mahoney], both on Epitaph Records, being borrowed a decade or so later, even though neither could be said to be stunning examples of the art. It could well be that Nofx took the idea from Bad Religion, and Stolen Youth from Nofx. Meanwhile Dead Silence just lifted the cover image lock, stock and. .

Artist : NOFX
Title : Surfer / 2001
EP / Fat Wreck Chords
Artwork : M. Desalvo

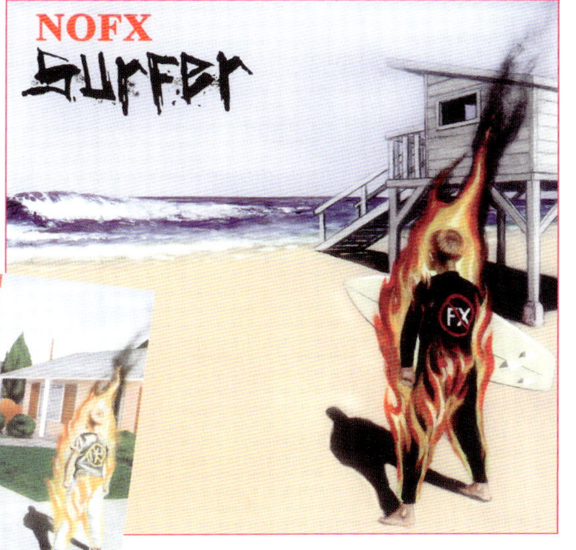

Artist : Los Planetas
Title : David & Claudia / La Verdadera Historia / 1995
Single / RCA / BMG Spain
Artwork : Javier Aramburu

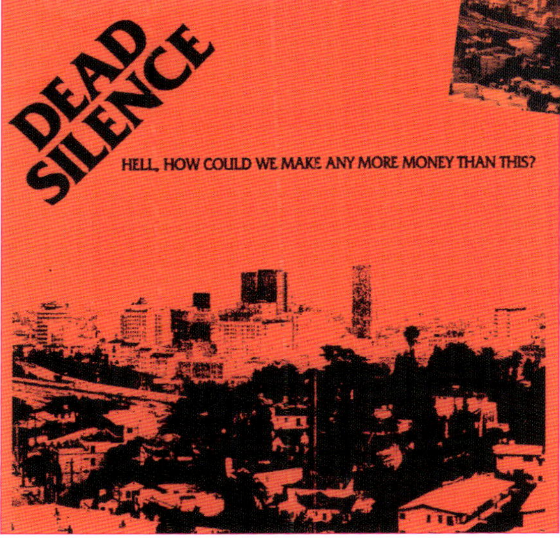

Artist : Stolen Youth
Title : Smurfer / 2003
EP / 2 Bucks Entertainment
Artwork : Luke Fazakerley

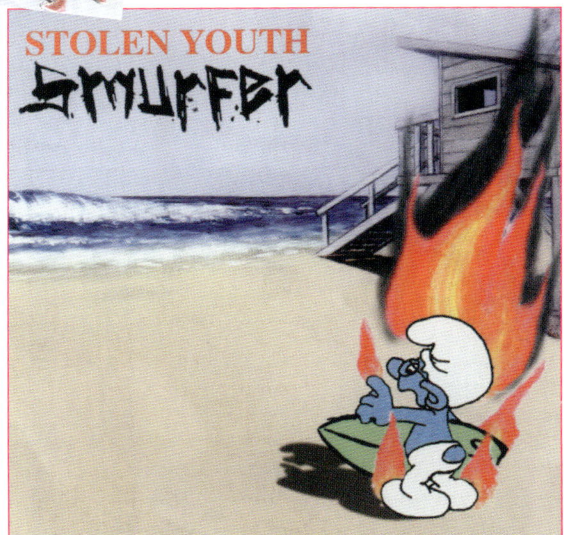

Artist : Dead Silence
Title : Hell, How Could We Make More Money Than This? / 1994
EP / Profane Existence
Artwork : Unknown

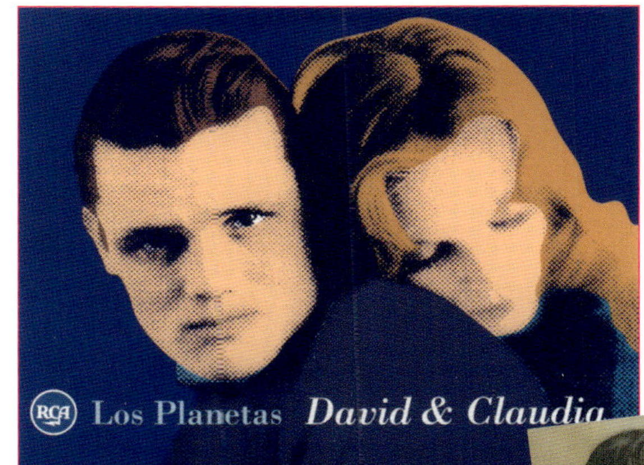

Chet Baker's album Chet [1969 : Riverside Records. Artwork : Paul Bacon / Ken Braren / Harris Lewine] has a washed out cover portrait of the trumpeter, a blonde resting on his shoulder. Spanish outfit Los Planetas have given it a modern Warhol look on their single which works well.

Les Baxter's easy albums have been collected for a long time; here his Space Escapade [1958. Artwork : Unknown] gets not so much a make-over by the Heartworms as nicked completely (with a Ferrante & Teicher cover for the backdrop - see page 58).

It's fascinating where some bands find their references; Barrel "Fingers" Barry's cheesy budget album Beer Garden Piano Swings The Classics [1964. Photo : George S. Whiteman] anybody? The '60s beer-drinking ladette image works for Pavement.

Artist :
Heartworms
Title : Space
Escapade /
1995
Album / Darla
Records
Artwork :
Unknown

Artist :
Pavement
Title : Cut
Your Hair + 2
/ 1994
Single / Big
Cat Records
Artwork :
Unknown

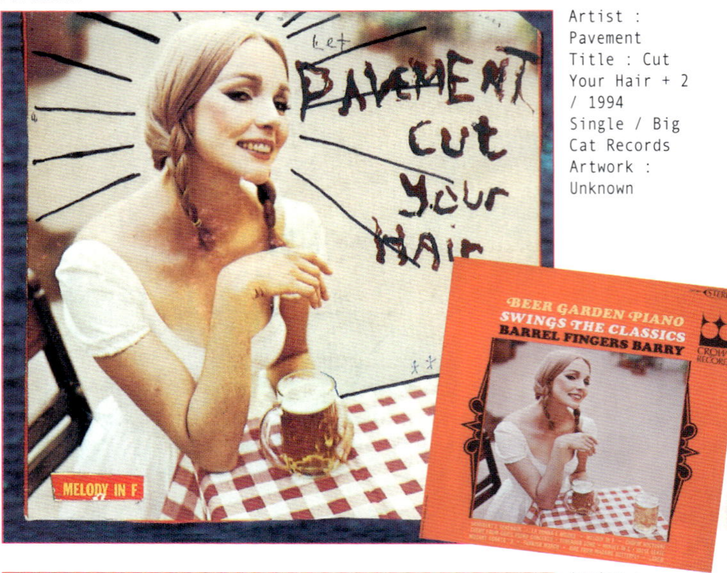

Artist : Cub
Koda
Title : Cub
Digs Chuck /
1989
Album /
Garageland
Records
Artwork :
Carmelin
Martin Photo :
Jim Oehl, Jan
Lindmark

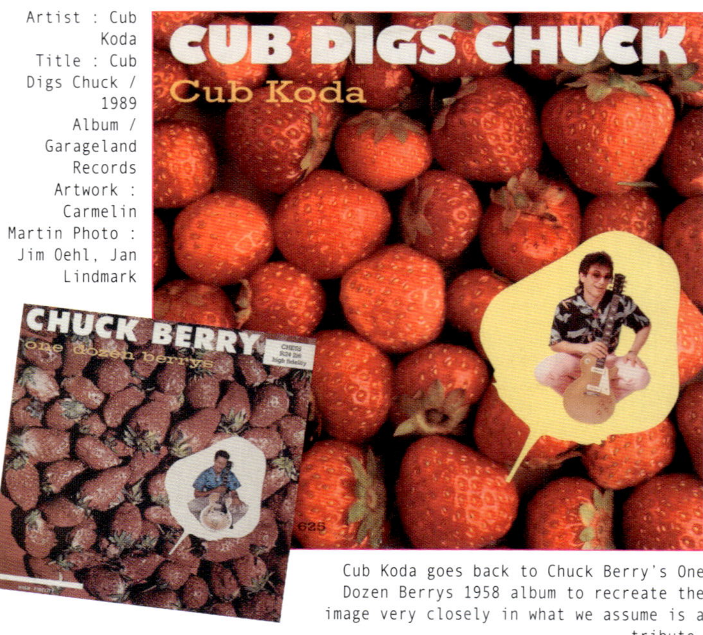

Cub Koda goes back to Chuck Berry's One Dozen Berrys 1958 album to recreate the image very closely in what we assume is a tribute.

Artist :
Electric
Frankenstein
Title : The
Chain + 1 /
2000
Single /
Safety Pin
Records
Artwork :
Marujographics
& The Redneck
Hillbillies
From Southern
Space

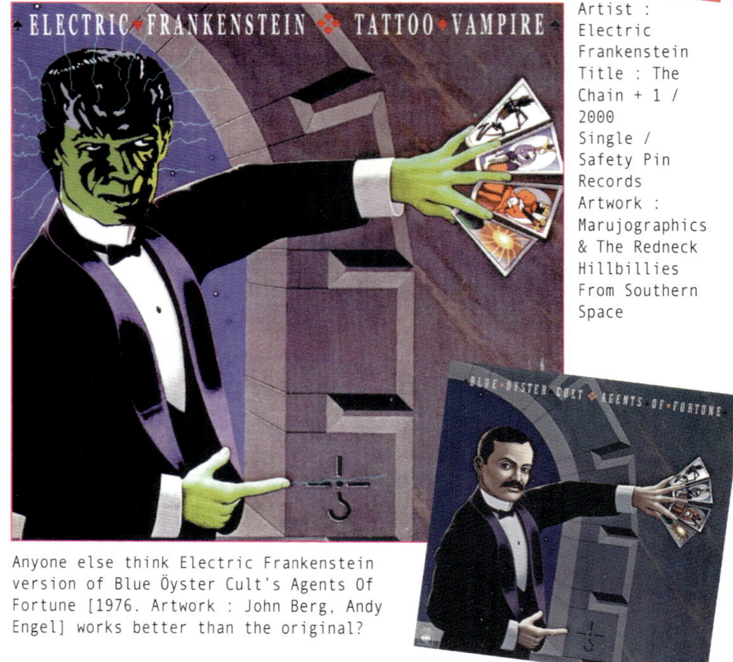

Anyone else think Electric Frankenstein version of Blue Öyster Cult's Agents Of Fortune [1976. Artwork : John Berg, Andy Engel] works better than the original?

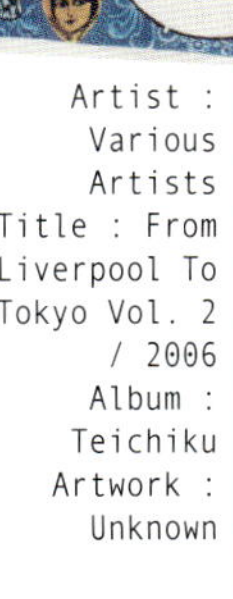

Sleeve wise (as well as musically) one of the most copied bands of all. When I first visited EMI's Manchester Square building in the late 70s, like everyone else who ever went there, I had to pause and look up the building, such is the power of that photo which decorated The Beatles 1962-1966 [1973 : Apple. Artwork : P. Linard Marketing]. Shampoo (who do it well) and The Bangles (with a dreadful sleeve) were similarly struck.

Artist : The
Bangles
Title :
1980-1983
Everything /
1990
Album / CBS
Artwork :
Unknown

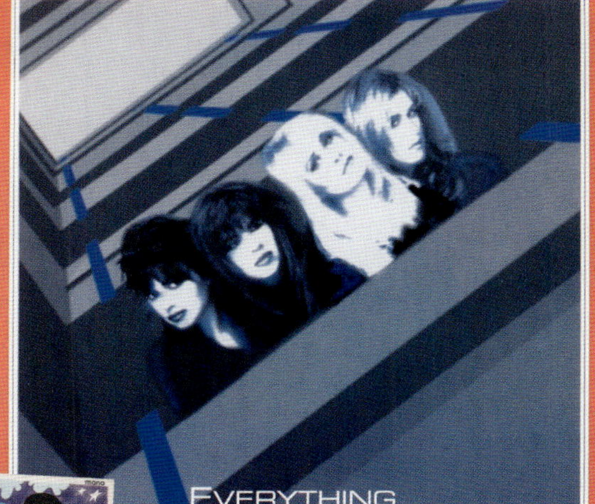

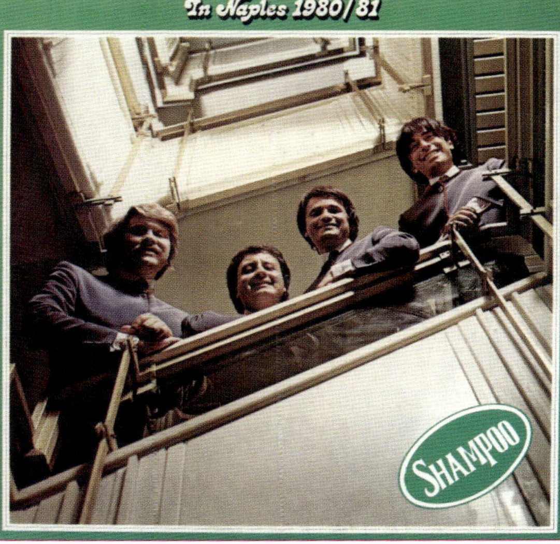

Artist :
Shampoo
Title : In
Naples 1980/81
/ 1980
Album / EMI
Artwork,
photo : Ennio
Antonangeli

Artist :
Various
Artists
Title : From
Liverpool To
Tokyo Vol. 2
/ 2006
Album :
Teichiku
Artwork :
Unknown

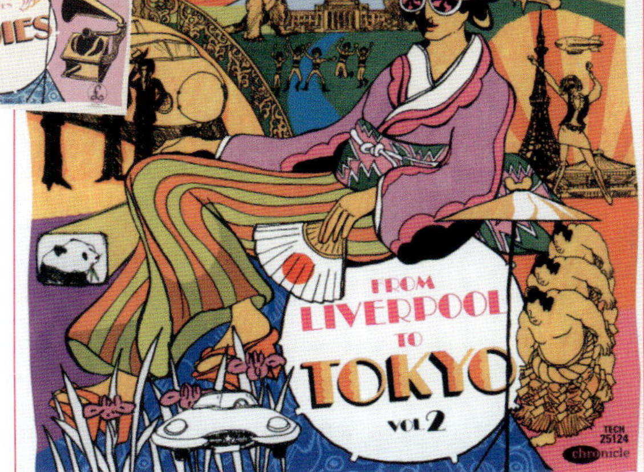

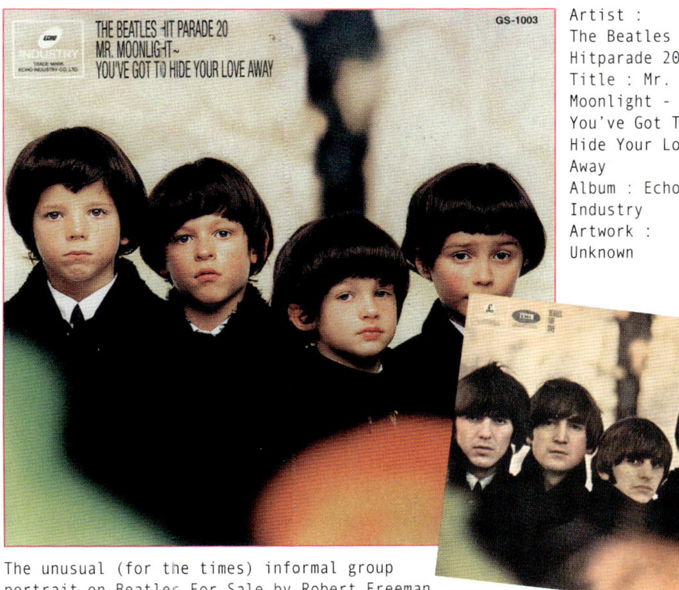

Artist :
The Beatles
Hitparade 20
Title : Mr.
Moonlight -
You've Got To
Hide Your Love
Away
Album : Echo
Industry
Artwork :
Unknown

A Collection Of Beatles Oldies [1966, Parlophone. Artwork : David Christian], a cover redolent of the times, given a twist on this Japanese CD - so the group are posed beside a Bullet Train not a veteran car, etc.

The unusual (for the times) informal group portrait on Beatles For Sale by Robert Freeman [1964 : Parlophone] is given a slightly Midwich Cuckoo look on this cover version remake.

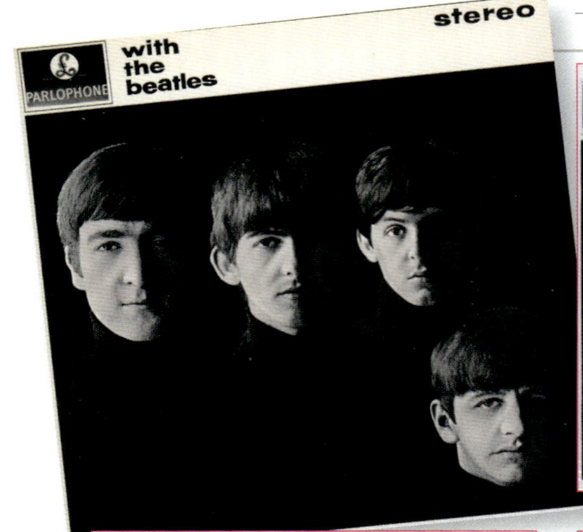
PARLOPHONE
with the beatles
stereo

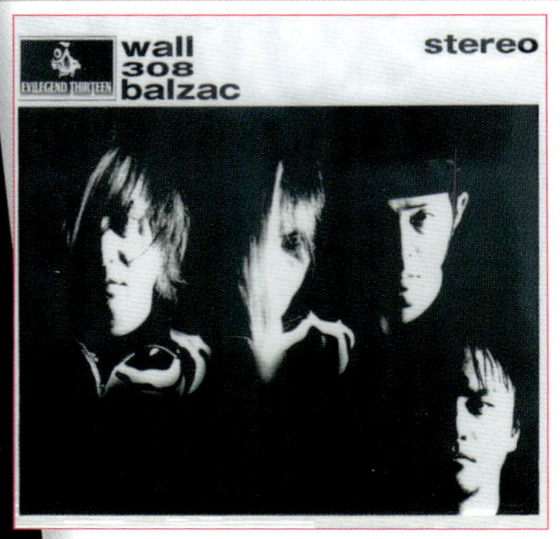
EVILFGEND THIRTEEN
wall 308 balzac
stereo

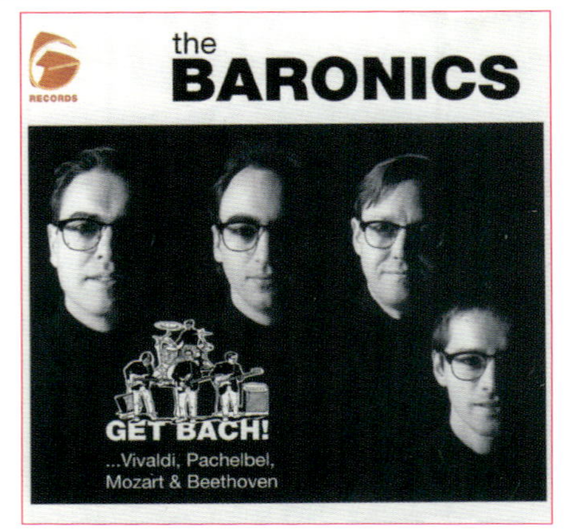
RECORDS
the BARONICS
GET BACH!
...Vivaldi, Pachelbel, Mozart & Beethoven

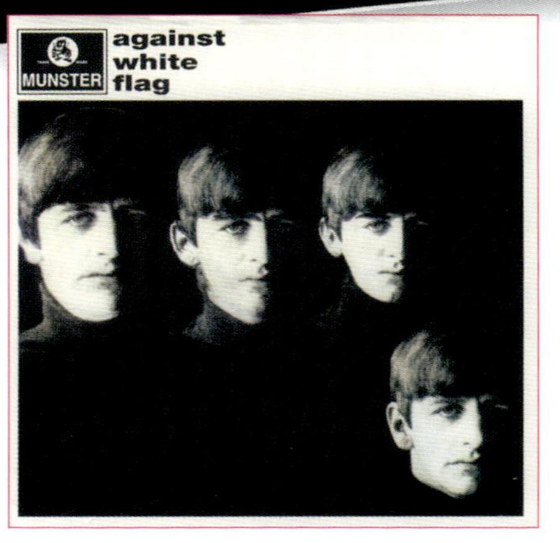
MUNSTER
against white flag

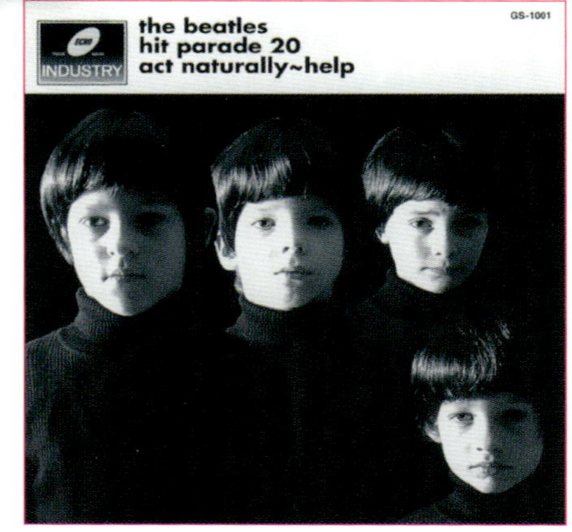
INDUSTRY
the beatles
hit parade 20
act naturally~help
GS-1001

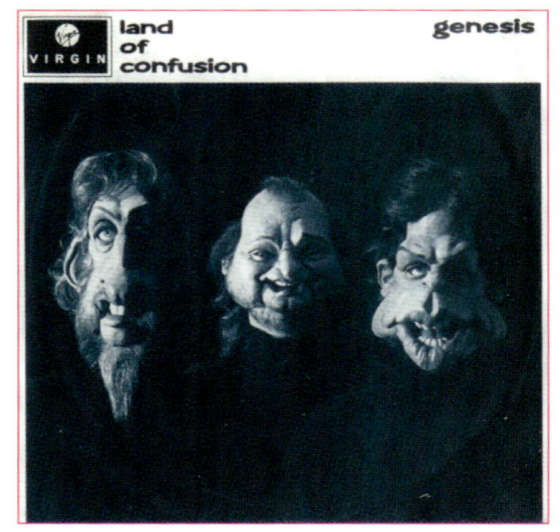
VIRGIN
land of confusion
genesis

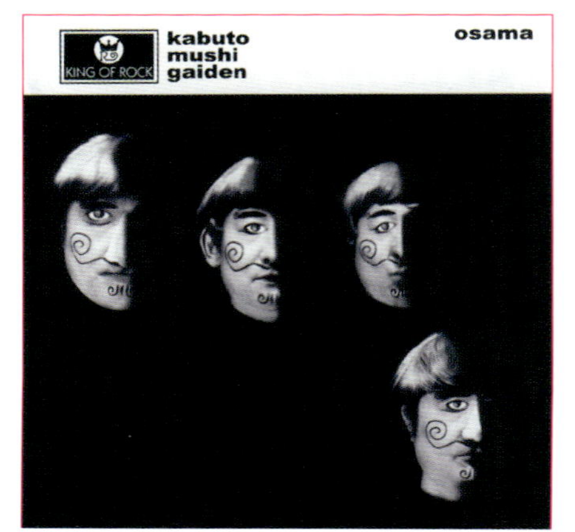
KING OF ROCK
kabuto mushi gaiden
osama

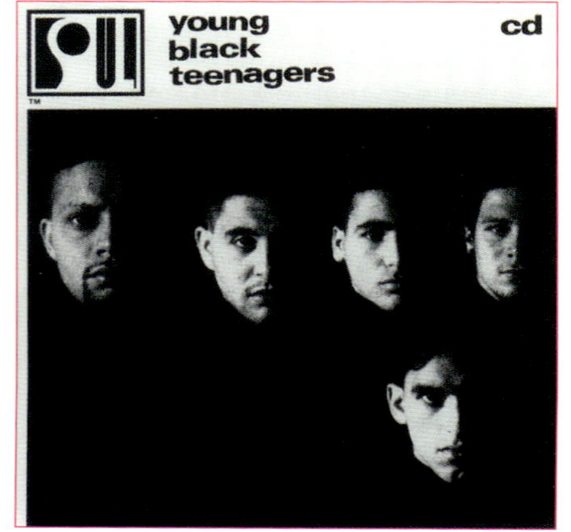
young black teenagers
cd

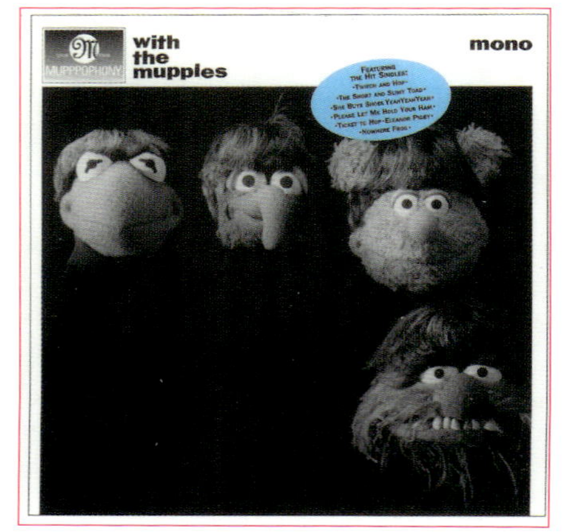
MUPPPOPHONY
with the mupples
mono

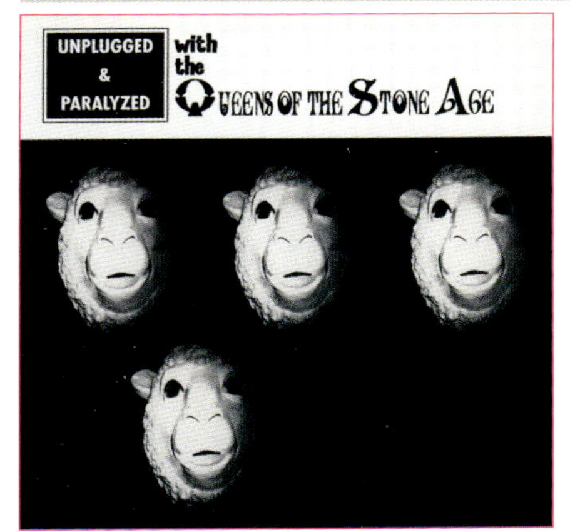
UNPLUGGED & PARALYZED
with the
QUEENS OF THE STONE AGE

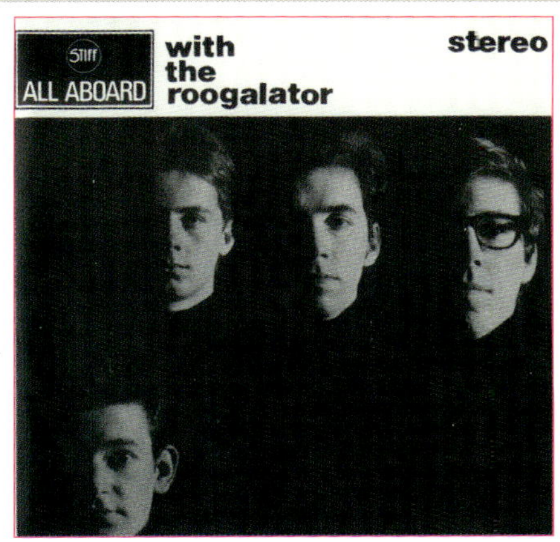
Stiff
ALL ABOARD
with
the
roogalator
stereo

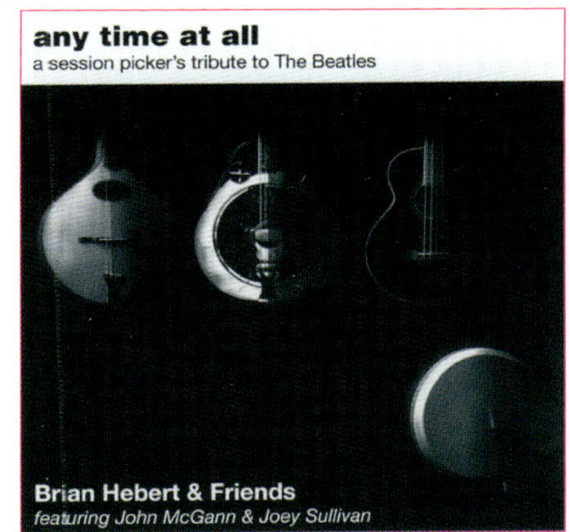
any time at all
a session picker's tribute to The Beatles
Brian Hebert & Friends
featuring John McGann & Joey Sullivan

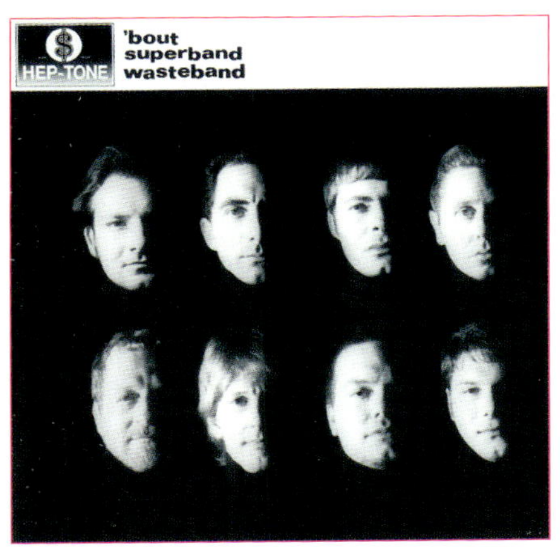
HEP-TONE
'bout
superband
wasteband

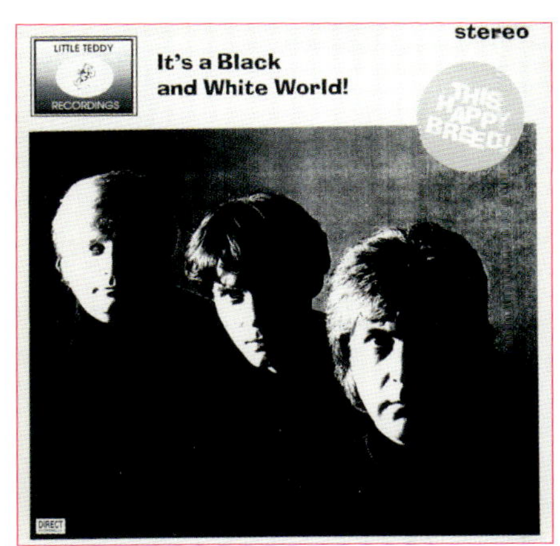
LITTLE TEDDY
RECORDINGS
It's a Black
and White World!
THIS
'APPY
BREED!
stereo
DIRECT

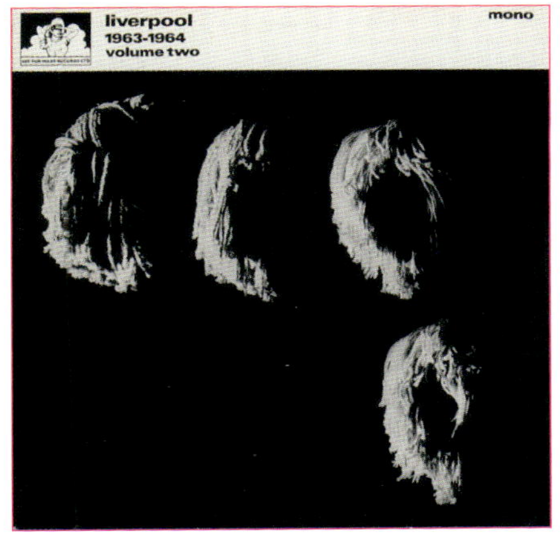
liverpool
1963-1964
volume two
mono

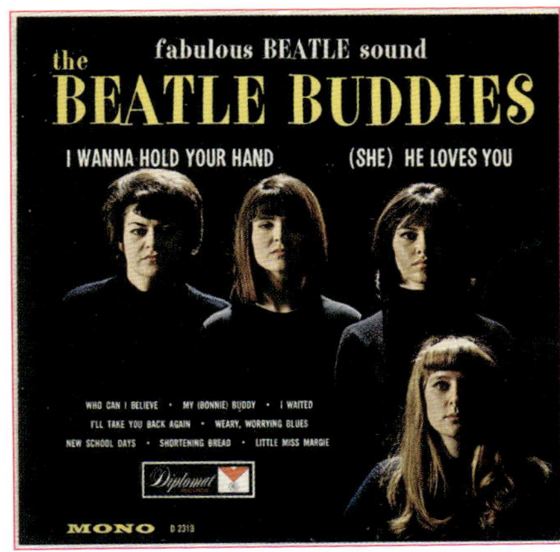
fabulous BEATLE sound
the
BEATLE BUDDIES
I WANNA HOLD YOUR HAND   (SHE) HE LOVES YOU
WHO CAN I BELIEVE · MY (BONNIE) BUDDY · I WAITED
I'LL TAKE YOU BACK AGAIN · WEARY, WORRYING BLUES
NEW SCHOOL DAYS · SHORTENING BREAD · LITTLE MISS MARGIE
Diplomat
MONO   D 2313

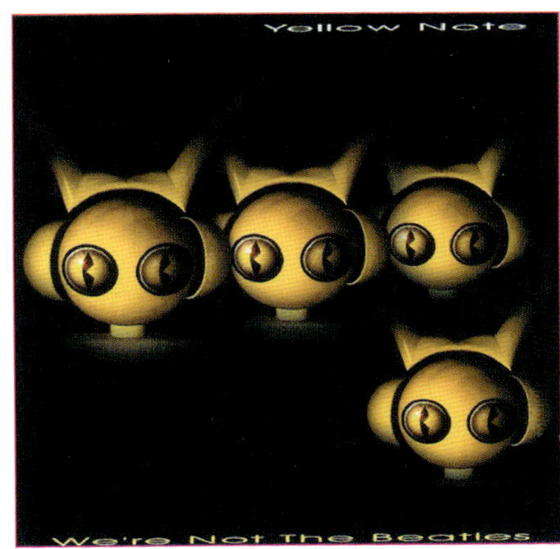
Yellow Note
We're Not The Beatles

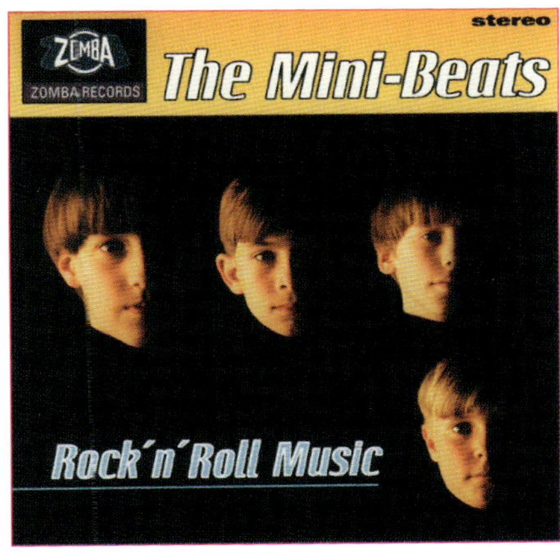
ZOMBA
ZOMBA RECORDS
The Mini-Beats
stereo
Rock 'n' Roll Music

Help! [1965 : Parlophone] sported another Robert Freeman portrait, also adapted for the US version (which carried graphics from the movie poster) on Capitol. Both have been widely copied, from the Vargas-style pin-ups on the V/A set to the Yoko Ono figure on Mono! though most bands just seem to like copying the semaphore poses.

Artist :
Asylum Party
Title : Ticket
To Ride / 1990
Single / LA
- New Rose
Artwork,
photo : Alain
Duplantier

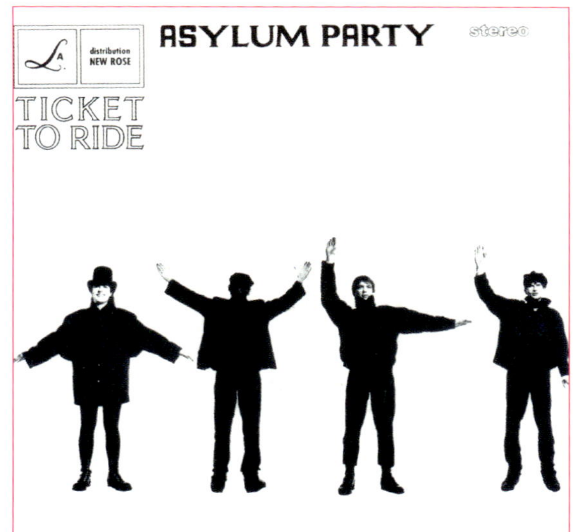

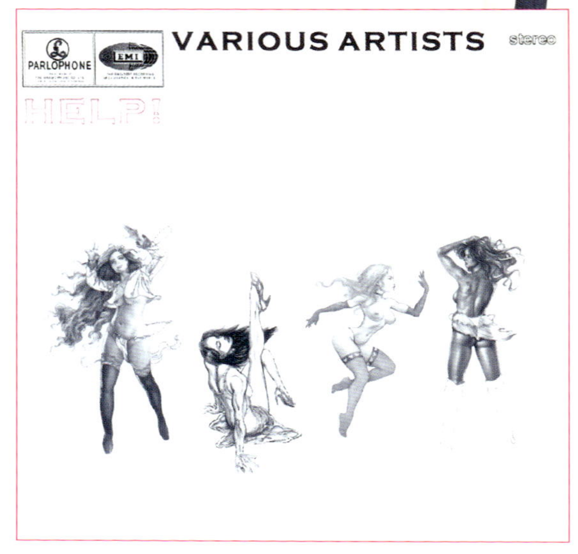

Artist
: Various
Artists
Title : Help!
/ 1994
Album :
Parlophone
Artwork :
Unknown

Artist : Tater
Totz
Title : Mono
/ 1989
Album : Giant
Records
Artwork : Bill
Bartell, Mike
Carter

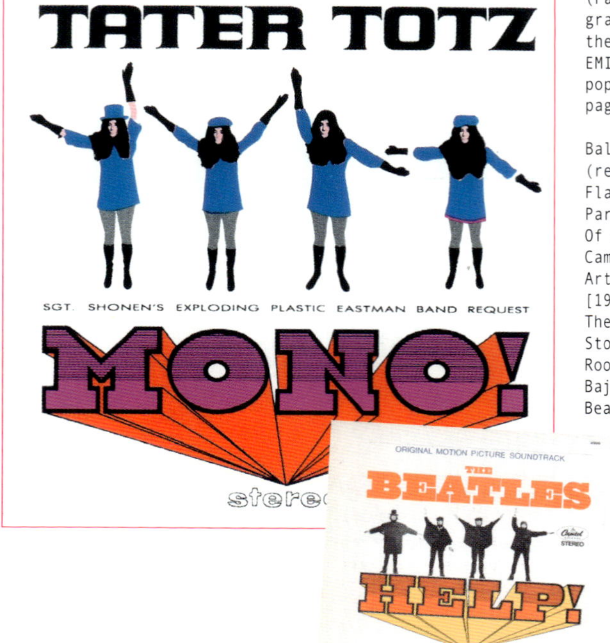

(Pages 18-19) With The Beatles [1963 : Parlophone] carried a striking grainy monochrome photograph of the band by Robert Freeman, set under the generic Parlophone logo and lower case bounced type title which was EMIs cover house-style at the time and could be seen on dozens of their pop album releases. None have been copied so much. On the last two pages we have (l-r, top to bottom):

Balzac : Wall 308 [1999 Artwork : Unknown] / The Baronics : Get Bach (reverse) [1996 Artwork : Jean-François Käfe, François Spénard] / White Flag : Ask Anybody + 1 [1995 Artwork : Pat Fear] / The Beatles Hit Parade 20 : Act Naturally - Help [Artwork : Unknown] / Genesis : Land Of Confusion + 1 [1986 Artwork : Genesis, Baker Dave. Photo : Andrew Cameron. Puppets by Fluck & Law] / Kabuta Mushi Gaiden : Osama [2005 Artwork : Hill Art] / Young Black Teenagers : Young Black Teenagers [1991 Artwork : Reiner Design Consultants. Photo : Perry Thompson] / The Muppets : With The Muppets [1994 Artwork : Unknown] / Queens Of The Stone Age : Unplugged & Paralyzed With [2005 Artwork : Unknown] / The Roogalator : All Aboard + 1 [1976 Artwork : Edward Barker. Photo : J.I. Bajzert] / Brian Hebert & Friends : A Session Picker's Tribute To The Beatles [2008 Artwork, photo : Henry Studios] / Superband Wasteband : Hear What You've Only Smelled (Inner sleeve) [1998 Artwork : Denny Burkes] / This Happy Breed : It's A Black And White World [1999 Artwork, photo : Barry the scouser] / Various Artists : Liverpool 1963-1964 [1983 Artwork : Unknown] / The Beatle Buddies : Fabulous Beatle Sound [1965 Artwork : Unknown] / Yellow Note : We're Not The Beatles [1998 Artwork : D. Barratt] / The Mini-Beats : Rock 'n' Roll Music [2000 Artwork : Fryderyk Gabowicz]

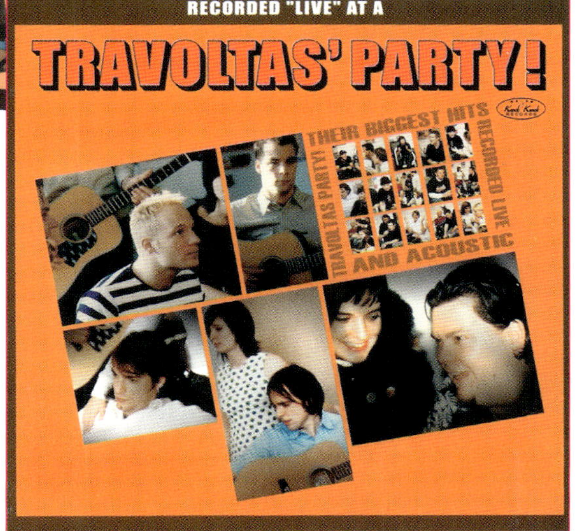

The rather dowdy album cover for Beach Boys' Party! in 1968 [Artwork : Tommy Steele / Chuck Ames] nevertheless prompted this knowing recreation for The Travoltas.

Artist :
Travoltas
Title :
Travoltas'
Party / 2005
Album / Knock
Knock Records
Artwork :
S. Venom at
MatthewStar.
com (Photos
: A. Van Der
Leer)

The 1974 album Endless Summer designed by Roy Kohare [Illustration : Keith McConnell] is another cover it's surprising to see borrowed, with The Toucans also adding Hokusai's famous Great Wave print to the mix (and even parodying the Pet Sounds title too).

Artist :
Toucans
Title : Beak
Sounds / 2003
Album /
Tropico
Records
Artwork : Leo
Daedalus

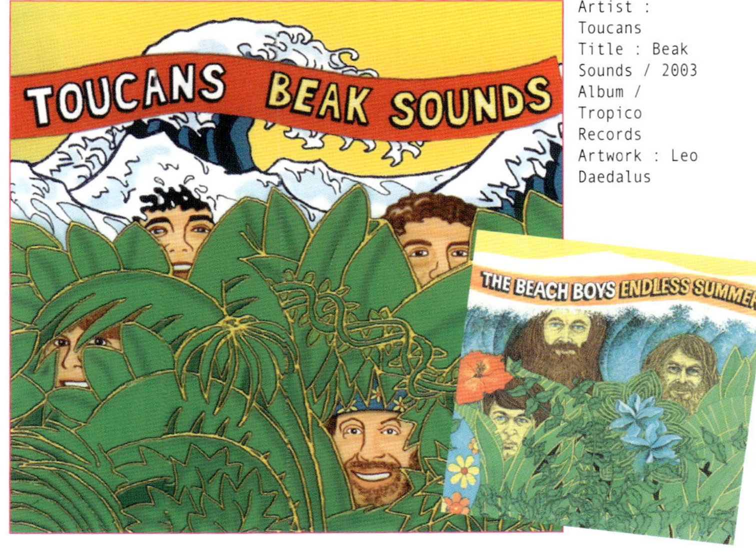

Artist :
Scratch
Bongowax
Title : Surfin'
Turd +3 / 1994
EP / Dionysus
Records
Artwork : SBW
Productions
(Photo : Craig
Weatherwax)

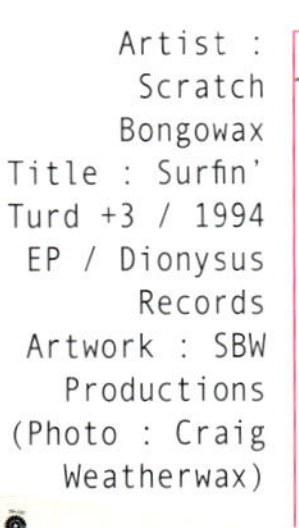

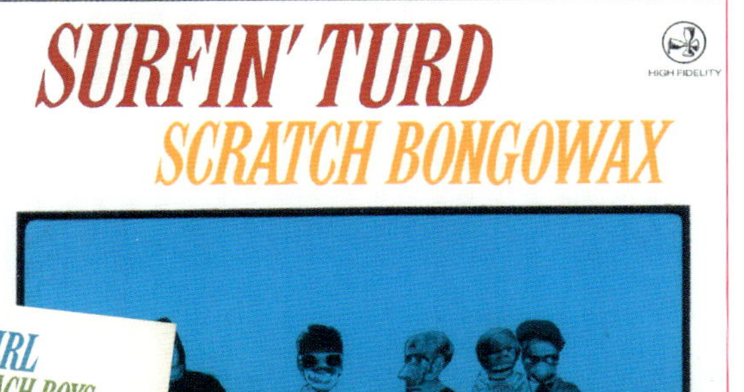

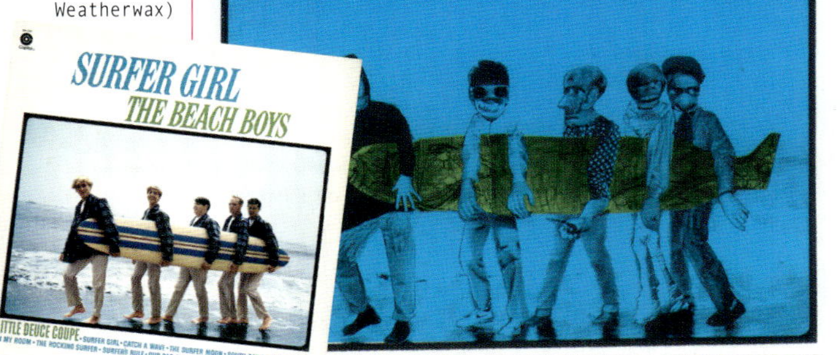

You would expect a seminal band like The Beach Boys to have had their art borrowed, though it's doubtful if back in 1963 they ever figured Surfer Girl (with the iconic cover shot by Ken Veeder) would end up looking like this!

Artist :
Beginner
Title : Gustav
Gans - Danke
/ 2003
Single /
Universal
Artwork :
Typeholics.KK1

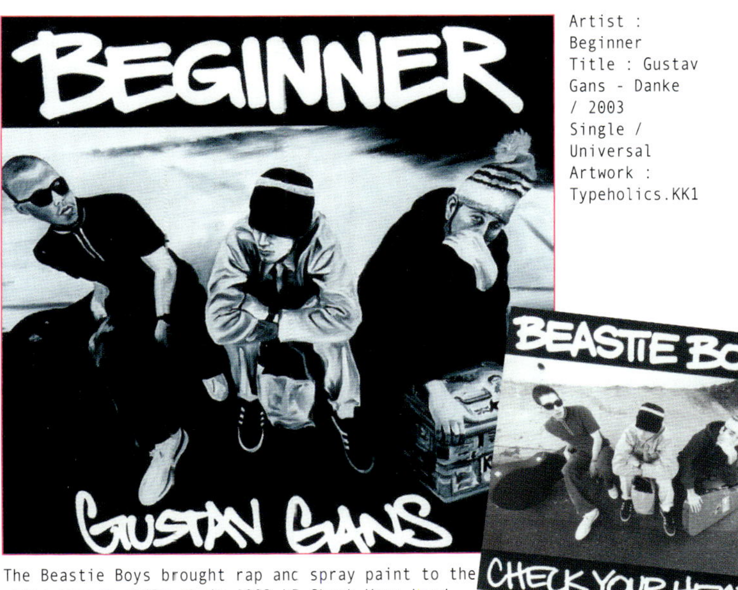

The Beastie Boys brought rap and spray paint to the white masses while their 1992 LP Check Your Head art by Haze Productions [Photo : Glen E. Friedman] also found imitators.

Karenlee Grant's sleeve for the Jeff Beck Group in 1972 [Photos : Richie Simpson] is simple but effective, and was used for this 1996 guitar compilation.

The poor old Bee Gees were much loved by impressionists and even inspired their own spoof tribute band, The Heebeegeebees, here parodying the 1976 Children Of The World sleeve [Designer : unknown].

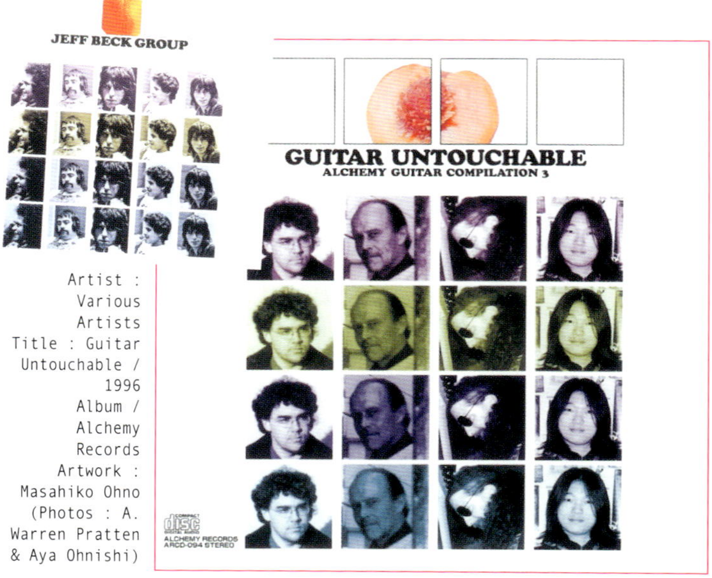

Artist : Various Artists
Title : Guitar Untouchable / 1996
Album / Alchemy Records
Artwork : Masahiko Ohno (Photos : A. Warren Pratten & Aya Ohnishi)

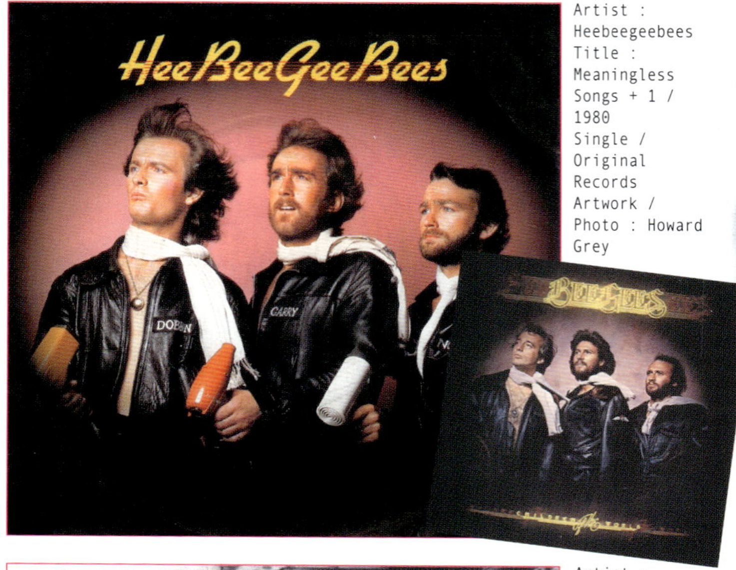

Artist : Heebeegeebees
Title : Meaningless Songs + 1 / 1980
Single / Original Records
Artwork / Photo : Howard Grey

Artist : The Quitters
Title : 1982 / 2006
Album / Garage-Pop Records
Artwork : Unknown

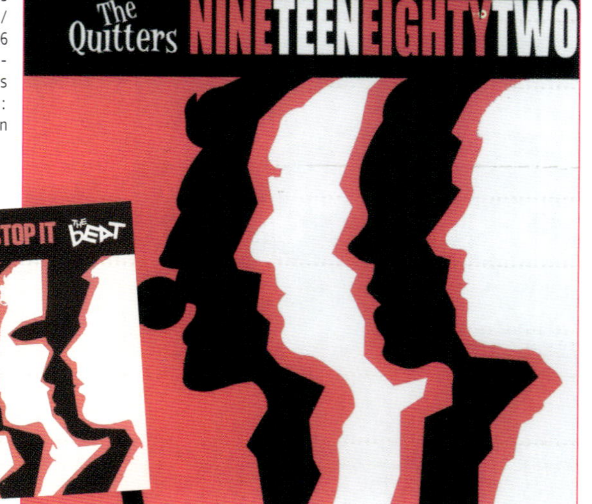

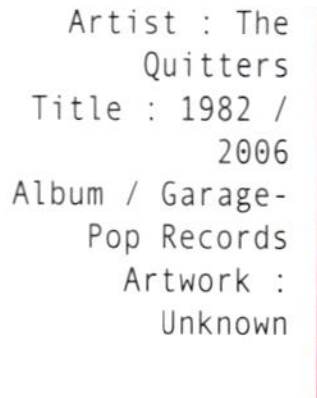

Artist : Lombardi
Title : Uno / 2002
Album / Warner Music Spain
Artwork : Rafa Sanudo (Photo : Jose Luis Santalla)

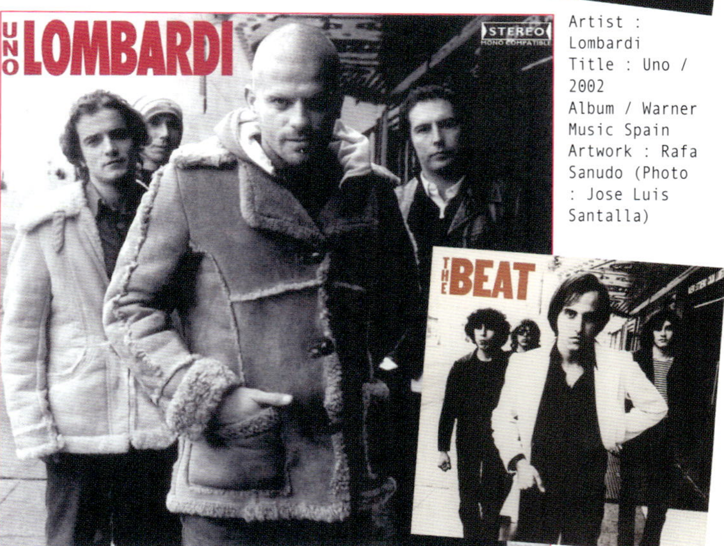

The Beat (U.K.) issued I Just Can't Stop It in 1980 on Go-Feet Records (through Arista) with a simple cover idea (uncredited for some reason) which was picked up over two decades later by The Quitters (also uncredited).

The Beat (U.S.A.) must have struck a chord with their 1979 debut, so much so that Lombardi even sought out the exact location of the cover photo (by Bob Seidemann) for their own version.

Beyoncé's Dangerously In Love [Photo : Markus Klinko & Indrani] was released in June 2003. Jintara's version hit Thailand shops in September, albeit she was more modestly clad to comply with Thai law (which given some of the seedier aspects of their tourist trade has to be ironic).

Graham Wright at the Cream agency (who put together a number of sleeves around this time) did the Sabotage cover in 1975, which for some strange reason gets closely replicated for the badly punned Camarosmith sleeve.

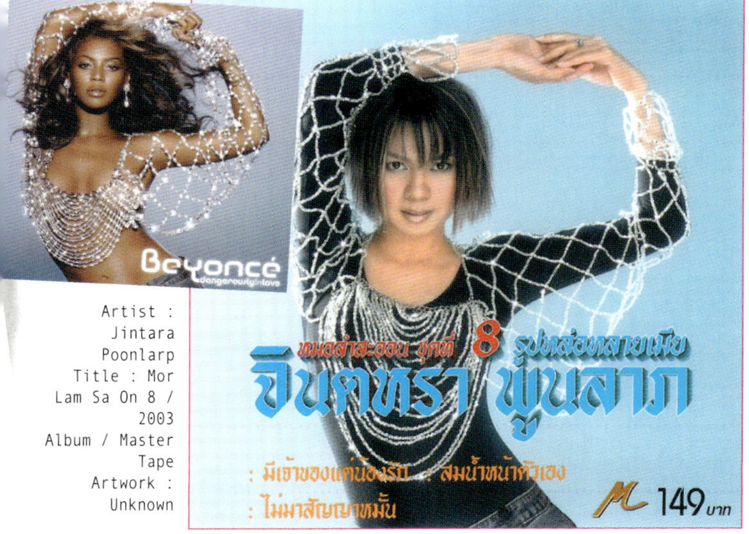

Artist : Jintara Poonlarp
Title : Mor Lam Sa On 8 / 2003
Album / Master Tape
Artwork : Unknown

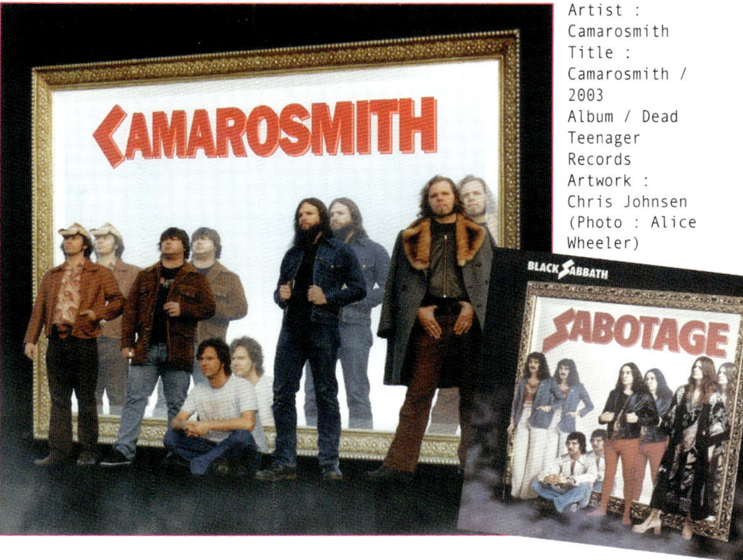

Artist : Camarosmith
Title : Camarosmith / 2003
Album / Dead Teenager Records
Artwork : Chris Johnsen
(Photo : Alice Wheeler)

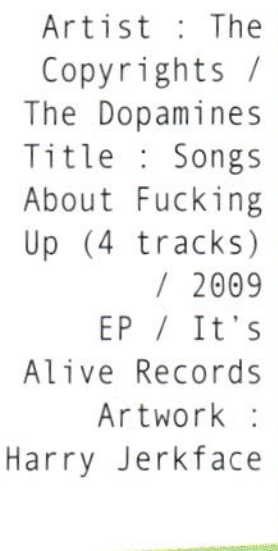

Artist : The Copyrights / The Dopamines
Title : Songs About Fucking Up (4 tracks) / 2009
EP / It's Alive Records
Artwork : Harry Jerkface

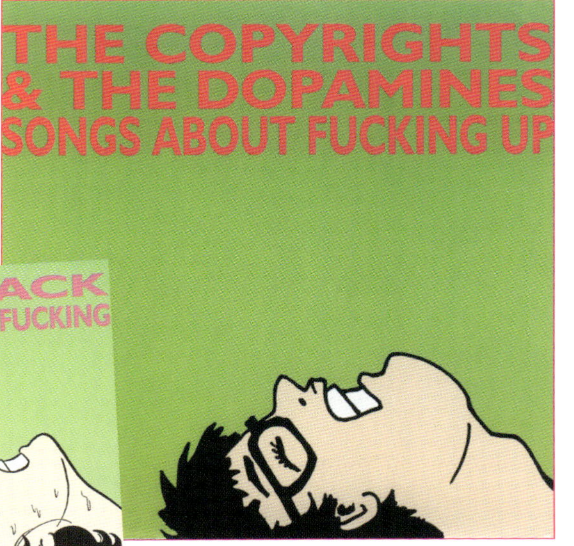

Big Black's 1987 album Songs About Fucking [Touch And Go Records. Designer : unknown] gets an obvious parody treatment on a two band 4 track EP.

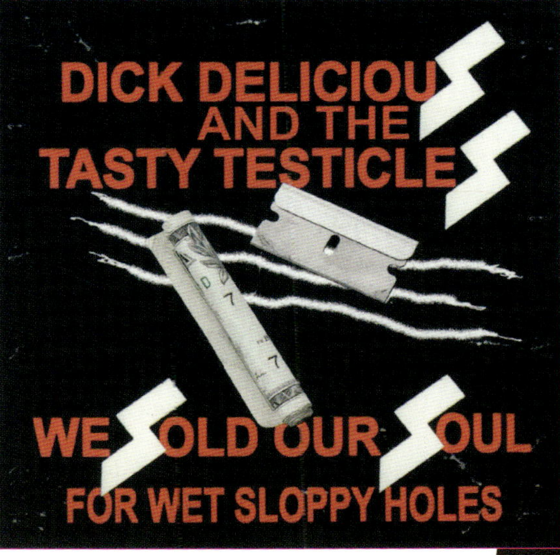

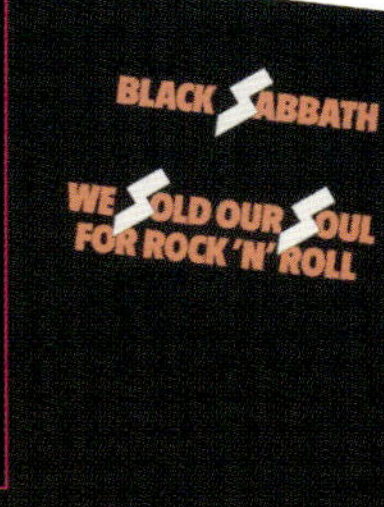

Artist : Dick Delicious & The Tasty Testicles
Title : We Sold Our Soul For Wet Sloppy Holes / 2001
Album / WFPTSO Records
Artwork : Dick Delicious

Sabbath's 1976 LP We Sold Our Soul For Rock 'N' Roll [Artwork : Results] has been lifted in part by the snappily named Dick Delicious & The Tasty Testicles - the parts in question being the Nazi-like 'S' and the title.

Black Sabbath's cunningly titled fourth album Vol. 4 [1972 : Vertigo] was designed by the Bloomsbury Group with a high contrast live snap of Ozzie by Keith McMillan. As you can see it has been copied. A lot. More than any of their other sleeves. Something about the simple layout just seems to strike a chord and it's a design which works at almost any size too. There are even people crawling the web looking for the exact font (in vain, it was hand-drawn for the cover).

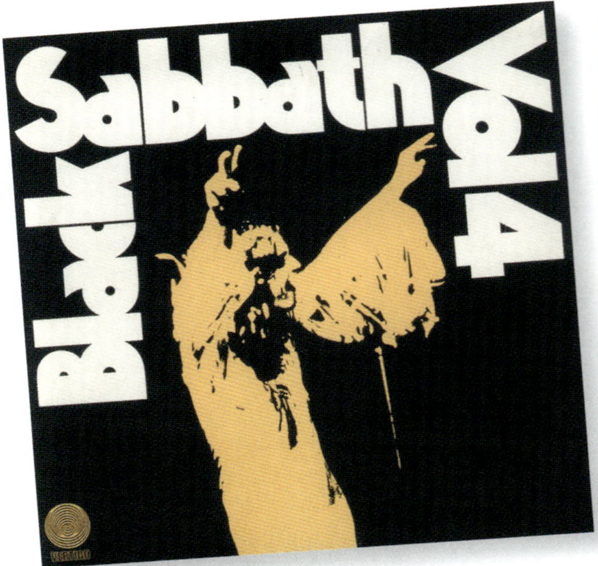

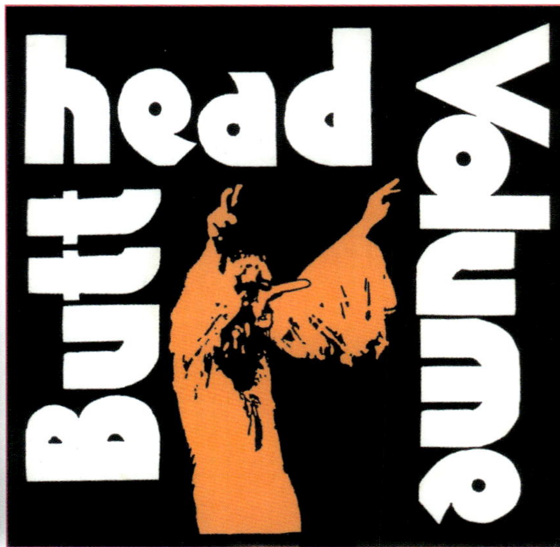

Artist : Butthead
Title : Volume (4 track) / 1992
EP / Heat Blast
Artwork : Unknown

Artist : Jim Florentine
Title : Terrorizing Telemarketers Vol. 4 / 2005
Album / Mulejuice
Artwork : Mike Morse

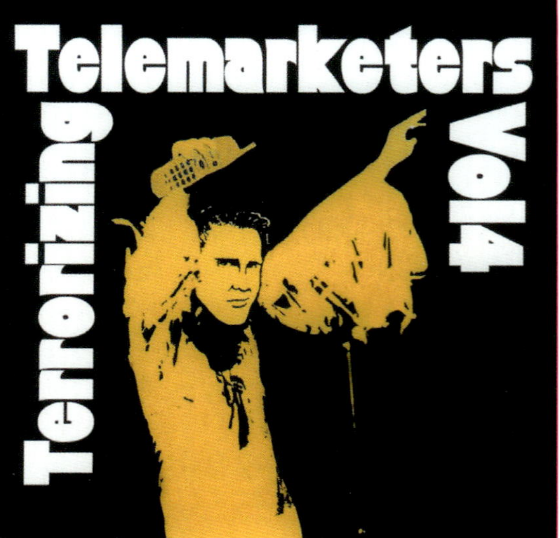

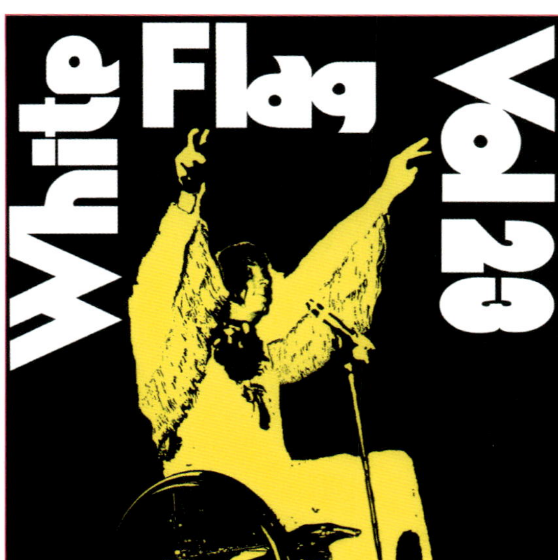

Artist : White Flag
Title : Vol. 23 / 2010
Single / Cupcake Records
Artwork : Pat Fear / Michael F. Glass (Photo : Kim McWhorter)

Some covers just copy the original photo (Butthead, Church of Misery), others add to it (the Telemarketers), and many parody it (White Flag, Peaceville). The Peaceville title here is actually a tribute CD, the least convincing sleeve of them all funnily enough.

Artist :
Various
Artists
Title :
Peaceville
Vol. 4 / 1992
Album /
Peaceville
Records
Artwork :
Anthony Young

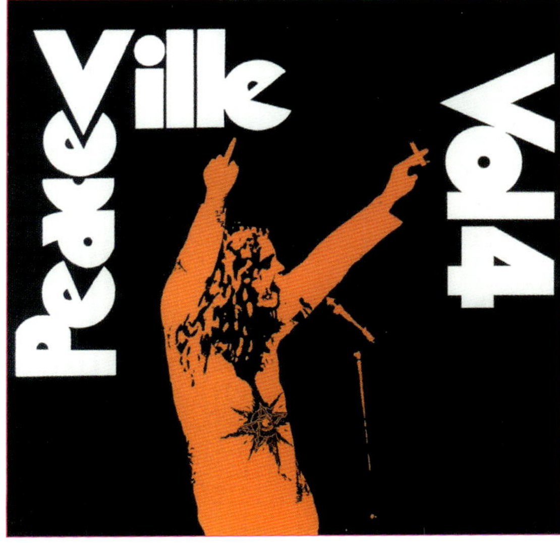

Artist :
Church Of
Misery
Title : Vol.
1 / ?
Album / Doom
Records
Artwork :
Unknown

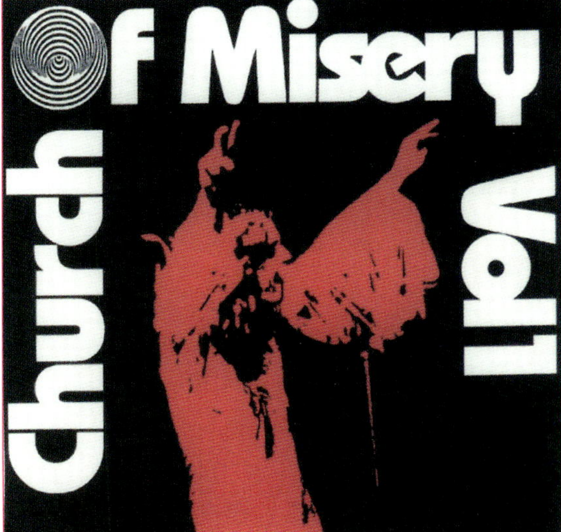

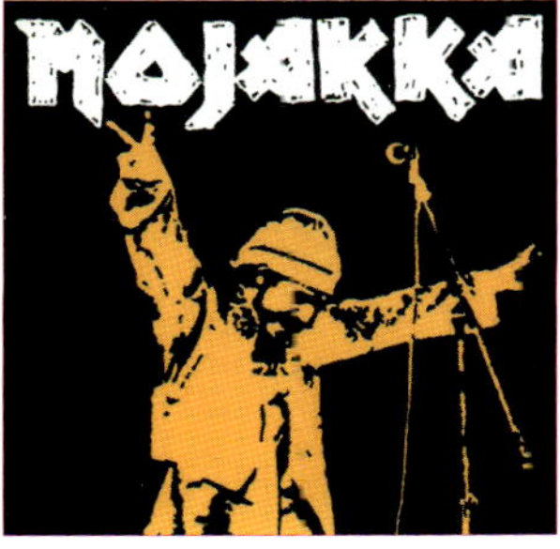

above

Artist : Rehupiikles
Title : Jatsin Kutso / 2003
Album / Edel Records

Artist : Mojakka
no more details

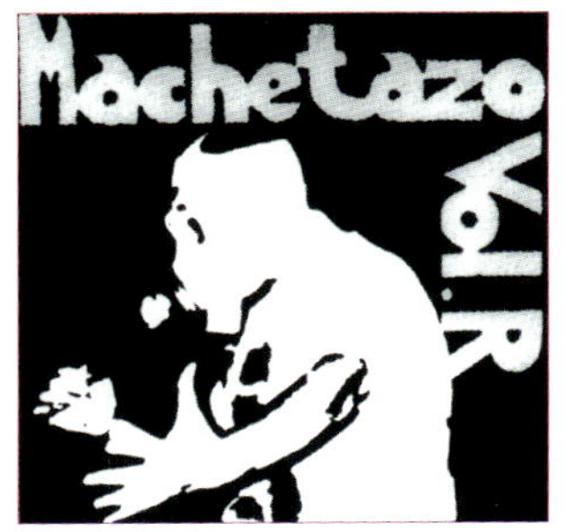

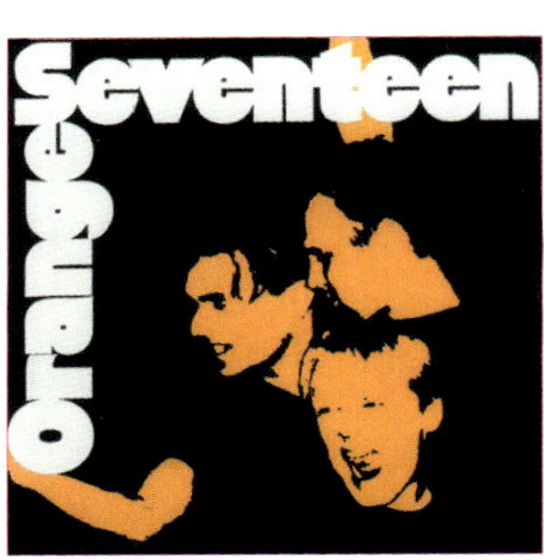

above

Artist : Machetazo / Abscess
Title : Vol. R
EP Label : Parade / Throne
Records
Artwork : Manel Craneo

Artist : Orange Seventeen
Title : (We Want) Rock N' Roll
Tonight + 1 / 2000
Single / Dart Records
Artwork : Karl (Photo : Brenda
D.)

Stylorouge did loads of great sleeves (and sadly a rubbish book documenting them all!). This slick offering for Blur [1995. Photo : Tom King] was parodied almost at once on a v/artists cover. Great title. Don't remember it happening.

Boney M's Love For Sale might have seemed risque for 1977 (when many major labels became more conservative), but what were the two whacky Poles thinking of twenty years on?

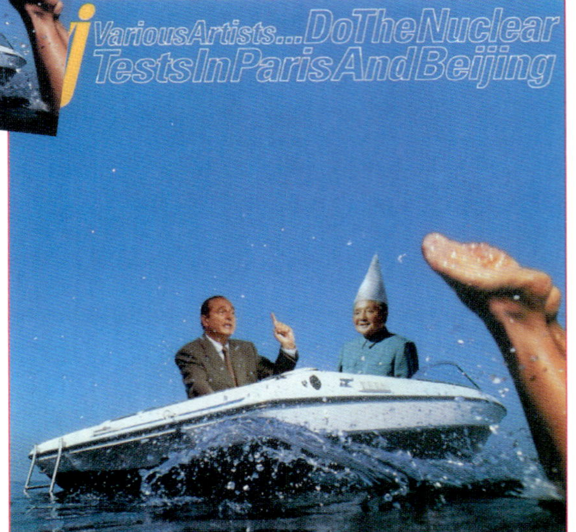

Artist : Various Artists
Title : Do The Nuclear Tests In Paris And Beijing / 1995
Album / Vinyl Japan
Artwork : Angie Boothroyd - Tetsuya

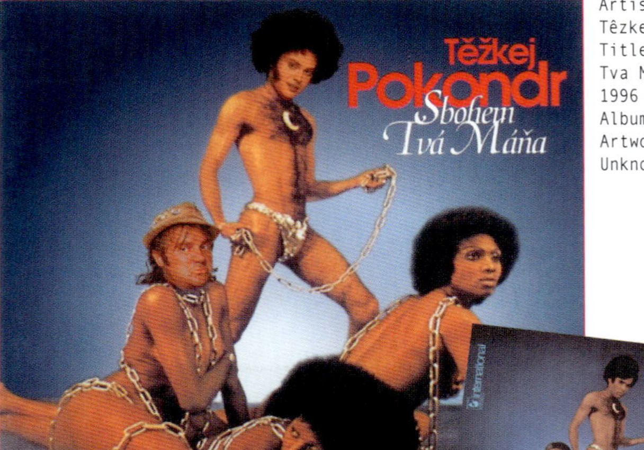

Artist : Tĕžkej Pokondr
Title : Shohem Tva M ña / 1996
Album / Sony
Artwork : Unknown

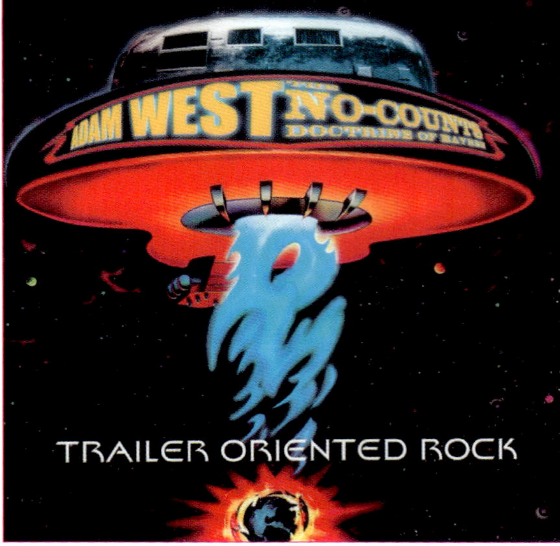

Artist : Adam West
Title : Trailer Oriented Rock / 2003
Album / Sleazey Records
Artwork : Mauamor (a.k.a. Edgar Raposo)

Artist : Foreskin 500
Title : More Tha A Feeling / Less Than A Feeling
Anno : 1996
Format : Single (Picture disc)
Label : GSL
Artwork : John Dunn

Boston's self titled 1976 debut had a cheesy sci-fi cover (by Roger Huyssen) redolent of the times, and was the subject of two ribbings; one by Adam West (not the Batman actor I assume) - sharing the album with The No-Counts Doctrine Of Mayhem - and a picture disc by Foreskin.

Blondie's massive selling 1978 Parallel Lines album [Design : Ramey Communications. Photo : Edo] came up with a novel group portrait and one which was instantly recognisable. No wonder a number of bands have borrowed the idea, with Lombardi (them again, see page 22) getting the prize for worst look-a-like. UK punk band Deadline take the prize for least likely to get listed in the charts German record label name (and have wisely shortened it for their website url).

Artist :
Deadline
Title :
Hanging On The
Telephone + 2
/ 2006
EP / I Used To
Fuck People
Like You In
Prison
Artwork :
Unknown

Artist : Germ
Attack
Title : A
Tribute To
Blondie / 1996
Album /
Wolverine
Records
Artwork : Def.
com (Photo :
Eva)

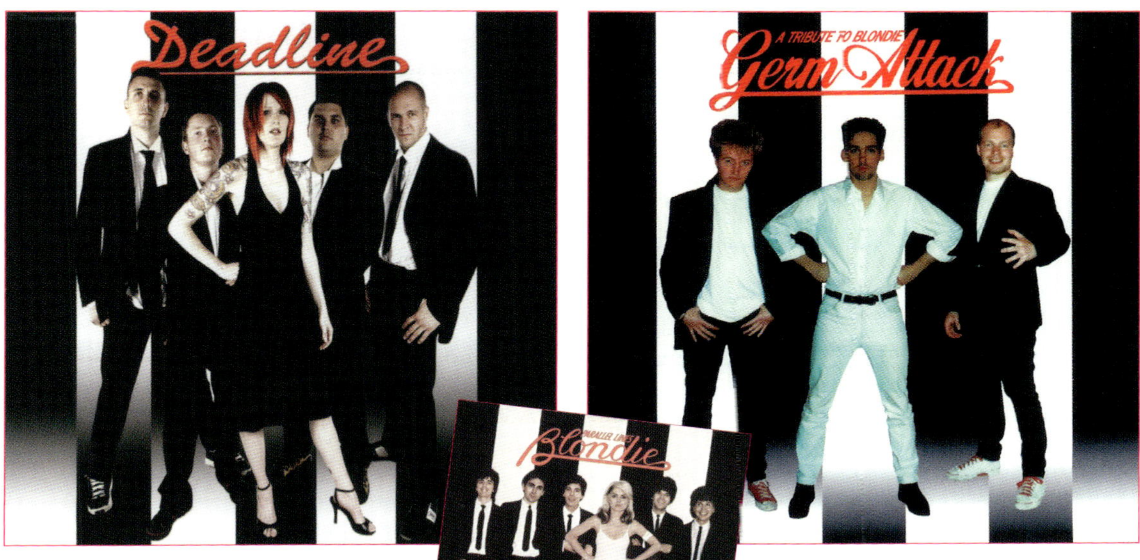

Artist :
Lombardi
Title : Uno
(Backside) /
2002
Album / Warner
Music Spain
Artwork : Rafa
Sanudo

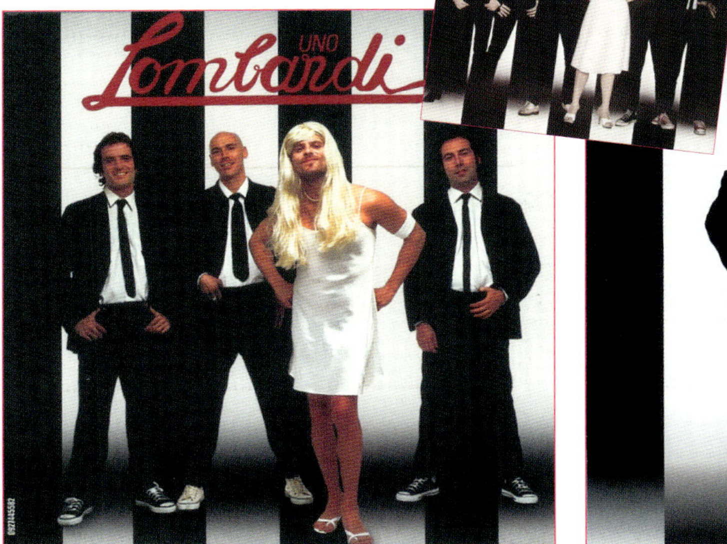

Artist :
Rantanplan
Title : Liebe
Minus Null /
2005
EP / Hamburg
All Styles
Recordings
Artwork :
Petra Wehling
(Photo :
Andrea
Küppers)

Two more inspired by Blondie originals, The Favourites using Eat To The Beat's stylish post-punk look from 1979 [Chrysalis. Artwork : Norman Seeff / Billy Bass], and Kishidan giving a slightly menacing interpretation of their debut Blondie [1976 : Private Stock. Artwork : David Perl. Photo : Shig Ikeida].

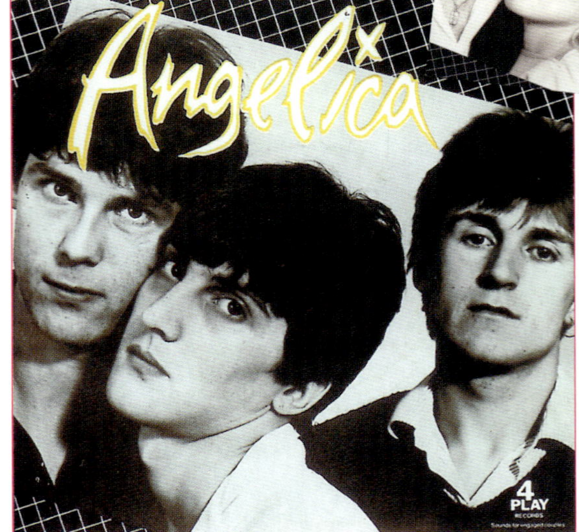

Artist :
Kishidan
Title : Boy's
Color / 2003
Album /
Capitol
Artwork :
Unknown

Artist : The
Favourites
Title :
Angelica + 1
/ 1979
Single / 4
Play Records
Artwork :
Unknown

Artist : Robyn
Ludwick
Title : Out Of
These Blues /
2010
Album / Late
Show Records
Artwork : Tom
Betts Photo
: Todd V.
Wolfson

D.J. Hop &
Mike Czech
Title : Neck
Excersize
Vol. 2
Album / Neck
Exersize
Records
Artwork : Rap
Town

Ludwick is going as much for the feel of Jackson Browne's Late For The Sky album from 1974 [Asylum Records. Artwork : Bob Seidemann / Jackson Browne] and the lettering is clearly based on SF poster supremo Rick Griffin's original trademark hand-lettering.

D.J. Hop & Mike Czech simply photoshopped themselves into a copy of Black Sheep's A Wolf In Sheep's Clothing [1991, Mercury. Artwork : Alli. Photo : Chris Callis]. Both covers are open to misinterpretation if you ask me.

No reason that I can see for this part copy, part reinvention of David Bowie's gatefold Diamond Dogs LP cover painting by Guy Peellaert [1974 : RCA], with what looks like Angie Bowie's head on. Belgian artist Peellaert specialised in airbrushed rock portraits at the time which were collected into a best selling book Rock Dreams.

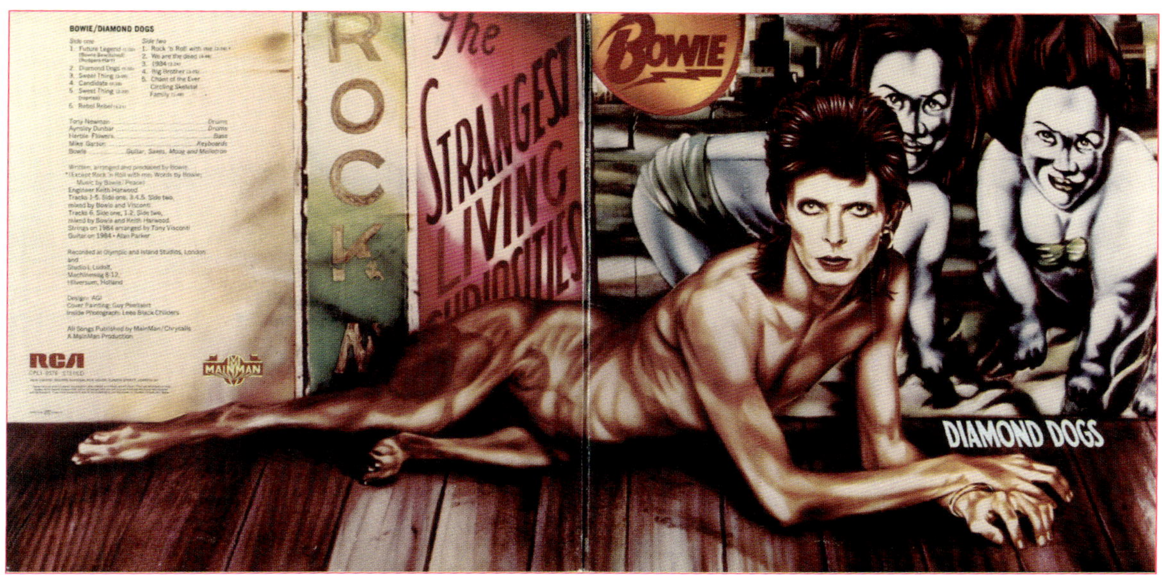

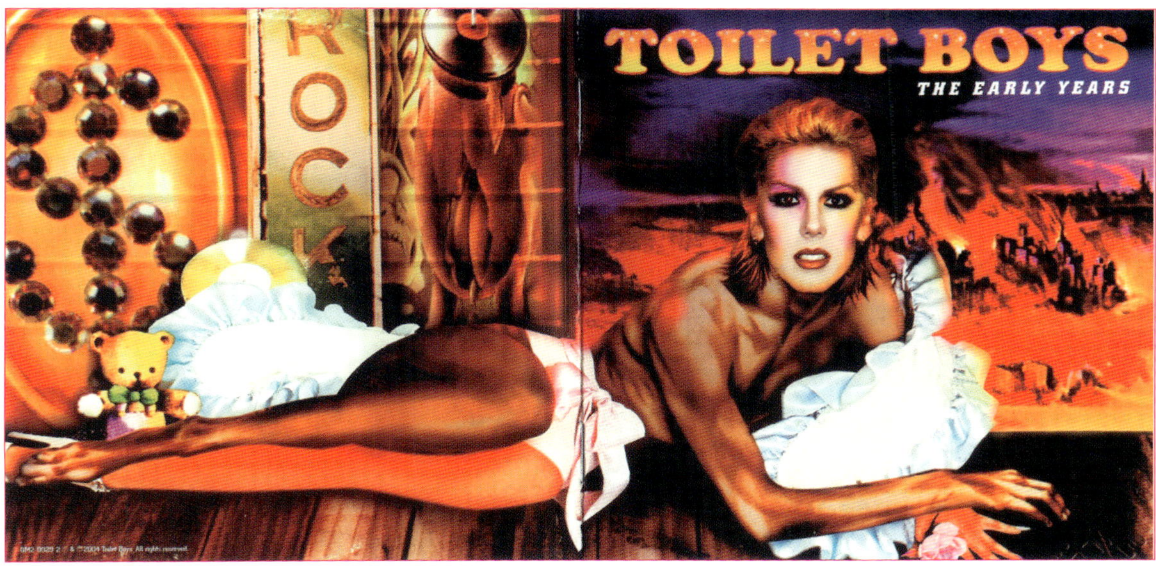

Artist : Toilet Boys
Title : The Early Years / 2004
Album / Ozit Morpheus Records
Artwork : Edward Odowd. Illustration : Scott Ewalt

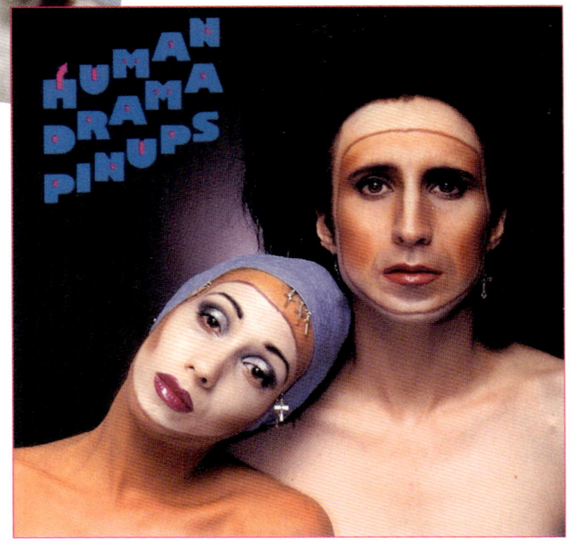

DAVID BOWIE

David Bowie has proved to be as influential with his covers as music. Pin-Ups from 1973 [Artwork : Mick Rock / Ray Campbell. Photo : Justin] is just lovingly referenced by Human Drama. The Man Who Sold The World [1970. Photo : Brian Ward] has the piss taken by Five Fifteen with an accurate pastiche, while Heroes [1977. Photo : Sukita] is imitated to good effect by Cex, who then very cleverly repeats the exercise for an instrumental edition of the same album after slapping gaffa tape across his mouth. Top!

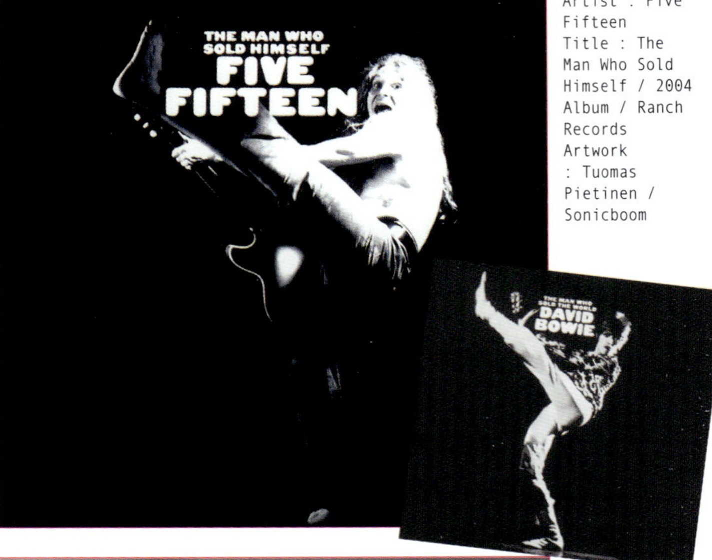

Artist : Human Drama
Title : Pinups / 1993
Album / Triple X Records
Artwork : Unknown

Artist : Five Fifteen
Title : The Man Who Sold Himself / 2004
Album / Ranch Records
Artwork : Tuomas Pietinen / Sonicboom

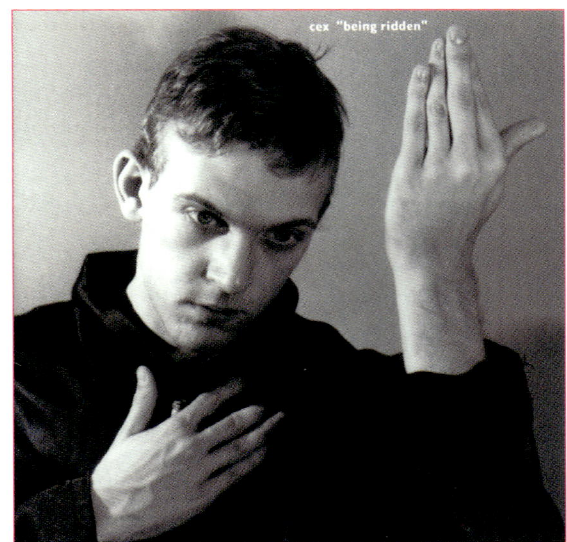

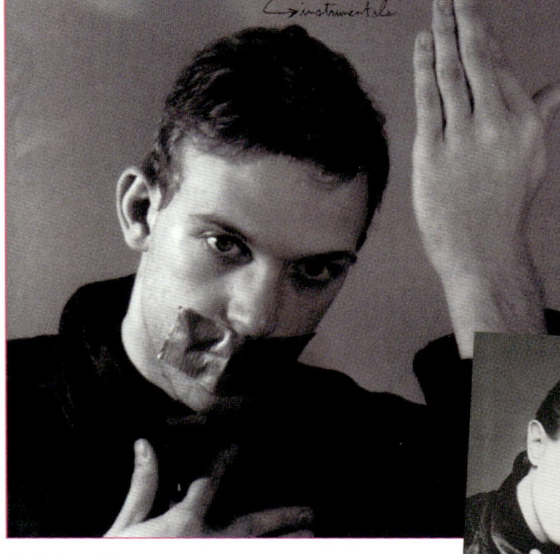

Artist : Cex
Title : Being Ridden / 2003
Album / Temporary Residence
Artwork : Jeremy Devine (Photo : Katie Rose)

Artist : Cex
Title : Being Ridden (Instrumental) / 2003
Album / Temporary Residence
Artwork : Jeremy Devine (Photo : Katie Rose)

The evocative cover to The Byrds country-rock classic Sweetheart Of The Rodeo album [1958 : Columbia. Artwork : Geller & Butler Advertising] relies on a great illustration from a 1933 book. In turn it has been borrowed by Petty Booka (with photos lifted from a book on old plastic radios), redrawn by a duo named after the album itself, and referenced on an album of celebrity vocalists by Rhino Records.

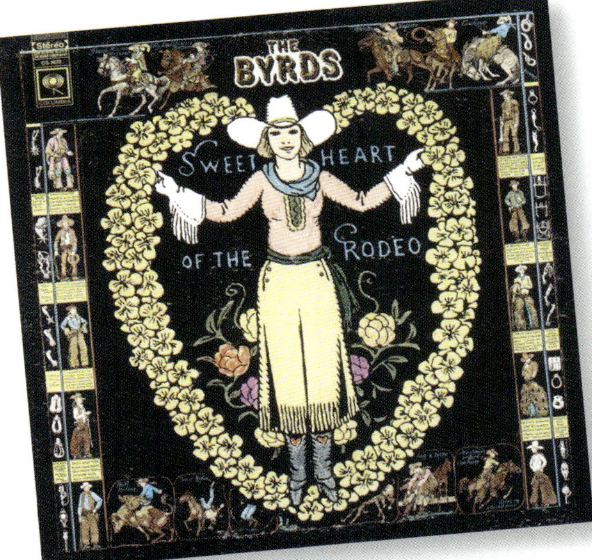

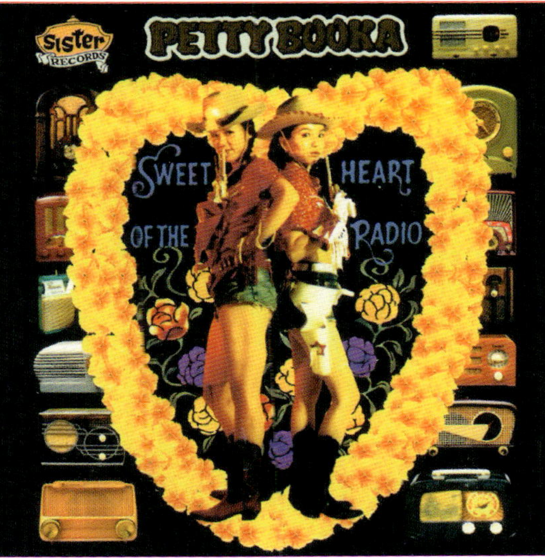

Artist : Petty Booka
Title : Sweetheart Of The Radio / 1997
Album / Sister Records
Artwork : Kato-chin club (Illustration : Rockin' Jelly Bean) (Photo : Bun-Shaka)

Artist : Various Artists
Title : Golden Throats - Sweethearts Of Rodeo Drive / 1995
Album / Rhino Records
Artwork : Monster X (Illustration : Drew Friedman)

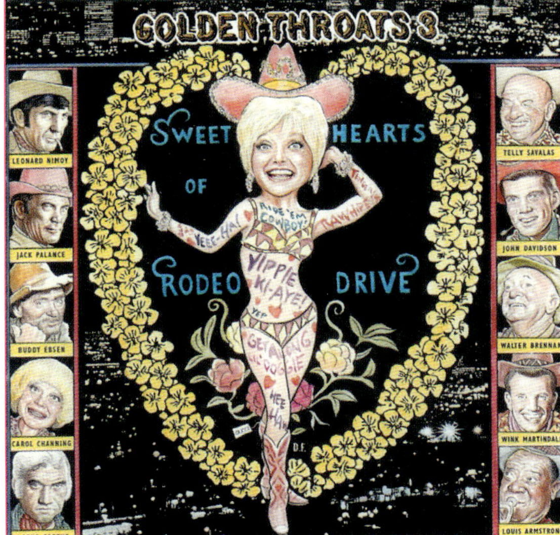

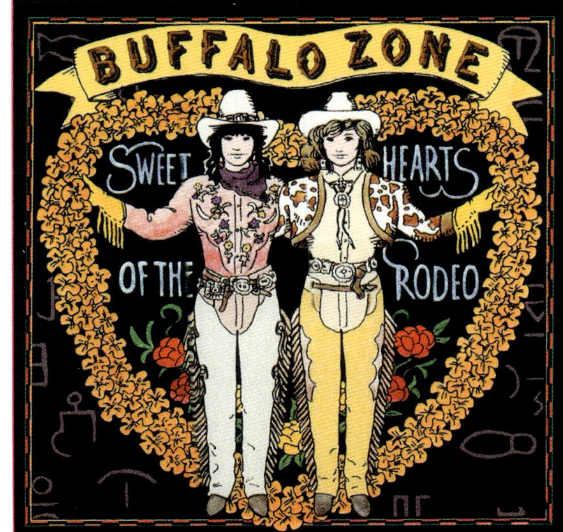

Artist : The Sweethearts Of The Rodeo
Title : Buffalo Zone / 1990
Album / Columbia
Artwork : Bill Johnson (Illustration : Dennas Davis)

Blue Cheer's Vincebus Eruptum pitched in at the centre of the psych movement in 1968 [Philips. Photo : John Van Hamersveld] with artwork by 'Gut' so redolent of the time it was bound to inspire others thirty plus years on, though none quite have quite the same mastery of lettering.

Artist : Dementia Thirteen
Title : Do The Snake + 2 / 2000
EP / Smilin' Bob Records
Artwork : Gut

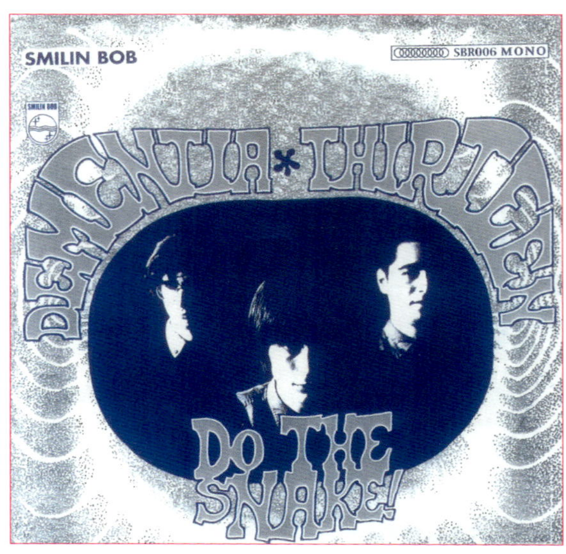

Artist : Reverend Bizarre
Title : Doom Meta / 2002
Album / Lohja Power
Artwork : Albert & John Gallo

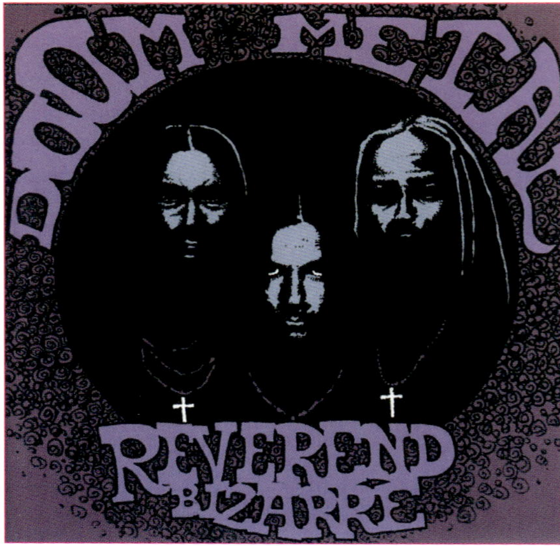

Artist : Thee Michelle Gun Elephant
Title : Chicken Zombies / 1997
Album / Triad
Artwork : Unknown

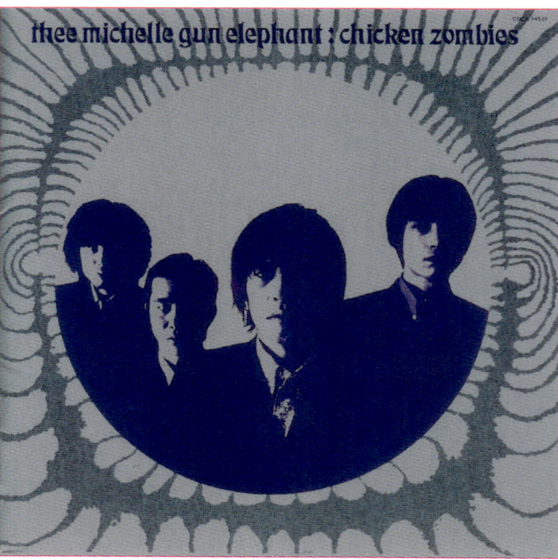

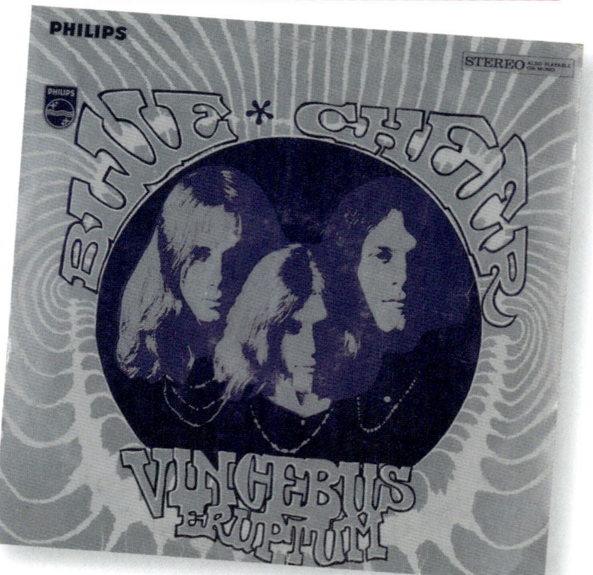

Borrowing Reid Miles graphics from his Blue Note cover designs is almost a cottage industry (this is the second example so far). His Tina Brooks 1960 cover for True Blue provides a blueprint for Blew (sorry).

Artist : Blew
Title : You're Not The Only One / 1998
Album / Broken Rekids
Artwork : Kumiko Suruki

The Dave Brubeck Quartet used a number of modern art works on their sleeves, including this from Time Out [1959. Columbia], designed by Randall Martin. Le Karlof replicate the typography and dropped in another piece of vintage art.

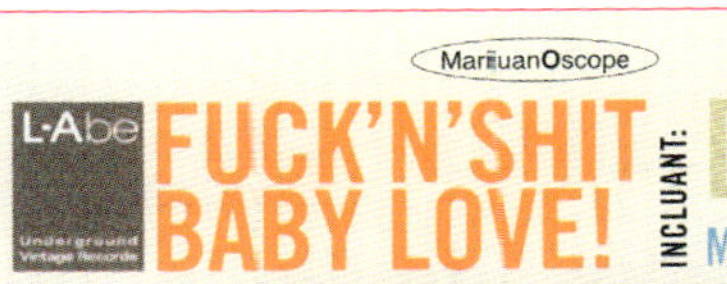

Artist :
Le Karlof Orchestra
Title : Fuck 'N' Shit Baby Love! / 2002
Album / Select
Artwork : François Coderre/Karim Blondy/Karlof Galovsky/ Crosso
Toile 'without Title # 17. Antoine St. James, New York, 1932

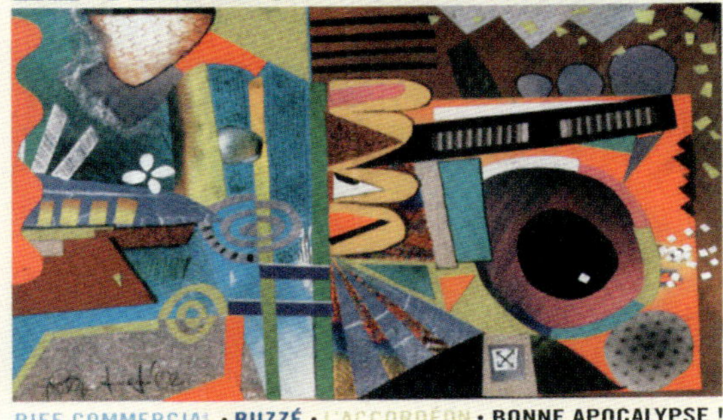

Artist : The Joggers
Title : Solid Guild / 2003
Album / Flameshovel
Artwork : Erica Bjerning & The Joggers (& Little e)

Buffalo Springfield's cover for Again [1967 : Atco] was put together by Loring Eutemey using an illustration by Eve Babitz, the idea being copied by The Joggers who get the type off nicely but miss the boat on the montage.

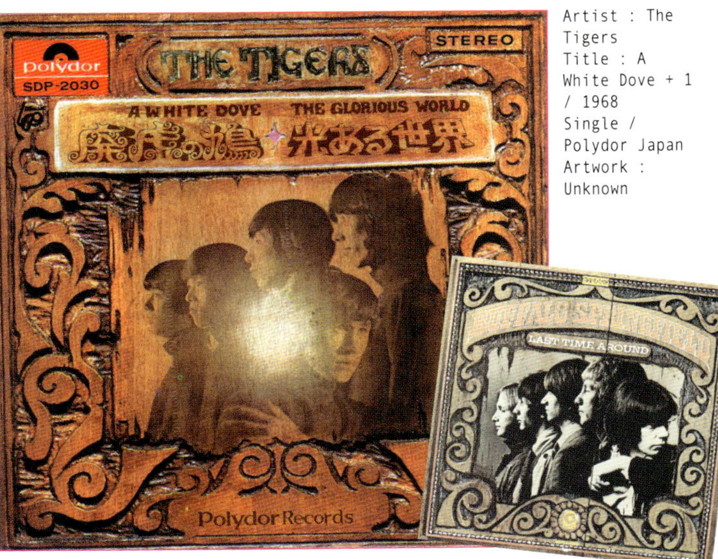

Artist : The Tigers
Title : A White Dove + 1 / 1968
Single / Polydor Japan
Artwork : Unknown

A strange one. Clearly both covers use a similar background photograph, it could just be coincidence especially since the Buffalo Springfield album Last Time Around [Artwork : Jimini Productions] and The Tiger's single both came out in 1968.

Big Brother & The Holding Company's Cheap Thrills is a rare example of underground comic artist (and all round genius) Robert Crumb working on an album sleeve back in 1968 [Artwork : Smay Vision. Illustration : Robert Crumb]. A quartet of bands have followed the layout and electric type but only the contemporary KYA collection begins to match up, though the Glory Hill art is a decent example of a more contemporary take.

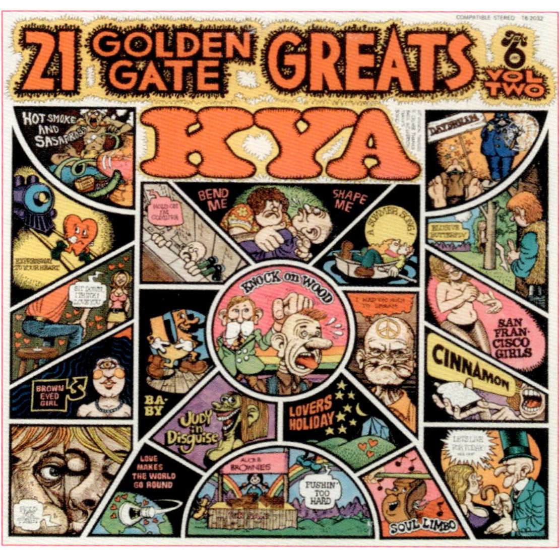

Artist : Various Artists
Title : KYA 21 Golden Gate Greats - Vol. 2 / 1968
Album / Take 6 Enterprises
Artwork : WT. Vinson

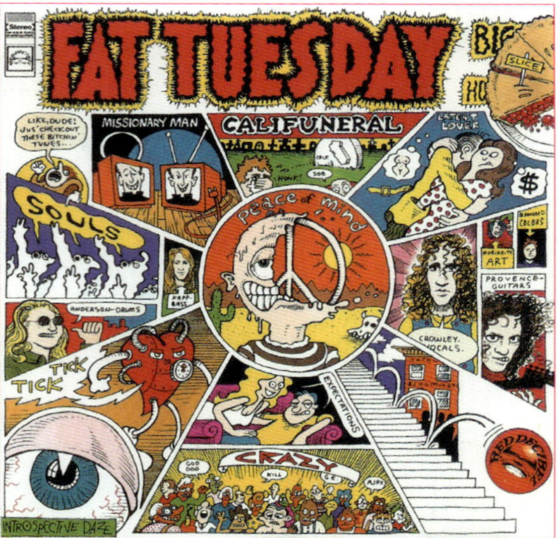

Artist : Fat Tuesday
Title : Califuneral / 1992
Album / Metal Blade Records
Artwork illustration : Pat Moriarity

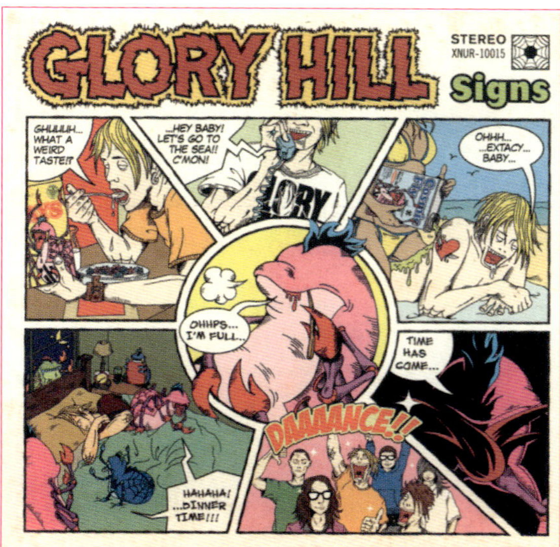

Artist : Glory Hill
Title : Signs / 2009
Album / Ultimate Recordings
Artwork : 7 Stars Design

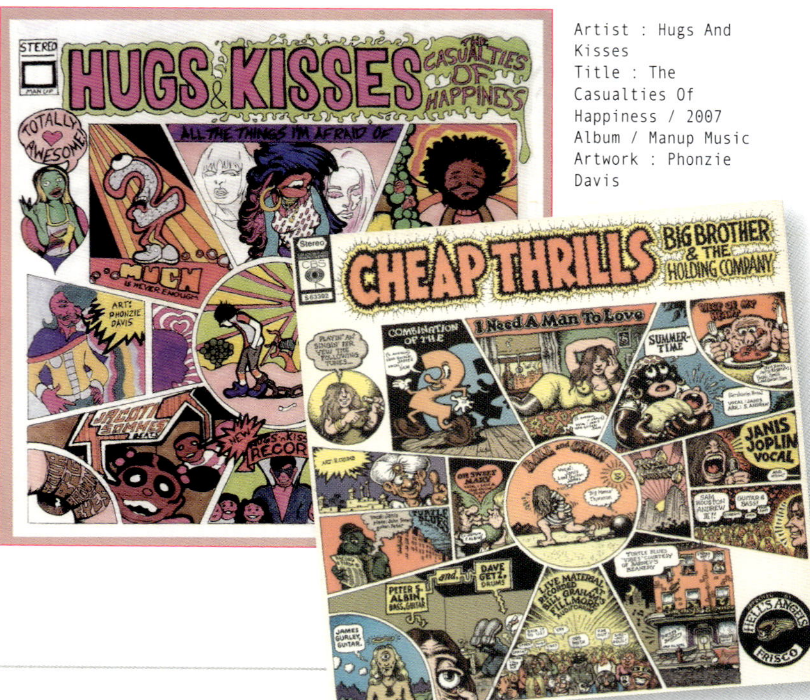

Artist : Hugs And Kisses
Title : The Casualties Of Happiness / 2007
Album / Manup Music
Artwork : Phonzie Davis

Two more examples of Reid Miles' work for Blue Note Records providing designers with their inspiration. Donald Byrd's A New Perspective [1963] is a typical example, with high-contrast black and white photography, the cool lines of an early E-Type Jag and clean type. You can forgive the James Taylor Quartet for copying it, and getting the vibe about right. However the 2004 Blue Note compilation below left merely shows how standards have slipped at the imprint since.

Artist : Various Artists
Title : Blue Note Revisited / 2004
Album / Blue Note - EMI
Artwork : Burton Yount
Photo : Till Kraut Krämer

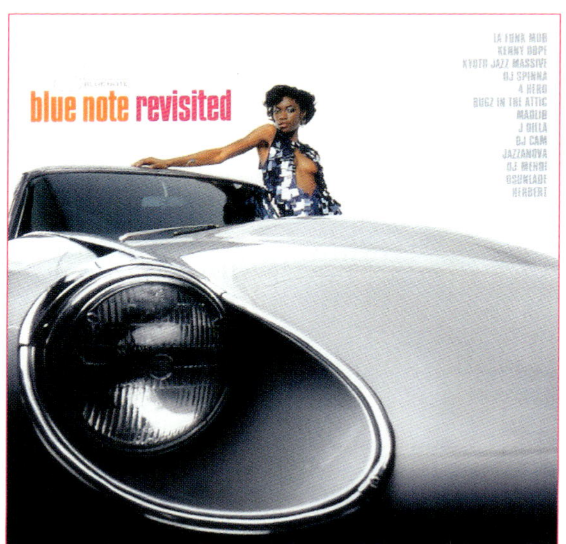

Artist : James Taylor Quartet
Title : Hammond-Ology / 2001
Album / Sanctuary Records
Artwork : Vegas

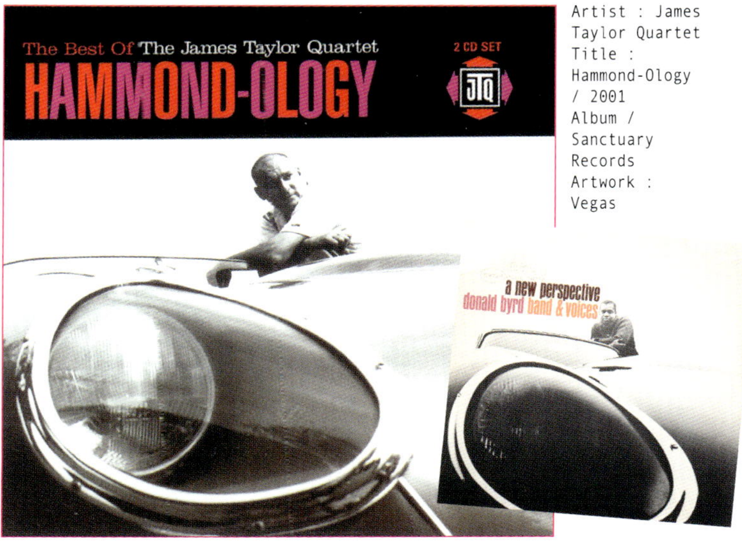

Artist : The Mortals
Title : Disintegration + 3
EP / Estrus Records
Artwork : Richard Head

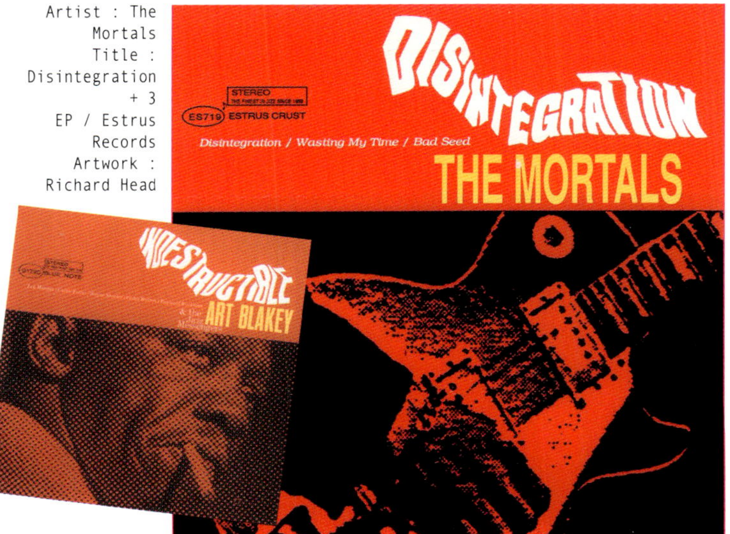

Artist : Chixdiggit! + Groovie Ghoulies
Title : Chronic For The Troops / 1998
Album / Delmonico Records
Artwork : Unknown

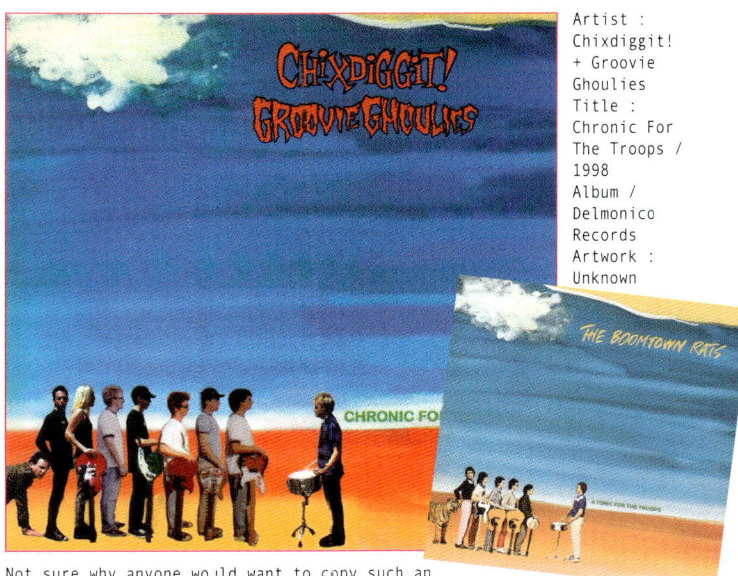

And here's another, the type and layout of Art Blakey & The Jazz Messengers' Indestructible [1964 : Blue Note. Artwork : Reid Miles. Photo : Francis Wolff] borrowed for an EP on Estrus, a label which crop a number of times in this book. And is Richard Head a real name?

Not sure why anyone would want to copy such an awful sleeve as The Boomtown Rats' A Tonic For The Troops [1978 : Mercury. Artwork : Chuck Loyola. Photo : Fin Costello] but Chixdiggit just lifted it outright for this album - shared with another band.

Bob Dylan's epic 1965 offering Bringing It All Back Home had a great cover photo by Daniel Kramer which has been much imitated. German writer and musician Christiane Rosinger and Belgian based King Koen have gone to great lengths to pay homage to the original, while the other two reinvent the image through illustration. And what is it with all these Reggae tributes? Jan's collection is full of them.

Artist : Christiane Rösinger
Title : Songs Of L. And Hate / 2010
Album / Staatsakt (Rough Trade)
Artwork : Unknown

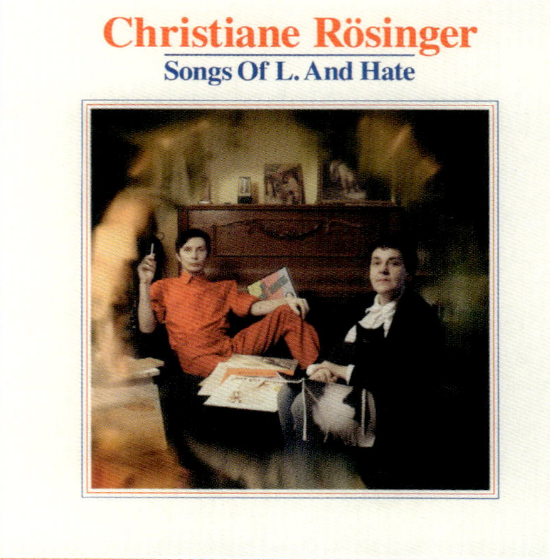

Artist : Cobra Skulls + 1
Title : Subterranean Homesick Blues + 1 / 2008
Single / Suburban Home Records
Artwork : Unknown

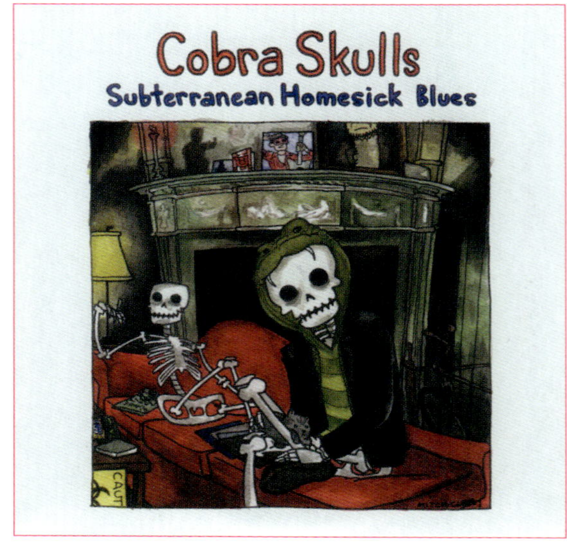

Artist : King Koen
Title : No Kicks On The Radio / 1988
12" Single / Punk Etc. Productions
Artwork : Unknown

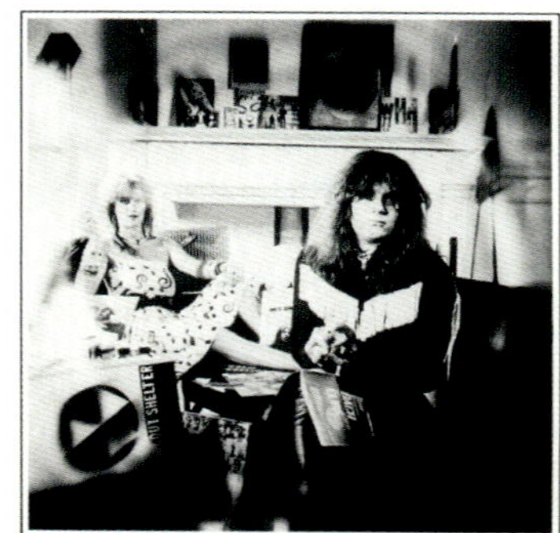

Artist : Various Artists
Title : Is It Rolling Bob? / 2005
Album / Ras Records
Artwork : Dick Bangham / Eric White

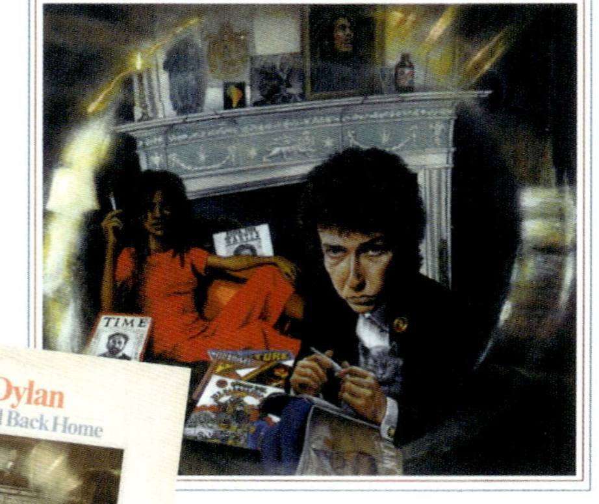

Dylan's other albums have also inspired cover designers and musicians. Richard Ashworth has paid homage to both Highway 61 Revisited [1965. Photo : Daniel Kramer] AND Nashville Skyline, copying Elliott Landy's 1969 image carefully (the Charlatans also clearly had the cover in mind on their North Country Boy release). Andy Boy goes more for the look by using very similar typography on his tribute to Barry Feinstein's cover for The Times They Are A-Changin' issued in 1964.

Artist : Richard Ashworth
Title : M3 Revisited
EP / Overdrive Records
Photo : Swill Beer

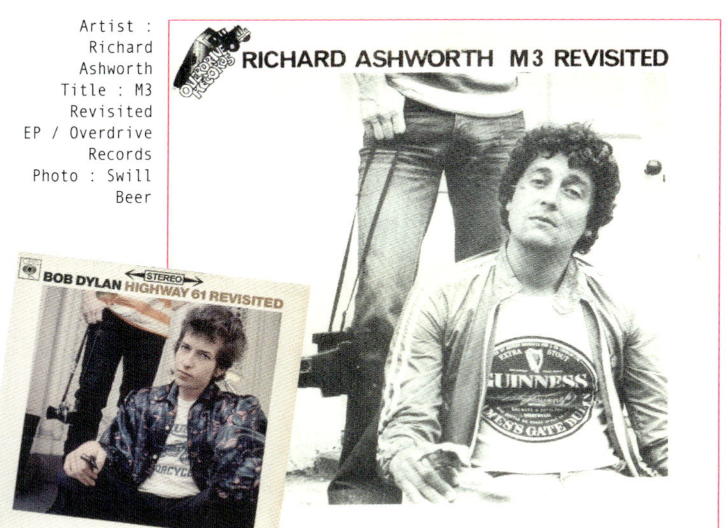

Artist : Andy Boy
Title : If Bob Dylan Had Balls He'd Be Me! / 1996
Album /In & Out
Artwork : Sean J. Wyett & AndyBoy (Photo : Michael Llewellyn)

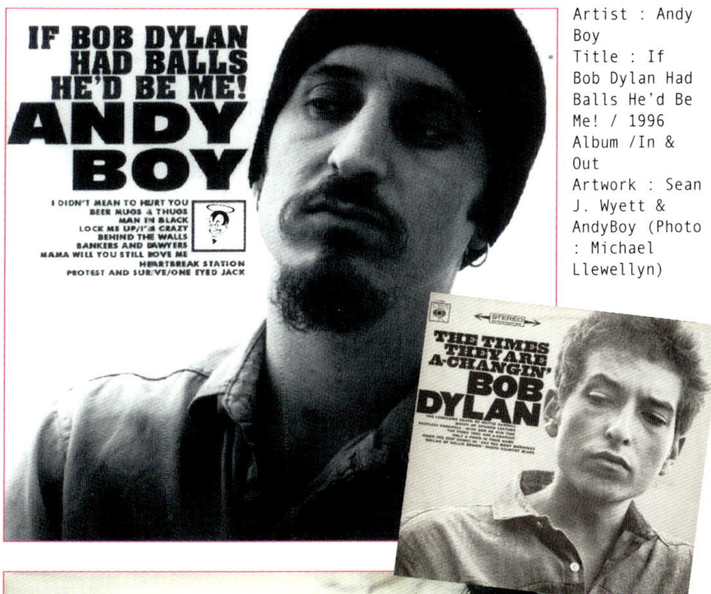

Artist : The Charlatans
Title : North Country Boy + 3 / 1997
EP / Beggars Banquet
Artwork : Negativespace (Photo : Tom Sheehan)

Artist : Richard Ashworth & White Dub
Title : Surrey Skyline / 1979
EP / Overdrive Records
Artwork : Pete Hobson (Photo : John Knight)

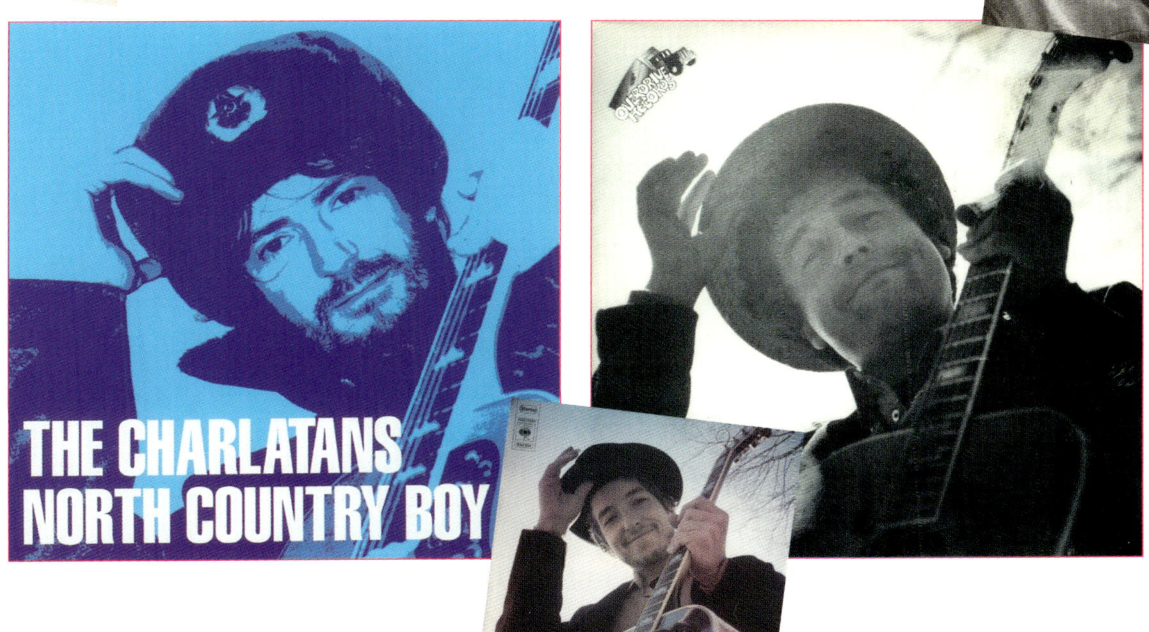

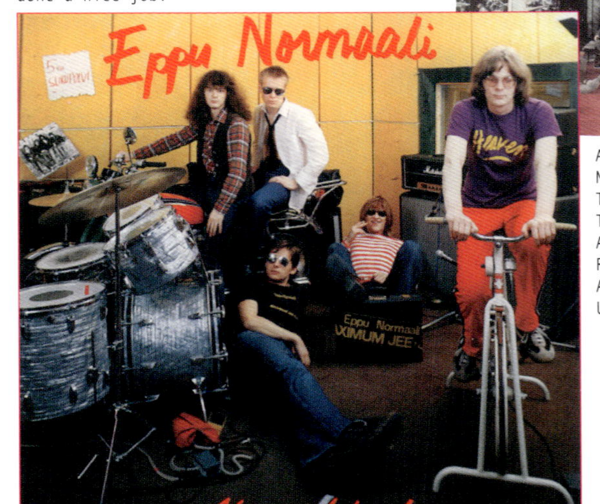

Crosby, Stills, Nash & Young enlisted Joni Mitchell to do the sketch for So Far [1974], with The Nightblooms doing their version twenty years on.

A cover clearly paying homage to Creedence Clearwater Revival's Cosmo's Factory album [1970 : Fantasy], put together by Bob Fogerty. The band have updated some of the kit, but done a nice job.

Artist : The Nightblooms
Title : 24 Days At Catastrofe Café / 1993
Album / Fire Records
Artwork : Merle Van Hees

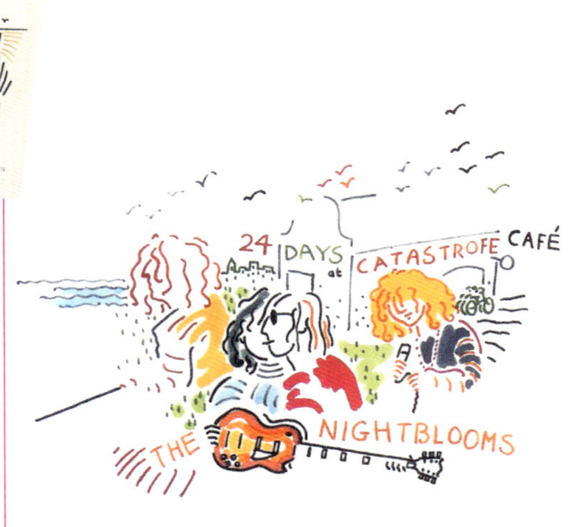

Artist : Eppu Normaali
Title : Akun Tehdas / 1980
Album / Poko Rekords
Artwork : Unknown

Artist : Various Artists
Title : In The Christmas Groove / 2009
Album / Strut Records
Artwork : Matt Thame

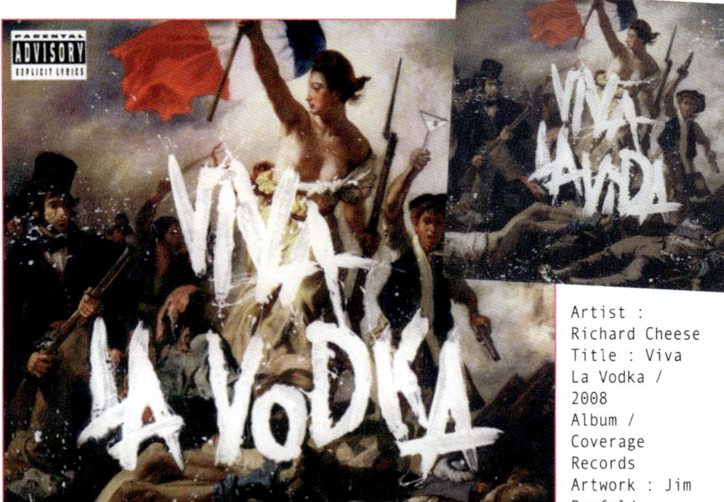

Artist : Richard Cheese
Title : Viva La Vodka / 2008
Album / Coverage Records
Artwork : Jim Rasfeld

This V/Artists title is clearly based on one of the later James Brown album sleeves, In The Jungle Groove, from 1986 [Polydor], put together by Ray Baradat/ Alan Leeds/ Matthieu Bitton / Vartan [Photo : Ryan Null].

Coldplay used Eugéne Delacroix's painting for their album Viva La Vida (Or Death And All His Friends) [2008 : Tappin Gofton/Coldplay], and Richard Cheese did the same - adding a cocktail glass in the hnds of one of the revolutionaries.

Bing Crosby's biggest selling single of all time, White Christmas, was rounded up on an album of the same name in 1970. The cover, with a Norman Rockwell style illustration of Bob on, has been trashed any number of times. An easy target perhaps but fun nevertheless.

Artist : Black Diamond
Title : White Christmas / 1995
Single / ARS
Artwork : Seven Productions
(Photo : Björn Tagemose)

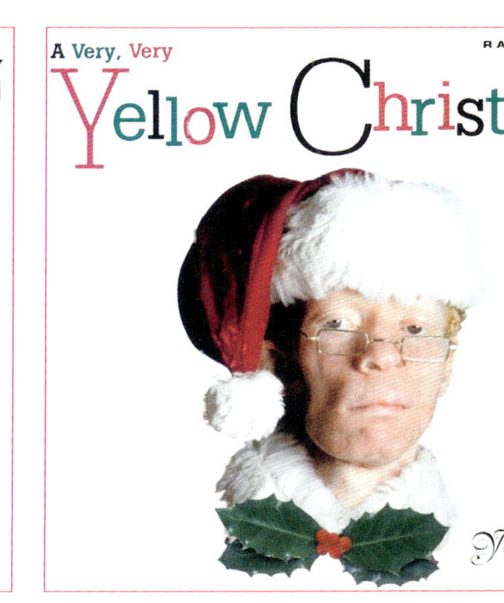

Artist : Yellowman
Title : A Very Very Yellow Christmas / 1998
Album / Ras Records
Artwork : JML Design (Photo : Jan Salzman)

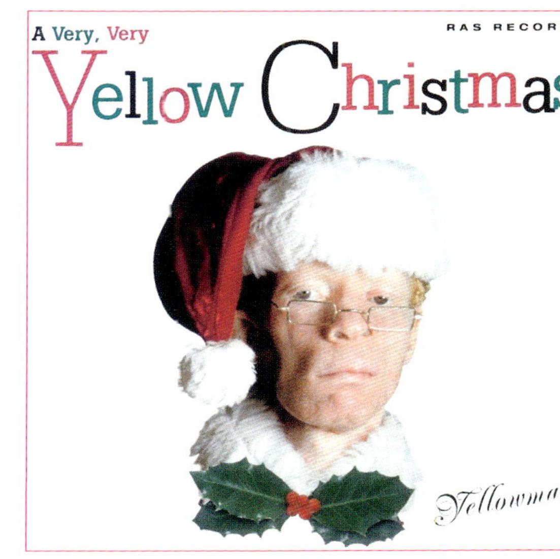

Artist : Bob Rivers
Title : White Trash Christmas / 2002
Album / Atlantic
Artwork : Webbervision
(Photo : Pink Monkey Studios)

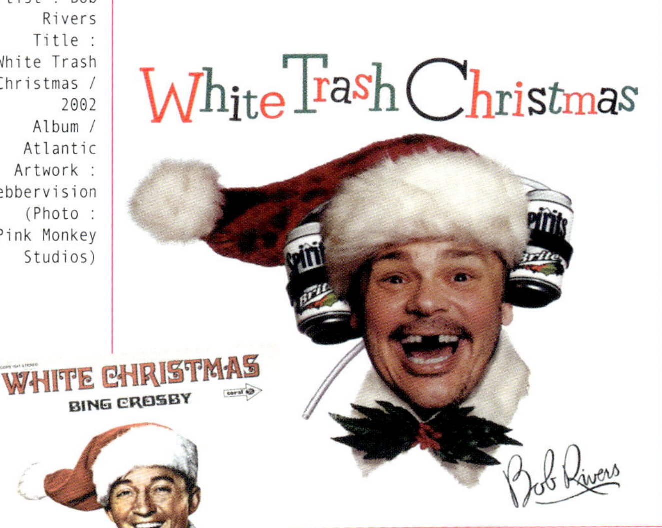

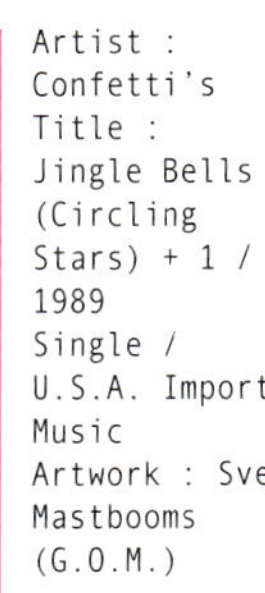

Artist : Confetti's
Title : Jingle Bells (Circling Stars) + 1 / 1989
Single / U.S.A. Import Music
Artwork : Sven Mastbooms (G.O.M.)

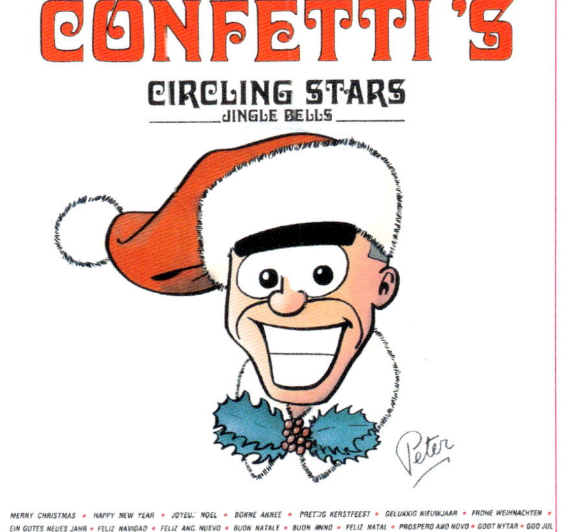

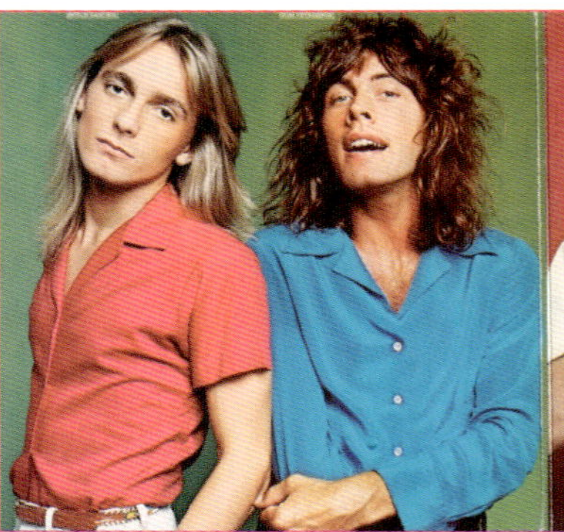 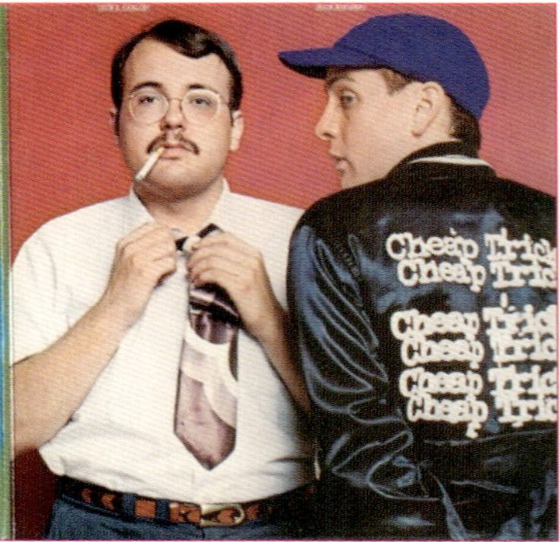 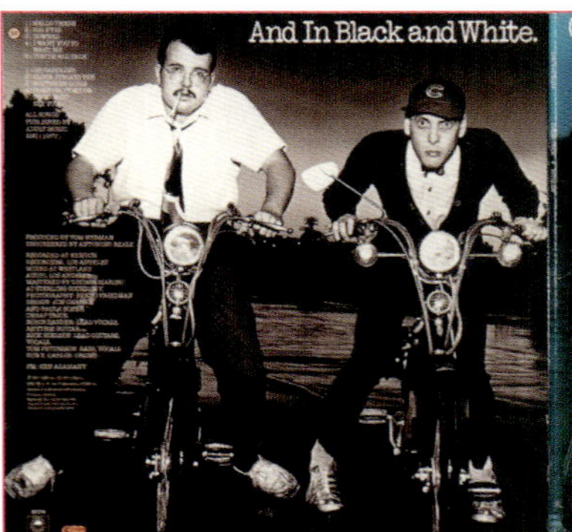 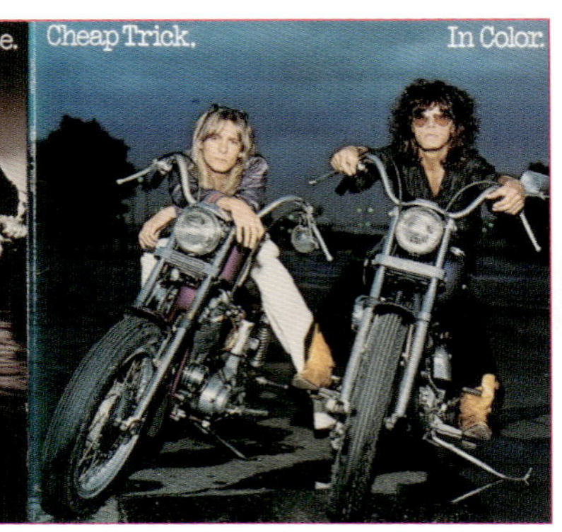

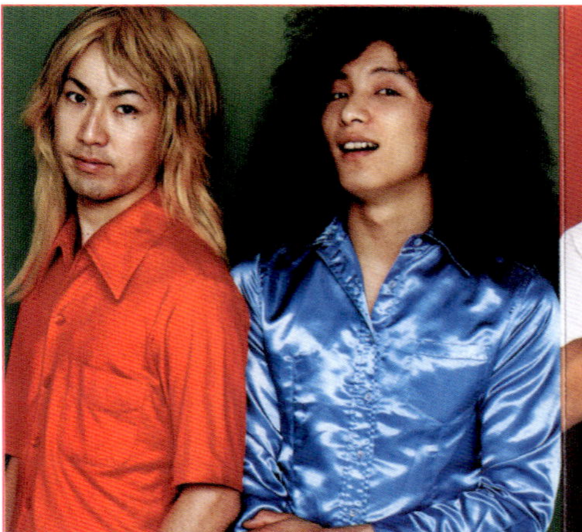 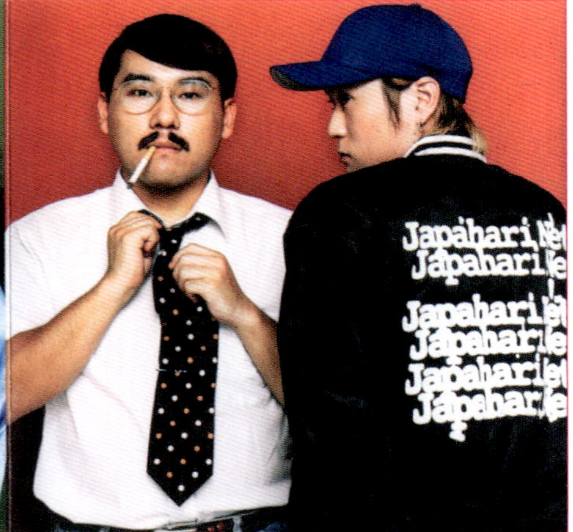

For sheer dedication to obsessively copying retro sleeves, JapahariNet must deserve some sort of prize. Cheap Trick's album In Color came out in 1977 on Epic. The gatefold sleeve carried album size photographic portraits of the band, taken by Benno Friedman (Jim Charne and Paula Scher are credited with the artwork). These photos split the 'nerdy' looking pair off from the rockers, so you get the former on bikes on the back, the hip dudes on big beefy motorcycles on the front.

The Japanese boys have copied it all so carefully, right down to the printed satin bomber jacket inside. You have to admire their devotion, even if I've no idea what inspired them to go to so much effort. Incidentally on the original gatefold, the back cover was printed upside down to give the feel of a reversable record (though this idea was spoilt by all the small print). JapahariNet even copied this on the CD. As it's hard to see in book form, I've cheated and shown it right side up, if you see what I mean.

Artist :
JapahariNet
Title :
HarukanaruHibi
/ 2004
Album / Toy's
Factory
Artwork :
Toshiyuki Kato
Photo: Masakazu
Yoshiba

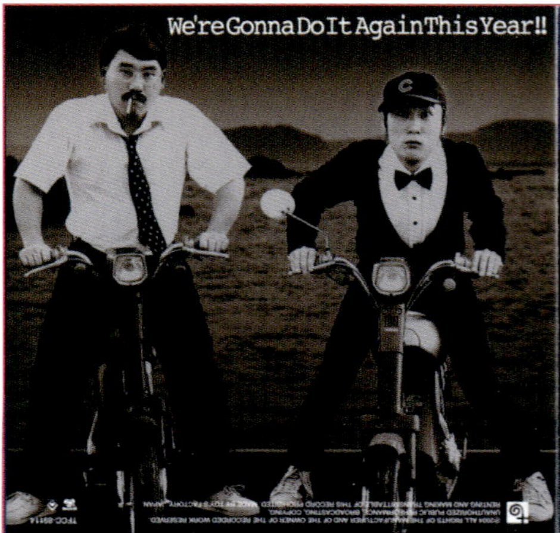 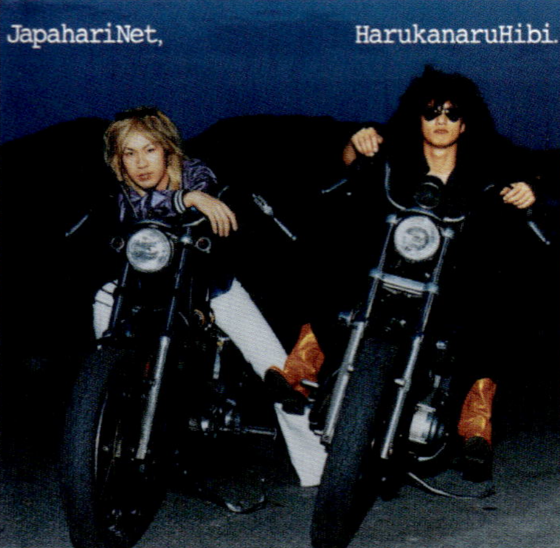

Hard to be certain exactly why Cheap Trick's 1977 album of the same name [Artwork : Paula Scher. Photo : Jim Houghton] should have been the one Big Black felt best served their purposes on this single.

Alberto Vargas had been drawing pin-ups for a few decades when The Cars asked him to illustrate their 1979 LP Candy-O. This in turn was used as a template for a detailed Beardsleyesque pen and ink crawing by Jen Ray which is arguably better.

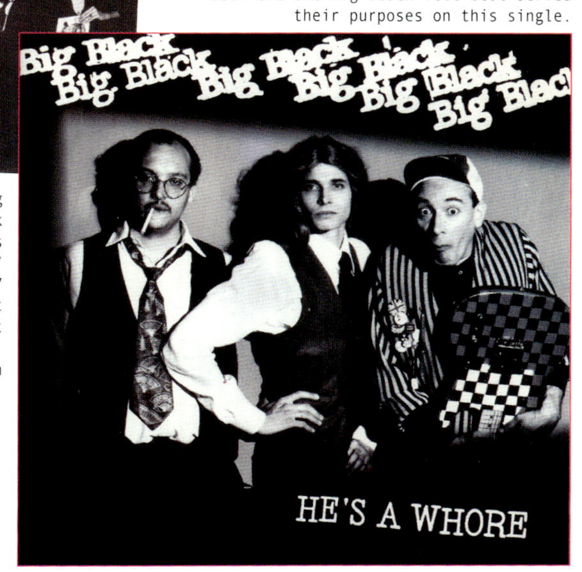

Artist : Big Black
Title : He's A Whore + 1 / 1987
Single / Blast First
Artwork : Unknown

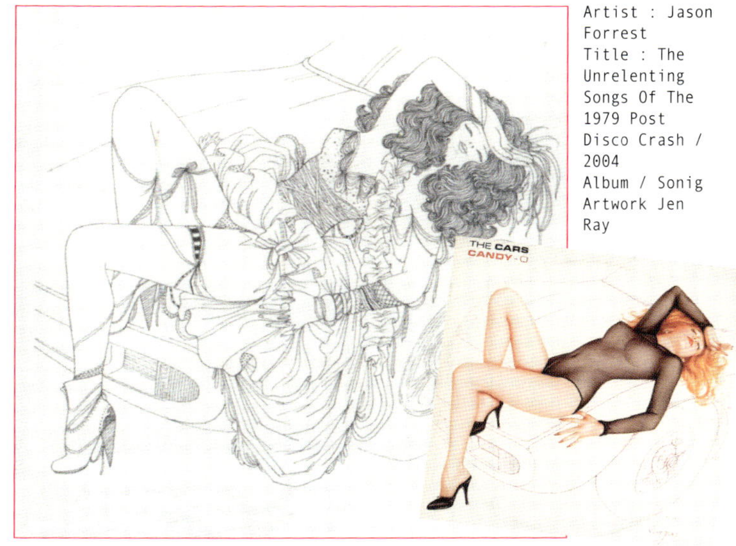

Artist : Jason Forrest
Title : The Unrelenting Songs Of The 1979 Post Disco Crash / 2004
Album / Sonig
Artwork Jen Ray

Artist : Martini Kings
Title : Intoxicating Sounds
Album / SwingOmatic
Artwork : Unknown

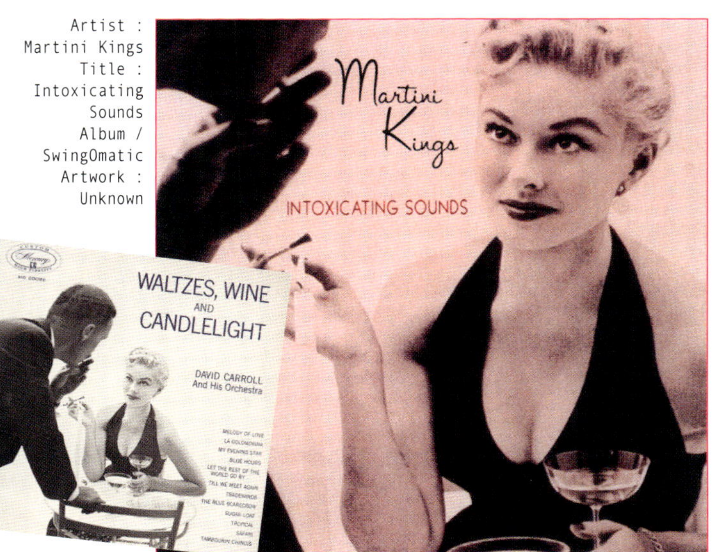

The Easy Listening scene of the 1990s saw a resurgence of interest in the glamourous cover images of the 1950s. Here a section lifted off David Carroll's 1955 LP Waltzes, Wine And Candlelight provides a new cover for the Martini Sounds.

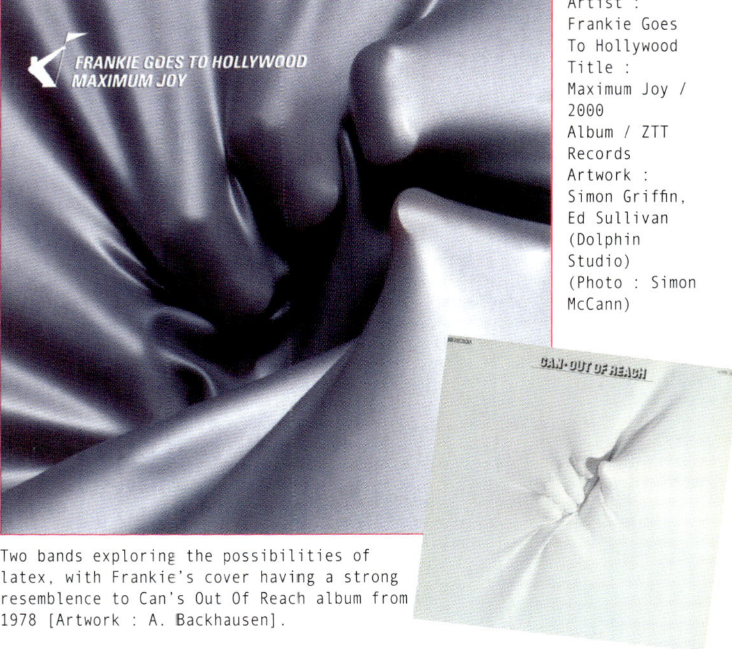

Artist : Frankie Goes To Hollywood
Title : Maximum Joy / 2000
Album / ZTT Records
Artwork : Simon Griffin, Ed Sullivan (Dolphin Studio) (Photo : Simon McCann)

Two bands exploring the possibilities of latex, with Frankie's cover having a strong resemblence to Can's Out Of Reach album from 1978 [Artwork : A. Backhausen].

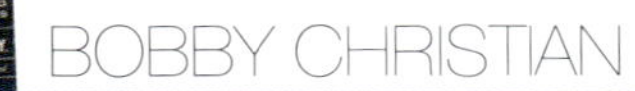

Bobby Christian's 1962 gem Strings For A Space Age [Audio Fidelity Records. Artwork : Unknown] is here lovingly redone, with the added twist of a nod to those Century21 EPs in the typography.

It took four people to come up with the original [Leonard Cohen : Death Of A Ladies' Man : 1977], even though the photo looked like an anonymous tourist souvenir shot. Quite why Mike wanted to mimic it so closely...

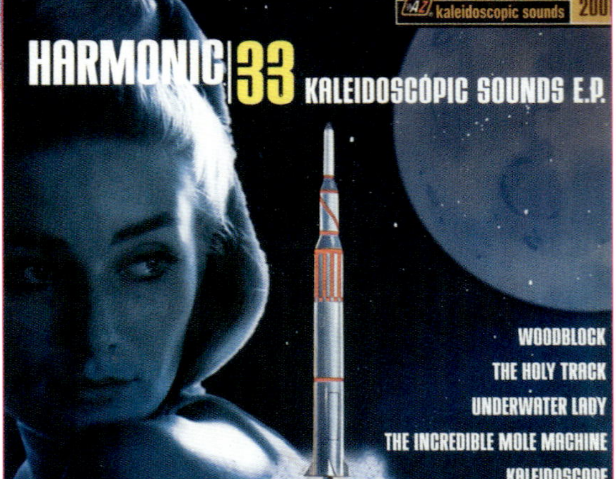

Artist :
Harmonic 33
Title :
Kaleidoscope
Sounds / 2001
EP / Alphabet
Zoo
Artwork : Lee
Framer

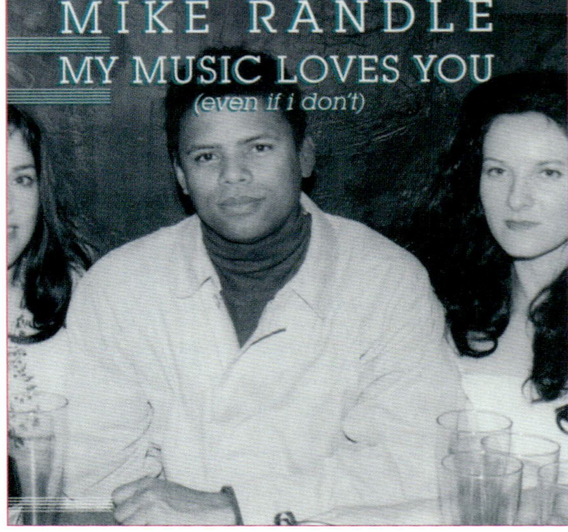

Artist : Mike
Randle
Title : My
Music Loves
You (Even If I
Don't) / 2000
Album /
Eggbert
Records
Artwork : Rita
Reischke Photo
: Matt Gainer

Artist : Boris
The Sprinkler
Title : Group
Sex / 1999
Album / Bulge
Records
Artwork : Nørb

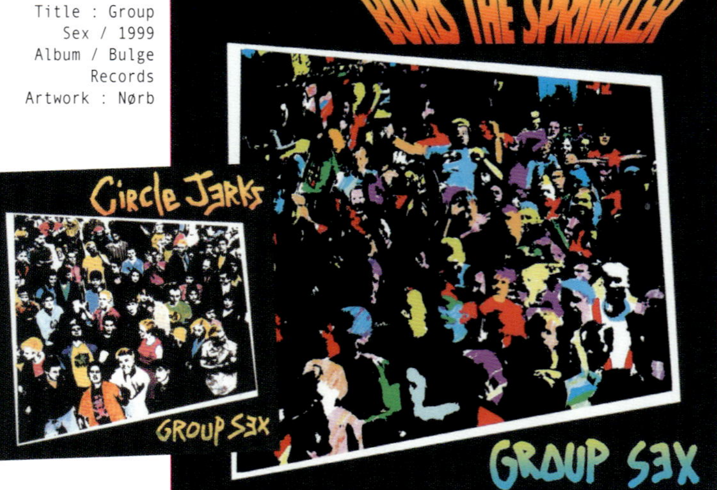

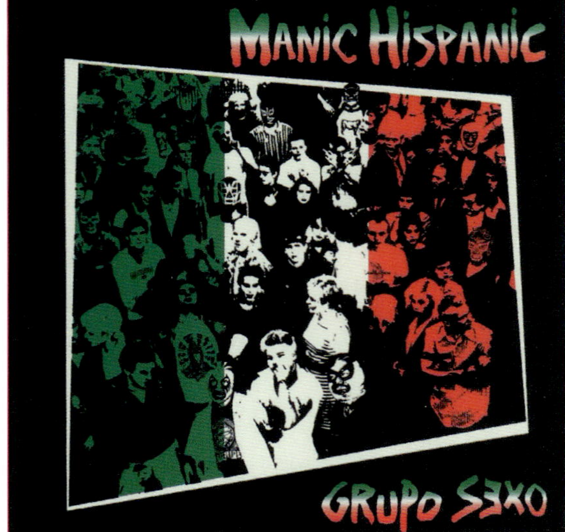

Artist : Manic
Hispanic
Title : Grupo
Sexo / 2005
Album / BYO
Records
Artwork :
Unknown

Strange one to copy, and notice how Manic Hispanic have sneaked in new t-shirt designs onto some of the crowd (as well as wrestlers masks!) off the original Circle Jerks LP Group Sex [1980 : Porterhouse Records. Artwork : Diane Zincavage], which would have been a great cover except for the 'lettering'.

Interesting that a sleeve design as simple, even basic, as John Jagel's work for Ornette! by The Ornette Coleman Quartet [1961 : Atlantic] should still remain so well regarded. These four may add their own twist, but most stick closely to the original, even down to the colours used on two of them.

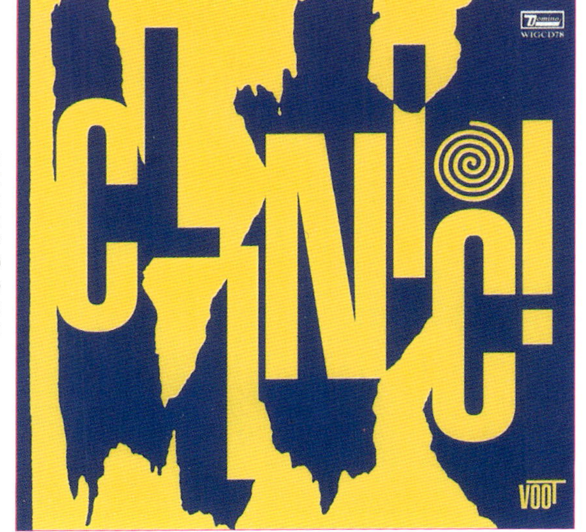

Artist :
Clinic
Title :
Internal
Wrangler /
2000
Album / Domino
Artwork :
Unknown

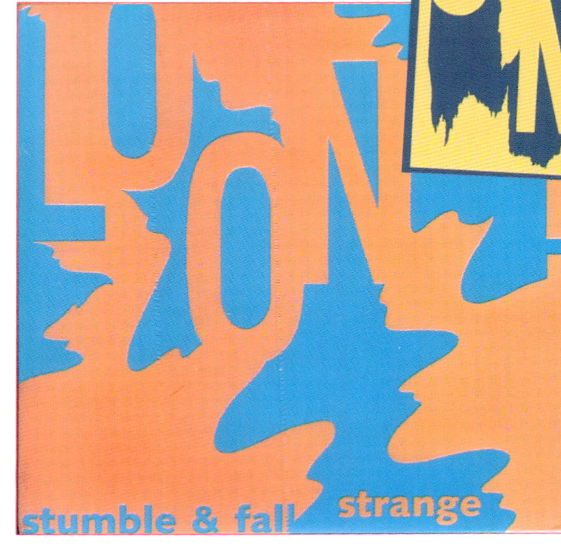

Artist : The
Loons
Title :
Stumble & Fall
+ 1 / 1998
Single / Max
Picou Records
Artwork :
Tracy Johnson

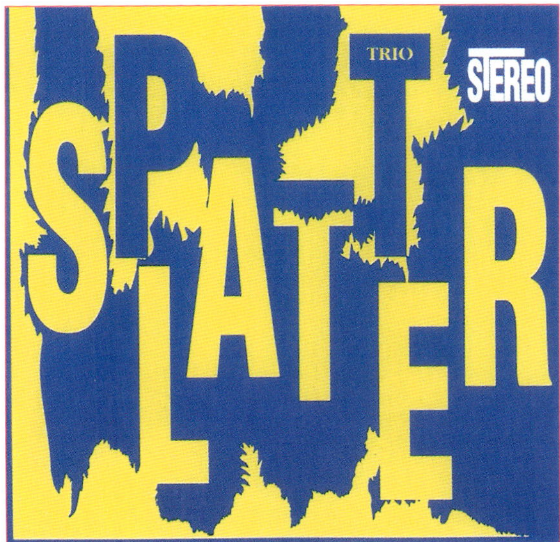

Artist :
Splatter Trio
Title :
Splatter Trio
/ 1990
Album /
Rastascan
Records
Artwork : Ed
Rachles

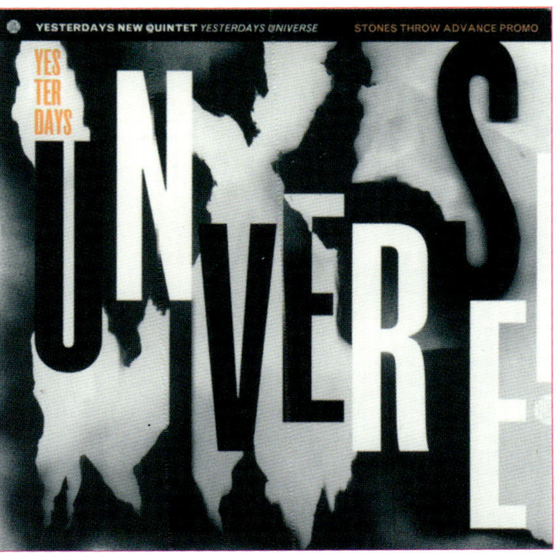

Artist :
Yesterdays New
Quintet
Title :
Yesterdays
Universe /
2007
Album / Stones
Throw Records
Artwork :
stonesthrow.
com

This is listed under Clash as the image is perhaps best known off the London Calling single sleeve, which is what the V/Artists cover Family 5 has copied. In fact The Clash themselves had borrowed it from a generic record sleeve used by Columbia UK for their 10" 78 rpm singles during the 1950s, an excellent commercial illustration and one of several used by the EMI Group at the time on their differnet bags. The Clash designer has filled in the missing art for the centre hole and used a similar script for the title.

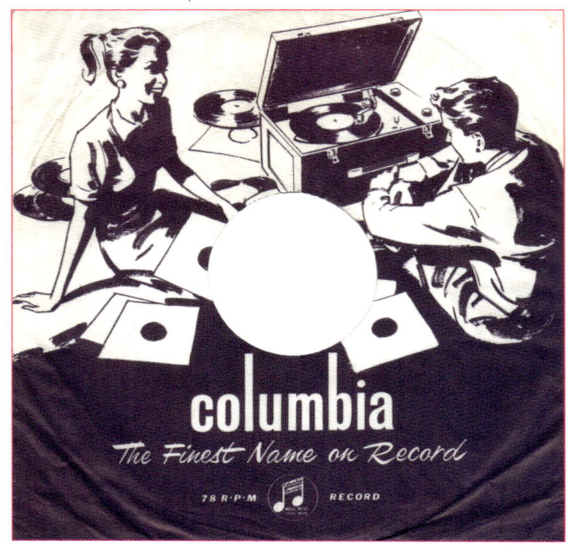

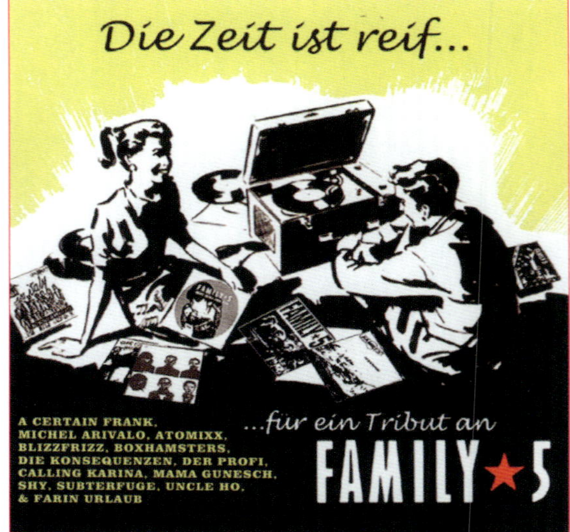

Artist : Various Artists
Title : Die Zeit Ist Reif...Für Ein Tribute An Family 5 / 2002
Album / Paul!
Artwork : Andreas Thiel / Knut Schötteldreier

Artist : The Clash
Title : London Calling + 1 / 1979
Single / CBS
Artwork : Unknown

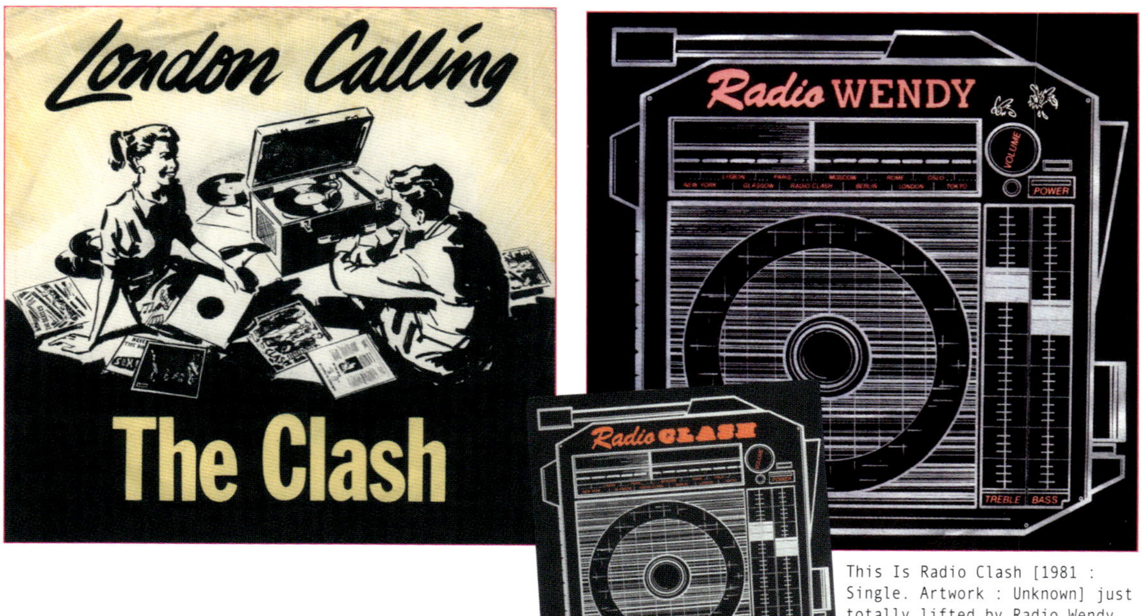

Artist : Radio Wendy
Title : Bad Asteroid / 19--
10" / Sympathy For The Record Industry
Artwork : P. Waters

This Is Radio Clash [1981 : Single. Artwork : Unknown] just totally lifted by Radio Wendy. What's sauce for the goose...

The Clash debut [CBS : 1977. Photo : Kate Simon] is their most copied sleeve, though their own debt to The Ramones first album (pg 113) is very clear (as it was to the music). It provided an instant punk look for these bands to follow in any case (the US and UK versions of the Clash LP were slightly different - the US label were scared of not having the title at the top...).

Artist :
C.H.E.
Title : Move
Like Pigeon /
2004
Album / I'm A
Cliché
Artwork : Jim
Delbes

Artist : My
So-Called Band
Title : My
So-Called Band
/ 1997
Album / Yesha
Artwork :
Steve Munsell
and Contagious
Graphics.
Photo : Robert
Lincoln

Artist : Thee
Stash
Title : Should
I Suck Or
Should I Blow
+ 1 / 1993
Single /
Shakin'
Street- Get
Hip Records
Artwork :
Unknown

Artist :
Various
Artists
Title : This
Is Rockabilly
Clash / 2002
Album /
Raucous
Records
Artwork :
Unknown

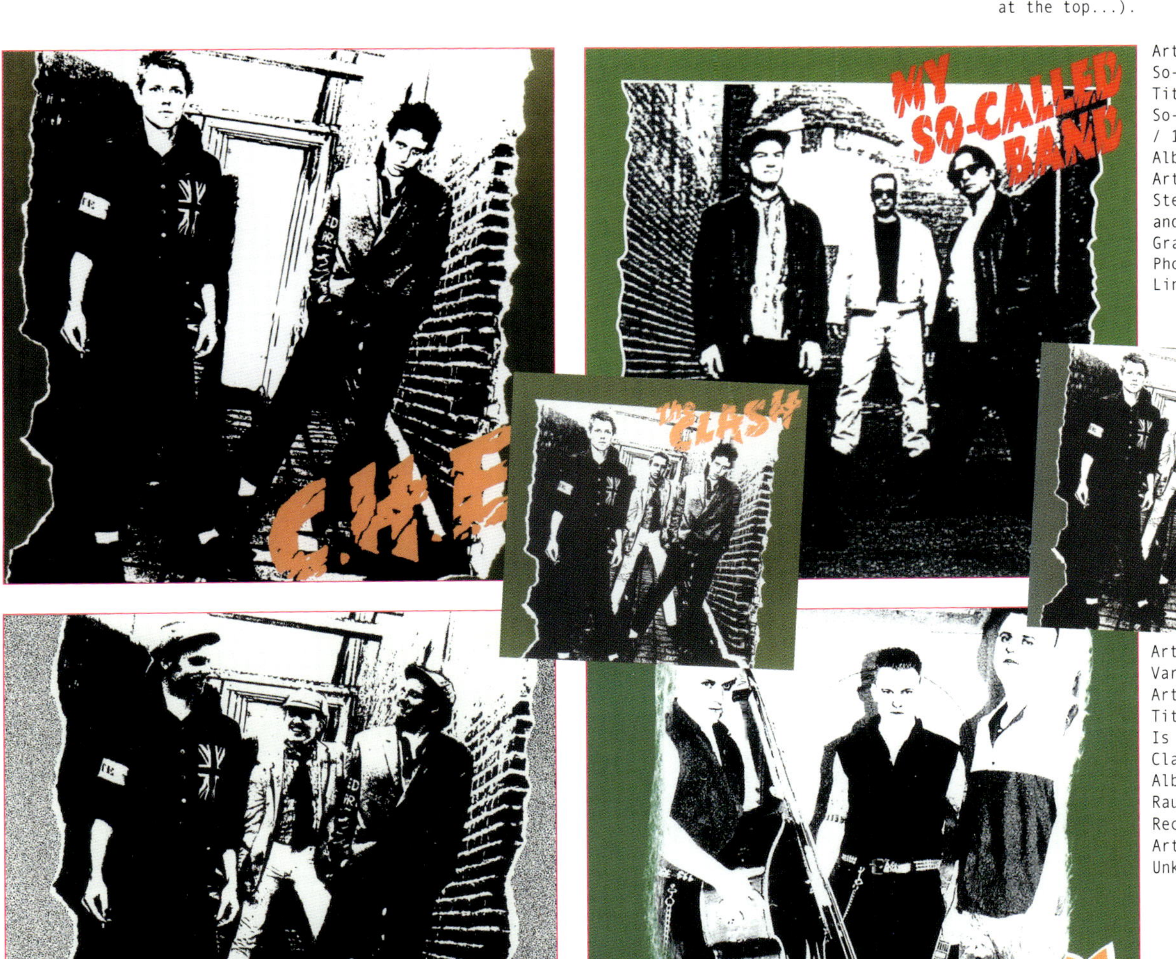

CREAM

Cream's Disraeli Gears [1967. Artwork : Martin Sharpe. Photograph : Bob Whitaker] was one of the key sleeve designs of the year, breaking new ground with the use of fluorescent inks. Perhaps because it was so unique, the copyists have been less successful. The recreations of the band's Goodbye [1969. Artwork Alan Aldridge Ink Studios / photo Roger Philips] and Wheels Of Fire [1968. Artwork : Martin Sharp / Stanislaw Zagorski] have been more authentic.

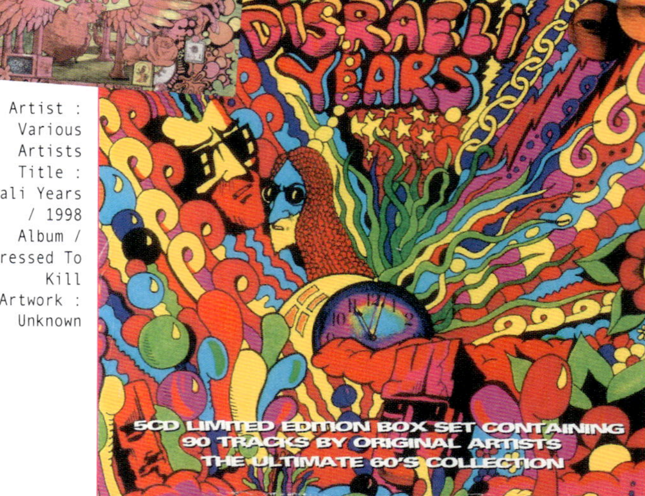

Artist :
Various
Artists
Title :
Disreali Years
/ 1998
Album /
Dressed To
Kill
Artwork :
Unknown

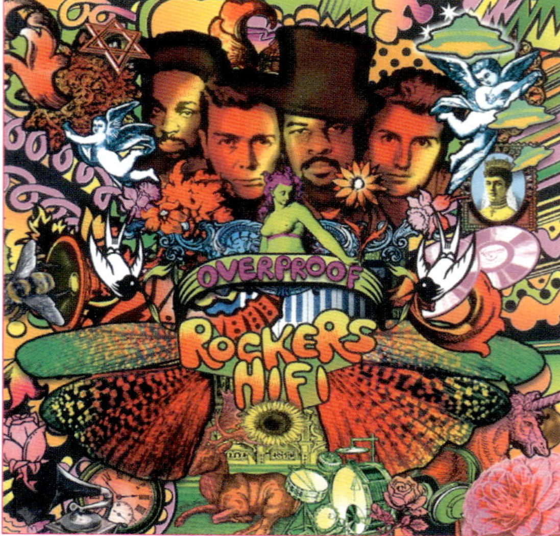

Artist :
Rockers Hifi
Title :
Overproof /
1998
Album /
Downbeat WEA
Artwork : Paul
Adams (Photo :
Trish Crumm)

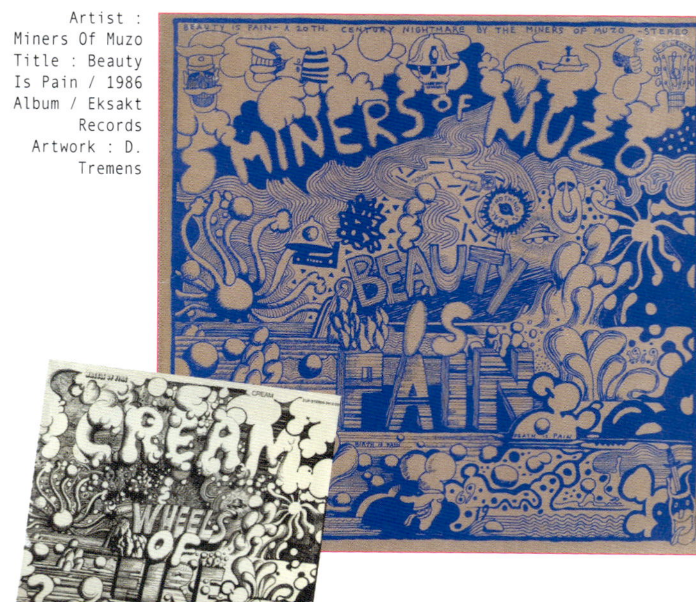

Artist :
Miners Of Muzo
Title : Beauty
Is Pain / 1986
Album / Eksakt
Records
Artwork : D.
Tremens

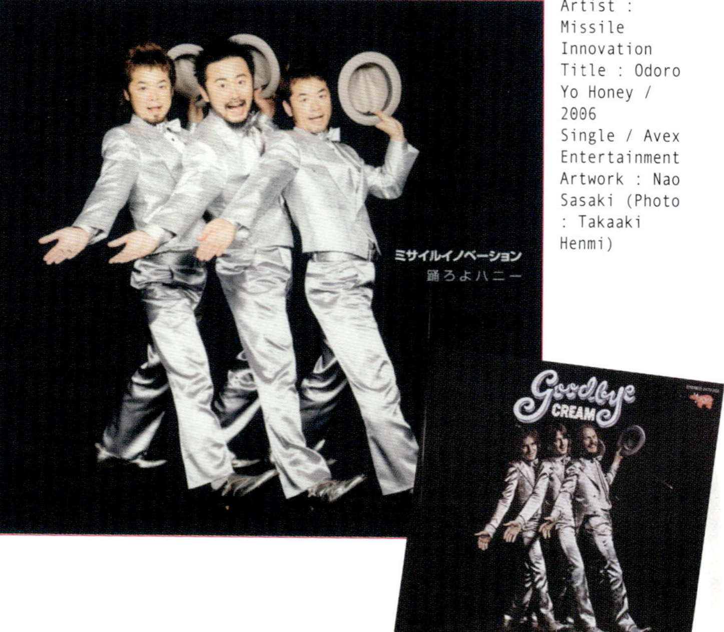

Artist :
Missile
Innovation
Title : Odoro
Yo Honey /
2006
Single / Avex
Entertainment
Artwork : Nao
Sasaki (Photo
: Takaaki
Henmi)

You just want to collect all the Chicago albums thanks to their logo. The V/Artist mail-order only set clearly liked the idea of Chicago 2 in steel [1970 : CBS. Artwork : John Berg / Nicholas Fasciano].

Gomez - the Texas punk band not the later UK outfit - borrow the Danzig sleeve [1988 : American Recordings. Artwork : Mark Weiss] but stick a Yoda on the front!

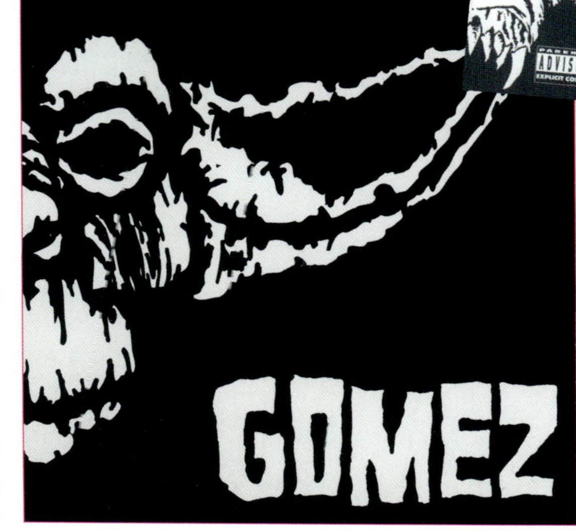

Artist :
Various Artists
Title :
Burbank: The
Warner Reprise
Loss Leaders /
1972
Album / Warner
Bros.
Artwork : Ed
Trasher

Title : Gomez
It's A Yoda
Not A Gremlin
/ 1995
Album / Little
Deputy Records
Artwork :
Unknown

Artist : Bryan
Adams
Title : So
Far, So Good
/ 1993
Album / A & M
Artwork : STAC
Photo : Andrew
Catlin

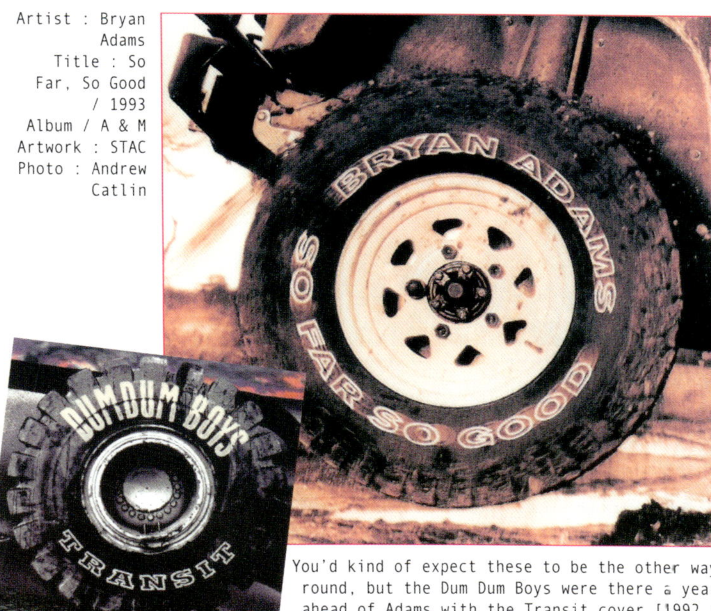

Artist :
Wargasm / 1994
Album /
Massacre
Records
Artwork :
Wargasm Photo
: Matthias
Herkle

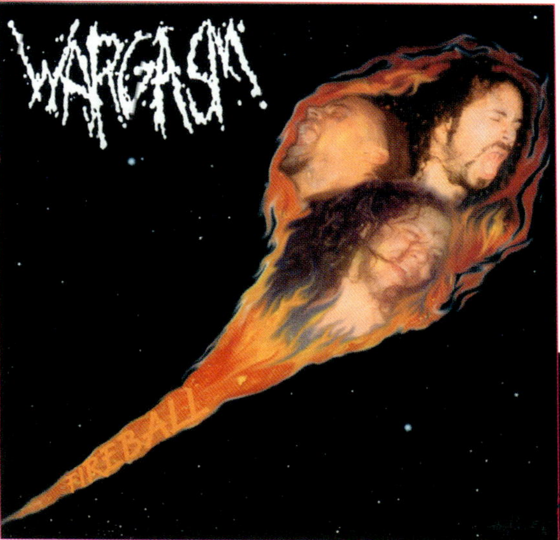

You'd kind of expect these to be the other way round, but the Dum Dum Boys were there a year ahead of Adams with the Transit cover [1992 : Oh Yeah. Artwork : Kine Røst & Bulldog Etter].

Deep Purple donate the title - Fireball - and cover idea (by bassist Roger Glover) from 1971 [Harvest. Artwork : Castle, Chappell & Partners Ltd. Photos : Tony Burrett] to Wargasm.

Deep Purple's breakthrough album In Rock featured a deceptively simple cover idea put together by their managers Tony Edwards (who hunted out the image of Mount Rushmore) and John Coletta (who organised the artwork). Many others bands have since gone back to the Rushmore carvings for artwork inspiration, but none did it so well; here are seven covers which clearly reference the Deep Purple cover directly.

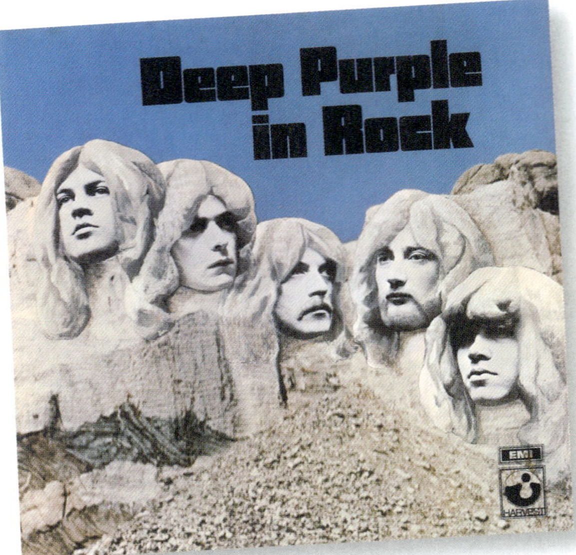

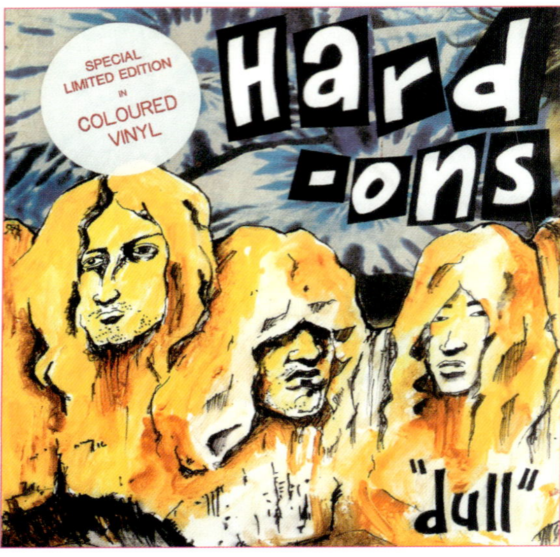

Artist : Hard-Ons
Title : Dull + 1 / 1991
Single / Waterfront Records
Artwork : Dickcheese Comic Company

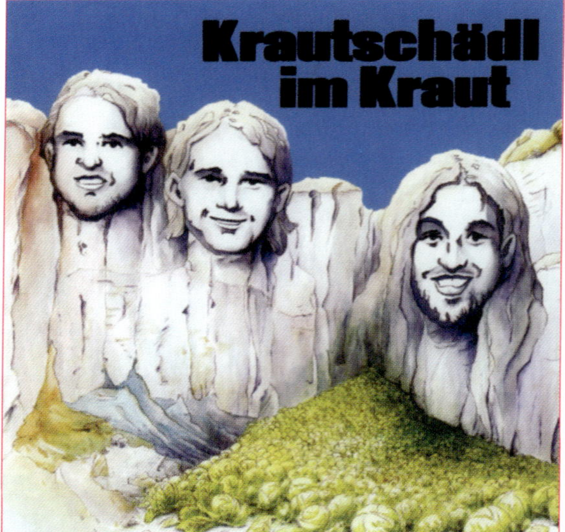

Artist : Krautschädl
Title : Im Kraut / 2007
Album / Sony
Artwork : Ronald Putzker / Gina Steffen

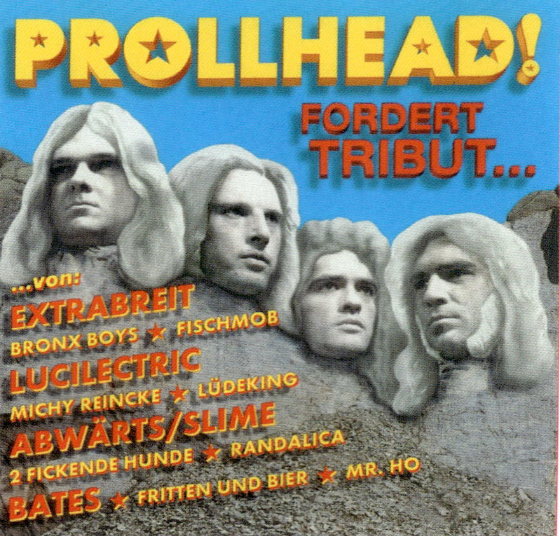

Artist : Various Artists
Title : Prollhead! Fordert Tribute / 1995
Album / Virgin
Artwork : Jörn Zimmermann
(Photo : Bela Hoche)

Even the singer on the album, Ian Gillan, had a go (bottom right); kicked out of the band in 1989 he commissioned a cover for his first solo 12" single which faded out all the rest of the band. Someone pointed out it might have repercussions and the cover was quickly withdrawn. He was asked back by Deep Purple a couple of years later. And the Japanese spoof? Mad guitarist King Curlee specialises in sending up rock bands in Japan.

Artist :
Various Artists
Title :
Strassenkreuzer
In Rock / 2003
Album /
Strassenkreuzer
e.V.
Artwork :
Arthur Engler
/ Wolfgang
Gillitzer
(Photo :
Michael
Matejka)

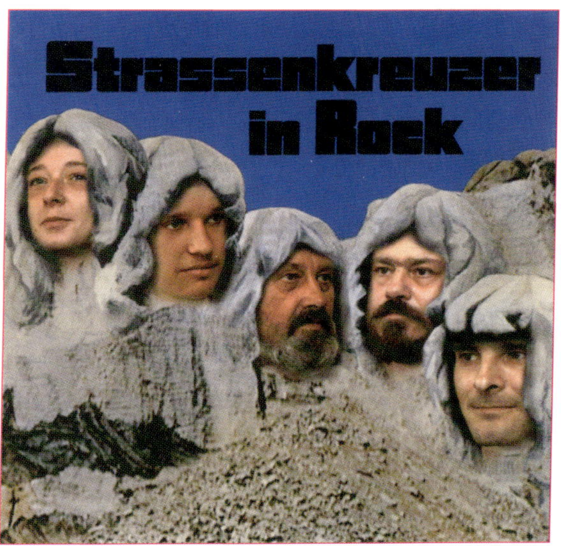

Artist : Vive
La Fête /
Andyasshole
Title : Child
In Time + 2 /
2007
12" Single
/ Surprise
- Lowlands
Artwork :
Unknown

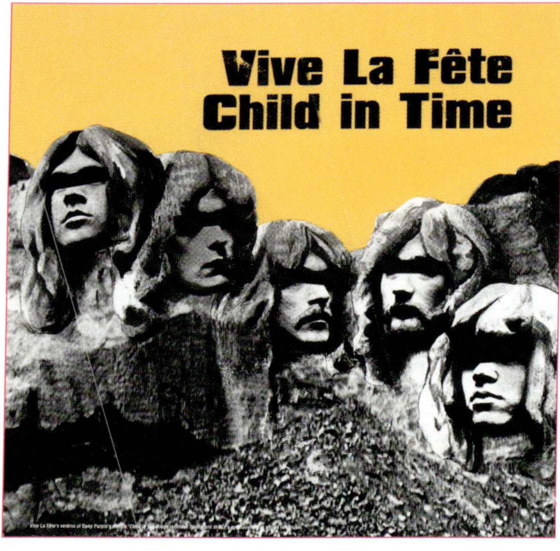

Artist : King
Curlee
Title :
Highway Star +
7 / 2005
Album / Fun
House
Artwork +
photos :
Akihiko Musha

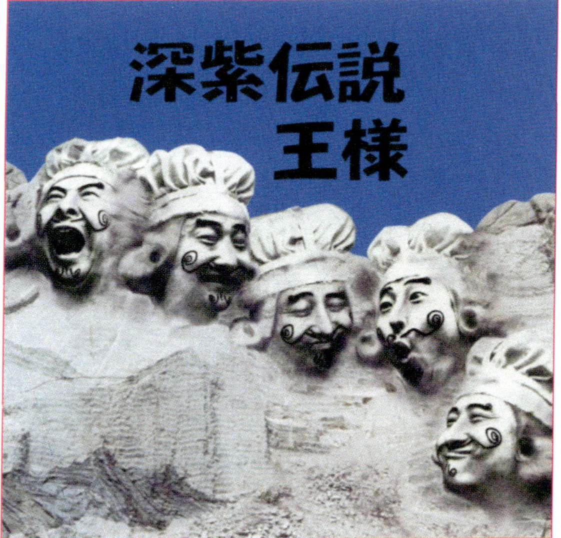

Artist : Ian
Gillan
Title : No
Good Luck + 2
/ 1990
12" Single /
Teldec
Artwork : Repo
Zest

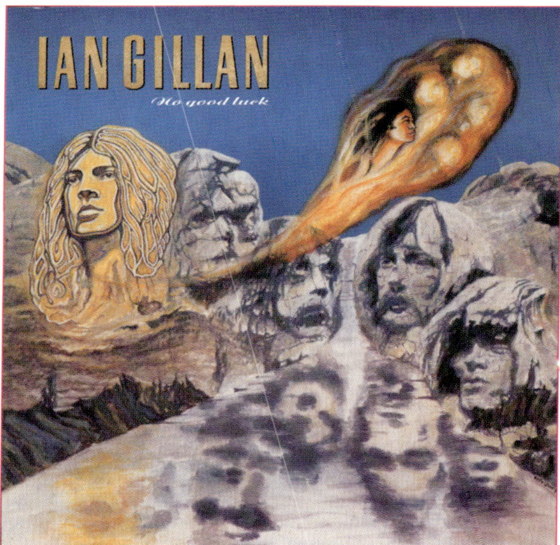

Lastly for Deep Purple, their live album Made In Japan from 1972 (cover idea bassist Roger Glover, photo's Fin Costello - taken in London not Japan) set a trend for double live rock albums, while the cover has also been heavily copied (desite the cost of running a gold colour as an extra). Dream Theater redid the whole of the album live in Japan in 2006 and issued it on their official bootleg series, the others just copied the cover and played their own material.

Artist : Die Goldenen Zitronen
Title : Das Ist Rock - Live In Japan / 1988
Album / Weserlabel
Artwork Marilyn

Artist : Dream Theater
Title : Made In Japan / 2006
Album / Ytsejam Records
Artwork : Hervé Pfeiffer / "Serlist Scotty" Hansen (Photo : Hiroyuki Yoshihama)

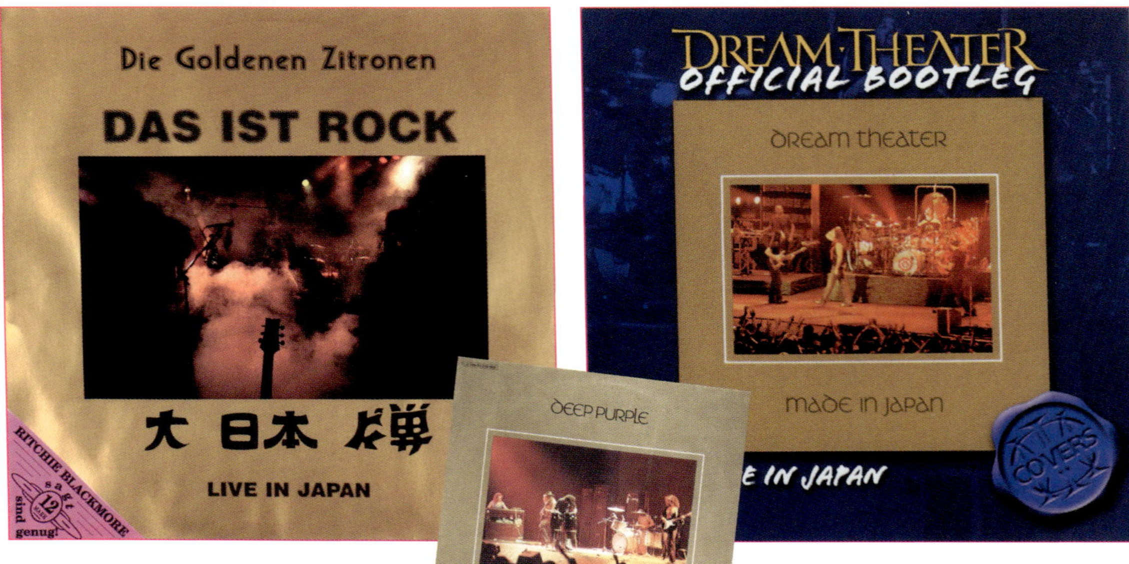

Artist : Elio E Le Storie Tese
Title : Made In Japan / 2001
Album / Aspirine - BMG
Artwork : Raffaella Riva (Photo : Giovanni Pinna)

Artist : The Nomads
Title : Made In Japan / 1995
Album / 1 + 2 Records
Artwork : R. Glover & Äckel-Ollie (Photo : Björn Nygårds)

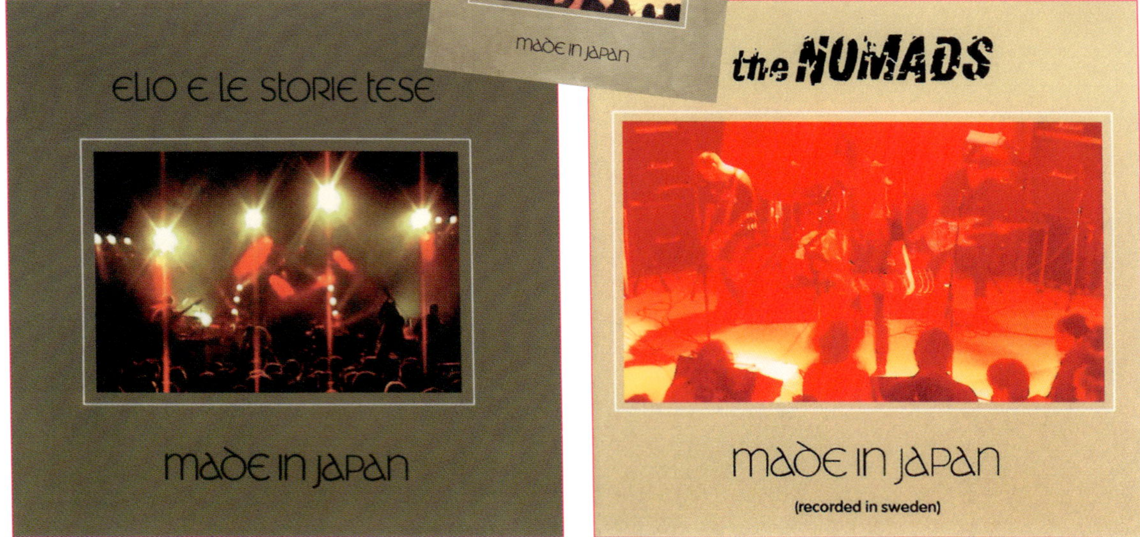

Garage rockers The Nomads issued their LP (recorded live in 1995 with no actual Purple tunes) in their native Sweden in 1996, while Hamburg punksters mixed MIJ and Purple's Last Concert In Tokyo sleeve together on a 1988 12" Das Ist Rock ("Ritchie Blackmore says this is enough" reads the corner sticker). To complete the international cover tributes, Elio e le Storie Tese hail from Italy, and cut their album at the Parco Capello - despite what the title says.

Not everyone can do hand-drawn typography. Compare the work on the cover of Donovan's Barabajagal album from 1969 [Artwork : Donovan & Sid Mauer at The Cottage, England. Photo : Sid Mauer] with the awkward letraset fonts on the Mark Fry copy.

Damned Damned Damned by The Damned came out in 1977 on the usually well decorated Stiff Records label, and had artwork by Peter Kodick, Judy Nylon and Pat Palladin. A few groups have indulged themselves to reproduce the photo shoot, the best (messiest?) being this one from The Automatics.

Artist : Mark Fry
Title : Dreaming With Alice / 1972
Album / RCA
Artwork : Giorgio Mangora / Tam Tam Studio

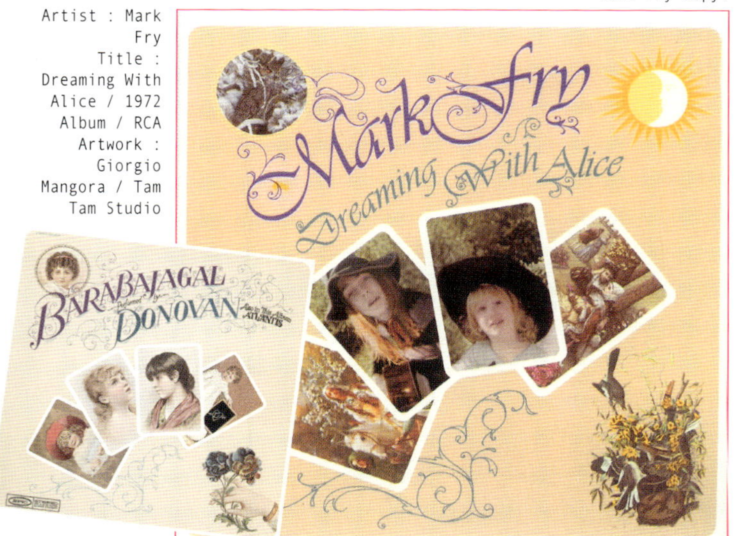

Artist : Automatics
Title : Go Bananas! / 1998
Album / Let's Dance Records
Photo : Meredith DeLoca

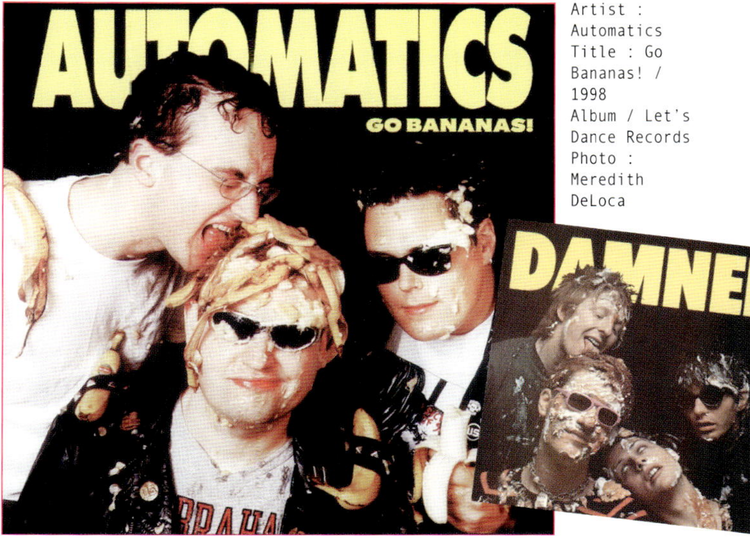

Artist : Boris
Title : Akuma No Uta / 2003
EP / Southern Lord
Artwork : Fangs Anal Satan (Photo : Eri Shibata)

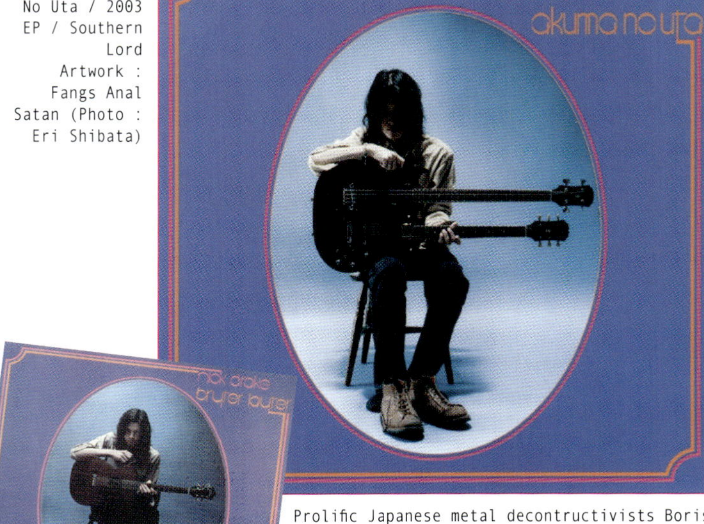

Prolific Japanese metal decontructivists Boris mix up stuff from decades of rock, so no surprise to see them paying tribute to Nigel Waymouth's Nick Drake cover for Bryter Layter [1970 : Island].

Artist : Demon Joker Junior
Title : Pa En Andere Stukken / 1997
EP / G-Force Records
Artwork : Unknown

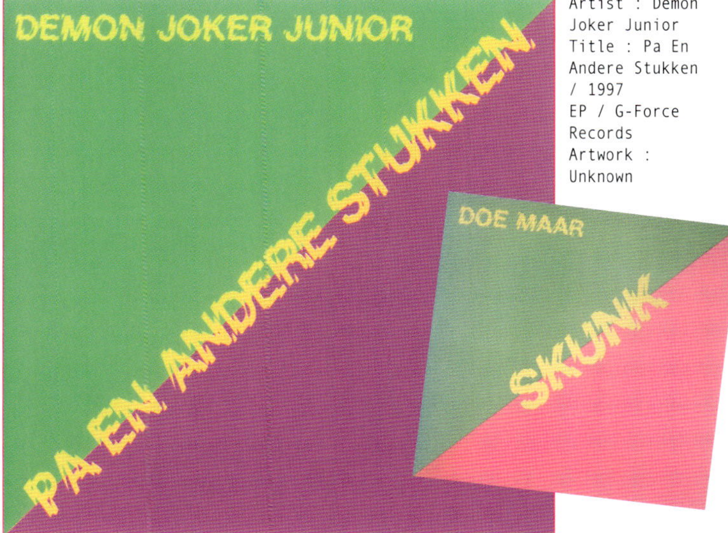

Letraset's Shatter typeface was insanely popular for a time (hello Kerrang), as here on Doe Maar's Skunk album cover in 1980, which in turn was carefully copied by Demon Joker Junior seventeen years on.

We don't know the name of the photographer of the solid looking 1957 Bo Diddley Chess label cover, or whether the rest of his band were hidden on purpose or not, but the V/Artists cover carefully repeats the pose.

The Dire Straits 1993 Vertigo album On The Night [Artwork Sutton Cooper / Paul Cummins] gets dragged into Photoshop's filter gallery and shoved back out by The Satellites. A real ten minute quickie!

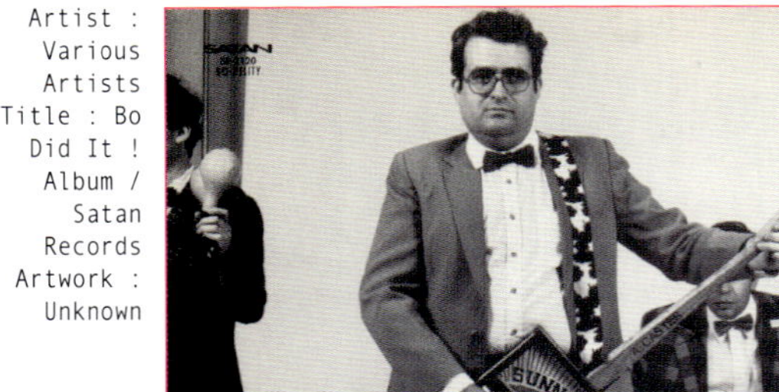

Artist : Various Artists
Title : Bo Did It !
Album / Satan Records
Artwork : Unknown

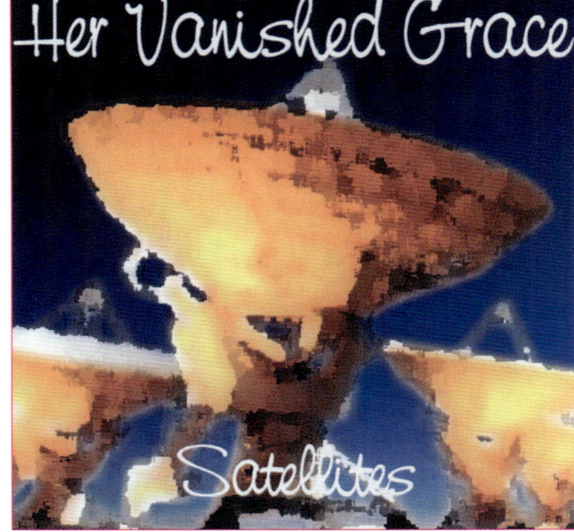

Artist : Her Vanished Grace
Title : Satellites / 2006
Album / Athame Music
Artwork : Charlie

Artist : Rubato (Terre Thaemlitz)
Title : Oh, No! It's Rubato / 2001
Album / Mille Plateaux
Artwork : Terre Thaemlitz

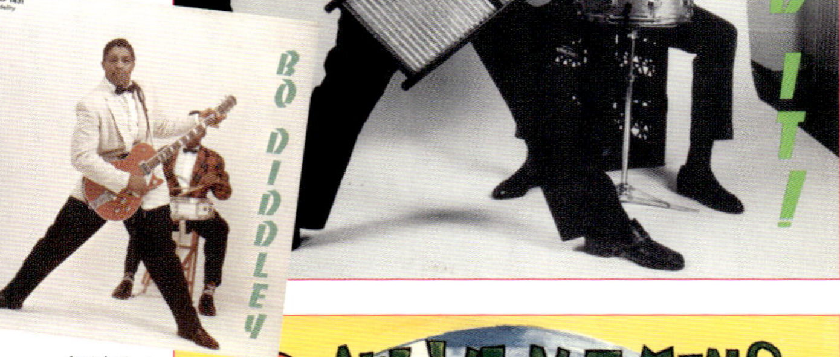

Artist : Clawhammer
Title : Are We Not Men? / 1991
Album / Sympathy For The Records Industry

Devo's sleeves were nothing if not unique, and the mixture of pop art and surrealism has found a lot of followers, with 1978's Are We Not Men? and Oh, No! It's Devo from 1982 [Artwork : Devo Inc.] clearly behind these two.

The Dictators' fabulously sexy Go Girl Crazy! cover from 1975 [Artwork : Johnny Montana / Gringo Huerta. Photo : David Gahr] turned into a 50s style comic illustration by The Bum.

The Romulans have montaged their heads into a repeat of the Zoom ice-lolly sucking nun from The Deviants classic and highly-charged 1969 LP cover [Artwork : Diogenic Attempts Ltd. Photo : Keith Morris]

Artist : Bum
Title : Your Disciple + 1 / 1992
Single / Au-Go-Go Records
Artwork : Pat McEown

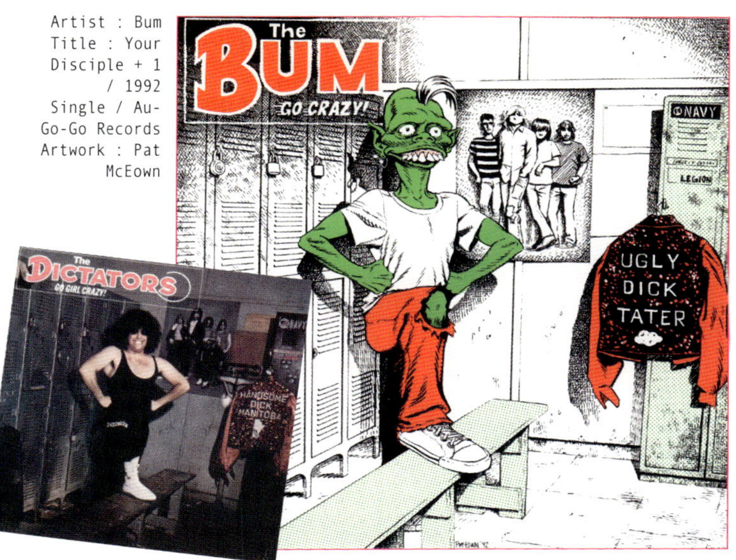

Artist : The Romulans
Title : Billy The Monster + 1 / 1993
Single / Prospective Records
Artwork : Unknown

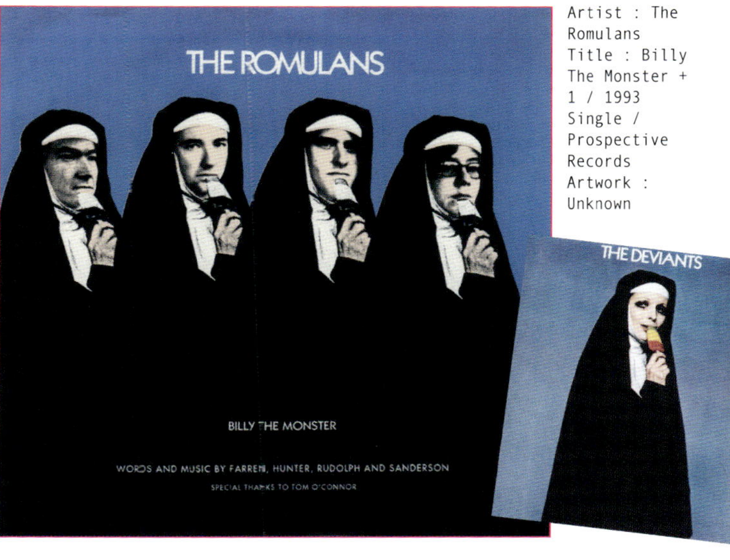

Artist : Smash Alley
Title : Too Late To Say No / 2007
Format :
Album Label : Kivel Records
Artwork : Tyler Bates / Stephen Jensen

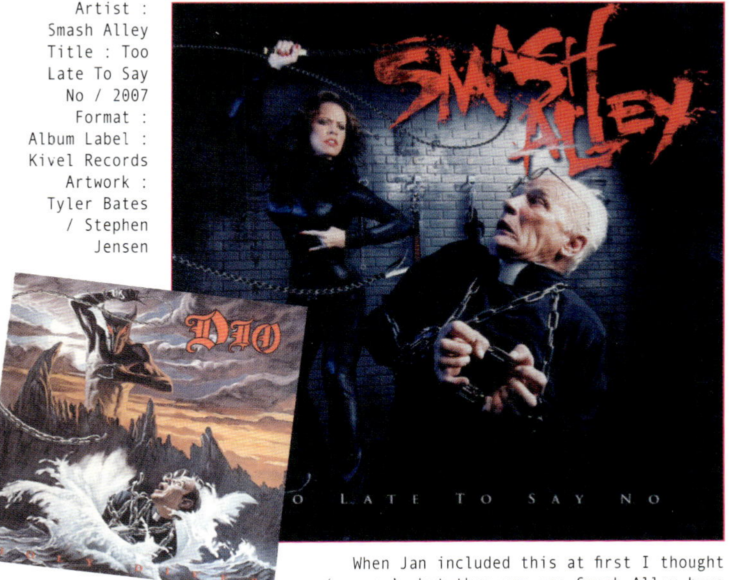

When Jan included this at first I thought 'no way', but then you see Smash Alley have replicated Randy Berrett's Métal Hurlant-style Vicar from Dio's 1983 Holy Diver exactly. The Devil's better looking mind.

Artist : D.J. Shadow
Title : Q-Bert Mix Live / 1997
12" Single / James Lavelle's Records
Artwork : Ben Drury & E.J. Dobson re-created by Kai Clements

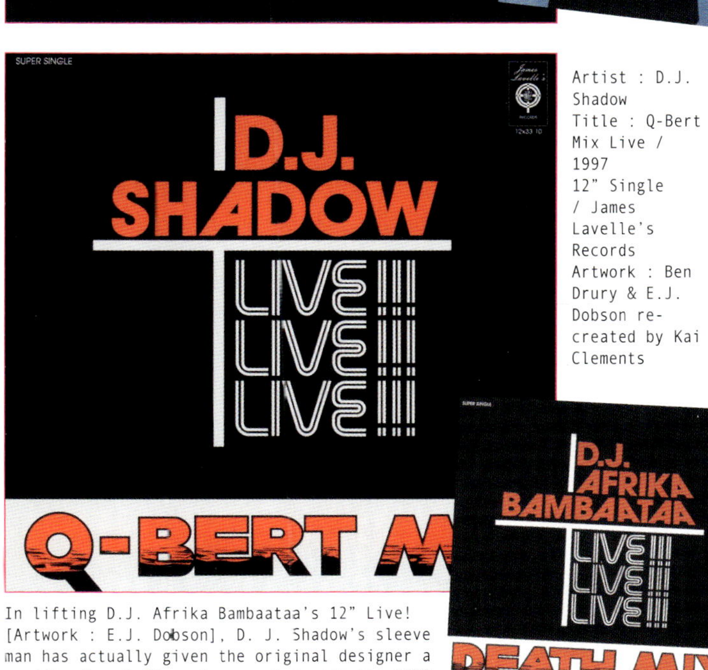

In lifting D.J. Afrika Bambaataa's 12" Live! [Artwork : E.J. Dobson], D. J. Shadow's sleeve man has actually given the original designer a credit, though I'm not sure what made the 1983 cover so inspirational.

DURAN DURAN

The slick look of Duran Duran's 1982 LP Rio, put together by Malcolm Garrett [Illustration : Nagel, Los Angeles] cleverly referenced by Rochester, New York garage fanatics The Quitters and mercilessly attacked by Alan Forbas for the V/Artists collection, which contains 15 covers by bands on the label.

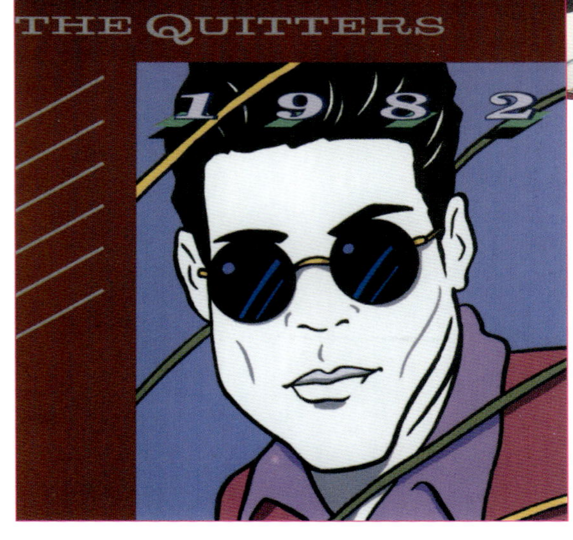

Artist :
Various
Artists
Title : Gag Me
With A Spoon
/ 1995
Album / Don't
Records
Illustration :
Alan Forbas

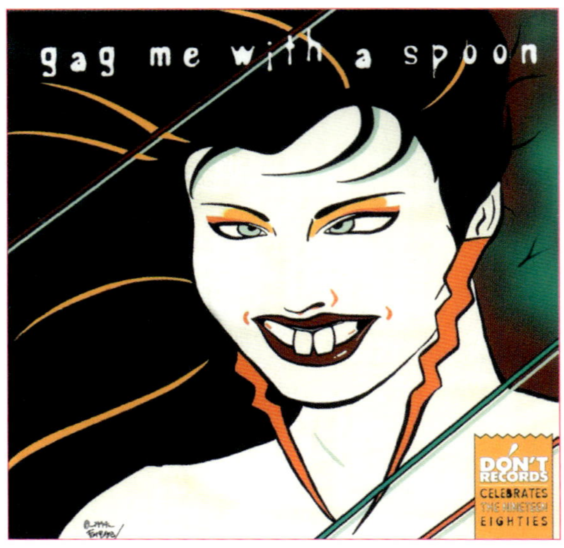

Artist :
The Quitters
Title : 1982
/ 2006
Album /
Garage-Pop
Records
Artwork :
Unknown

Artist :
Babamania
Title :
Pornmuzik /
2001
Album /
Imperial
Records
Artwork :
Tohru Asou
(Photo : Mikio
Ariga)

Artist :
Soundtrack
Title :
Elizabethtown
- Songs From
The Brown
Hotel / 2005
Album/ RCA
Artwork :
Motion Picture
Artwork

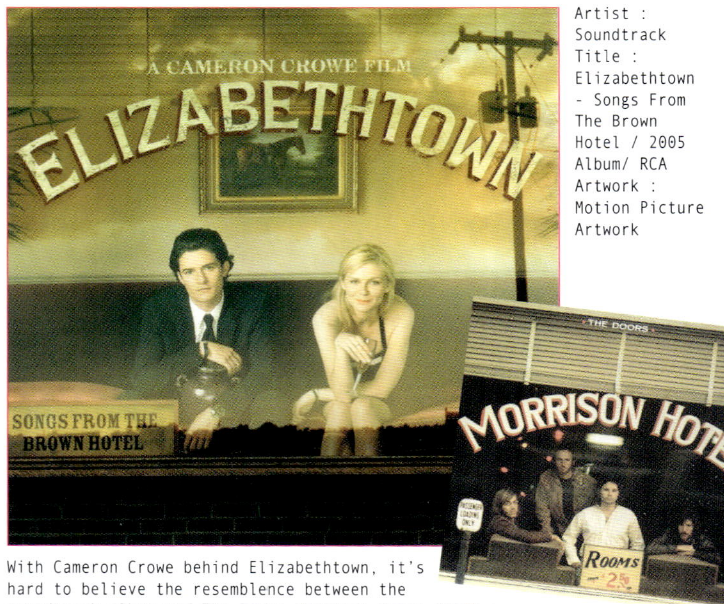

The Doors' Strange Days album from 1967 was made by Joel Brodsky's teriffic cover shot, here the inspiration for Babamania's cover, right down to the fake gig poster on the wall.

With Cameron Crowe behind Elizabethtown, it's hard to believe the resemblence between the soundtrack album and The Doors Morrison Hotel [1970 : Elektra. Artwork : Gary Burden. Photo : Henry Diltz] wasn't very deliberate, although it doesn't convince.

More Blue Note inspired covers? Not exactly, as all three use a famous uncerwater photograph by Toni Frissell (1939) now owned by the Library Of Congress, though the Bill Evans / Jim Hall Undercurrent cover got there first in 1962. Whether the other designers were aware of this cover or if it's a coincidence isn't clear.

Artist :
Osvaldo
Golijov
Title : Oceana
/ 2007
Album /
Deutsche
Grammophon
Artwork :
Chika Azuma /
Fred Münzmaier

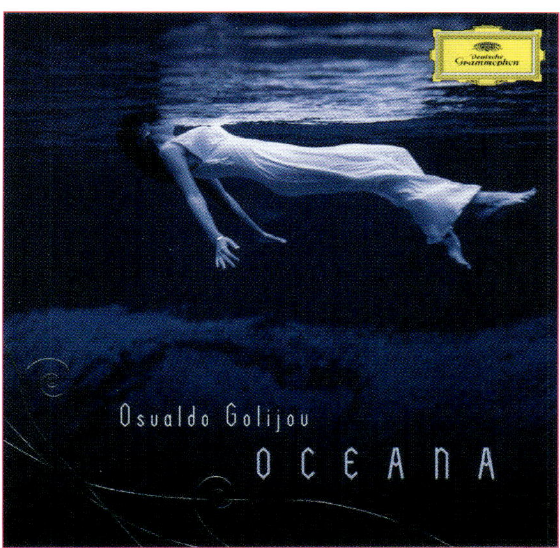

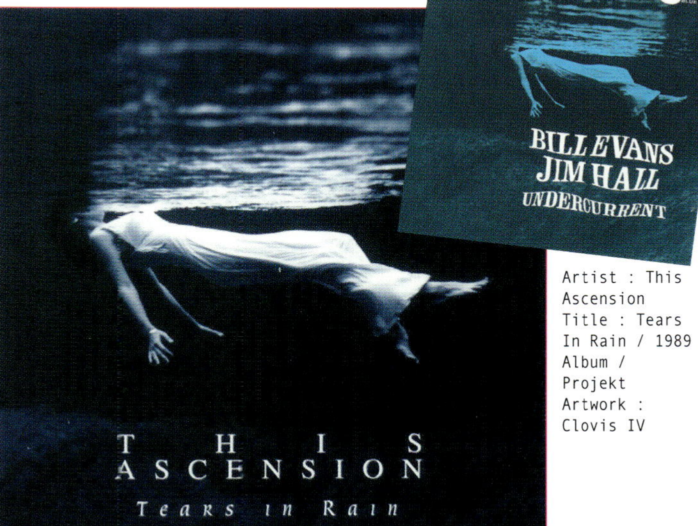

Artist : This
Ascension
Title : Tears
In Rain / 1989
Album /
Projekt
Artwork :
Clovis IV

Artist : Black
Sabbath
Title : Born
Again / 1983
Album /
Vertigo
Artwork :
Steve Joule /
Steve Barrett

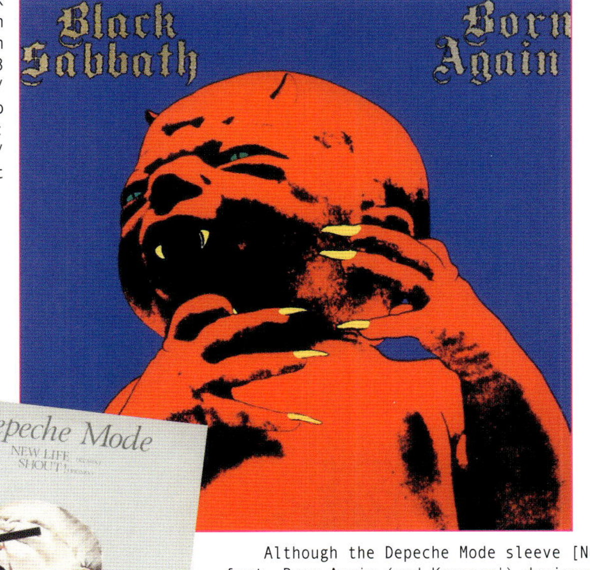

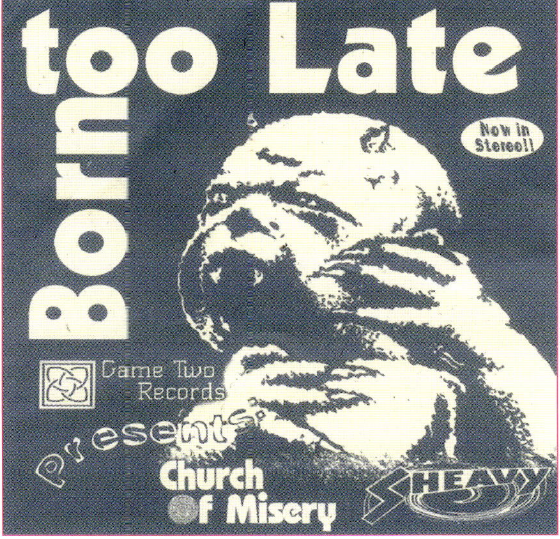

Artist :
Church Of
Misery (+ 1)
Title : Born
Too Late /
1991
Album / Game
Two Records
Artwork :
Ritchie Perez

Although the Depeche Mode sleeve [New Life, 1981 12" Single, Illustration : Simon Rice] came out first, Born Again (and Kerrang!) designer Steve Joule says he'd never seen it, and based his cover on a photo from Mind Alive, a 1968 weekly Illustrated Encyclopedia magazine cover - so the similarity is coincidence. He photocopied it, stuck the horns on and was surprised (he admits he didn't want the job) when the label said how much they liked it. Church of Misery must also have been fans.

A number of designers have used images of flight cases on covers, but The Eagles Live sleeve [1980. Photo : Aaron Rapoport] was clearly the inspiration for the Wolle Kriwanek Band's slightly less well-known release.

Electric Light Orchestra's A New World Record [1976] made much of the detailed logo [Artwork : Kosh / Ria Lewerke] which because so much linked to ELO that you'd wonder why someone might want to copy it so closely.

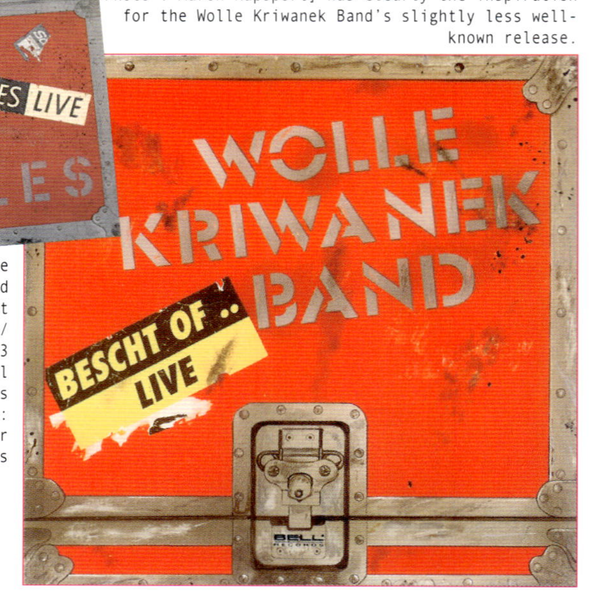

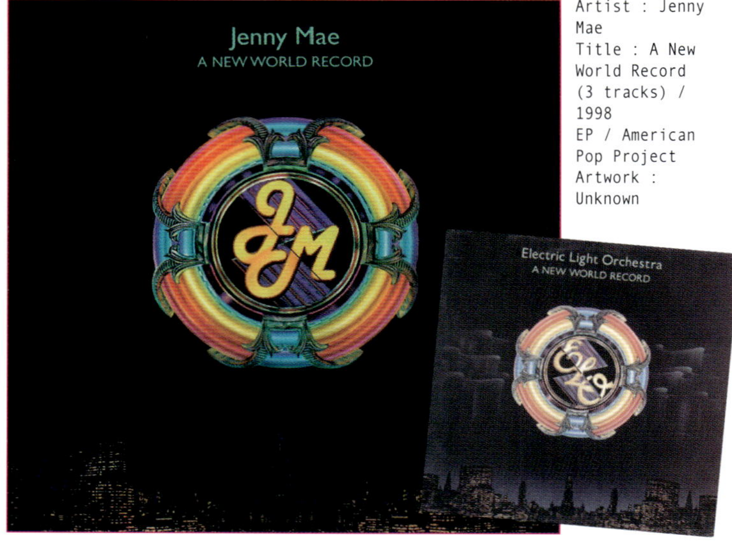

Artist : Wolle Kriwanek Band
Title : Bescht Of - Live / 1993
Album / Bell Records
Artwork : Gaukler Studios

Artist : Jenny Mae
Title : A New World Record (3 tracks) / 1998
EP / American Pop Project
Artwork : Unknown

Artist : Love Tractor
Title : Before And After Christmas / 2006
Album / Fundamental Records
Artwork : Michele Shadrick / Billy Holmes / Mike Richmond

Artist : The Becks Street Boys
Title : Pop's Not Dead / 2005
Album / Matulas Records
Artwork : Unknown

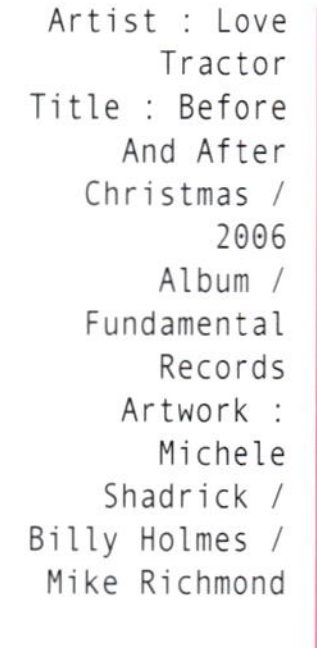

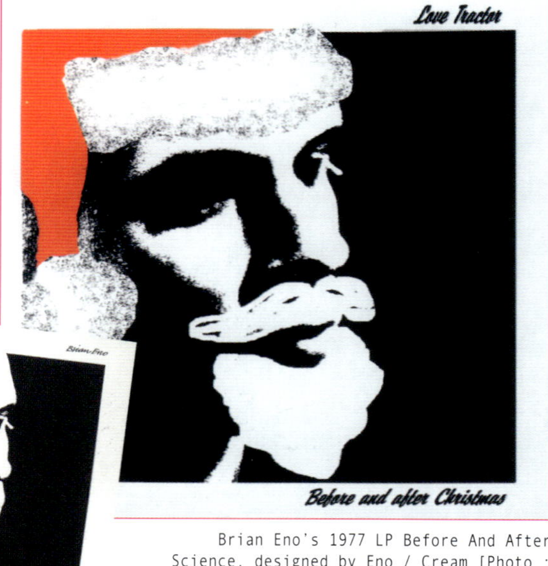

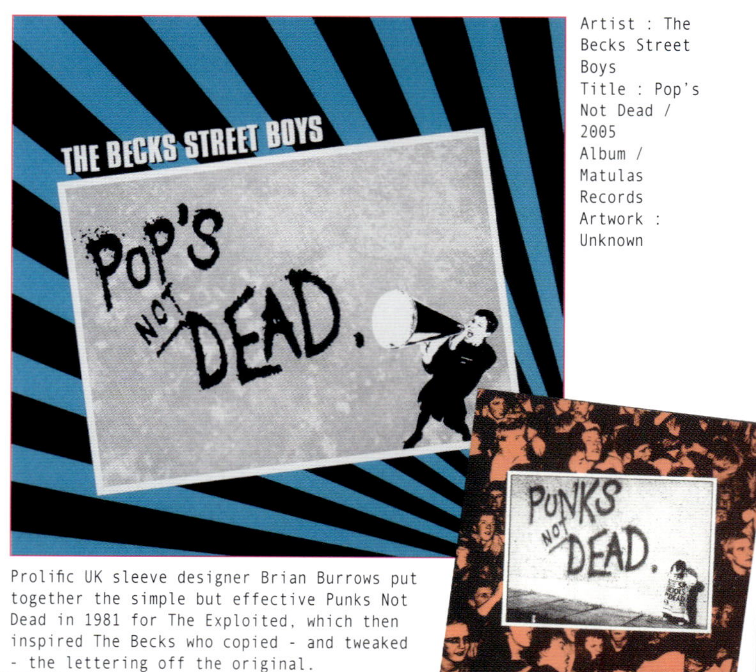

Brian Eno's 1977 LP Before And After Science, designed by Eno / Cream [Photo : Ritva Saarikko] gets a less than reverential Christmassy make-over by Love Tractor.

Prolific UK sleeve designer Brian Burrows put together the simple but effective Punks Not Dead in 1981 for The Exploited, which then inspired The Becks who copied - and tweaked - the lettering off the original.

Duke Ellington's music on the 1959 soundtrack album Anatomy Of A Murder may have been good, but the film poster designed by Saul Bass is what makes it very collectable - and imitated - today (Howard Fritzson adapted it for the sleeve). Here are four of the more interesting users who have all leaned on the original in one way or another.

Artist : Elvis Costello With The Metropole Orkest
Title : My Flame Burns Blue / 2005
Format : Album
Label : Deutsche Grammophon
Artwork : Coco Shinomiya (Illustration : Edwin Fotheringham)

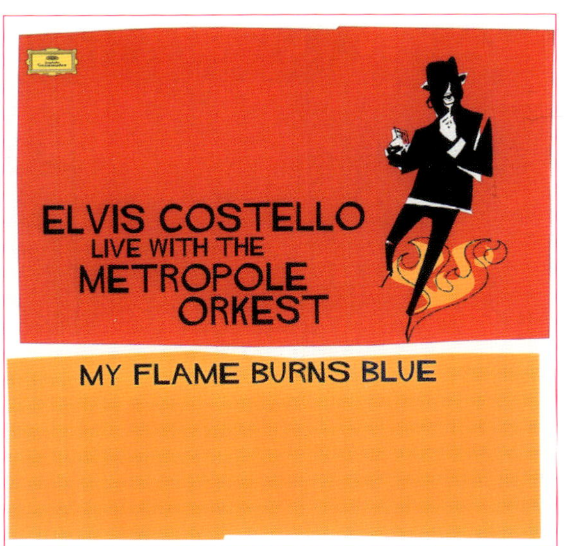

Artist : Paul Chastain & Ric Menck
Title : Hey Wimpus - The Early Recordings Of... / 1987
Album / Action Music
Artwork : Kaufman / Menck / Merritt

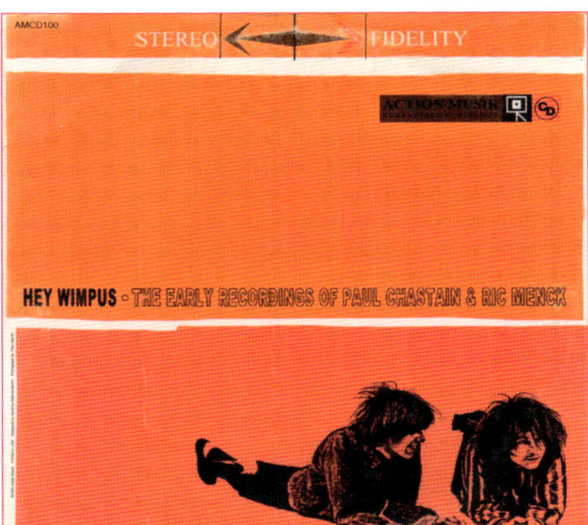

Artist : Stan Ridgway
Title : Anatomy / 1999
Album / New West Records
Artwork : UMod007 for Allied Chemical.com

Artist : Tindersticks
Title : Donkeys 92-97 / 1998
Album / Island
Artwork : Island Records Ltd.

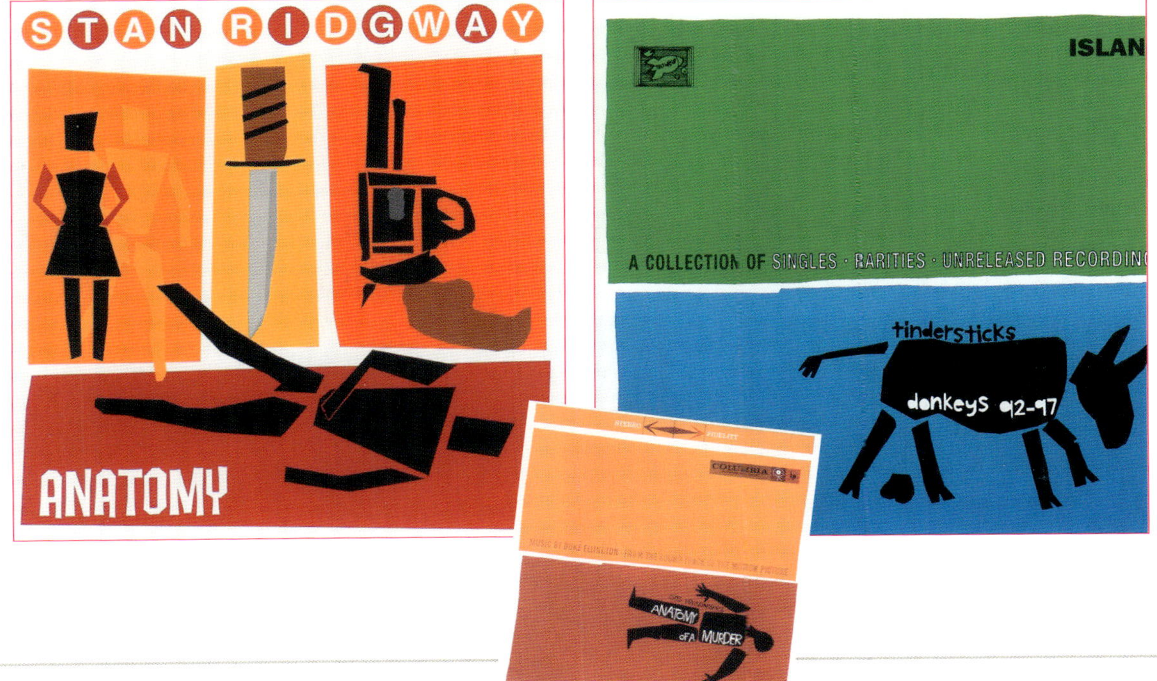

Frampton Comes Alive! gets a bit of a rough ride these days, as the less than reverential sleeves here show, but in its day [1976 : A&M. Artwork : Roland Young & Stan Evenson. Photo : Richard E. Aaron] it was an enormous album, selling well over six million copies for the former Humble Pie guitarist. Melba Comes Alive is a very strange collection of American crank radio phone-in calls placed by Brother Russell (well worth hunting the web for a listen).

Artist :
Brother
Russell
Title : Melba
Comes Alive! /
1997
Album / Vinyl
Communications
Artwork :
Unknown

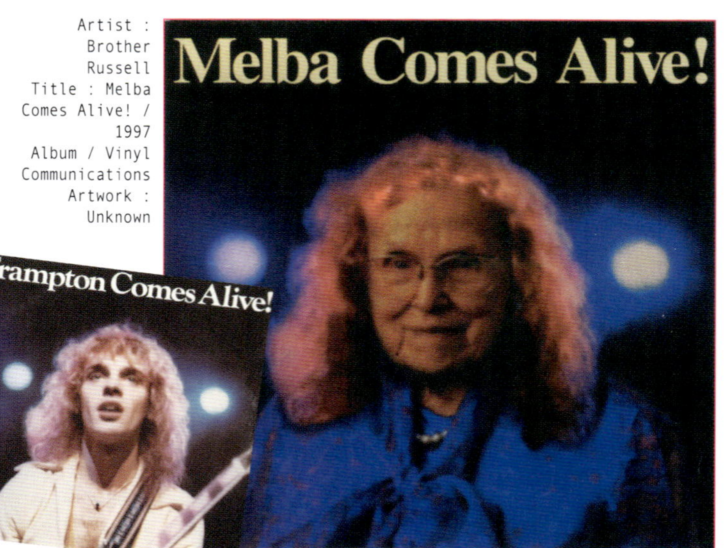

Artist :
Various
Artists
Title : Fiesta
Comes Alive!
/ 1997
Album / Slap A
Ham Records
Artwork :
Lydia Dodge

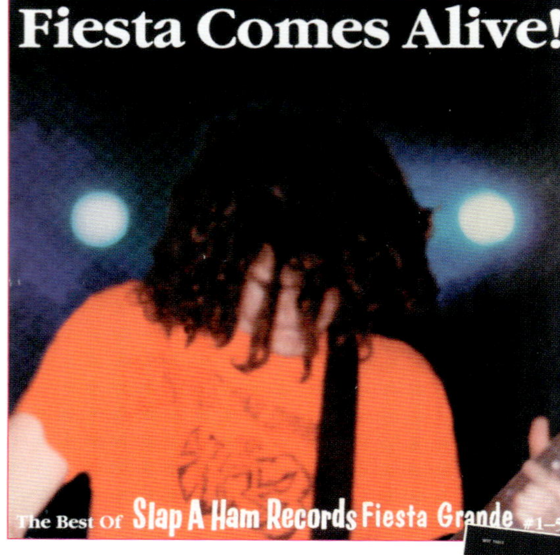

Artist :
Cococoma
Title :
Cococoma /
2007
Album / Goner
Records
Artwork : Bill
Roe

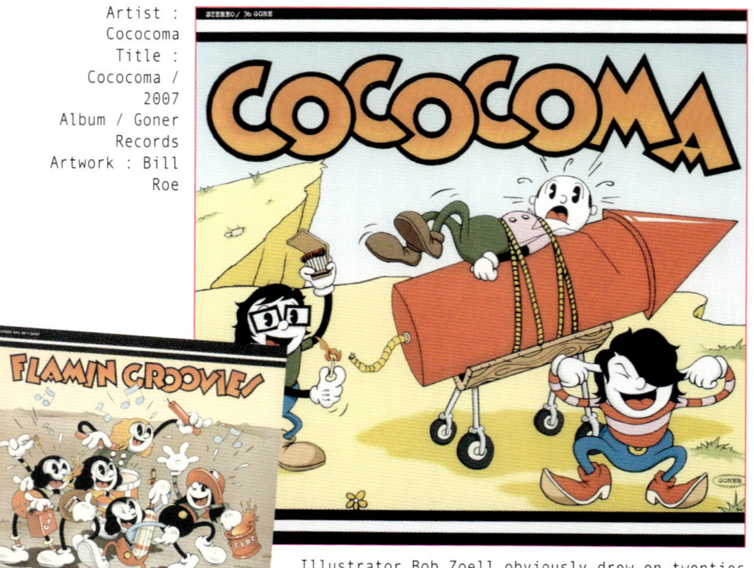

Artist :
Casiocore
Title : The
Sound Of
Tomorrow Today
/ 2000
Album / Slabco
Artwork :
Susan Robb

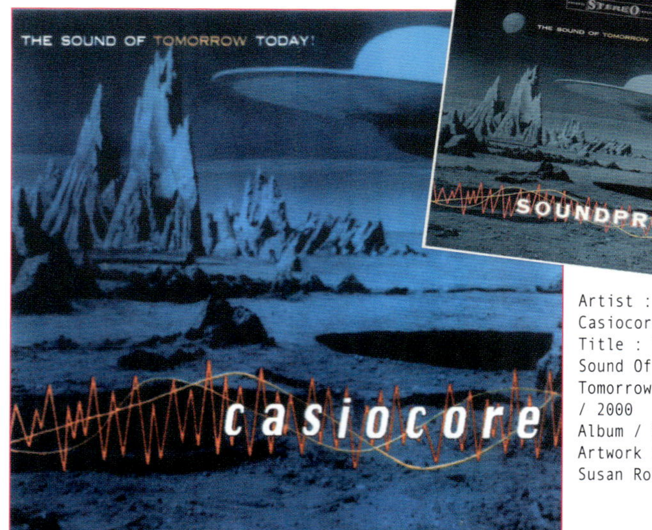

Illustrator Bob Zoell obviously drew on twenties cartoons for the Flamin' Groovies' Supersnazz LP [1969 : Epic], and Cococoma were in turn inspired by the artwork (and thank Zoell in their credits).

Ferrante & Teicher's Soundprocf - The Sound Of Tomorrow Today sleeve is another sci-fi vinyl classic from 1956 [Westminster. Artwork : Unknown], reworked closely by Casiocore, right down to the subtitle.

Well, you gotta have a bit of fun. Not so much a tribute more an almost exact replica! Funkadelic's Free Your Mind ... And Your Ass Will Follow was important musically and pushed boundaries cover-wise, especially for 1970 [Westbound Records. Artwork : The Graffiteria / Stanley Hochstadt]. Sadly for Nocturnal Rage they lacked the option of gatefold vinyl and also had to suffer one of those 'parental advisory lyric' warnings. As if any parents bought it. I'm now so fed up of these that I digitally removed it.

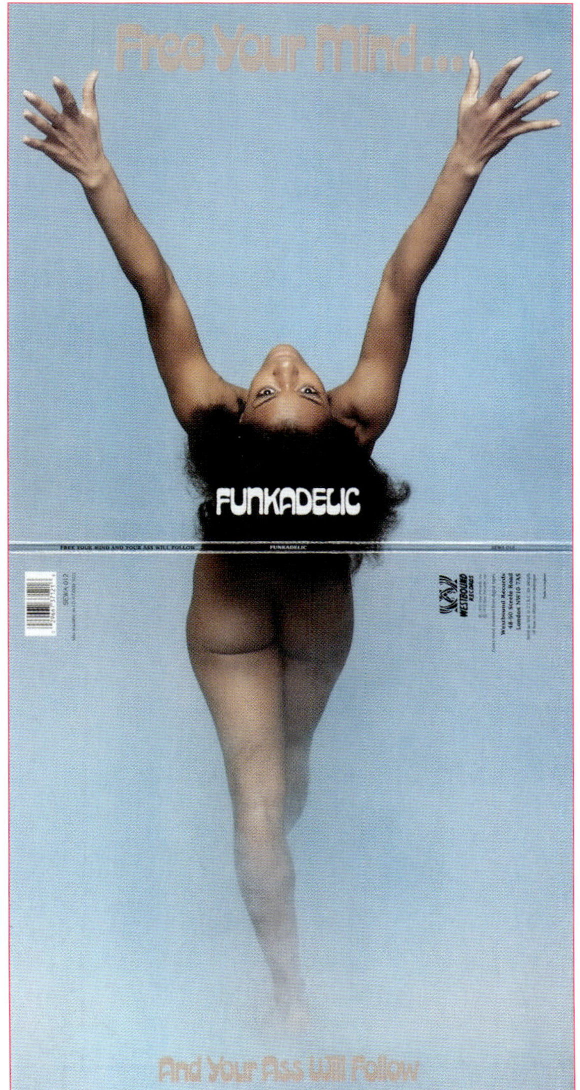

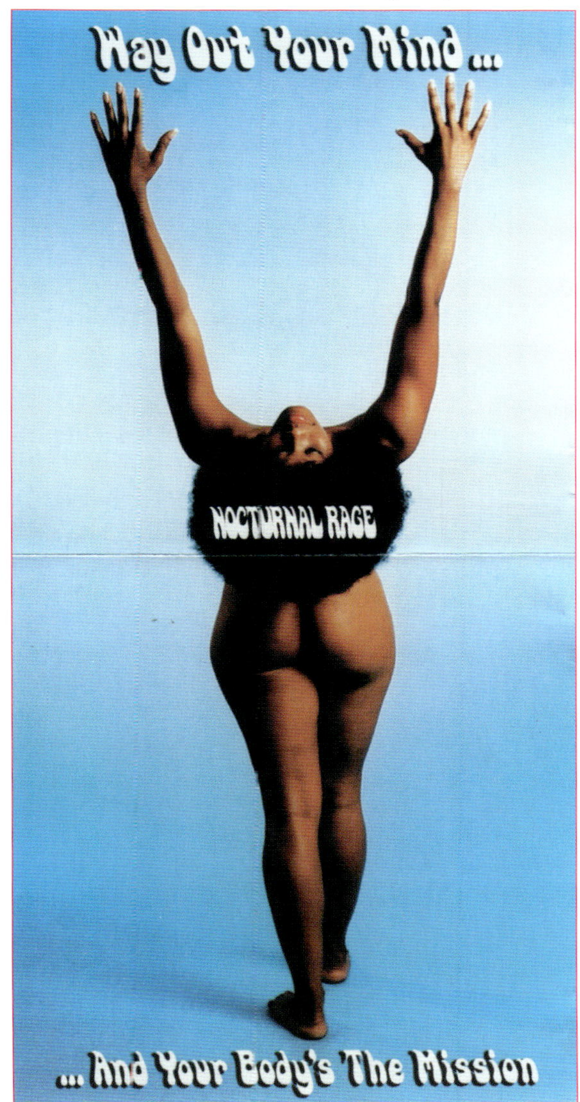

Artist : Nocturnal Rage
Title : Way Cut Your Mind / 2005
Album / Noc Cn Wood Recorcs
Artwork : Rokert C. Wood & Jovan Price.
Photo : Paige Craig-Apodaca

Island Records did great sleeves for many of their acts, but this one for Marianne Faithfull's remarkable Broken English LP in 1979 [Artwork / Photo : Dennis Morris] is one of their simplest and best. The copy is well done too.

Bryan Ferry's post-Roxy sleeves were often just plain dull, but In Your Mind [1977] was on form, courtesy Nicholas de Ville & Bob Bowkett at C.C.S. [Photo : Monty Coles]. Certainly far more contemporary than Fleetwood Mac's LP from the same year (below).

Artist : Kid & Khan
Title : Bad English / 2004
Album / Transsolar Records
Artwork : Danuta
(Photo : Bela Borsodi)

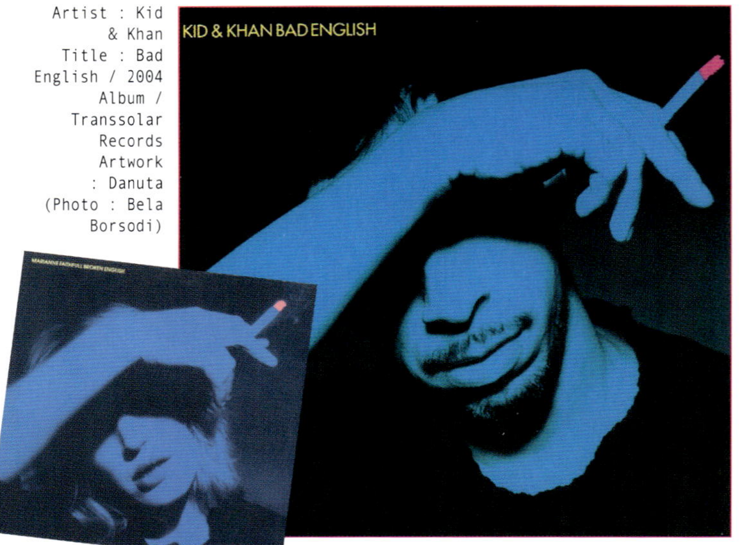

Artist : Tiga
Title : Sexor / 2006
Album / PIAS
Artwork : Pawel Karwowski
(Photo : Marek Vogel)

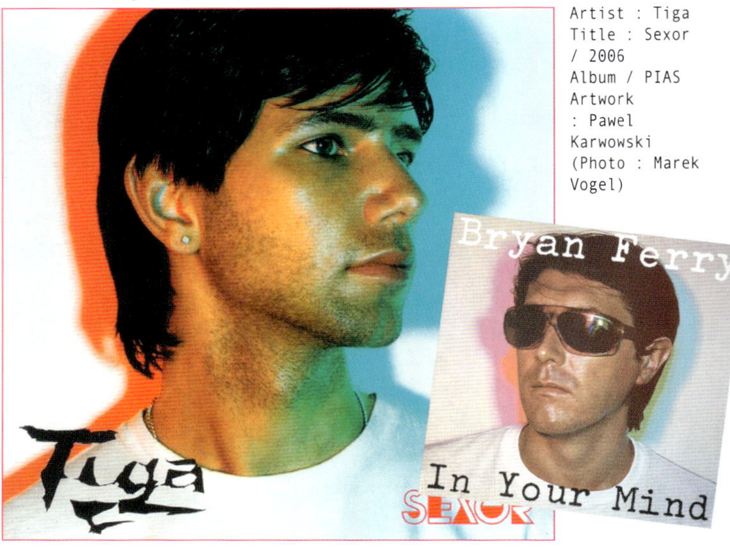

Artist : Schlong
Title : Tumours / 1993
EP / Bun Lenght Records
Artwork : Hugh Janus (Photo : Farzad Owrang)

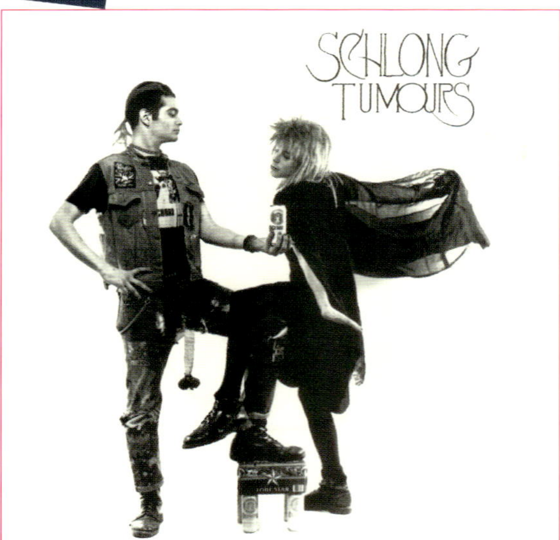

Artist : Dougal Reed
Title : Rumours / 2001
Album / The Kitty Kitty Corporation
Artwork / Photo : Melanie Standage

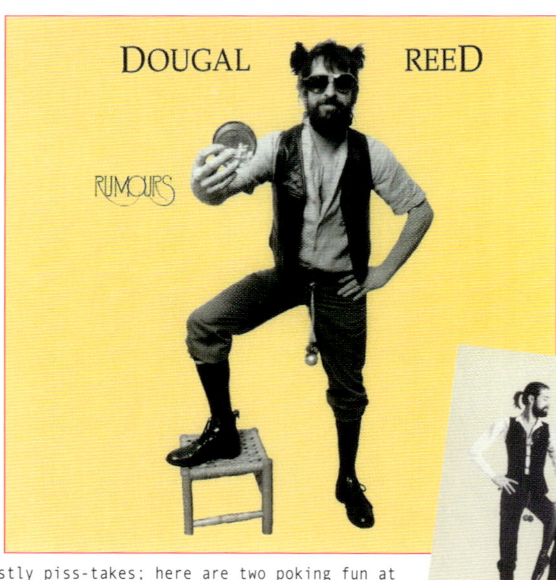

Fleetwood Mac's Rumours [1977] cover seems to have prompted mostly piss-takes; here are two poking fun at Desmond Strobel's design and / or Herbert Worthington's cover pic.

The Glitter Band always struggled without their leader, but Rock 'N' Roll Dudes [1975 : Bell Records. Artwork : MLT Marketing Associates. Photo : J. Trapman] is a great summation of mid-seventies male fashion. The Cruel Sea adapted and montaged it up twenty years on.

The rather lack-lustre cover to Green Day's Dookie [1994   Reprise Records] by Richie Bucher clearly worked for some, and re-rendered here for a two track / two band single on the aptly named Under The Influence label.

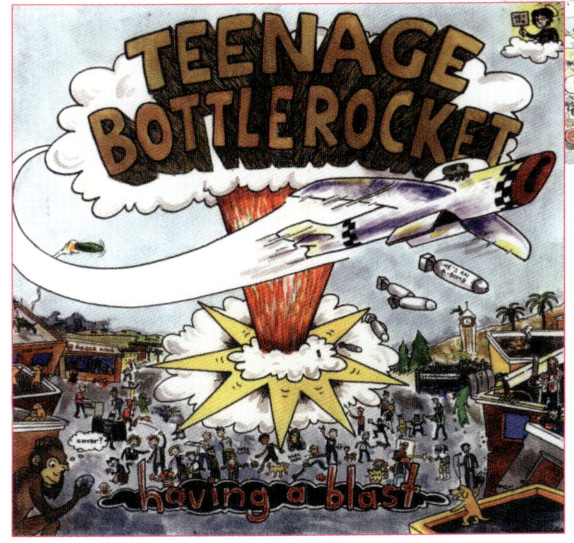

Artist : The Cruel Sea
Title : Rock 'N' Roll Duds / 1995
Album / Polydor
Artwork : Tex & J.F.

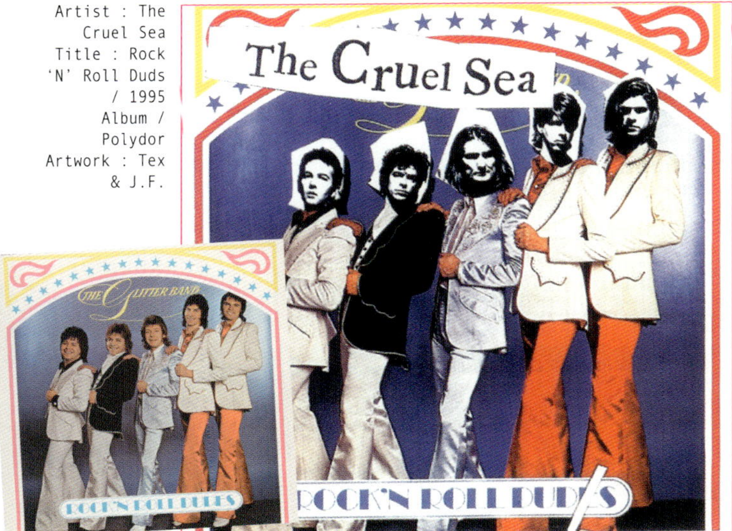

Artist : Teenage Bottlerocket + 1
Title : Having A Blast + 1 / 2008
Single / Under The Influence
Artwork : Unknown

Artist : Bracket
Title : Appetite For Food / 1997
EP / High Output Records
Artwork : Unknown

Artist : The Mono Men
Title : Shut Up! / 1993
Album / Estrus Records
Artwork : Unknown

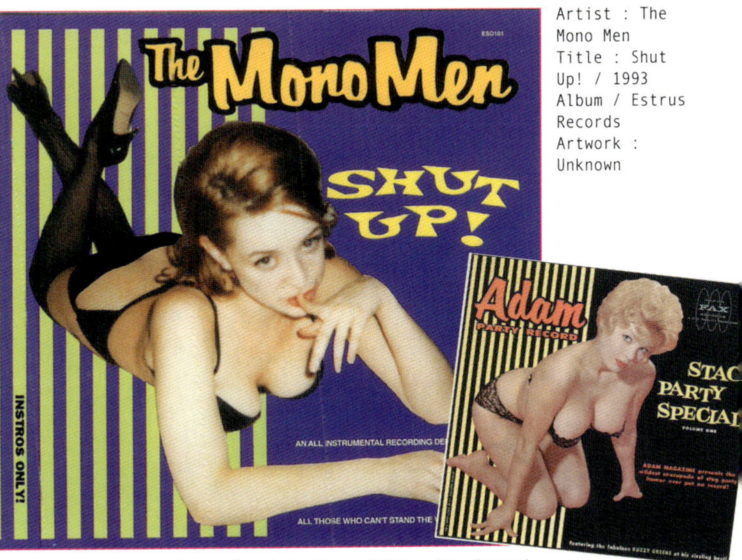

The cover to big-selling Guns n' Roses album Appetite For Destruction [1987 : Geffen. Artwork : Michael Hodgson. Pairting : Robert Williams], itself owing something to Kiss, inspired a lot of copyists, most of which were even duller. Bracket's at least had a sense of humour about it.

Buzzy Greene's Stag Party Special album [1960 : Fax Record Company] is sought after by cheesecake sleeve collectors and cleavage fans for obvious reasons. The Mono Men were obvious admirers and did their own tribute.

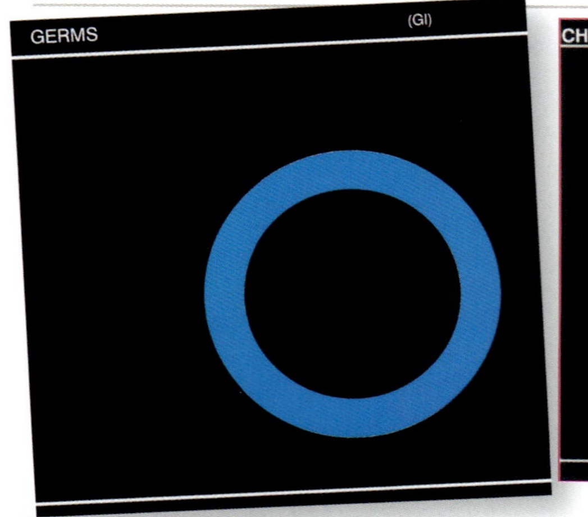

GERMS
(GI)

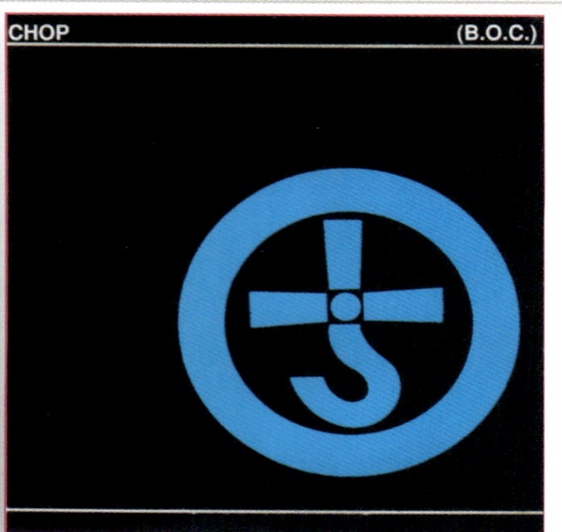

CHOP
(B.O.C.)

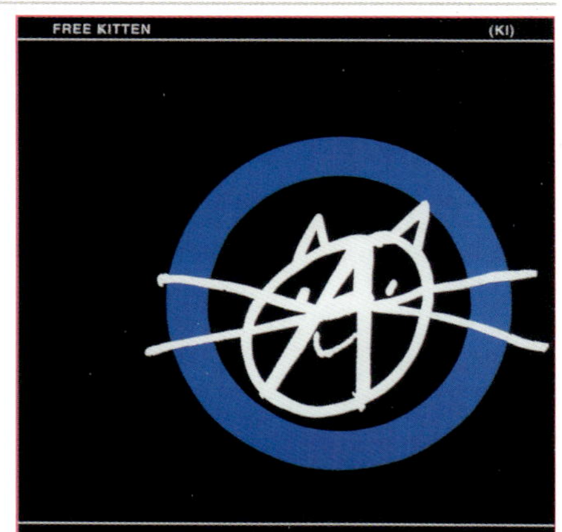

FREE KITTEN
(KI)

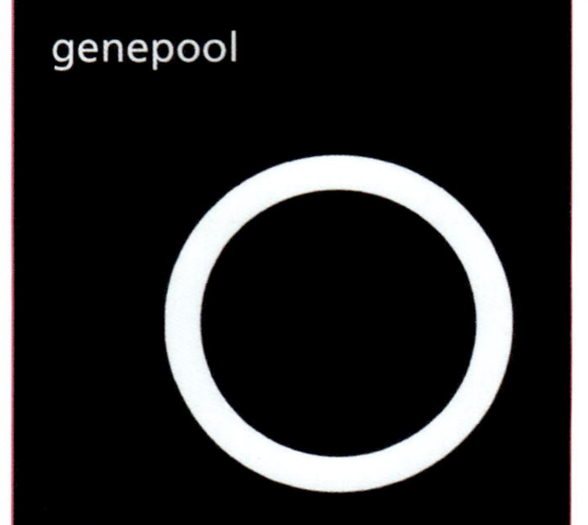

genepool

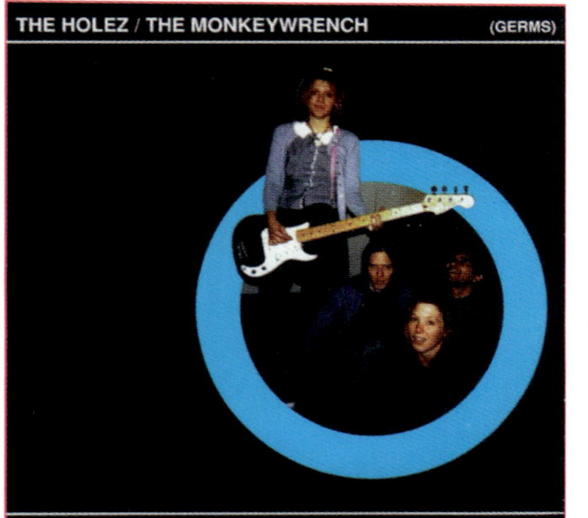

THE HOLEZ / THE MONKEYWRENCH
(GERMS)

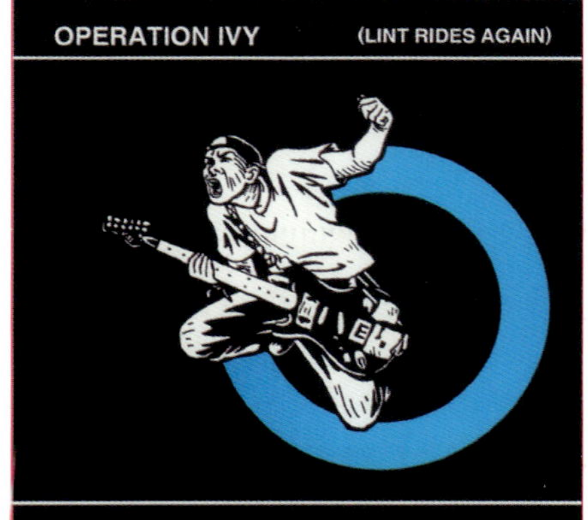

OPERATION IVY
(LINT RIDES AGAIN)

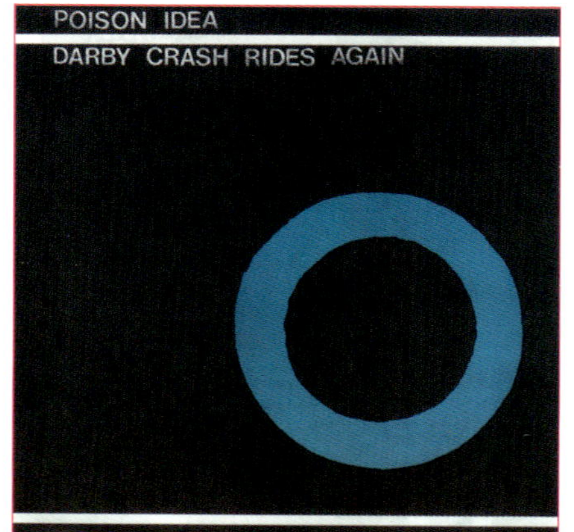

POISON IDEA
DARBY CRASH RIDES AGAIN

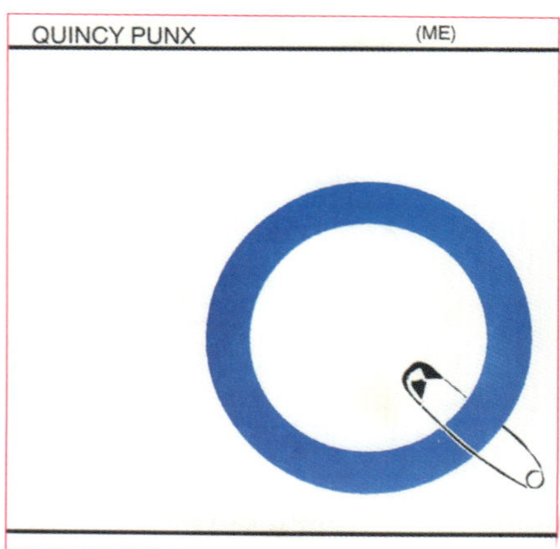

QUINCY PUNX
(ME)

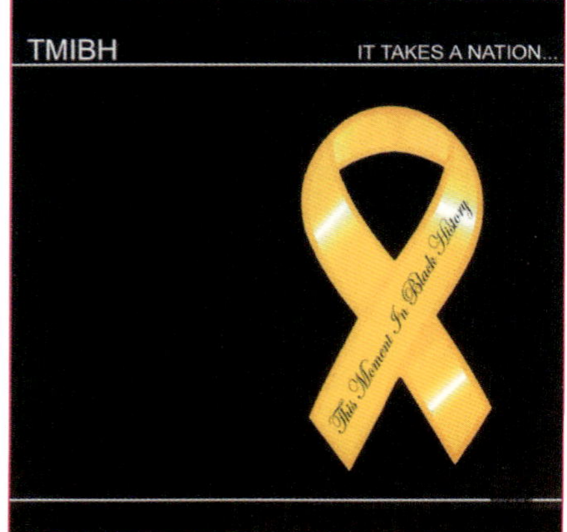

TMIBH
IT TAKES A NATION...
This Moment In Black History

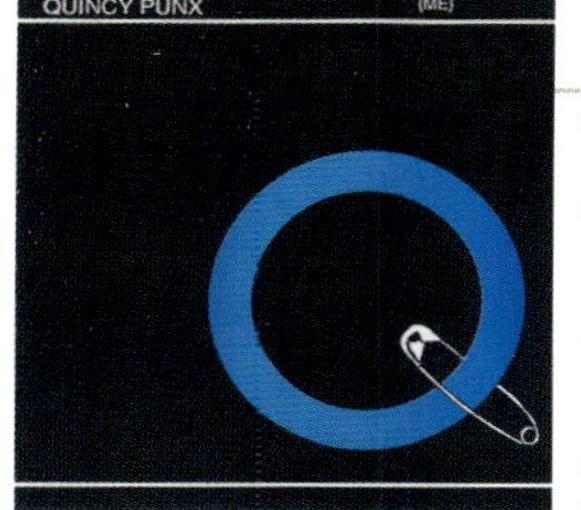

While early LA Punk band The Germs - formed in 1977 - debut (and only) studio album [QI : 1979] missed the mainstream arrival of punk by a year or two, it was a cult success and proved influential. As a result dozens of bands have paid tribute to them both musically and by copying the very simple cover design [Slash Records. Artwork : Melanie Nissen]. For a lot of these bands it was a simple shorthand to tell prospective buyers where they were coming from. Pages 62 top l- r / 63 show some of the variations (Quincy Punks are in twice as they issued the cover in white and black versions). Singer Darby Crash killed himself in 1980.

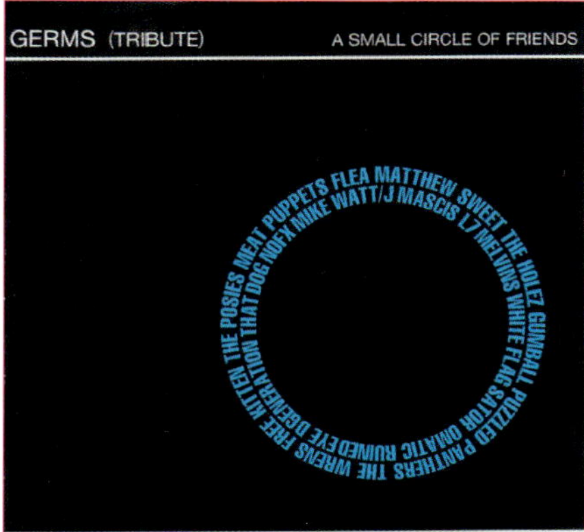

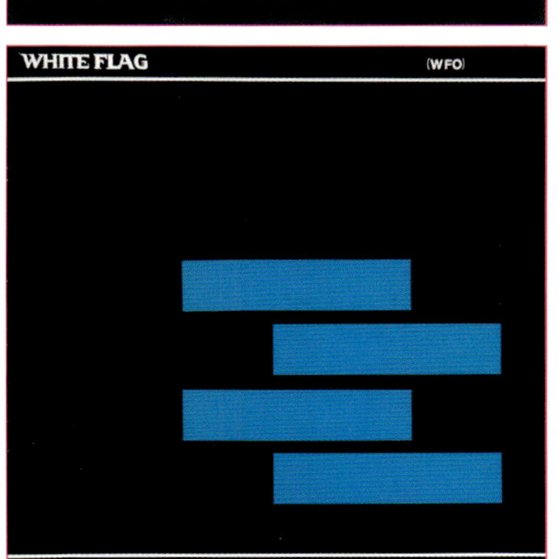

Artist : Chop
Title : (B.O.C.) / 1993
2 track Single : Dutch East India Trading
Artwork : Unknown

Artist : Free Kitten
Title : (KI) / 1994
Single / Radiation Records
Artwork : Unknown

Artist : Genepool
Title : Everything Goes In Circles / 2004
Album / Noisolution - Indigo Records
Artwork : Timmy Nawrot & Genepool

Artist : The Holez (+ 1)
Title : Circle 1 + 1 / 1995
Single / Gasa Tanka
Artwork + photo : Bill / Charles Peterson

Artist : Operation Ivy
Title : (Lint Rides Again) / 1989
Album / Slashout ! Records
Artwork : Unknown

Artist : Poison Idea
Title : Darby Crash Rides Again / 1989
EP / American Leather Records
Artwork : Unknown

Artist : Quincy Punks
Title : (ME) / 1994
EP / Recess Records
EP / THD Records
Artwork : Unknown

Artist : This Moment In Black History
Title : It Takes A Nation Of Assholes To Hold Us Back / 2006
Album / Cold Sweat Records
Artwork : Buddy Akita / Tiny Patron Press

Various Artists Germs Tribute
Title : A Small Circle Of Friends / 1996
Album / Grass Records
Artwork : David Landry Jr. / Lazy Chicken Design / Bill Bartell

Artist : White Flag
Title : (WFO) / 1985
Album / Gasatanka Records
Artwork : Bill Bartell / White Flag

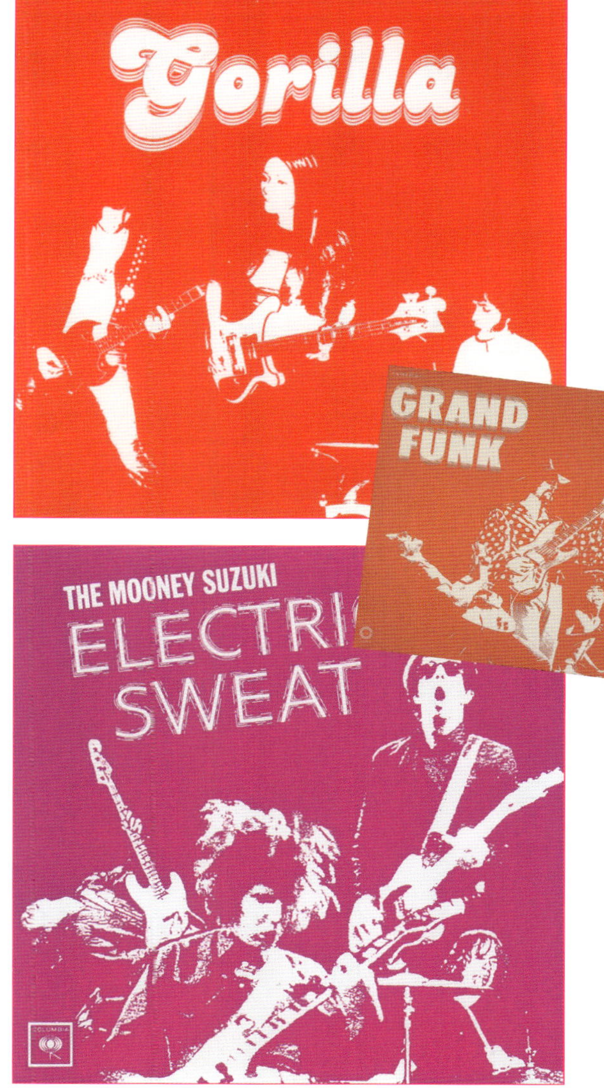

Grand Funk Railroad's 1969 debut cover, simple and direct [Capitol. Artwork : Silvia Gmür] with just a little tinting of the title to convey LOUD NOISE.

Artist : Gorilla
Title : Gorilla / 2001
Album / Lunasound Recording
Artwork : Jenni Sinclair

Artist : The Mooney Suzuki
Title : Electric Sweat / 2002
Album / Columbia
Artwork : Mike Fornatale, Jessica Arp, Todd Osborne

BELOW : Artist : Die Toten Hosen
Title : Reich & Sexy / 1993
Album / Virgin
Artwork : Johann Zambryski & Die Hosen
Cover AG (Photo : Gabo)

OPPOSITE PAGE :
Artist : Die Toten Hosen
Title : Love , Peace &
Money / 1995
Album / Virgin
Artwork : Johann
Zambryski & The Hosen
Cover AG (Photo : Gabo)

Artist : Fun Lovin'
Criminals
Title : King Of New York
(US) / 1977
Single / Chrysalis
Artwork : Morph
Iconography / Gerb /
Dr. Revolt (Photo : Bob
Gruen)
Outer and inner sleeve
shown.

Artist : Sex Pistols
Title : Substitute + 1
/ 1977
Single / Virgil Records
Artwork : Unknown

Artist : John 5
Title : Remixploitation
/ 2009
Album / Mascot Records
Artwork : Piggy D. (Photo
: Neil Zlozower)

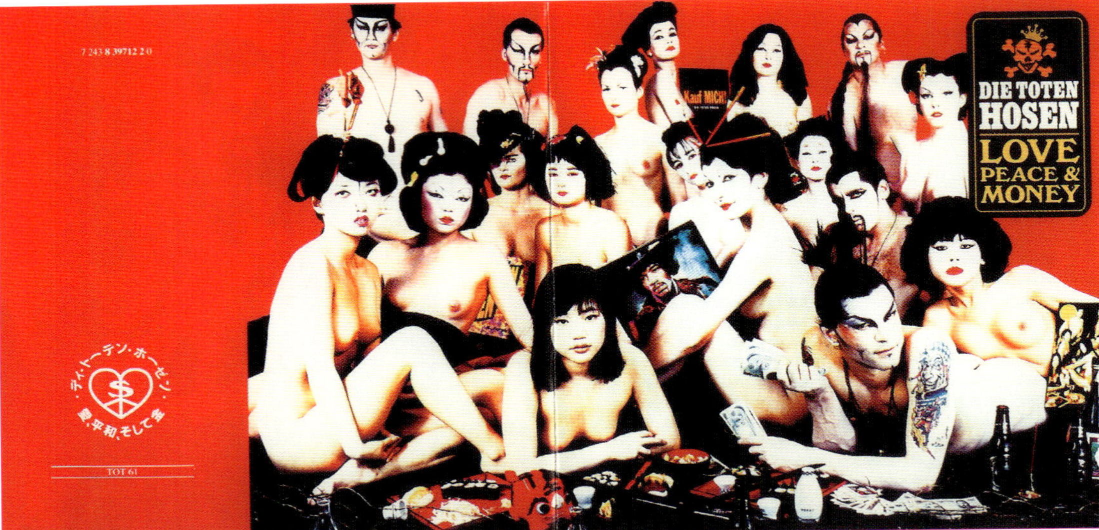

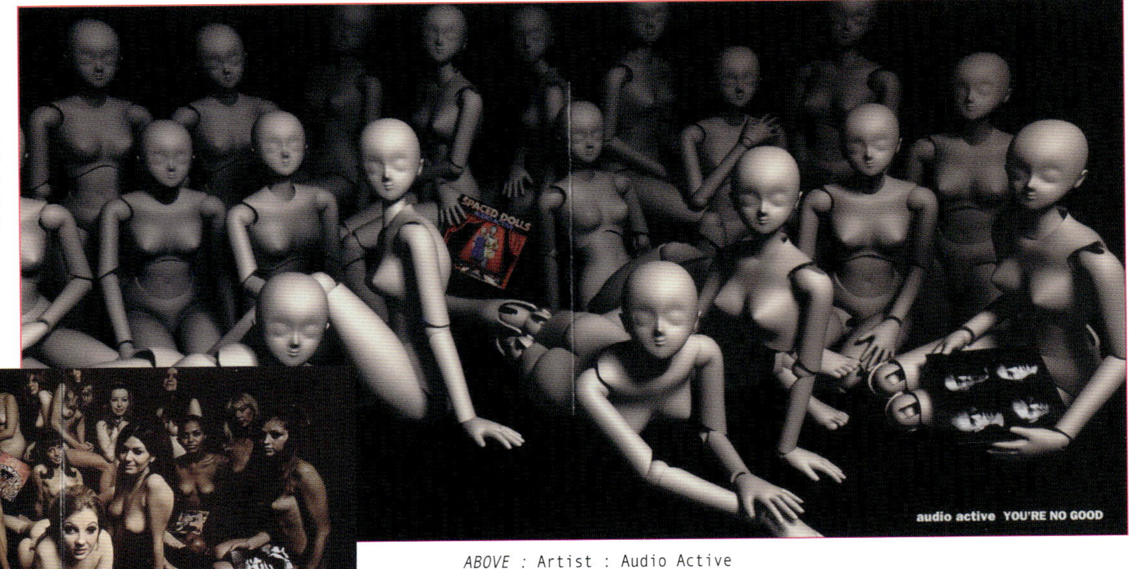

ABOVE : Artist : Audio Active
Title : You're No Good / 2000
EP / Dream Machine
Artwork : Tatsuya Horinouchi (Atami Graphics)

David Montgomery's cover shot for the Jimi Hendrix Experience Electric Ladyland album [1958. *Page 65 bottom left*] needs little introduction. It works because it is just ordinary people, no airbrushing or fakery whatsoever. This didn't stop some trying to ban it of course, and others wanting to replicate the photo shoot, twice in the case of Die Toten Hosen (though it loses so much on a CD). The crash test dummies concept is one of the most interesting, while the Sex Pistols' appropriation marks the sheer desperation of that band's end game.

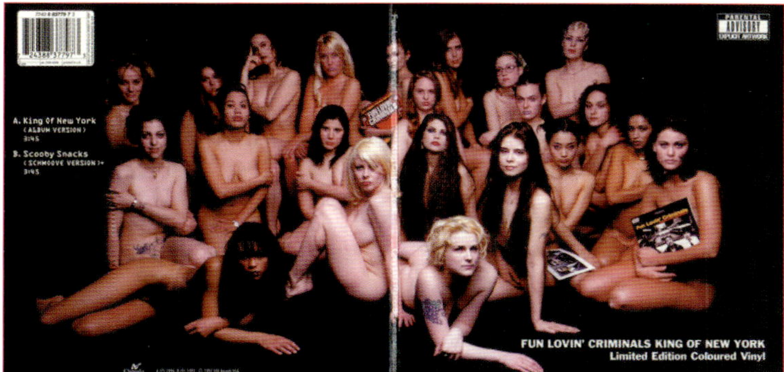

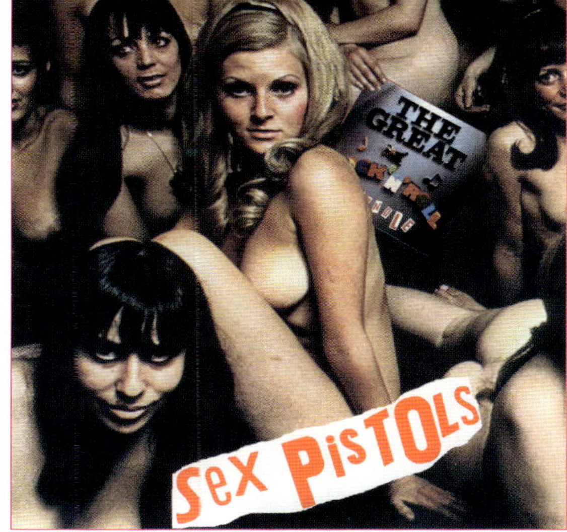

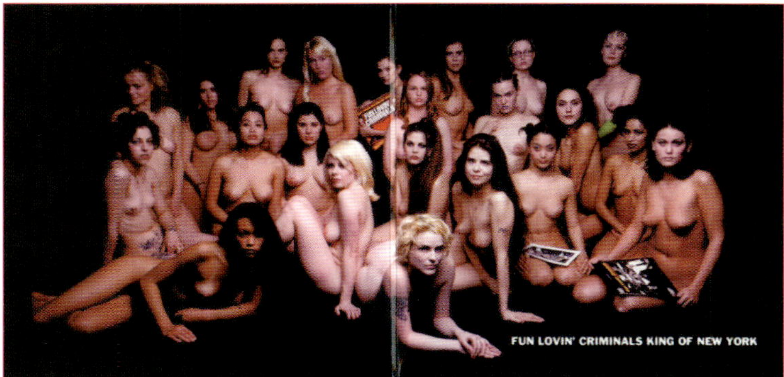

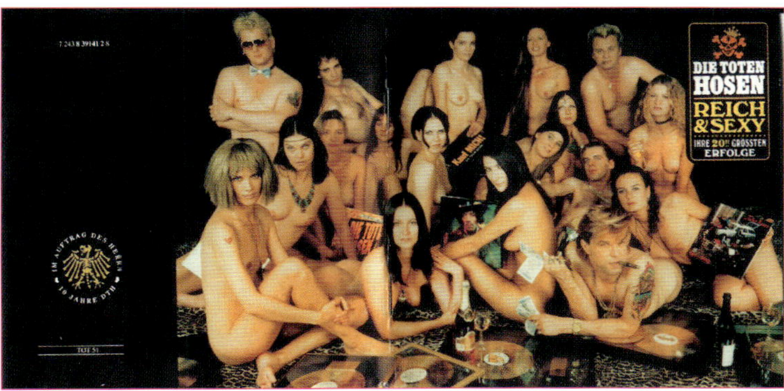

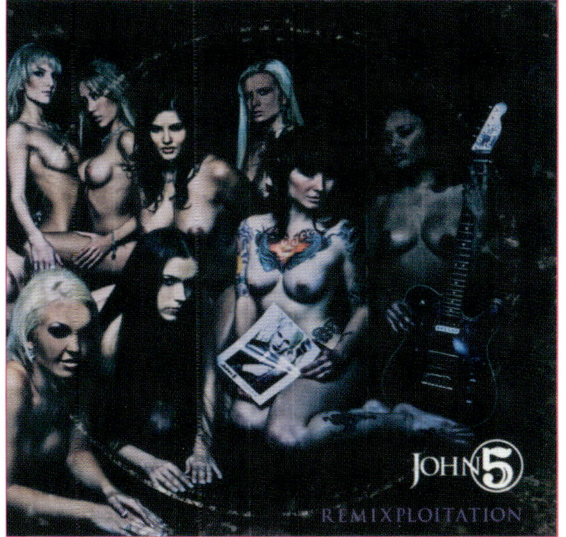

The American cover of the first Jimi Hendrix Experience album Are You Experienced by [1967 : Reprise. Art director : Ed Trasher] was different to elsewhere (as was the track listing), and the artwork (done by cover photographer Karl Ferris) is very SF poster-era in feel. The two copyists here draw on the lettering and infra-red photo aspects respectively, but not the fish-eye lens look.

Artist : The Jimi Homeless Experience
Title : Are You Homeless / 2007
Album / MK-Ultra Records
Artwork : Big Tasty / Jon Kinyon

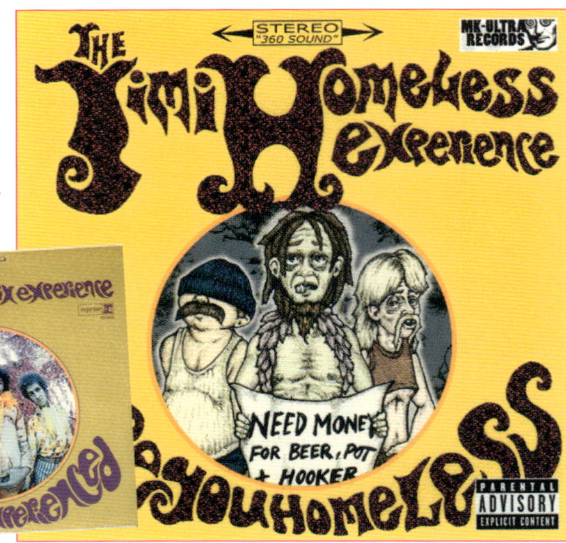

Artist : Tha Liks (Alkaholiks)
Title : X.O. Experience / 2001
Album / Loud Records - Epic
Artwork : Jason Clark.
Photo : Daniel Hastings

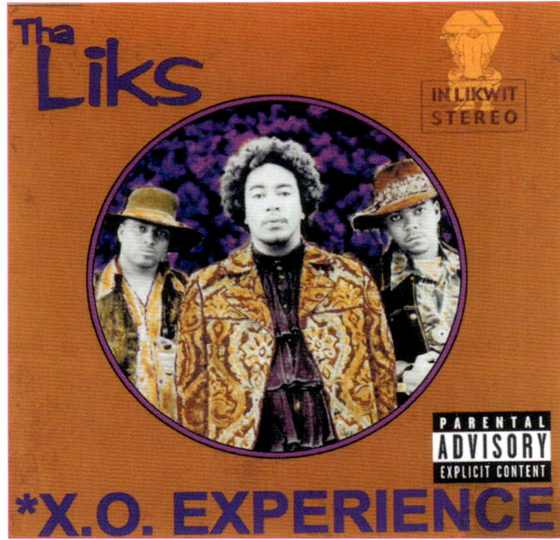

Artist : Jon Auer & Ken Stringfellow
Title : Private Sides / 2003
EP / Arena Rock Recording Company
Artwork : Dawn Pierson / Jon Auer / Ken Stringfellow
(Photo : Nathan Breskin-Auer)

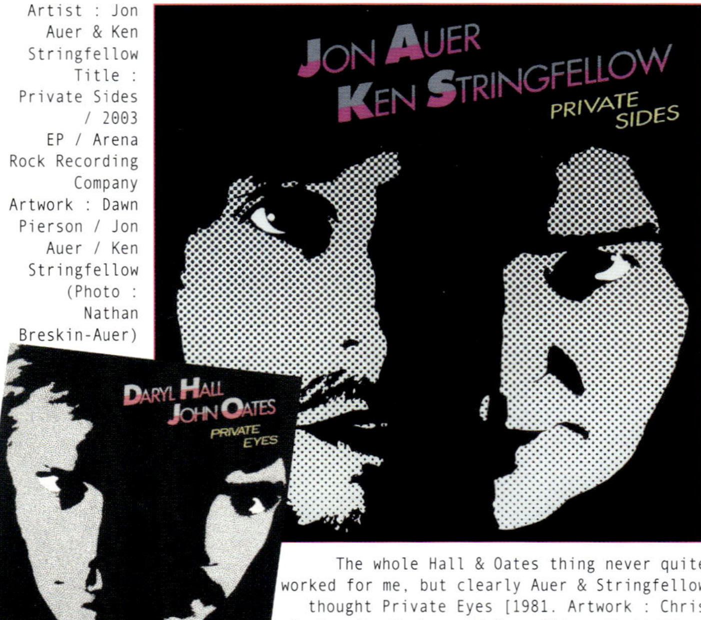

The whole Hall & Oates thing never quite worked for me, but clearly Auer & Stringfellow thought Private Eyes [1981. Artwork : Chris Eselgroth. Photo : Ed Caraeff] worth lifting.

Artist : Girls On Top
Title : Being Scrubbed + 1 / 2000
Single / Black Melody
Artwork : Unknown

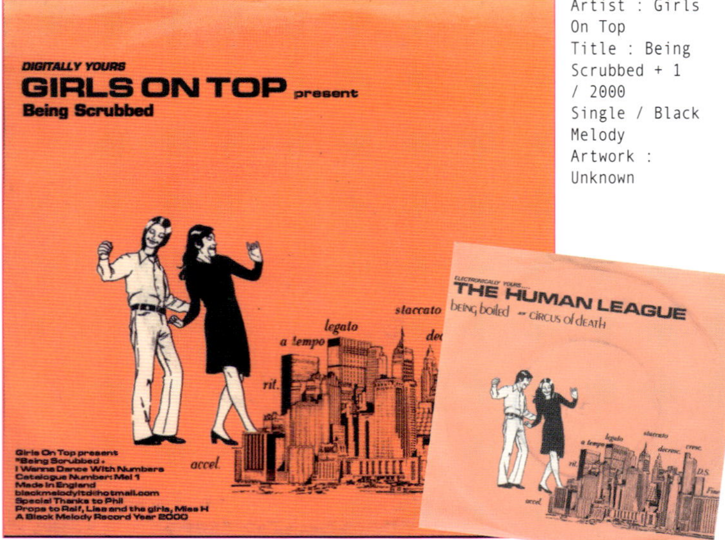

The Human League adopted Eurostyle type for their early release such as the Being Boiled EP [1978]. Their cover with the comic style illustration is slightly tweaked by Girls On Top on a 'can you spot the difference' sort of level.

Never underestimate the power of the blues, though it is interesting to see just how diverse a bunch of musicians have borrowed elements from this 40 year old self-titled 1962 Lightnin' Hopkins album, issued by Folkways in a typically (for the label) classy cover [Artwork : Ronald Clyne. Photo : Samul B. Charters]. It's the graded colour overlaid by black and white photos which proves the big draw, with Brimstone Howl's typography deliberately all over the place we trust.

Artist : Brimstone Howl
Title : Guts Of Steel / 2007
Album / Alive Records
Artwork : Rachel (Photos : Julia)

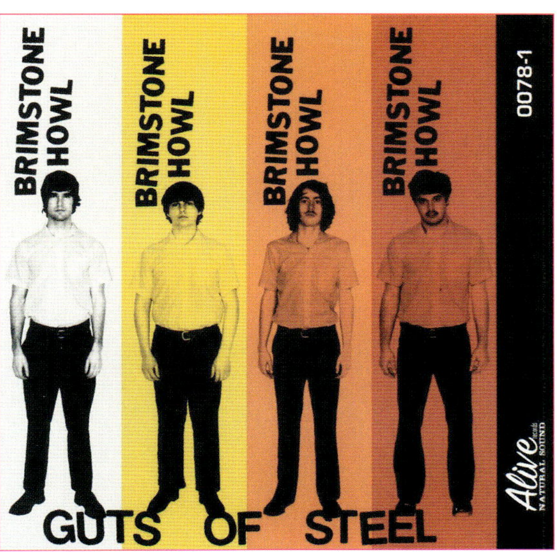

Artist : Jester
Title : Not Ready For The World / 2003
Album / DJ Sets
Artwork : Himbeertoni (Photo : Reflectorium. com)

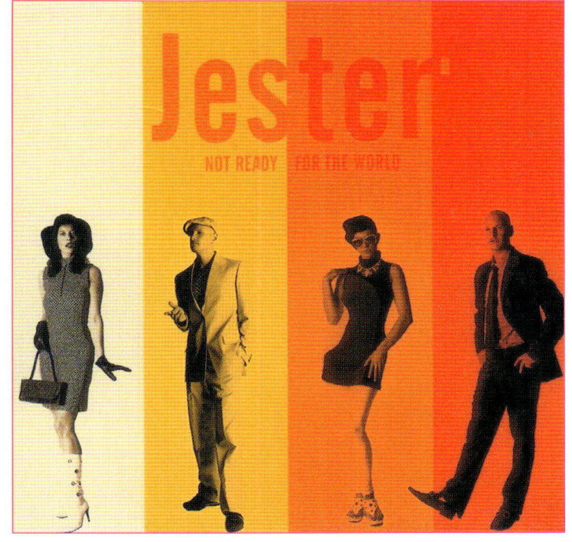

Artist : The Chronics
Title : Soulshaker / 2000
Album / Bad Afro Records
Artwork : Peter Markham (Photos : Andreas Mikkel Hansen)

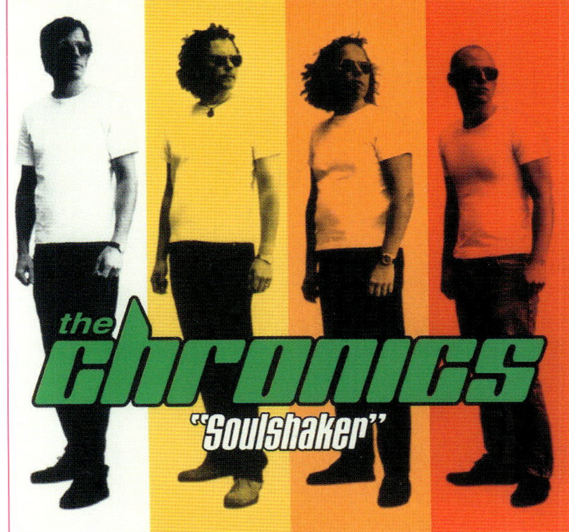

Artist : Paolo Nutini
Title : These Streets / 2006
Album / Atlantic
Artwork : Dominic Leung / Jez Potter (Photo : Paul Wesley Griggs)

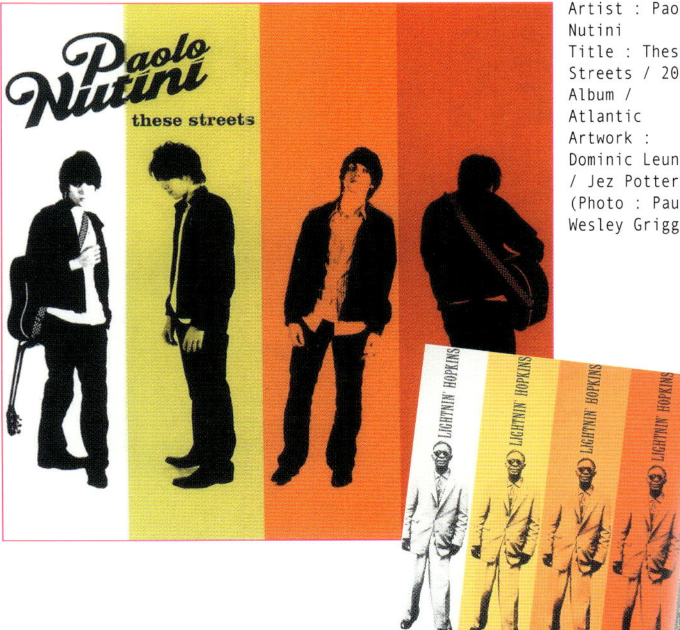

The South American Françoise Hardy EP [1967 : Vogue], with the titles translated (common practise there for European artists), is copied by ninties Argentinian rockers Los Brujos - the song looks like it might be a tribute to the French chanteuse.

A groovy fifties cover for Jerry Murad's Harmonicats' South American Nights [Mercury] - with the worlds' least convincing ethnic Bongo player - is the source of a 1995 single, though the vivd colours of the original have been toned down somewhat!

Artist : Los Brujos
Title : Françoise / 1996
EP / Rock Indiana
Artwork : Miguel Angel

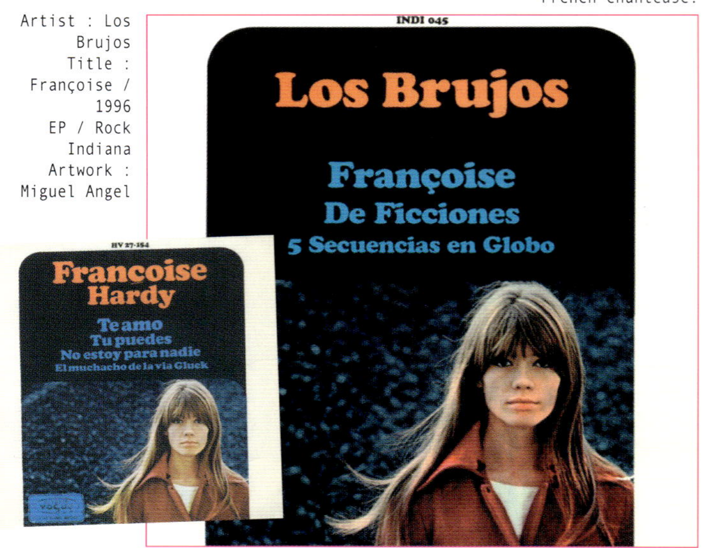

Artist : Me First & The Gimme Gimmies
Title : Denver + 2 / 1995
Single / Fat Wreck Chords
Artwork : Unknown

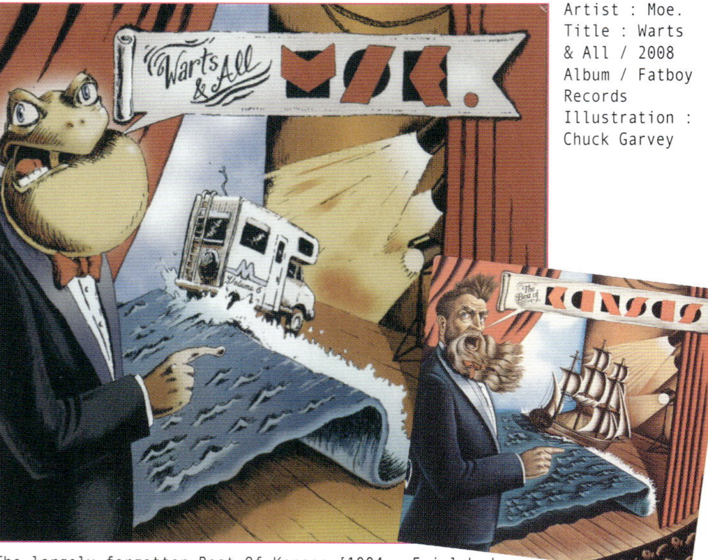

Artist : Pearl Jam
Title : Someday At Christmas + 1 / 2004
Single / Tenclub
Artwork + photos : Jeff Ament

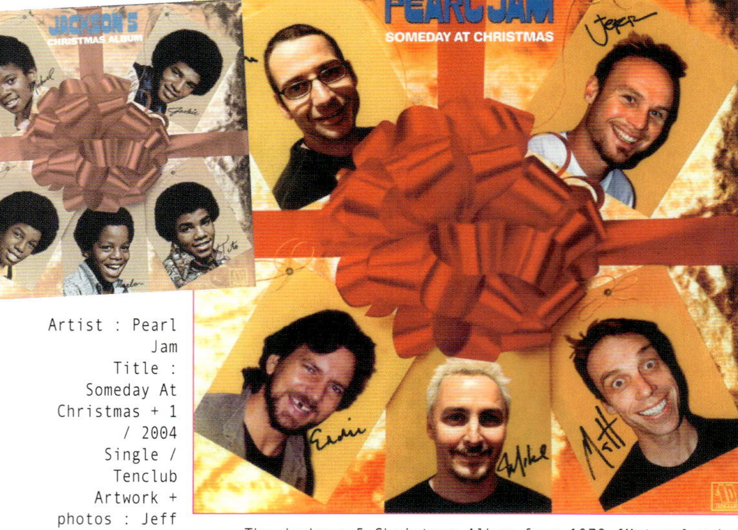

The Jackson 5 Christmas Album from 1970 [Motown] makes an unlikely choice for Pearl Jam to borrow from, but nevertheless it looks like they just dropped their own mug shots on and went for it on this single.

Artist : Moe.
Title : Warts & All / 2008
Album / Fatboy Records
Illustration : Chuck Garvey

The largely forgotten Best Of Karsas [1984 : Epic] had a strange enough cover illustration (by Steve Carver), but the look-a-like is perhaps even weirder, though the layout follows the original very closely.

I still look on Iron Maiden's childish cover output with bemusement. I like a bit of OTT sci-fi illustration as well as the next person, but Derek Rigg's work was always very sub-EC Comics. It has been copied a lot though and here are four examples, taking inspiration from Iron Maiden [1980], The Number Of The Beast [1982] and a single The Trooper [1983]. Auto Repeat manage to airbrush out "Eddie" altogether (though his ghost sort of remains) but otherwise use the same art, while Scudelia Electro go for one of those air-brushed robot pieces so popular in Japan.

Artist : Auto Repeat
Title : The Unbearable Lightness Of Auto Repeating / 1998
Album / Crammed Disc
Artwork : Unknown

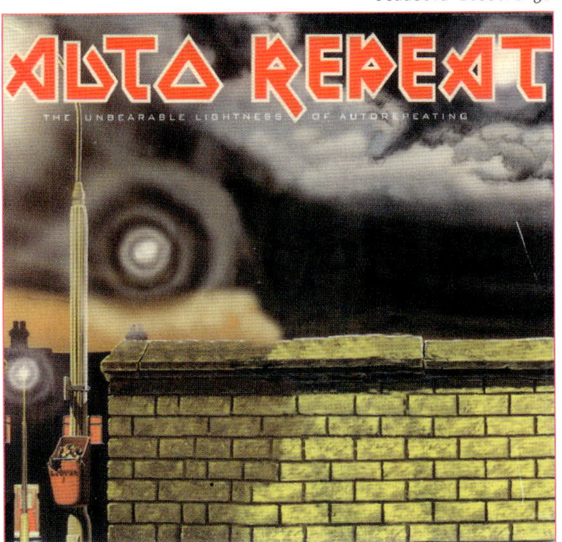

Artist : Scudelia Electro
Title : Miss / 1998
5"CDS / Polystar
Artwork : Takafumi Maeda (Cracker Design).

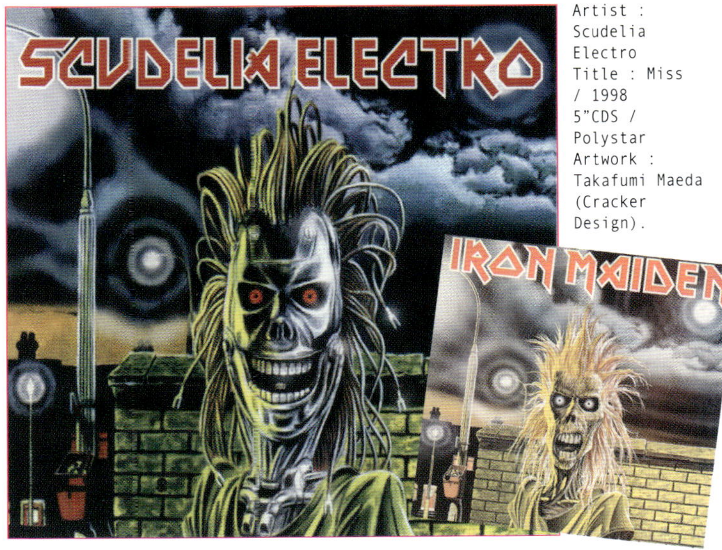

Artist : Porn Flakes
Title : The Number Of The Beef / 1998
Album / Grappler Unlimited
Artwork : Joe D. / Todd

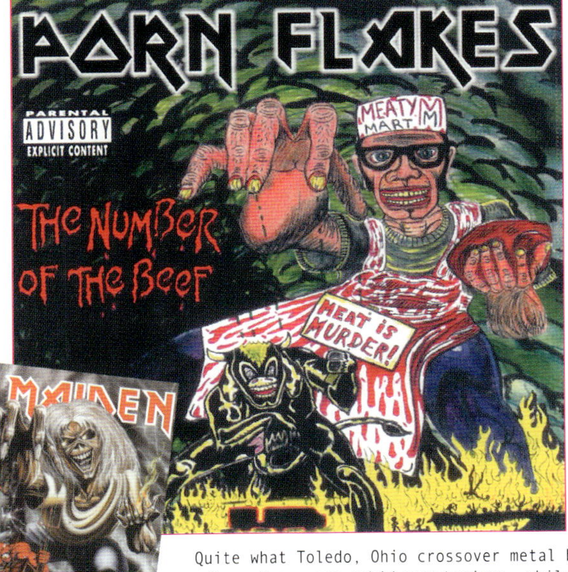

Artist : Marc Live
Title : This Is Street Music / 2004
EP / Live Seven Recordings
Illustration : Kacy

Quite what Toledo, Ohio crossover metal band Porn Flakes set out to do I'm not sure, unless they were rabid vegetarians, while Marc Live clearly nicks the cover idea off The Trooper but reworks it as a baseball cap wearing street zombie.

The Incredible Bongo Band's 1972 album Bongo Rock on MGM had a cover titled Music inspired by The Thing With Two Heads, done by Michael Viner. DJ Hype has taken the hands and dropped them onto two mixing desks rather than the bongos.

A great piece of 60s technology, combining a record with illustrations (somehow), on a decicated piece of retro kiddie hardware which likely fetches a small fortune now. A joint project by General Electric and budget label Pickwick International, the 7" single 'book' sleeve has ▼

Artist : DJ Hype
Title : 1973 - Recon / 2003
Album / Masters On Broadway
Artwork : Unknown

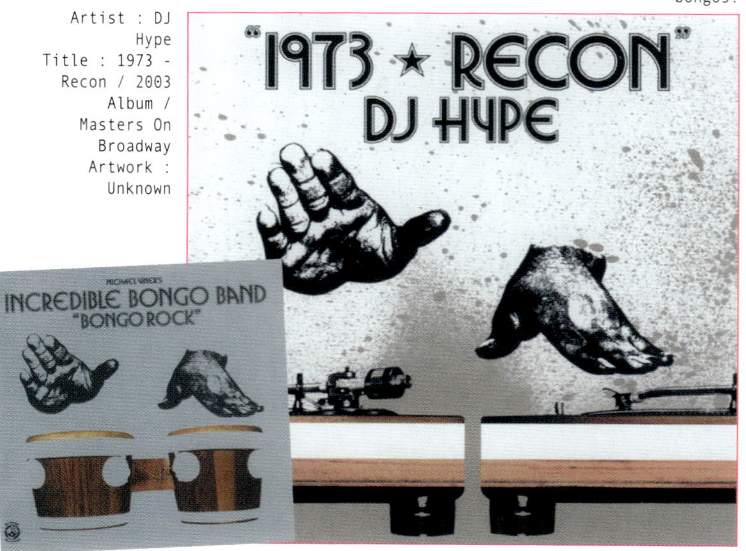

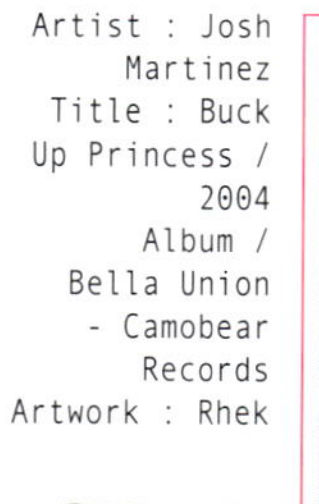

Artist : Self
Title : Gizmodgery / 2000
Album / Spongebath Records
Artwork : Kii Arens

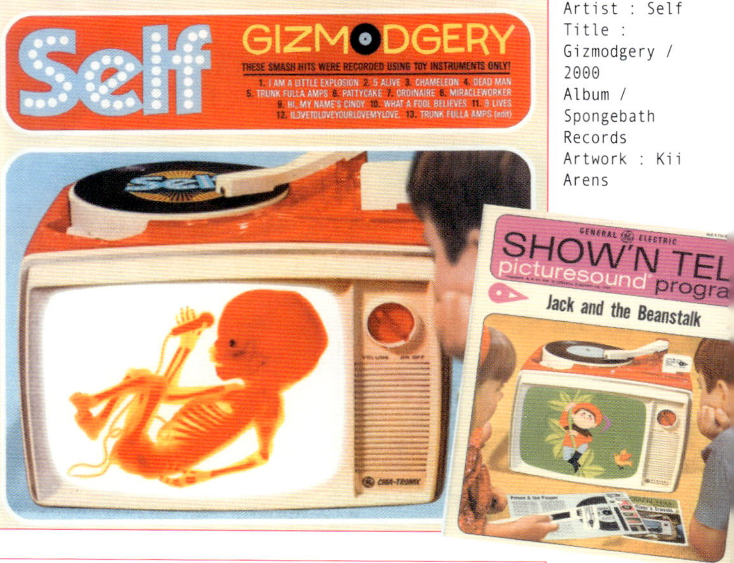

Artist : Josh Martinez
Title : Buck Up Princess / 2004
Album / Bella Union - Camobear Records
Artwork : Rhek

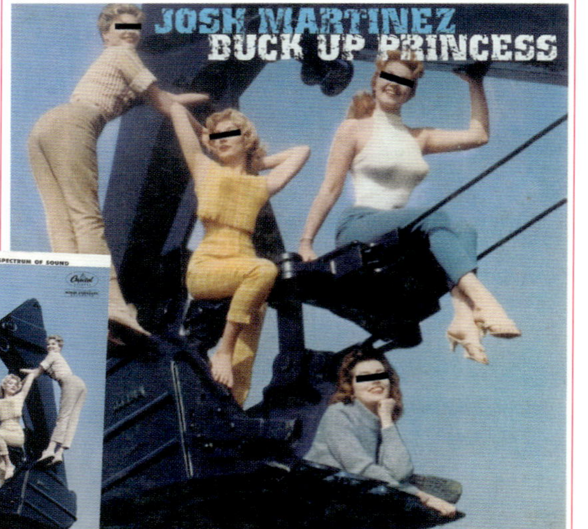

Artist : Scared Of Chaka
Title : Scared Of Chaka / 1996
Album / 702 Records
Artwork : Ron & Dave

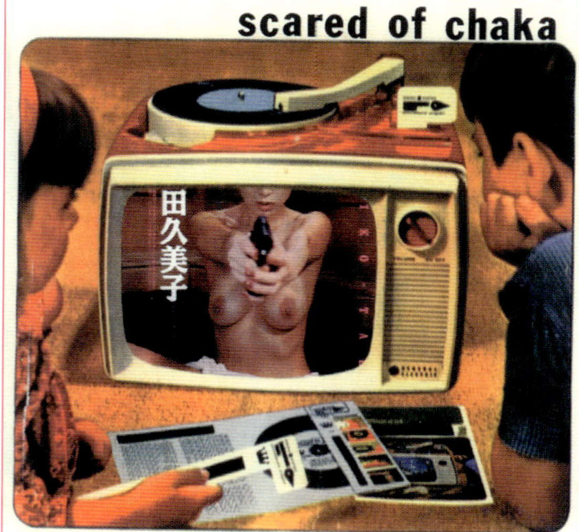

You've got to love some of these very literal easy listening sleeves; It's called I Dig Chicks? We'll hire a digger and some chicks, job done. This was for a Jonah Jones 1958 album on Capitol, the person responsible remains unknown! The Josh Martinez cover copies it lock stock.

been plundered for these two albums, including a self-referential offering recorded using vintage children's toys.

Parodying Michael Jackson gave some comfort to those who never really got the singer, especially when you took Quincy Jones away. Weird Al Yankovic had his finest moment with elaborate digs at both Bad [1987. Artwork : Tony Lane / Nancy Donald. Photo : Sam Emerson] AND Thriller [1982. Artwork : Mac James / Valadé Photo : Dick Zimmerman], able to use state of the art Japanese illustrators for the latter and Jackson's photographer for the former.

Artist : Tech
N9ne
Title : Killer
/ 2008
Album /
Strange Music
- Fontana
Artwork : Sean
Branagan.
Photo : Joshua
Hoffine

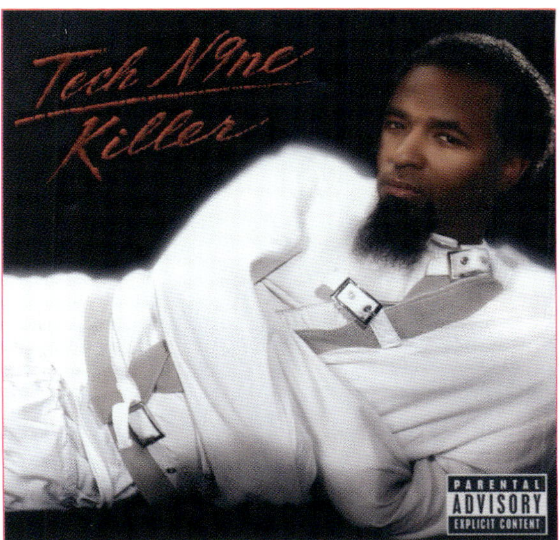

Artist : Weird
Al Yankovic
Title : Eat It
/ 1984
Album / Scotti
Bros.
Artwork :
Yasuo Kuni-
Eda / Takaomi
Shibayama.
Illustration :
Hideharu Ishii

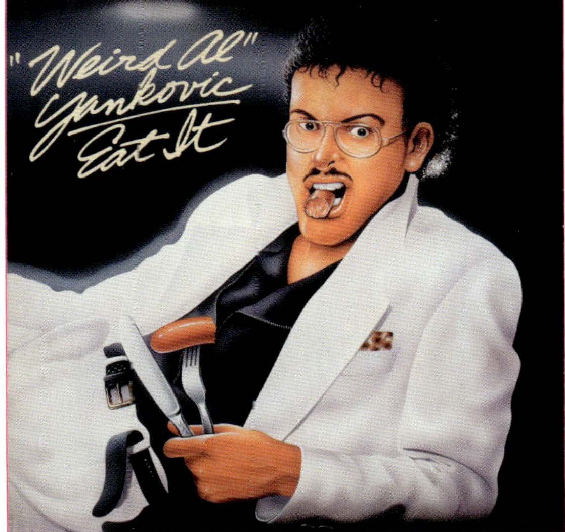

Artist : Weird
Al Yankovic
Title : Even
Worse / 1988
Album / Scotti
Bros.
Artwork :
Tony Lane /
Nancy Donald
/ Christine
Wilson. Photo
: Sam Emerson

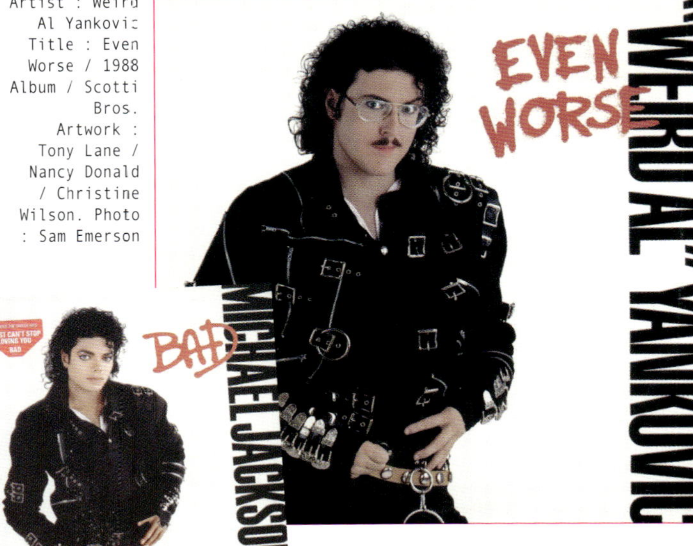

Artist : Bob
Sapp
Title : Sapp
Time + 1 /
2003
Single / For
Life Music
Entertainment
Artwork :
Mitsuru
Komagata
/ Daisuke
Suzuki. Photo
: Ryu Tamagawa

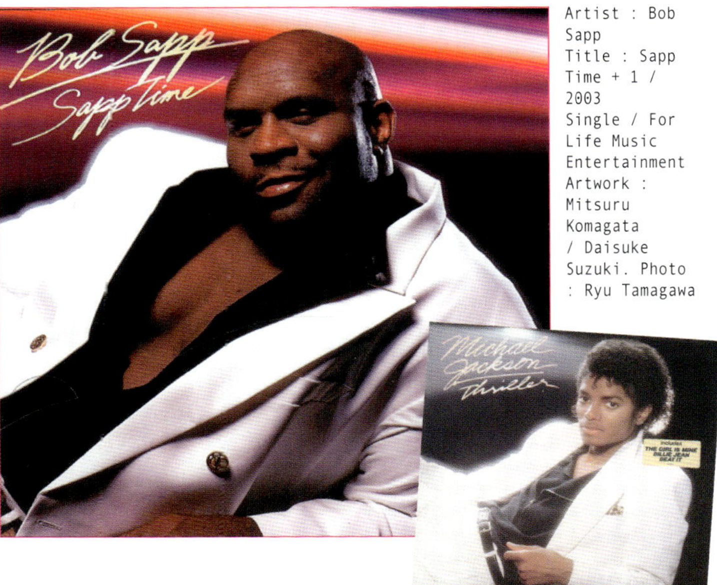

Tom Jones was his own worst enemy for many years, so little surprise that the two covers here take the mickey and steal the original sleeves. John Otway just defaces Green Green Grass Of Home [1967 : Decca] while Coolidge Records graft a gurning face onto Live In Las Vegas [1969 : Decca. Photo : Terry O'Neill], a follow up to their first local Philadelphia bands compilation, with four tracks by each band as a limited edition CD. Volume 1 had been vinyl.

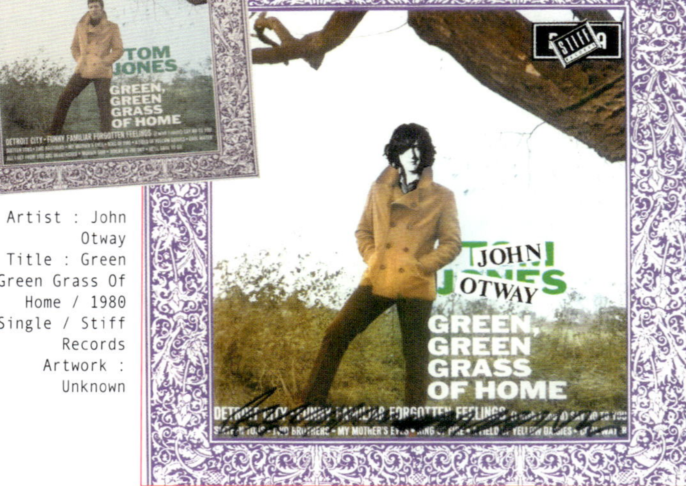

Artist : John Otway
Title : Green Green Grass Of Home / 1980
Single / Stiff Records
Artwork : Unknown

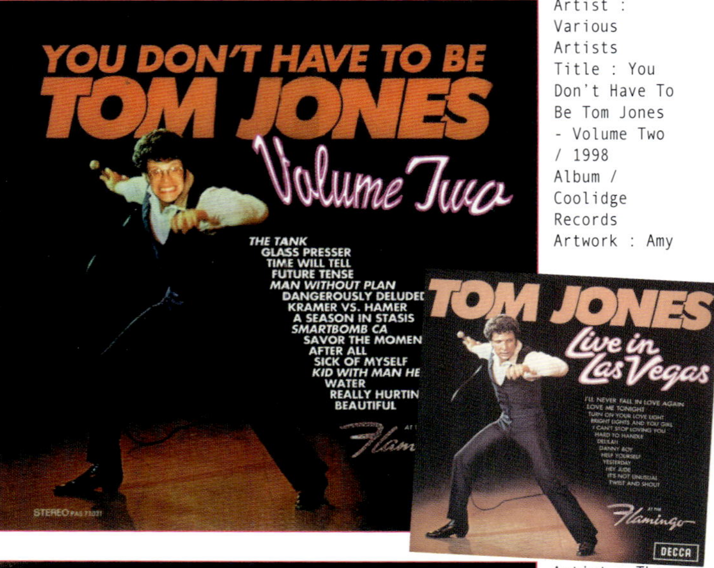

Artist : Various Artists
Title : You Don't Have To Be Tom Jones - Volume Two / 1998
Album / Coolidge Records
Artwork : Amy

Artist : Hatebeak +1
Title : Beak Of Putrefaction + 2 / 2004
EP / Reptilian Records
Artwork : Unknown

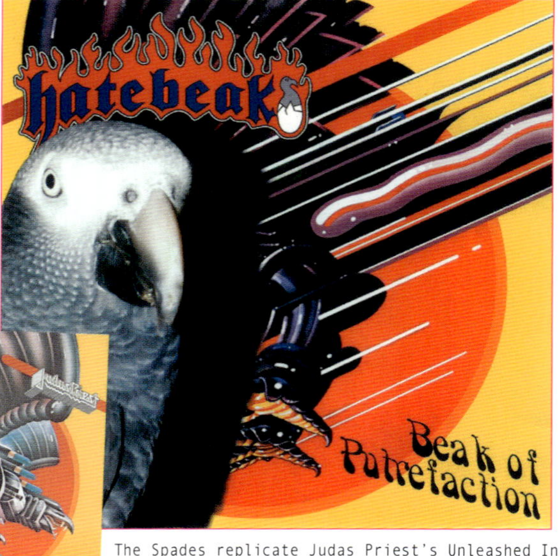

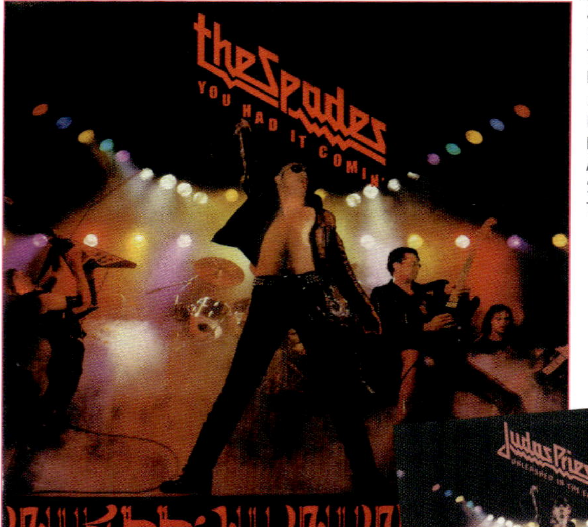

Artist : The Spades
Title : You Had It Comin' / 2003
EP / Suburban Records
Artwork : Dick Spade Photo : Tessa Koot

The Spades replicate Judas Priest's Unleashed In The East (Live In Japan) cover closely [1979 Photo : Fin Costello] but we're not sure what is behind the overlaying of a budgie onto the same band's Screaming For Vengeance artwork [1982. Artwork : Doug Johnson & John Berg] by Hatebeak...

James Gang Rides Again [1970. Artwork : Bob Lockhart] isn't an obvious cover to copy, but Jeanjacket Shotgun even duplicated the back sleeve as well.

Artist :
Jeanjacket
Shotgun
Title :
Collides Again
/ 2001
Album /
Houston Party
Records
Artwork :
Brian Young

Likewise White Flag pay homage to both the front and back covers of Jefferson Airplane's Surrealistic Pillow [1967. Artwork : Jeff Smith. Photo : Herb Greene]

Artist : White
Flag
Title : White
Rabbit + 2 /
2---
Single /
Sympathy For
The Record
Industry
Artwork : Pat
Fear & Marty
Balin. Photo :
Vicki Berndt

Artist : Fitz
Of Depression
Title : I'm
The Man + 1 /
1995
Single / Yoyo
Recordings
Photo : Reuben
Lorch-Miller

Artist :
Adriano
Canzian
Title :
Pornography /
2005
Album /
International
Deejay Gigolo
Records
Artwork : Go
Lab. Photo
: Makoto
Nakashima

Joe Jackson's spivvy look for I'm The Man [1979. Artwork : Michael Ross / Joe Jackson. Photo : Bruce Rae] closely copied by Fitz Of Depression for a 45.

Grace Jones' Slave To The Rhythm [1985. Artwork : Jean-Paul Goude / Greg Porto. Photo : Jean-Paul Goude] provides inspiration for Adriano Canzian (what you can see behind the advisory notice).

The sleeve for the Kiss album Rock And Roll Over [1976. Artwork : Michael Doret] was arguably the band's best, blending top quality design, colourful illustration and type in a way which was very original. Small wonder so many bands have tried their own versions and it has to be said, often with a lot of panache. Many are at least as well put together as ▷

Artist :
Clowns For
Progress + 1
Title : Insect
+ 1 [1996]
Single /
Diablo Musica
Artwork :
Unknown

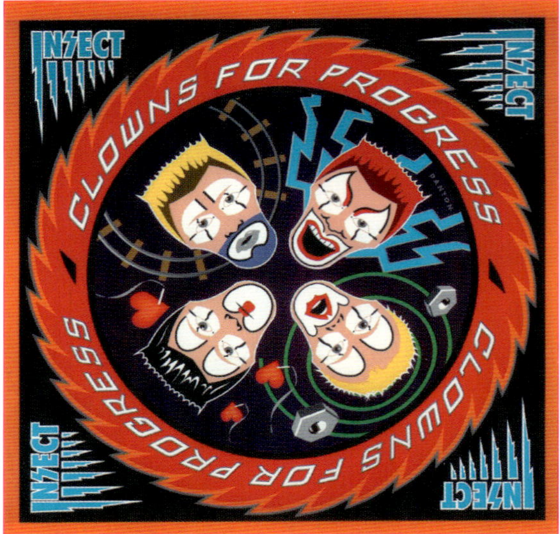

Artist :
Crunch
Title : Rock
And Roll
Doping / 1999
EP / TOHC
Records
Artwork :
Unknown

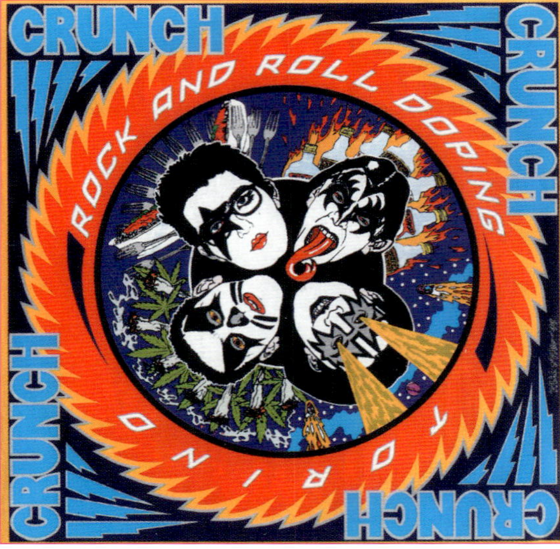

Artist : Hard
Ons
Title : Suck
And Swallow /
2002
Album / Rookie
Records
Artwork : Sam
Egan / Ray Ahn

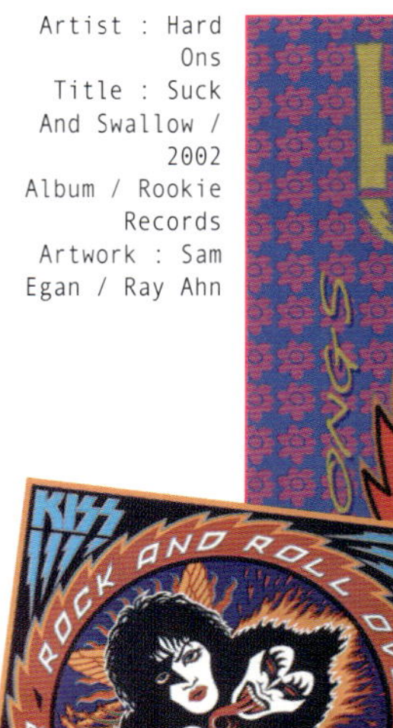

Artist :
Japaharinet
Title : Best
Fire Of Heaven
/ 2007
Album / Toy's
Factory
Artwork :
Kyoko Nakano
(Gotz)
Illustration
: Kazuhiro
Watanabe

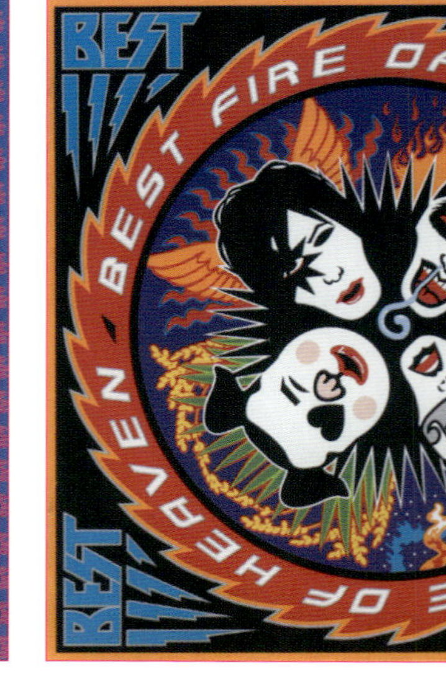

the Kiss cover (especially as some are just singles) and even those which are doing it on the cheap (such at the Muscle Bitches shared 45 and Second Hand) still have a sense of fun. The Hard Ons have been in the book before, as indeed have White Flag, while the String Quartet tribute cover adds a new element to the mix - cellos. Crunch self-released their EP.

Artist :
Muscle Bitches
+ 1
Title : Save
The Nymphos +
2 / 1990
EP / Baptist
Cracker
Artwork :
Robin Driscoll

Artist :
Second Hand
Title : Puke
And Fall Over
/ 1996
EP / Recess
Records
Artwork :
Little Stevie

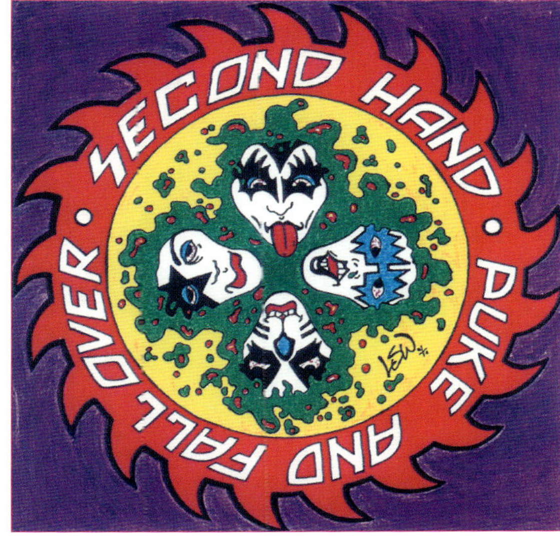

Artist : The
String Quartet
Title :
Tribute To
Kiss / 2004
Album /
Vitamin
Records
Artwork : Ron
Sievers /
Martin Cimek

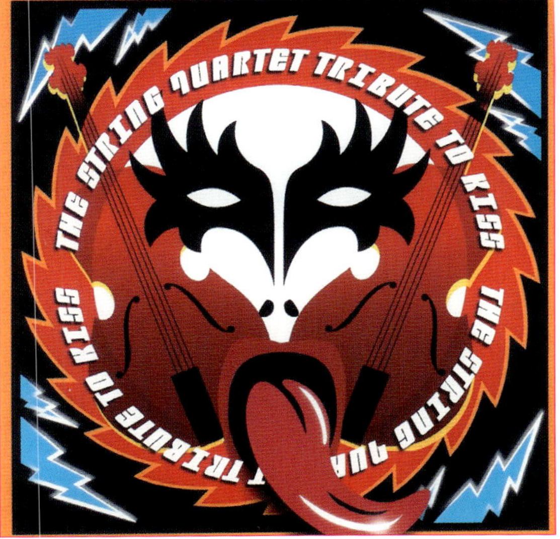

Artist : White
Flag
Title : Benefit
For Cats /
2010
Album /
Cupcake
Records
Artwork :
Chris Shary
/ Michael F.
Glass / Pat
Fear

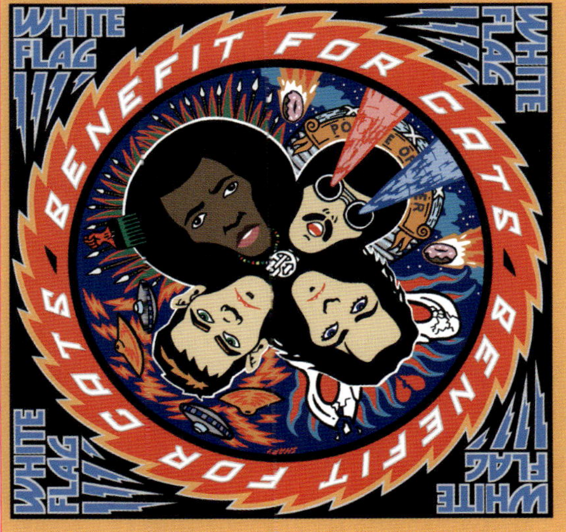

Taking their inspiration from the Kiss Dynasty album cover [1979 : Casablanca Records. Artwork : Howard Marks Advertising Inc. Photo : Francesco Scavullo], this disparate bunch include the very funny Australian comedian Norman Gunston (playing all four members, complete with shaving nicks), Sack Trick, replacing the band with sheep, and the catchily titled i # $; ! by Fearless leader, who seem to be enjoying themselves.

Artist : Fearless Leader
Title : " i # $; ! " / 1992
Album / Hell Yeah Records
Artwork : Ann Marie Aubin.
Photos : Robin Okman, Brad Smith & Alien Rock

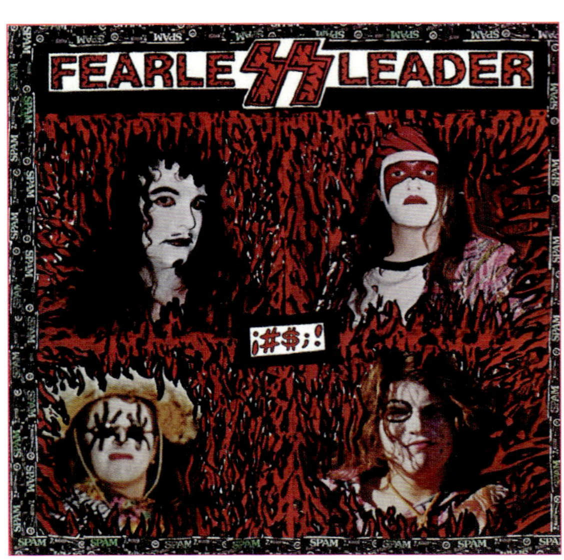

Artist : Sack Trick
Title : Sheep In Kiss Make-Up / 2004
Album / Sack Trick
Artwork : Andy Hunns / Chris Paulo Dale / Reuben Gotto

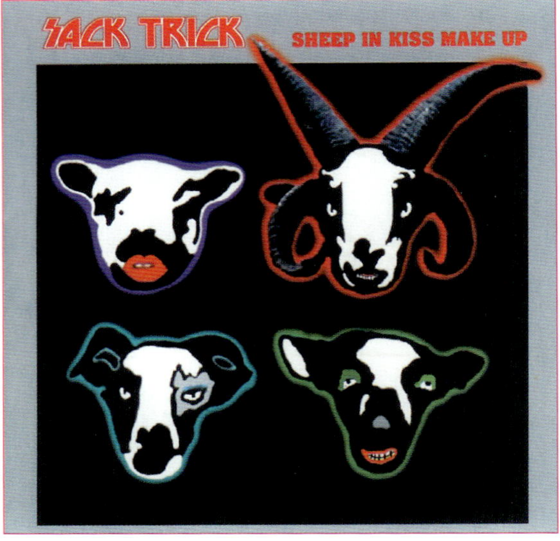

Artist : Norman Gunston
Title : Kiss Army + 1 / 1980
Single / 7 Records
Artwork : Unknown

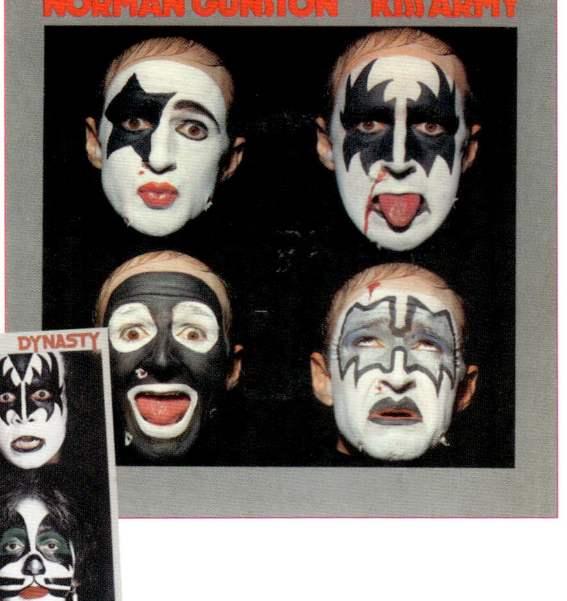

Artist : The Three O'Clock Heroes
Title : Over The Dump / 1996
EP / We Bite Records
Artwork : Unknown

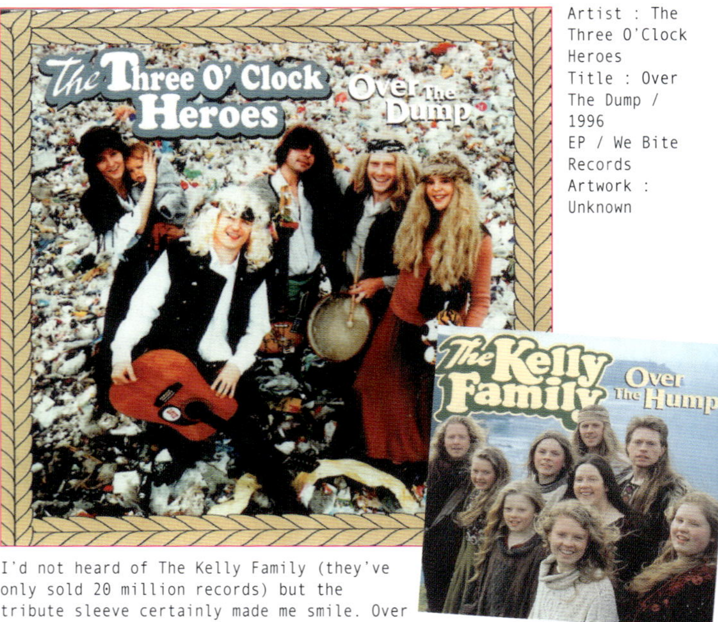

I'd not heard of The Kelly Family (they've only sold 20 million records) but the tribute sleeve certainly made me smile. Over The Hump was issued in 1994 [Kel-Life Production / EMI. Artwork : Dan Kelly. Photo : Thomas Stachelhaus]

The KELLY FAMILY

A couple of Kinks albums unfamiliar to the European market, as they were reconfigured and redressed by the American label. Greatest Hits [1966 : Reprise] sports an Ed Trasher design, The Kink Kontroversy [1965 : Reprise] designer is unknown. Both sleeves have been borrowed to give sixties authenticity to more recent bands, The Jynx in particular going to great lengths to get their version just right.

Artist : The Jynx
Title : Greatest Hits / 2000
10" Album / Norton
Artwork : Pete Ciccone

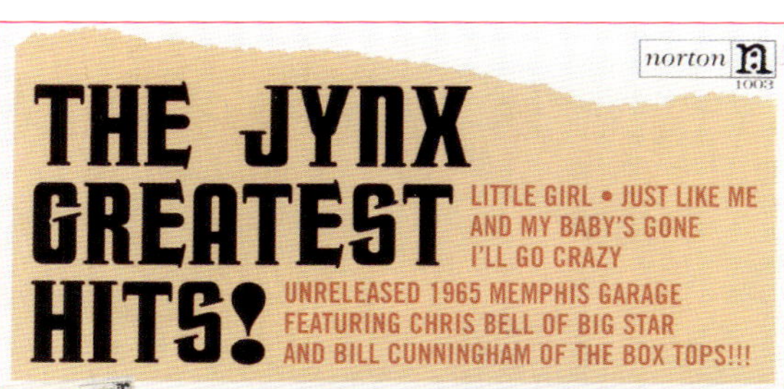

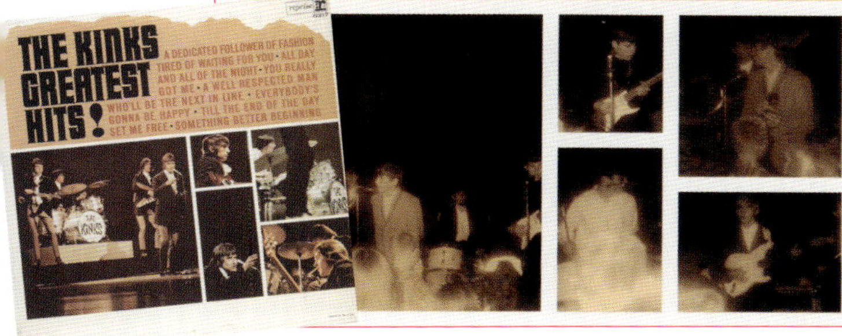

Artist : The Chesterfield Kings
Title : Trippin' Out / 1997
10" Album / Imposible Records
Artwork + photo : Mary Ellen Gardiner

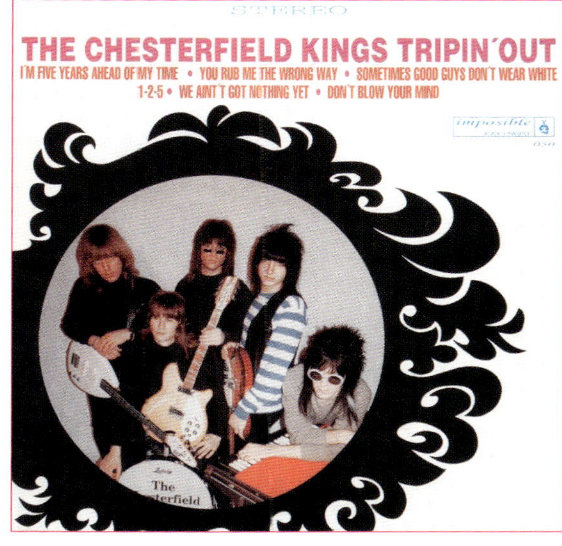

Artist : Frenchbloke & Son
Title : Sexy Model - Neon Love / 2004
Single / Half Inch Recordings
Artwork : Unknown

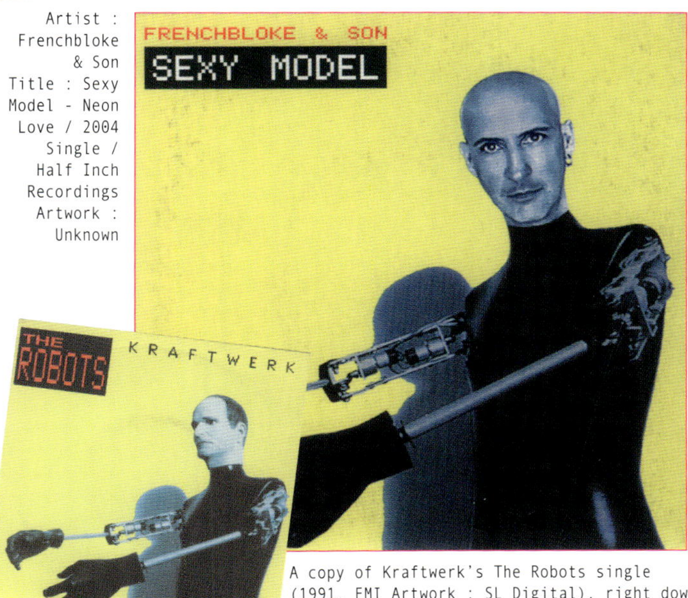

A copy of Kraftwerk's The Robots single (1991. EMI Artwork : SL Digital), right down to the typeface, with just a replacement head. A Cyberdyne Systems upgrade perhaps.

Artist : Golden Smog
Title : America's Newest Shitmakers Fake Album in box 35 Years Of Golden Smog / Ryko Disc
Artwork : Unknown

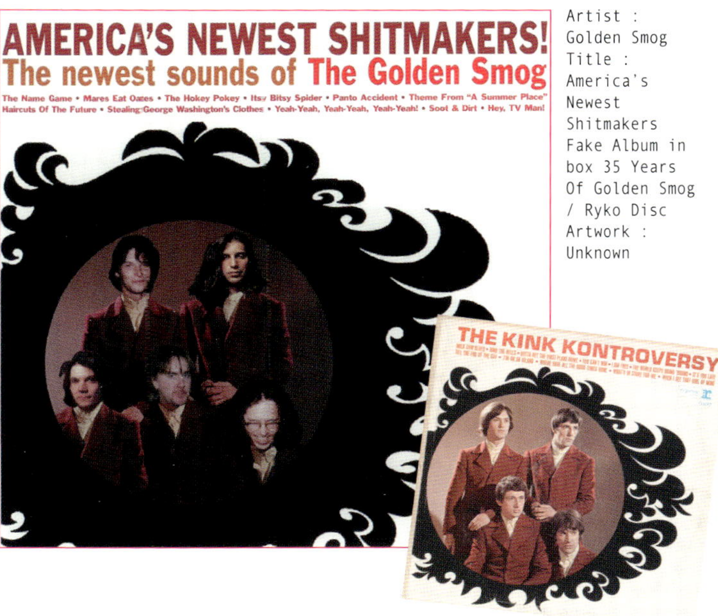

Teaching new-wave brit bands that it was OK to plunder pre-War German Bauhaus design for cover ideas, Kraftwerk's The Man-Machine [1978. Artwork : Karl Klefisch. Photo : Günter Fröhling] is a very familiar cover image which has had some strange copyists, with only musicians / comedian Bill Bailey really putting in the effort to get it right. Richard X (Girls On Top) actually mixed together Whitney Houston's I Wanna Dance (hence her pic on the cover) with Kraftwerk's Numbers. NME thought it so good they made it their single of the week. They often were easily pleased.

Artist :
Various
Artists
Title : F.E.A.
CD Version-
Dosmilcuatro
/ 2004
Album /
Sinnamon
Records
Artwork
: Feos y
Lafamiliafeliz

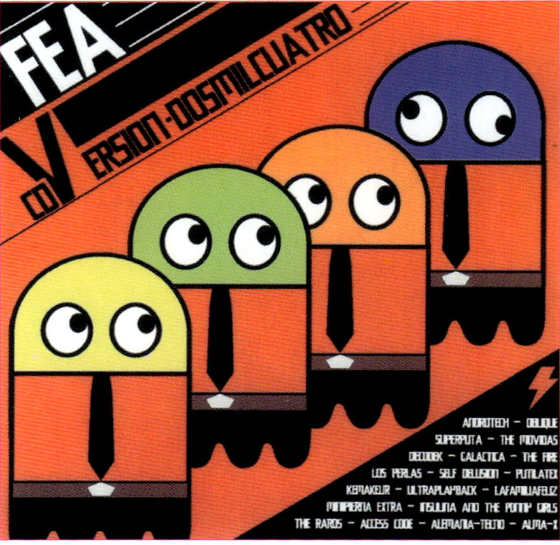

Artist :
Milemaker
Title : Sex
Jams / 2000
4 track EP
/ Bloodlink
Records
Artwork :
Unknown

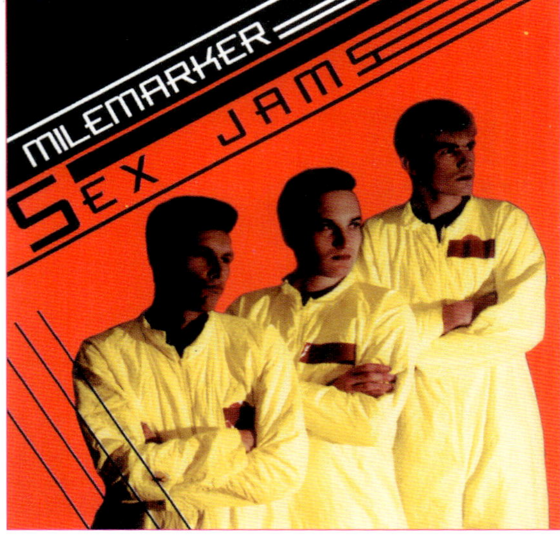

Artist : Girls
On Top
Title : Being
Scrubbed + 1
/ 2000
Single / Black
Melody
Artwork :
Unknown

Artist : Bill
Bailey
Title : Das
Hokey Kokey /
2006
Single / BBM
Artwork : Sam
Oakley

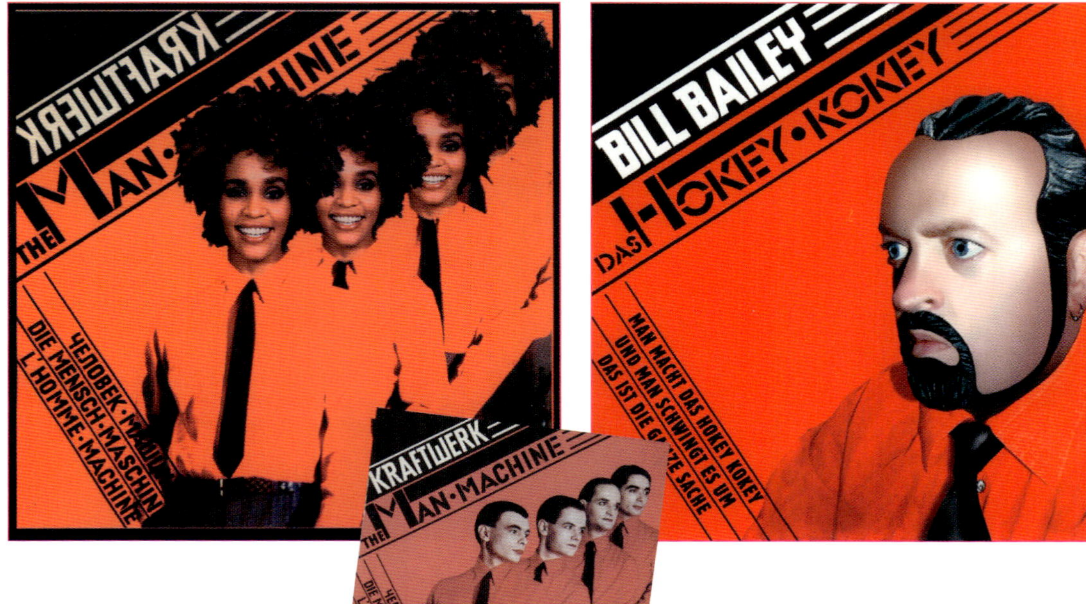

Hopefully you're familiar with Barry Godberg's dramatic and unsettling painting which decorated King Crimson's awesome album In The Court Of The Crimson King back in 1969 [Island]. Here are a quartet of sleeves which have used it to work from, including a very clever reworking of the original or the inevitable tribute CD (many of which are very dull) and the very disturbing image courtesy of Japanese speed metal folk the Sex Machineguns.

Artist : Various Artists
Title : Schizoid Dimension : A Tribute To King Crimson / 1997
Album / Purple Pyramid
Artwork + painting : Grenas

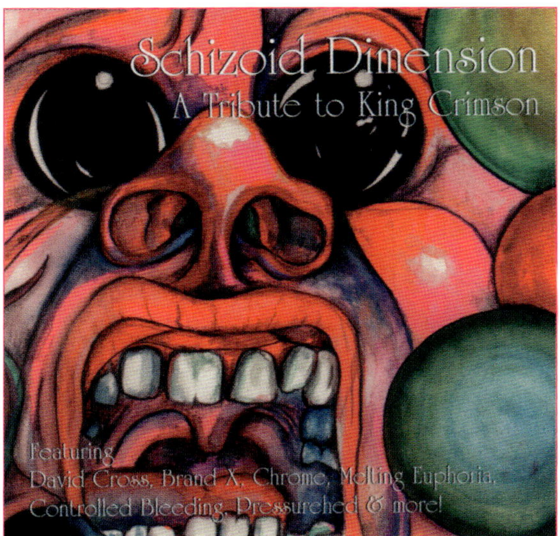

Artist : Various Artists
Title : Have A Nice Die (A Tribute To Hi Technology Suicide) / 2007
Album / P-Vine Records
Artwork : Unknown

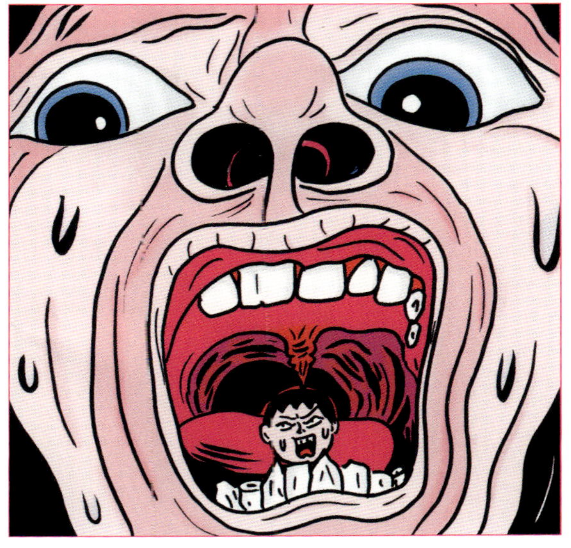

Artist : Sex Machineguns
Title : S.H.R. + 1 / 2001
Single / EMI Japan - Express
Artwork : Unknown

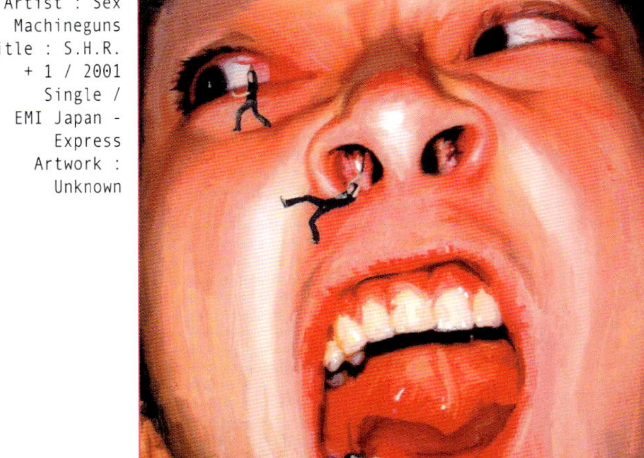

Artist : Various Artists
Title : G.Lasts - Tribute To Godzilla / 2004
Album / Monster Music - Universal
Artwork : Kenji Saiki / 7 Stars

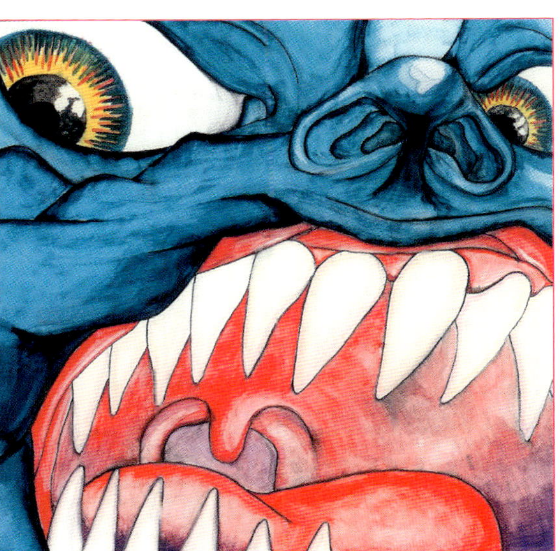

One of the biggest rock acts of all time, unsurprisingly Led Zeppelin have often seen their artwork copied or plundered. David Juniper's cover for LZ2 in 1969 was very distinctive and forms the basis for both a close copy and reggae funsters Dread Zeppelin's cover photo shoot.

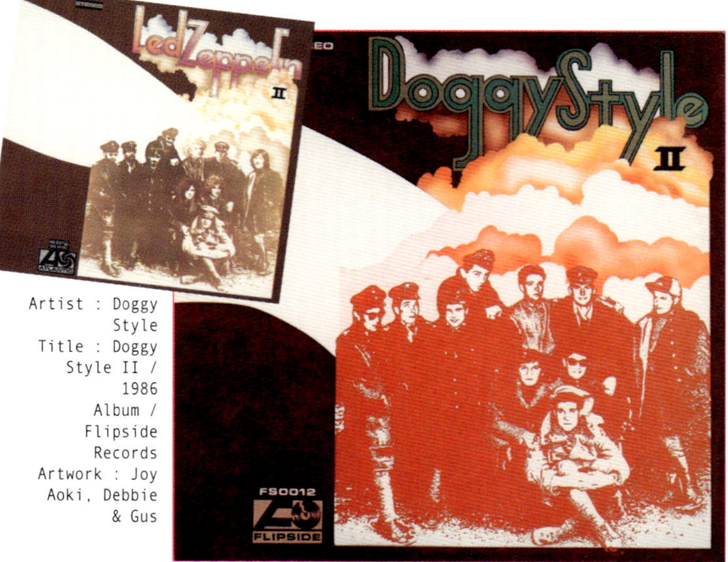

Artist : Doggy Style
Title : Doggy Style II / 1986
Album / Flipside Records
Artwork : Joy Aoki, Debbie & Gus

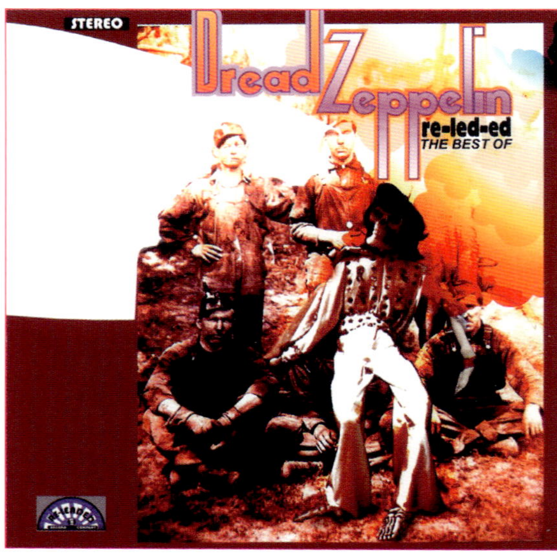

Artist : Dread Zeppelin
Title : Re-Led-Ed - The Best Of / 2004
Album / Cleopatra Records
Artwork : Unknown

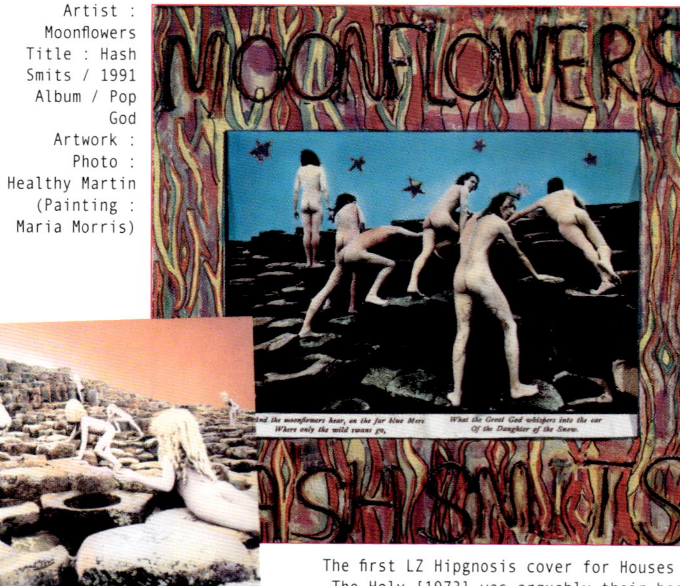

Artist : Moonflowers
Title : Hash Smits / 1991
Album / Pop God
Artwork : Photo : Healthy Martin (Painting : Maria Morris)

The first LZ Hipgnosis cover for Houses Of The Holy [1973] was arguably their best, and is clearly the basis for the Moonflowers less than reverential version.

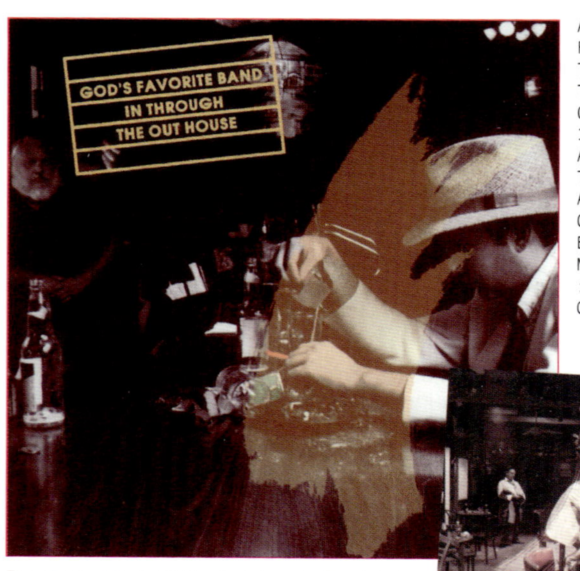

Artist : God's Favorite Band
Title : In Through The Out House / 1992
Album / Twin/Tone Records
Artwork : God's Favorite Band / Jill McLean (Photo : Daniel Corrigan)

The Hipgnosis designed In Through The Out Door in 1979 provides both the cover and title for God's Favorite Band, though I assume they didn't do five different editions (or however many LZ originally foisted on their fans!).

The elaborate cover created for Led Zeppelin III in 1970 (complete with die-cut sleeve and revolving centre piece) has been revisited by a number of bands, including a very obvious version by The Leslies (a Swedish band but here compiled for a US relese), a somewhat chaotic rendition by Pete Holly, and the Jazz Orchestra who use the scrapbook idea but skipped the lettering altogether for a more modern look.

Artist : The
Leslies
Title : That's
Me + 3 / 1997
EP / American
Pop Project
Artwork :
Unknown

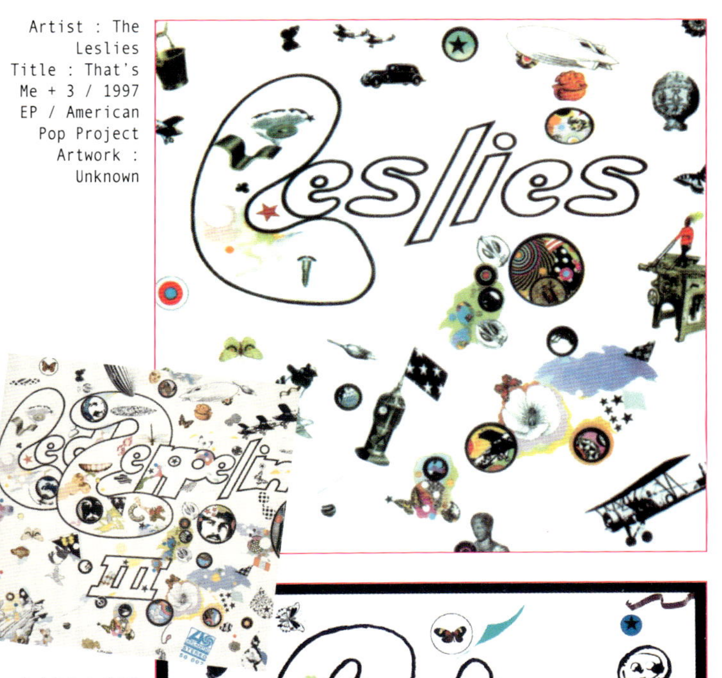

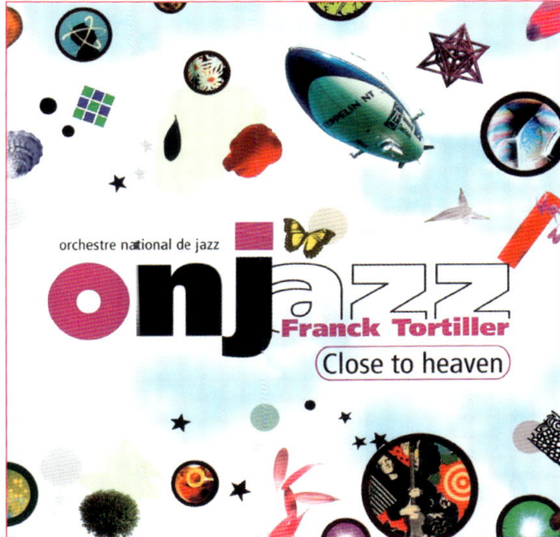

Artist :
Orchestre
National De
Jazz (Franck
Tortiller)
Title : Close
To Heaven /
2005
Album / Le
Chant Du Monde
Artwork :
Caty Rousseau
(Photos :
Mephisto)

Artist : Pete
Holly
Title : III /
2002
Album / Look's
Music
Artwork :
Unknown

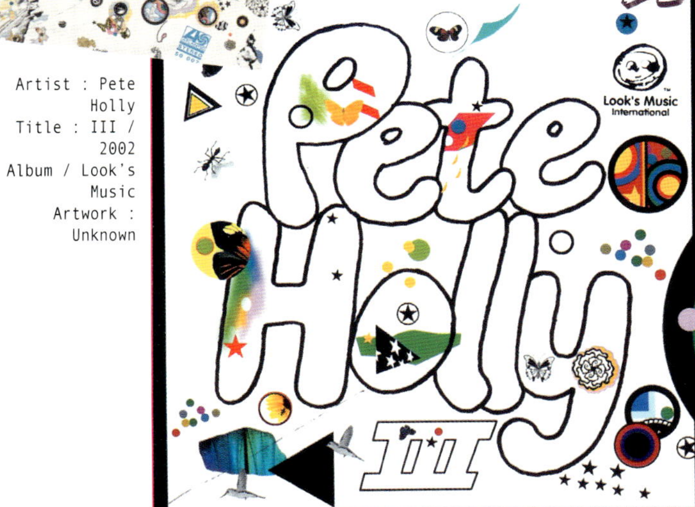

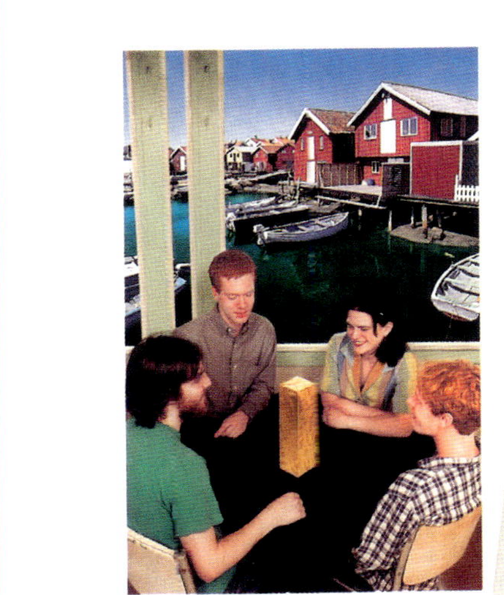

Artist :
Sardina
Title :
Presents /
1995
Album / Hitit
Recordings
Artwork :
Bob Plant
(Photo : Gary
Hannabarger)

Personally the band's later Hipgnosis sleeves
always seemed a little too overblown but 1976's Presence
was the basis for this version by Sardina (with artwork
credited to Bob Flant!).

Lastly, 4 Non Blondes play fast and loose with Led Zeppelin IV [1971] by the Graphreaks design team, just dropping in a different - but similarly themed - photo.

Edward O'Connell replicates the US sleeve for Nick Lowe's Jesus Of Cool [1978 : Riviera. Artwork : Unknown], then sticks a bag on his head in case you mistake them.

Artist : 4 Non Blondes
Title : Misty Mountain Hop / 1994
EP / Atlantic
Artwork : Cally on Antar Hangman (Aubrey Powell). Photo : Hulton library

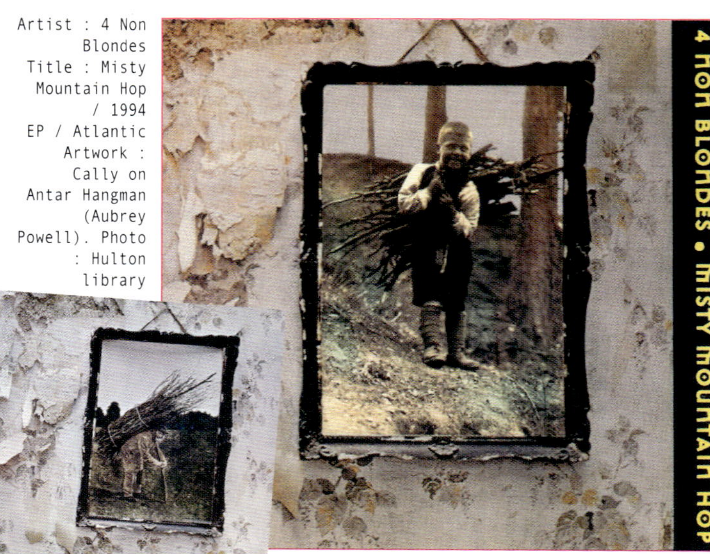

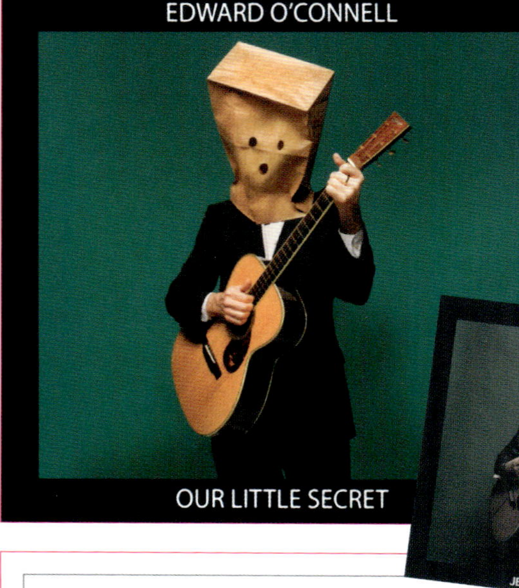

Artist : Edward O'Connell
Title : Our Little Secret / 2010
Album / Dangerous Oaf Ramp
Artwork : Seemeen Hashem, Aqueous Studio
Photo : Max Taylor

Artist : Make Up
Title : Sound Verite / 1996
Album / KLP
Artwork : Unknown

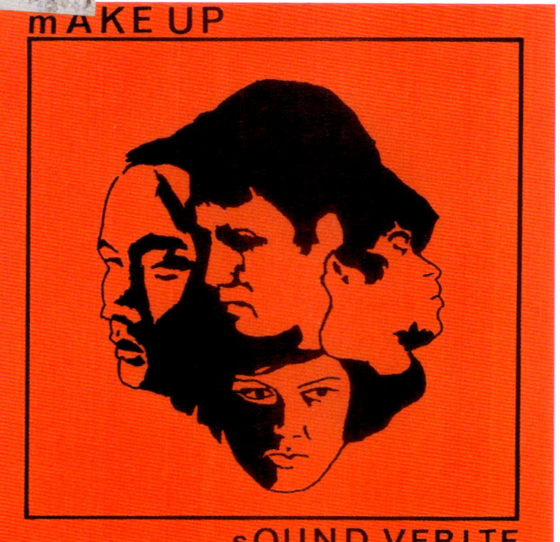

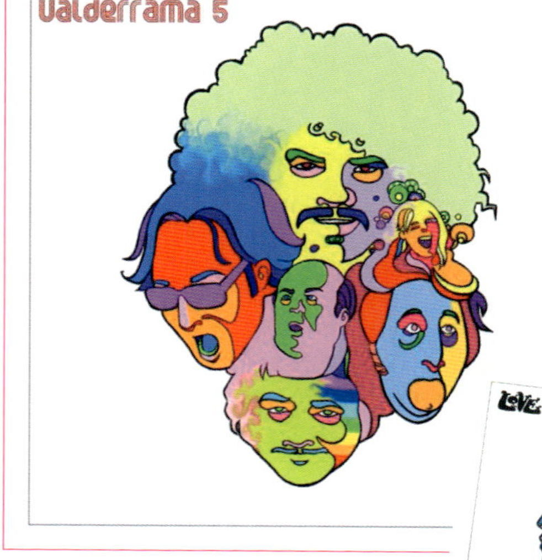

Artist : Valderama 5
Title : Forever Asses / 2004
Album / self released
Artwork : Unknown

Love's Forever Changes, their third album, [1968 : Electra. Artwork : Bob Pepper / William S. Harvey] is another simple but effective cover image which is still being borrowed four decades on.

John Lennon & Yoko Ono's Two Virgins cover in 1968 caused a bit of a stir as you might imagine, and both the front and back cover have inspired others, including the pastiche by The Squirrels (who also appear on page 124), covering the hits of Johnny Kidd - Seattle style. Don't fancy yours much!

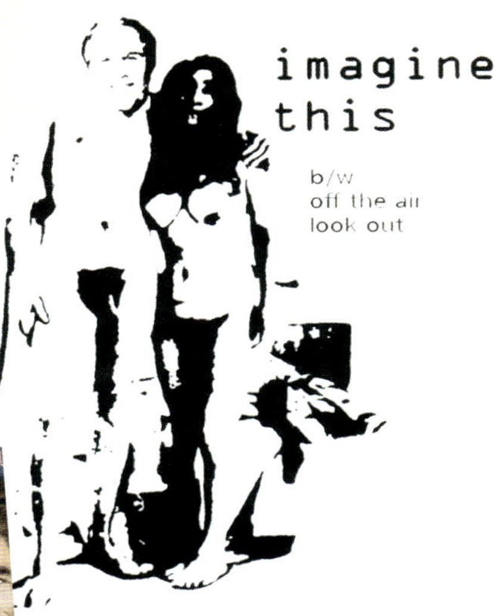

Artist : Wax
Audio
Title :
Imagine This +
2 / 2005
Single / Metal
Postcard
Artwork :
Unknown

New Age Urban Squirrels   "Five Virgins"

"When two great saints meet it is a humbling experience. Five Squirrels, on the other hand, is pretty darn stupid." - Scott McCaughey. Refurbished Music Numero Uno. All Rights Reserved. PopLlama Products P.O. Box 95364 Seattle, WA 98145-2364

Artist : The
New Age Urban
Squirrels
Title : Five
Virgins / 1985
Album / Pop
Lama
Artwork : Ayne
St. Martin /
Marty Perez

Artist :
Assfactor 4
Title : Sports
Anno : 1997
Format : Album
Label : Old
Glory Records
Artwork : Gabe
Madden / Chad
Miller

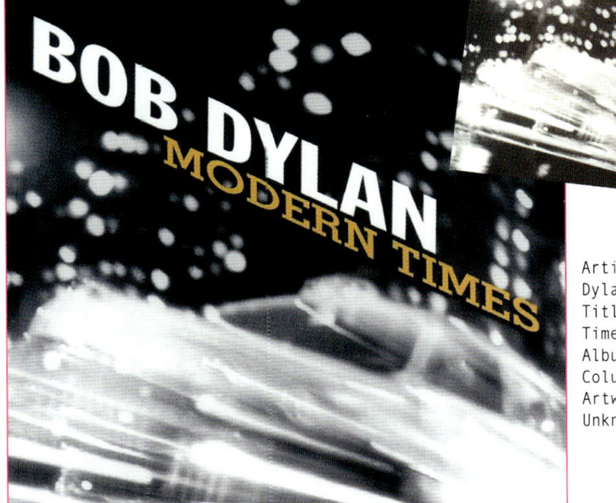

Artist : Bob
Dylan
Title : Modern
Times / 2006
Album /
Columbia
Artwork :
Unknown

For some reason the cover to Huey Lewis & The News' album Sports [1983. Artwork : Bennett Hall / Bunny Zaruba] has always annoyed me, so the piss take here was always going to make the book.

The designer of Dylan's Modern Times might have been aware of Luna's 45 a decade earlier, but more likely just used the same picture library, both being captivated by Ted Croner's wonderful vintage image of a New York taxi at night.

The suitably trippy (yet slightly academic looking, in the way of vintage language lesson albums) cover to Dr. Timothy Leary Ph.D's album L.S.D. [1966. Pixie Records] relies on an op-art swirl used by any number of covers, but the two bands here have clearly been staring at the original.

Artist :
Porcupine Tree
Title : Voyage
34 - The
Complete Trip
/ 2000
Album /
Delirium
Records
Artwork :
Aleph (design
: Richard
Allen)

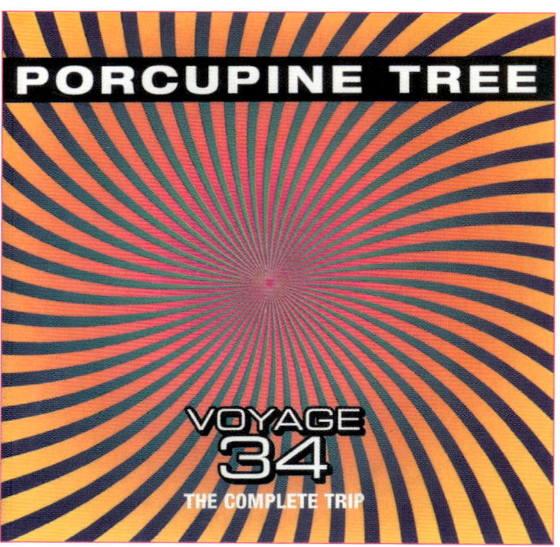

Artist
: Reverb
Motherfuckers
Title : L.S.D.
+ 1 / 1991
Single / Vital
Music Records
Artwork :
Terhorst /
Edrosa

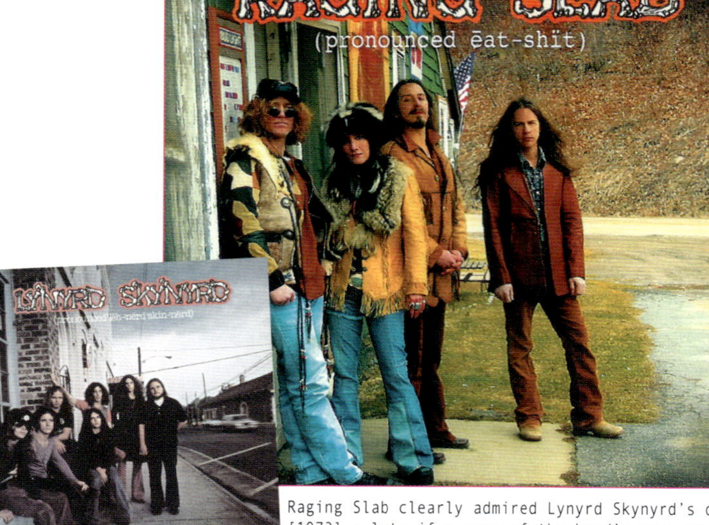

Artist :
Raging Slab
Title :
Pronounced Eat
Shit / 2002
Album / Tee
Pee Records
Artwork /
Photo : Laura
Sypien
Front and back

Raging Slab clearly admired Lynyrd Skynyrd's debut album Pronounced Leh-nerd Skin-nerd [1973] a lot; if a copy of the band's pose on the front, the typography and the title weren't enough, they even replicated Emerson-Loew's back cover design as well (shown right).

Nigel Weymouth's sleeve for John & Beverley Martyn's Stormbringer LP [1970] was quite a change from his earlier summer of love style [Photo : Hiroshi] and was closely imitated by Wooden Wand.

John Mayall & The Bluesbreakers With Eric Clapton used a Decca publicity shot but the 1966 layout remains period enough to have inspired Cable, right down to one of them reading The Beano comic.

Artist : Wooden Wand & The Sky High Band
Title : Second Attention / 2006
Album / Kill Rock Stars
Artwork : Shayde Sartin (Photo : Keith Wood)

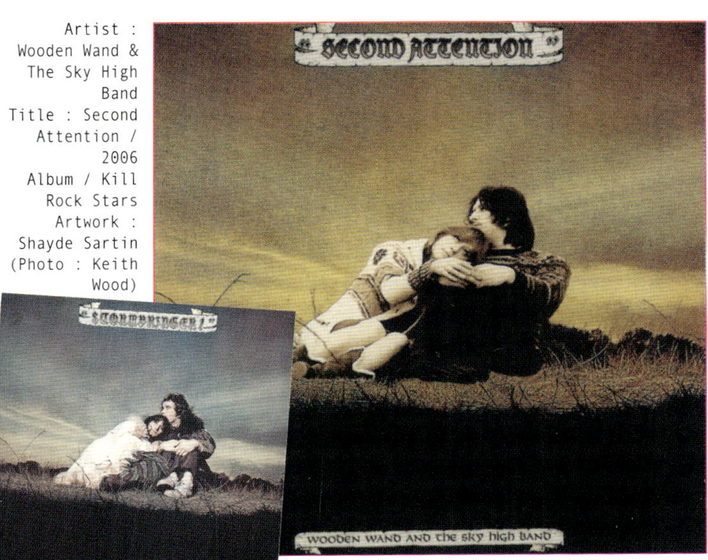

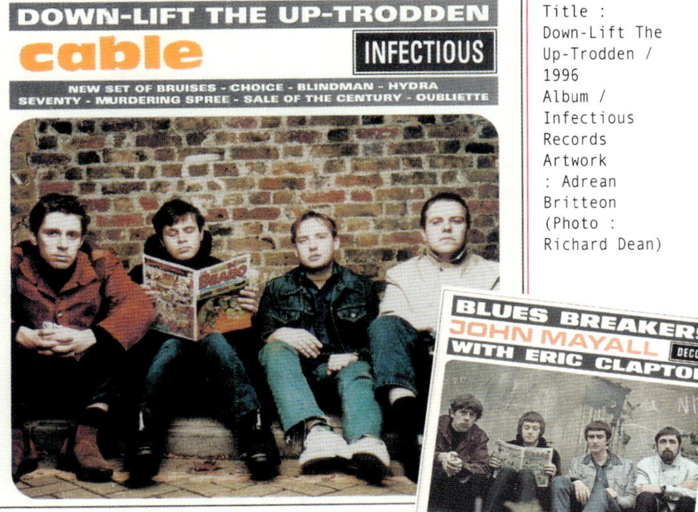

Artist : Cable
Title : Down-Lift The Up-Trodden / 1996
Album / Infectious Records
Artwork : Adrean Britteon (Photo : Richard Dean)

Artist : Sylk Smoov
Title : Sylk Smoov / 1991
Album / PWL Records
Artwork : Rick Dehaan/ Alison Ashley (Photo : Renaldo)

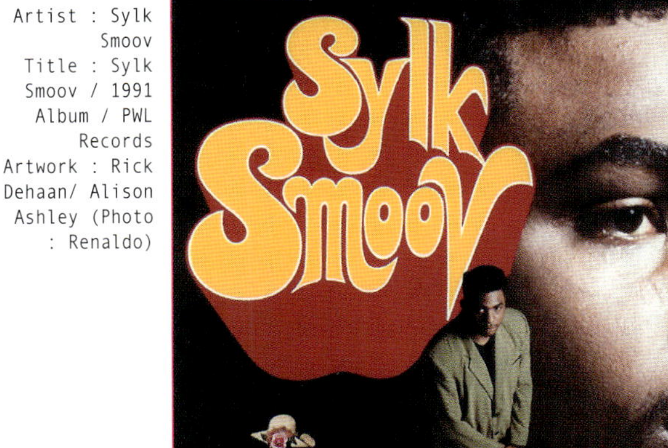

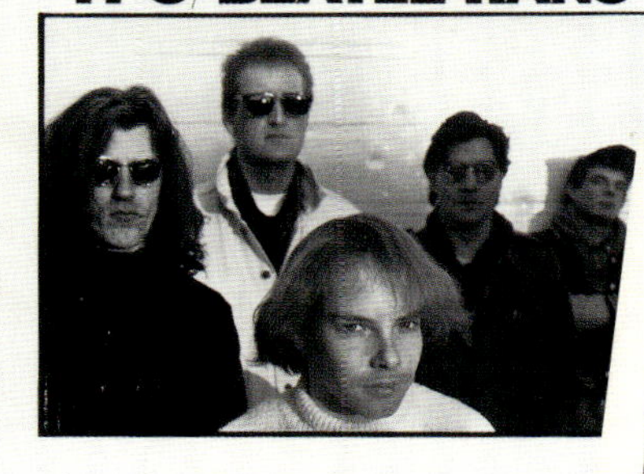

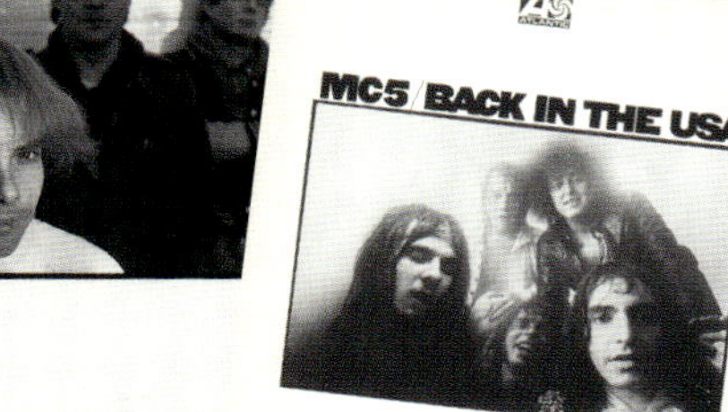

Artist : Beatle Hans
Title : It's / 1990
Album / Fierce Records
Artwork : Joan Marker (Photo : Frank Dries)

Curtis Mayfield's Super Fly cover [1972] was something of a Blaxploitation landmark, with artwork by Glen Christensen and photos by David Parks, and inspired this Sylk Smoov cover.

Flying the flag for simple design and high quality b/w portrait photography, MC5's Back In The U.S.A [1970] is hard to top [Elektra. Artwork : Joan Marker. Photo : Stephen Paley], as Beatle Hans found out.

Richard Corben's fantasy illustration for Meat Loaf's Bat Out Of Hell [1977] fits the album like a glove, and few labels would have the money for such a commission these days. Witness the low-budget look-a-like from Arthur Kay (the substitution of a scooter for Meat's hog is a nice touch) and the even lower budget Pork Dukes, a UK punk band (begun by old hippies from the folk rock era if their history is to be believed).

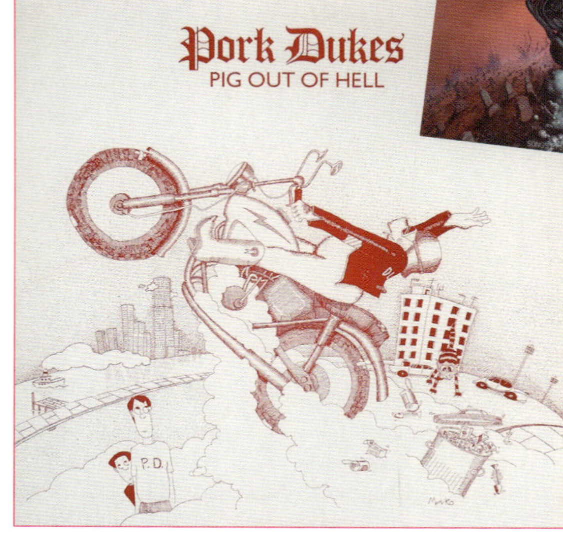

Artist :
Arthur Kay's
Originals
Title :
Sparkes Of
Inspiration /
1989
Album / Skank
Records - Link
Records
Artwork :
Steve Friel

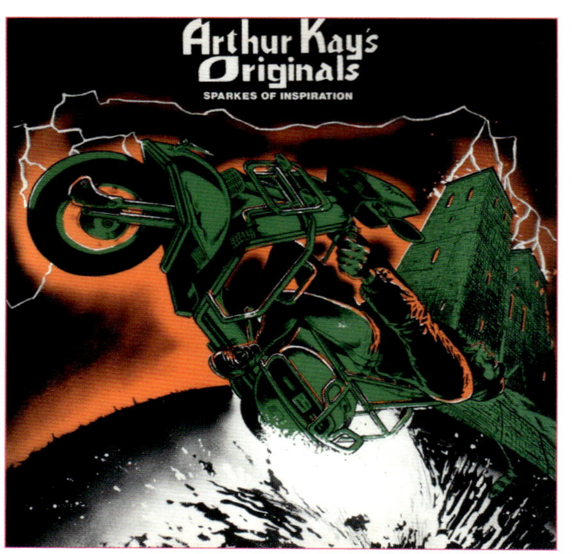

Artist : The
Pork Dukes
Title : Pig
Out Of Hell /
1979
Album / Wood
Wreckchords
Artwork :
Marco

Artist :
Otasco
Title : Hubris
/ 2007
Album /
Apocalypse The
Apocalypse
Artwork :
Unknown

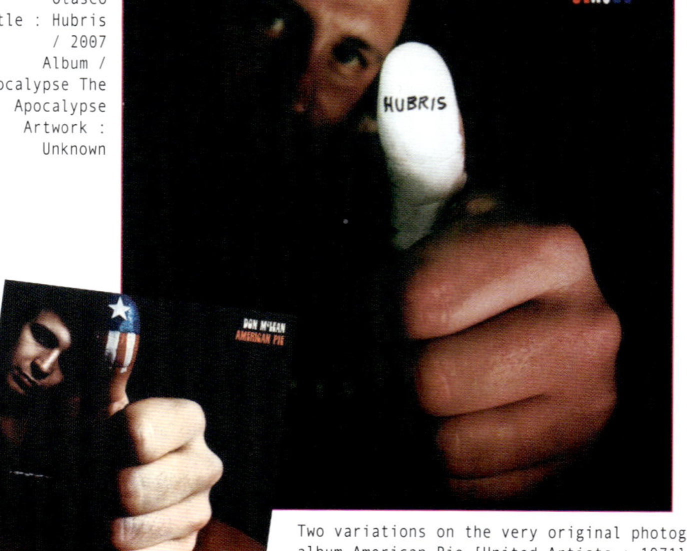

Artist : Slag
Title :
American Fuck
/ 1994
Album / Great
Big Kiss
Records
Artwork Photo
: Judy Wildman

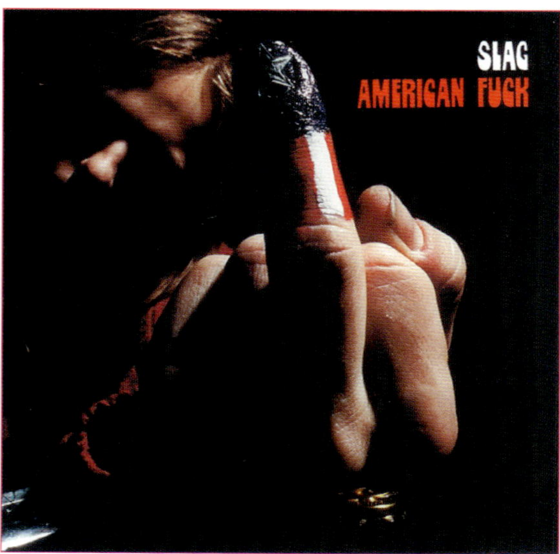

Two variations on the very original photograph and design [S. Whiteman] which decorated the Don McLean album American Pie [United Artists : 1971], with Slag getting straight to the point.

Come the HM revival of the late 70s, no band could show their face without a badly designed logo of some sort to slap on covers and merchandise, Metallica's grim effort being typical. Their Master Of Puppets LP [Elektra : 1986. Artwork : Metallica / Peter Mensch] clearly inspired Hewhocorrupts, and Sleepasaurus - though they may also have had the Jim Henson Master of Muppets cover in mind as well. We'll spare you that.

Artist : Sleepasaurus Title : Master Of Muppets / 1994 EP / Big Words Records Artwork : Unknown

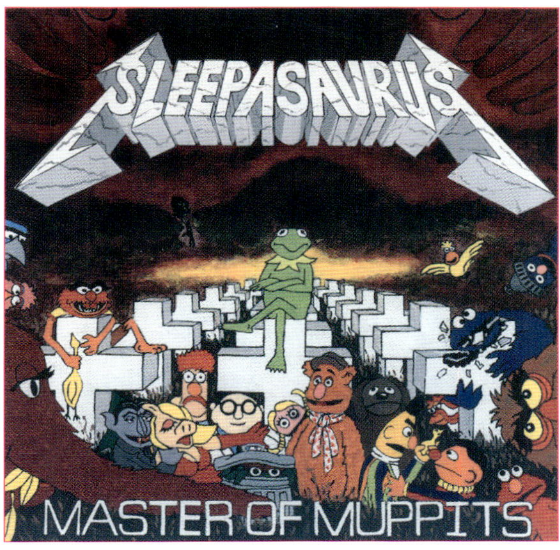

Artist : Hewhocorrupts Title : Master Of Profits / 2002 EP / Forge Again Artwork : Hewhocorrupts / Spencer James Thayer

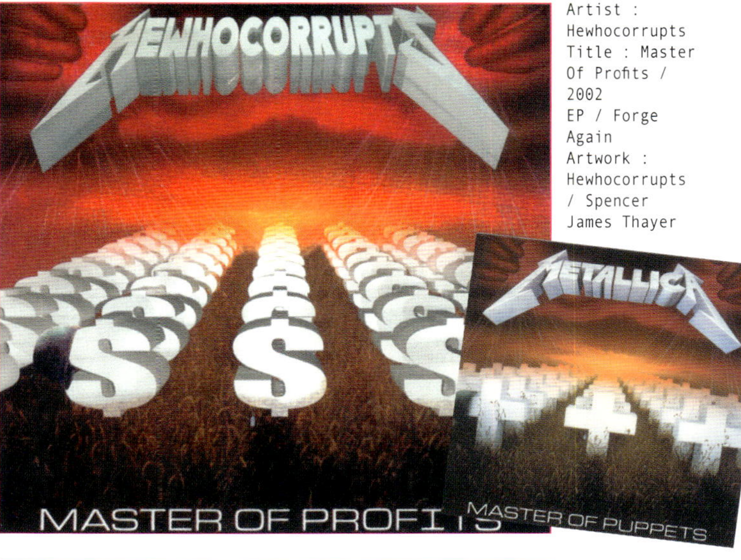

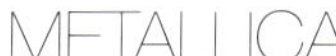

Artist : Sloppy Seconds Title : Garbage Days Regurgitated / 2000 Album / NIT Records Artwork : Mike Kreffel (Photo : Rich Miller)

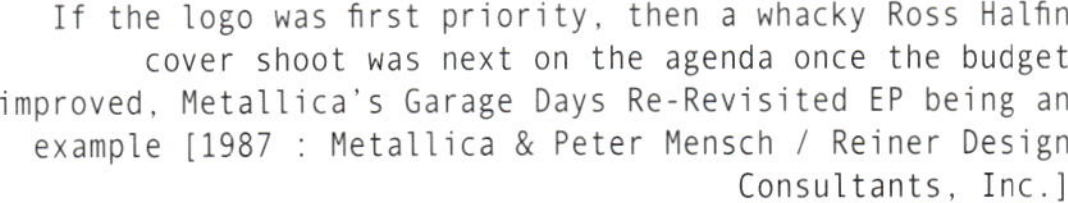

Artist : Richard Cheese Title : I'd Like A Virgin / 2004 Album / Ideatown Artwork : Unknown

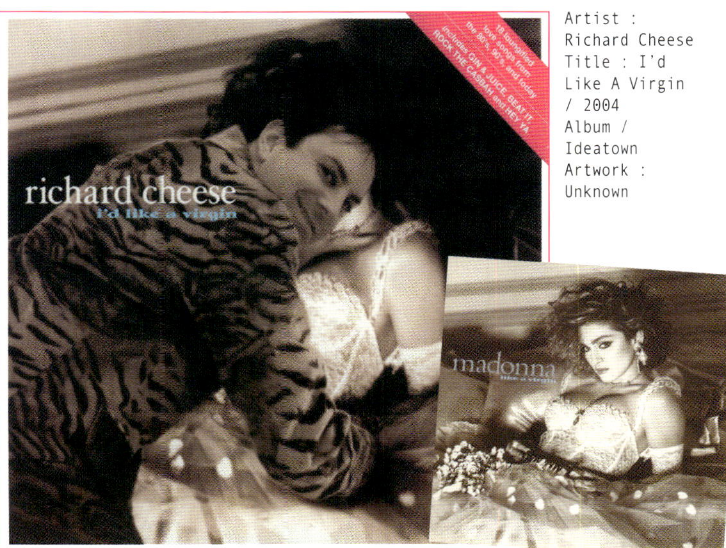

If the logo was first priority, then a whacky Ross Halfin cover shoot was next on the agenda once the budget improved, Metallica's Garage Days Re-Revisited EP being an example [1987 : Metallica & Peter Mensch / Reiner Design Consultants, Inc.]

Madonna's Like A Virgin sleeve [Sire : 1984. Artwork : Jeri McManus. Photo : Steven Meisel], shot in a New York hotel room, gets a photoshopped workover twenty years on from Mr. Richard Cheese, pushing his luck (and perhaps punching above his weight?).

Motörhead's famous logo, designed by Joe Petagno in 1977 (with a little help from Phil Smee who turned it into the heavy negative image) for their debut, is what all those band's like Metallica were after but lacked the vision to commission. Now one of the most recognised band logos of all time, variations of it decorate just about every album they have released. It has also been widely copied and borrowed... here are four from single sleeves.

Artist : Bömbers
Title : Bergen / 2004
4 track EP / Hearse Records
Artwork : BM

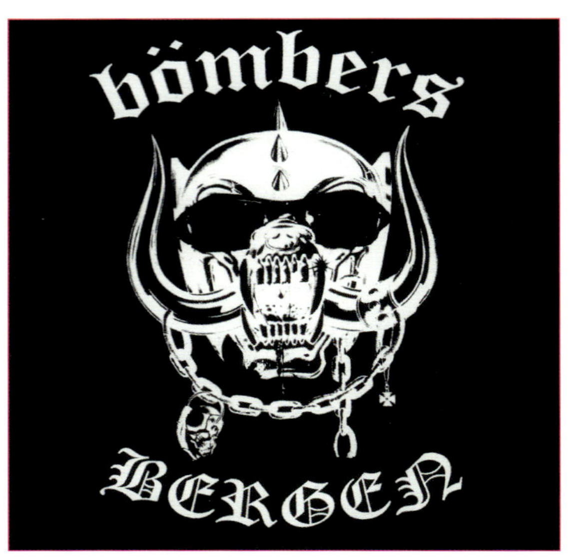

Artist : Dikke Dënnis & Friends
Title : De Schoppen-Aas / 2001
EP / Suburban Records
Artwork : Bartman / Killerkustom

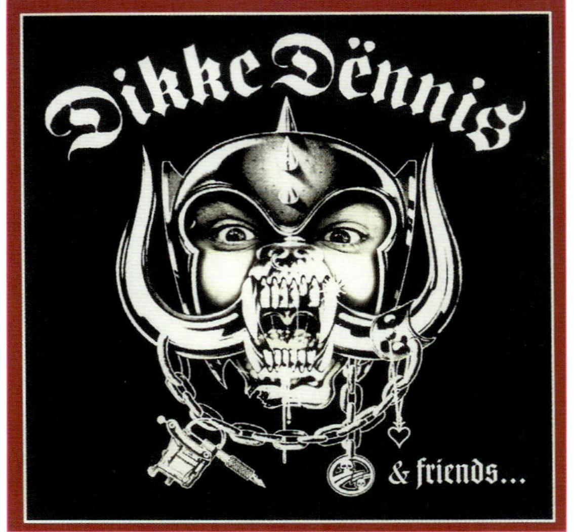

Artist : Goöber Patrol
Title : Eight Of Spades / 1998
EP / Fat Wreck Records
Artwork : Unknown

Artist : Motörhoney
Title : Take + 2 / 2000
EP / Lance Rock Records
Artwork : Jim Sorenson

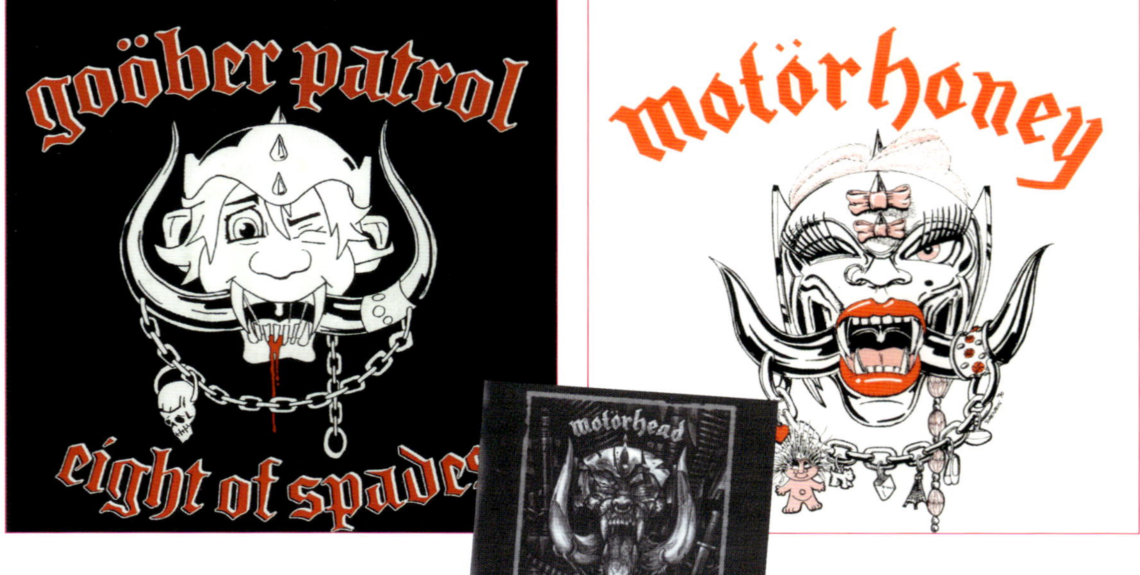

It's interesting that albums which you would not immediately think of as copy-worthy have proved inspirational for some. The cover of Van Morrison's second album Astral Weeks [1968 : Warner Bros] by the prolific American art director Ed Trasher [Photo : Joel Brodski] and itself inspired by an Irish painting, is one.

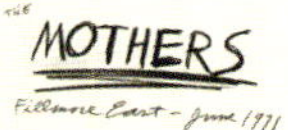

Artist : Alias Ron Kavana
Title : This Is The Night + 2 / 1990
12" Single / Chiswick
Artwork : Phil Barker Design (Photo : Denis Lewis)

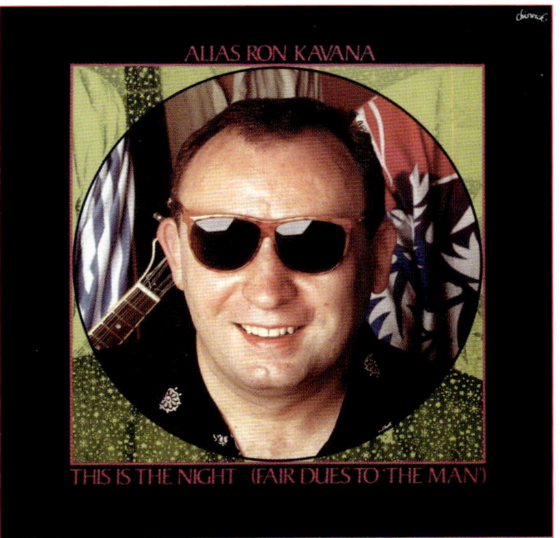

Artist : Robert Nacken
Title : Majomin + 1 / 2001
12" Single / Spectrum Works
Artwork : Lars Dorsch / Stefan Rose (Photo : Lutz Voigtländer)

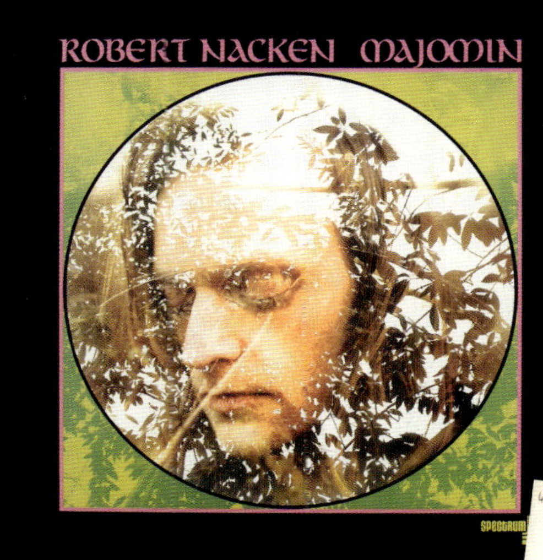

Artist : John Lennon & The Plastic Ono Band
Title : Some Time In New York City (Inner sleeve) / 1971
Album / Apple
Artwork : Cal Schenkel / Al Steckler

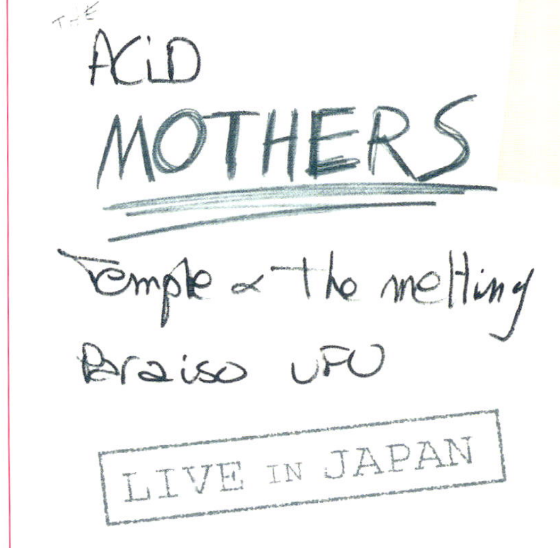

Artist : Acid Mothers Temple & The Melting Paraiso UFO
Title : Live In Japan / 2001
Album / Acid Mothers Temple - Eclipse
Artwork : Sachiko@ELF

The Mothers live album Fillmore East [1971 : Bizarre / Reprise] had a clever bootleggy cover by their regular designer Cal Schenkel, which has been copied and transformed by some, including on the inner sleeve of the Lennon album shown here (inner sleeves being a little off our remit but this is worth an exception).

This DIY take on The Mothers Of Invention album Freak Out! [1966 : Verve. Artwork : Jack Anesh. Photo : Ray Leong] is quite nicely executed. Clearly Liam Gallagher's new outfit Beady Eye have been checking this cover out too....

A straight copy of Van Morrison's Moondance cover layout here [1970 : Warner Bros. Artwork : Bob Cato. Photos : Elliott Landy].

Artist : The Morticians
Title : Freak Out With The Morticians / 1987
Album / Tin Soldier
Artwork + photo : Lisa Redfern

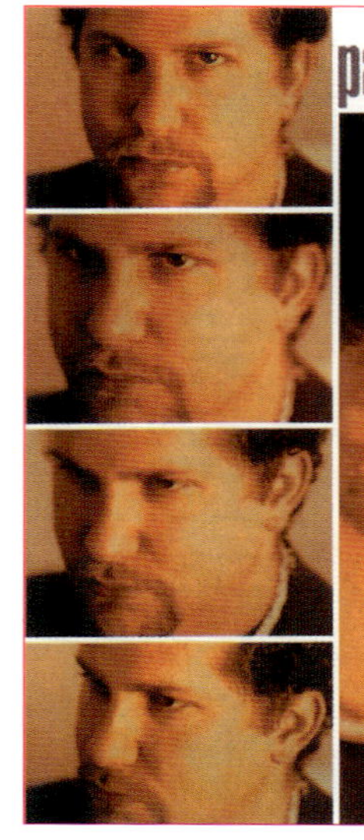

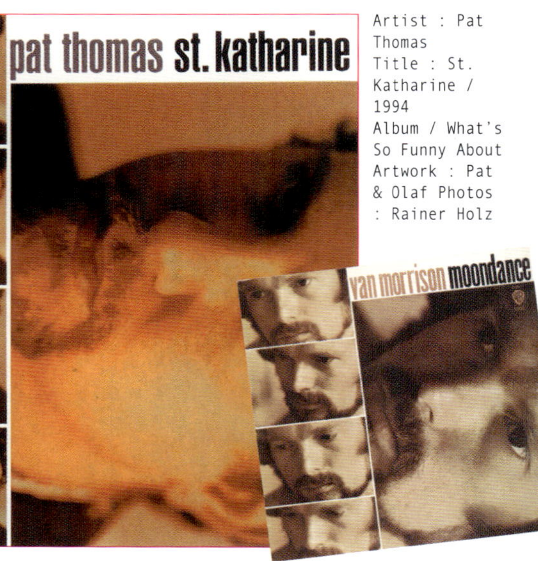

Artist : Pat Thomas
Title : St. Katharine / 1994
Album / What's So Funny About
Artwork : Pat & Olaf Photos : Rainer Holz

Artist : The Rockingbirds
Title : Jonathan, Jonathan + 1 / 1992
Single / Heavenly - Columbia
Artwork : Vegas

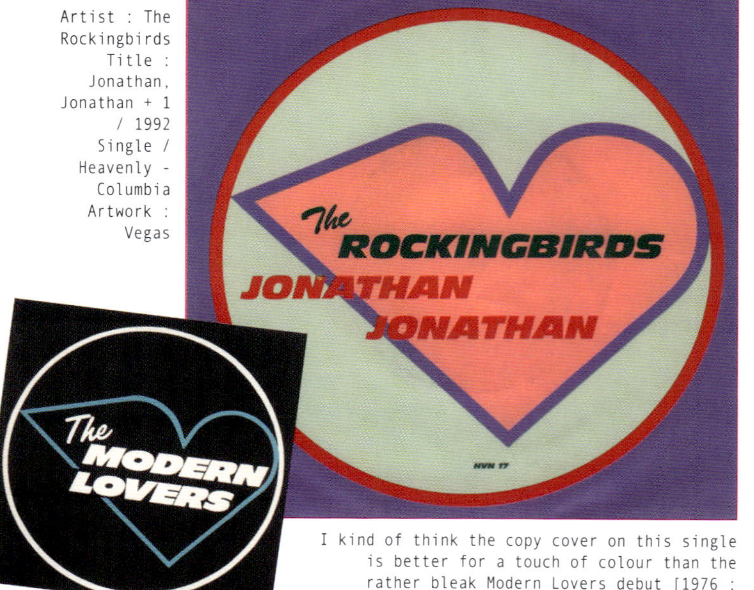

Artist : Totenmond
Title : Auf Dem Mond Ein Jener / 2001
Album / Massacre Records
Artwork : Juliart

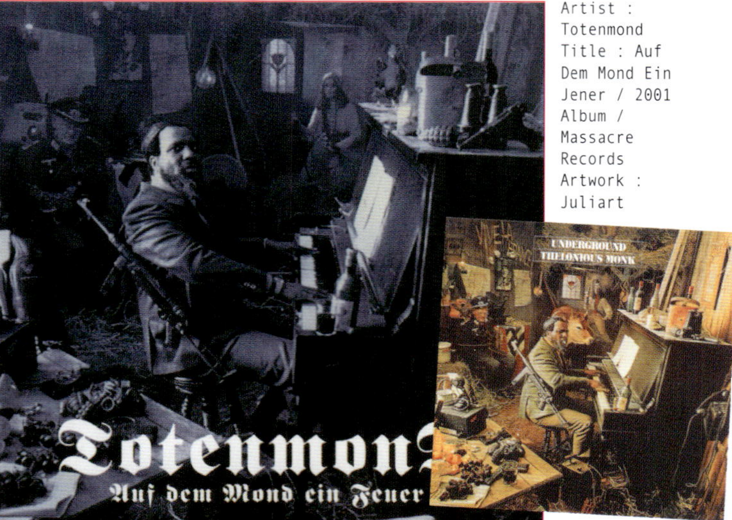

I kind of think the copy cover on this single is better for a touch of colour than the rather bleak Modern Lovers debut [1976 : Beserkley. Artwork : Unknown].

Thelonious Monk's elaborate cover shot for Underground [1967 : Columbia. Artwork : John Berg / Dick Mantel. Photo : Horn / Griner] is closely recreated for German metal band Totenmond.

Bob Mitchum's 1958 LP Calypso was a simple cash-in job, he doesn't sing on the LP, merely compiled it. Quite why Philippe would want to copy the cover so closely we don't know.

A great cover shot for The Miracles '61 LP Hi, We're The Miracles [Artwork : Karl Klefisch. Photo : Günter Fröhling] closely copied by the Bo Gumbos.

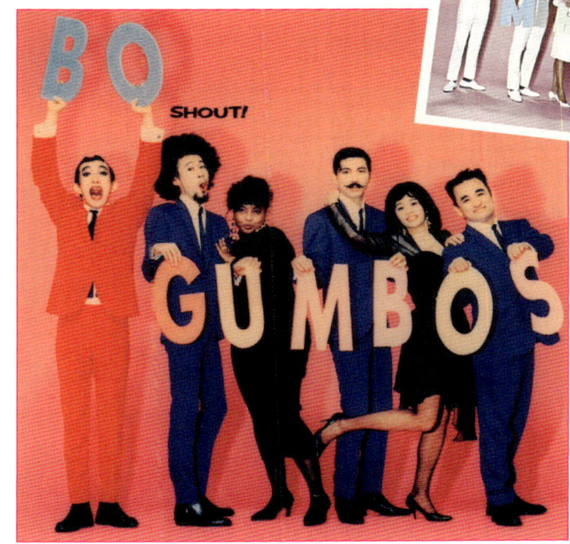

Artist :
Philippe Lavil
Title :
Calypso / 2007
Album / RCA
Artwork /
Photos :
Thierry Layani

Artist : Bo Gumbos
Title : Shout!
Anno : 1994
Format : Album
Label : Bo Records / File Records
Artwork : Yasuo Yagi (Photo : Masafumi Sakamoto)

Artist :
Current 93
Title : Halo
/ 2004
Album / Durtro Jnana
Artwork :
Paul Jackson
(Painting
: Jennifer
Maguire)

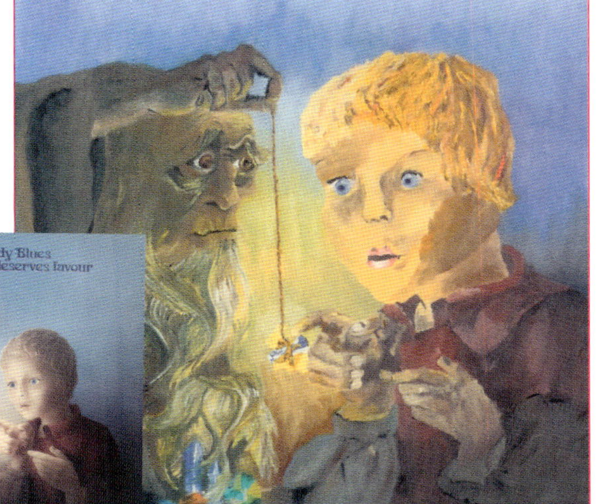

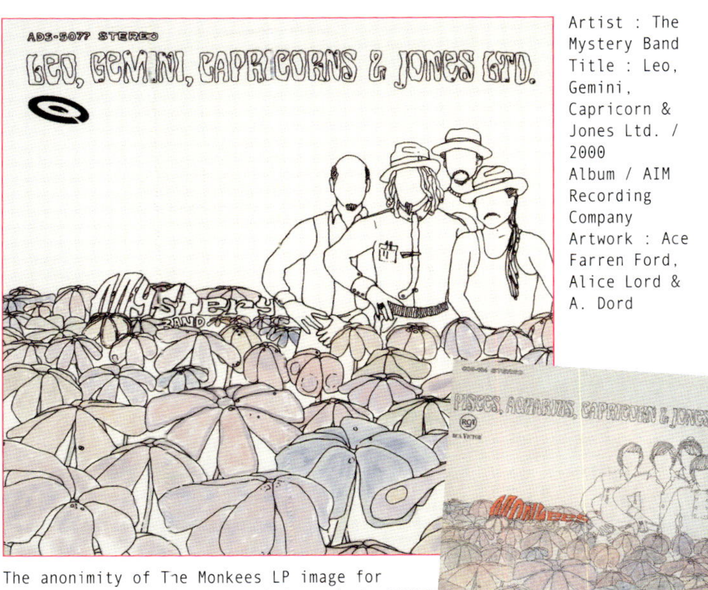

Artist : The Mystery Band
Title : Leo, Gemini, Capricorn & Jones Ltd. / 2000
Album / AIM Recording Company
Artwork : Ace Farren Ford, Alice Lord & A. Dord

The painting by Phil Travers which decorated the Moody Blues LP Every Good Boy Deserves Favour [1971 : Threshold] is obviously the inspiration for the Current 93 cover, but exactly what chord it struck...

The anonimity of The Monkees LP image for Pisces, Aquarius, Capricorn & Jones Ltd. [1967 Artwork : Bernard Yeszin] obviously suited The Mystery Band, who replicated every element.

Stereolab often looked to the vinyl past for cover ideas, here taking Gary McFarland's The In Sound [1965. Artwork : Win Bruder. Painting : Peter Shulman] for inspiration, but did at least credit the original designer.

I always admired the Hoodoogurus sleeve but didn't spot until recently that it owed much to Jackie McLean's Right Now [1965 : Blue Note], another great Reid Miles design.

Artist :
Stereolab
Title : The In
Sound / 1998
3 track EP /
Independent
Project
Records
Artwork
Painting :
Peter Shulman

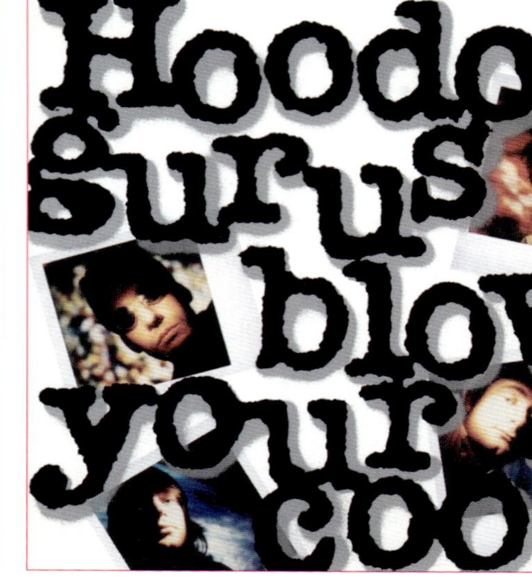

Artist :
Hoodoogurus
Title : Blow
Your Cool! /
1987
Album / Big
Time - Elektra
Artwork :
Richard Allan
Photos : Robyn
Stacey

Artist :
Arthur Mullard
& Hylda Baker
Title : Band
On The Trot /
1978
Album / Pye
Artwork :
Unknown

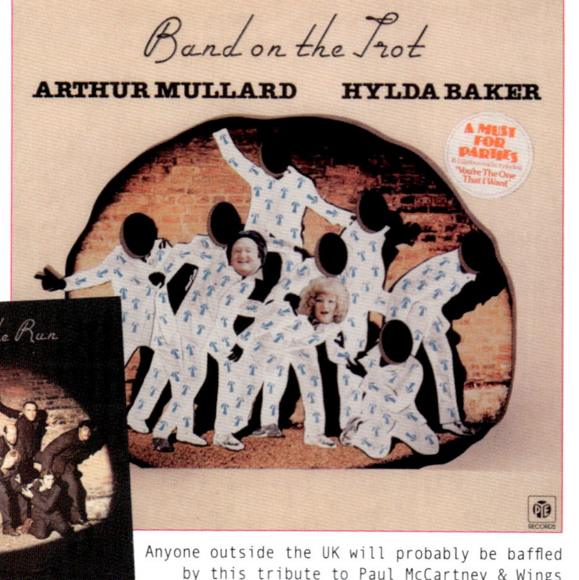

Artist : Boyd
Rice
Title : The Way
I Feel / 2000
Album /
Caciocavallo
Artwork :
Unknown

Anyone outside the UK will probably be baffled by this tribute to Paul McCartney & Wings Band On The Run [1973 : Apple. Artwork : MPL Communications Inc.], the rest of us will just groan quietly.

Boyd Rice borrows both the idea and some of the images from the smart cover to Leonard Nimoy's The Way I Feel [1969 : Dot. Artwork : Christopher Whorf / Ron Wolin. Photo : Fred Poore], but his effort lacks finesse.

A very recognisable cover, The New York Dolls self-titled 1973 debut album [Artwork : Album Graphics, Inc. Photo : Toshi] has been referenced by several groups, albeit each adding their own twist on the image, with Spanish pop glam outfit Nancys Rubias (all the members used the Christian name Nancy!) clearly working the hardest of this batch.

Artist : Devil Dolls
Title : We Are The Devil Dolls / 2002
Album / Corduroy Records
Artwork Photo : Anita Frank

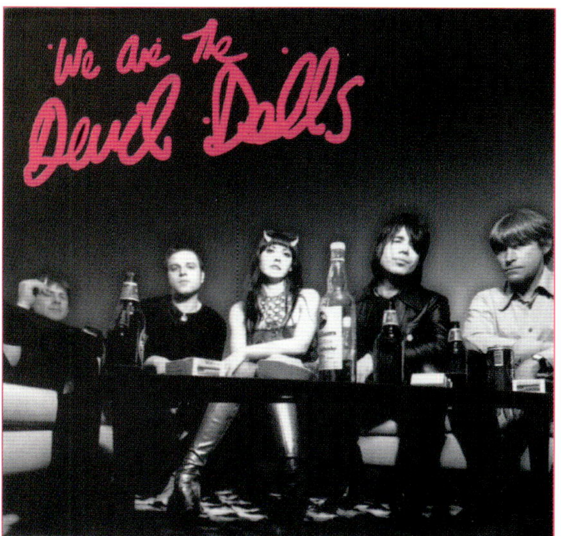

Artist : Nancys Rubias
Title : Nancys Rubias / 2005
Album / Dro East West
Artwork : Juan Gatti

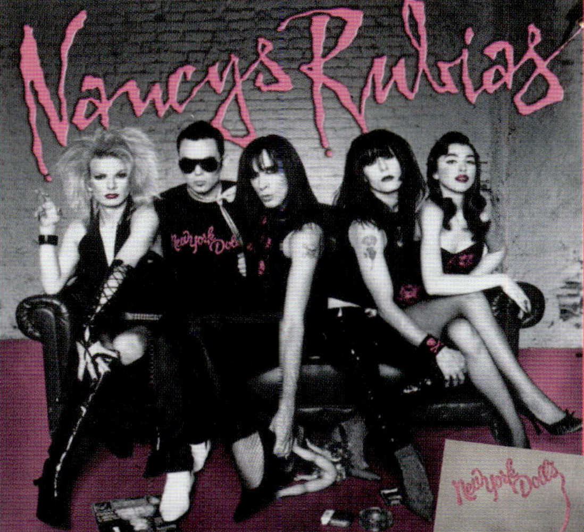

Artist : New Wave Hookers
Title : New Wave Hookers / 1998
Album / Junk Records
Artwork : Nancy Farber / Jason Hill
Photo : Tom Huckabee / Tim McGary

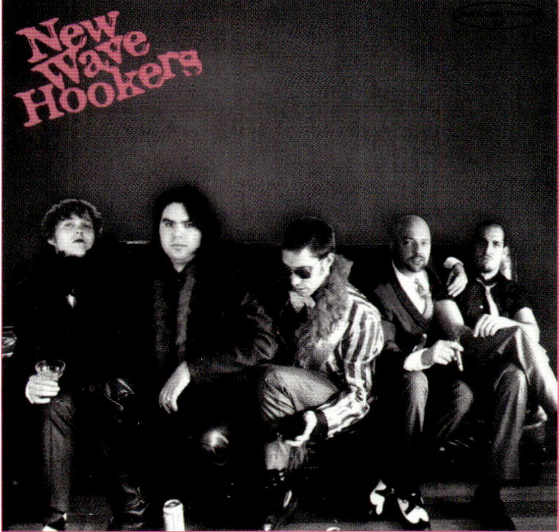

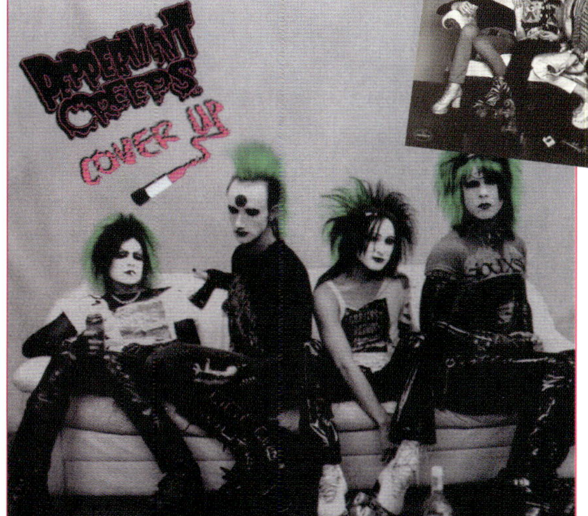

Artist : Peppermint Creeps
Title : Cover Up / 2008
Album / Deadline Music - Cleopatra
Artwork Photo : Regina Henderson

Nazareth's 1971 debut was designed by C.C.S. Associates [1971 : Pegasus. Photo : Jim Wilson], responsible for a number of classy sleeves. It's not an obvious cover to borrow, but Nashville Pussy were clearly big fans.

Nirvana's 1991 debut album (is it really twenty years gone?) was so influential musically that it's no wonder the cover (by Robert Fisher, with Kirk Weddle the one getting his feet wet and Spencer Elden having his first swim) has been borrowed and parodied over a dozen times. ▶

Artist :
Nashville
Pussy
Title : Say
Something
Nasty / 2002
Album /
Artemis
Artwork :
Jeff Wood
(Photo : Evan
Bartleson)

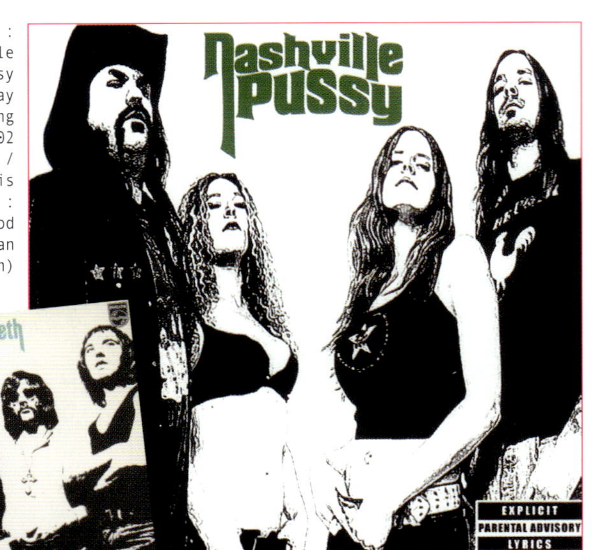

Artists : Los
Straitjackets
(+ Southern
Culture On The
Skids)
Title : Smells
Like Teen
Spirit / 2009
Single /
Spinout
Records
Artwork :
Michael
Triplett

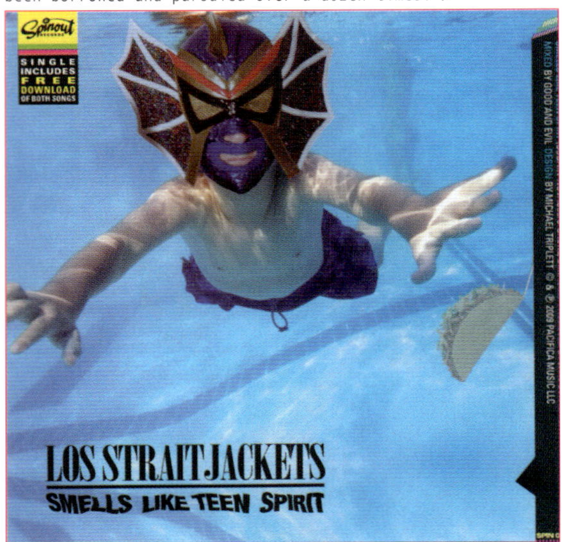

Artist :
Andrew Jackson
Jihad
Title : Two
Headed Boy
- 2008
Single /
Suburban Home
Records
Artwork :
Mitch Clem

Artist :
Gacy's Place
Title : Smells
Like... / 1998
EP / Spiral
Objective
Artwork : Ben
Chalmers /
Gacy's Place /
Ned Kelly

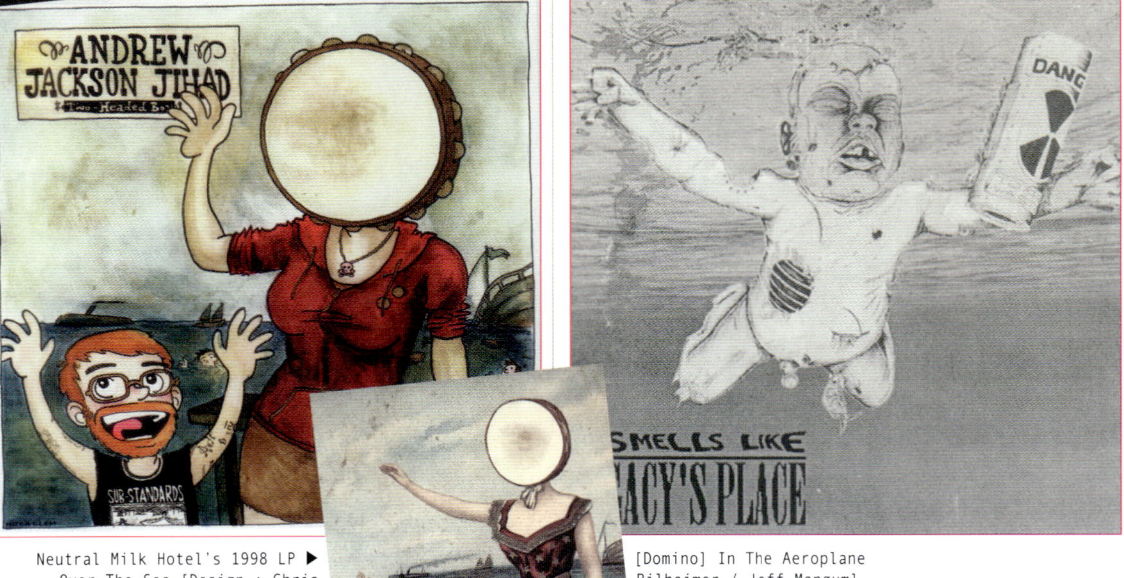

Neutral Milk Hotel's 1998 LP ▶ Over The Sea [Design : Chris used a Victorian postcard into a photo, and referenced here in a

[Domino] In The Aeroplane Bilheimer / Jeff Mangum], which the buyer could add hand-drawn illustration.

We've chosen five of the more obvious variations, though cannot help but wonder if one of the Nirvana crew had maybe taken a look at the 1973 Hipgnosis designed cover for Argent's In Deep L⸮ (*right*)?
Weird Al is chasing a doughnut rather than a dollar bill, and went to the trouble of using the same photographer as Nirvana for both the album and this single taken from it (and checking with the designer for ▼

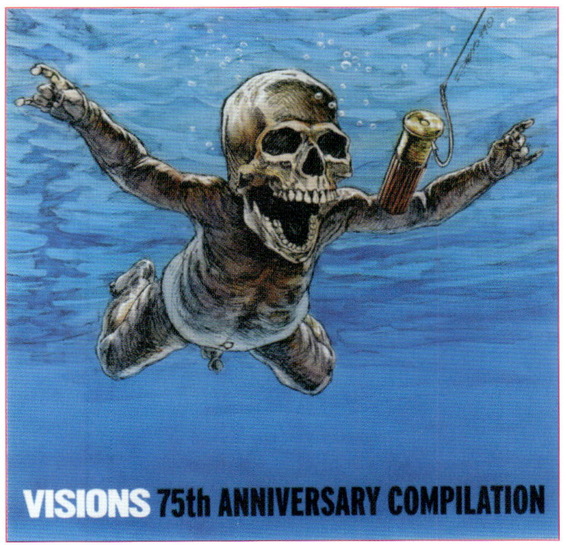

Artist : Various Artists
Title : Visions - 75th Anniversary Compilation
Album / Visions
Artwork : Unknown

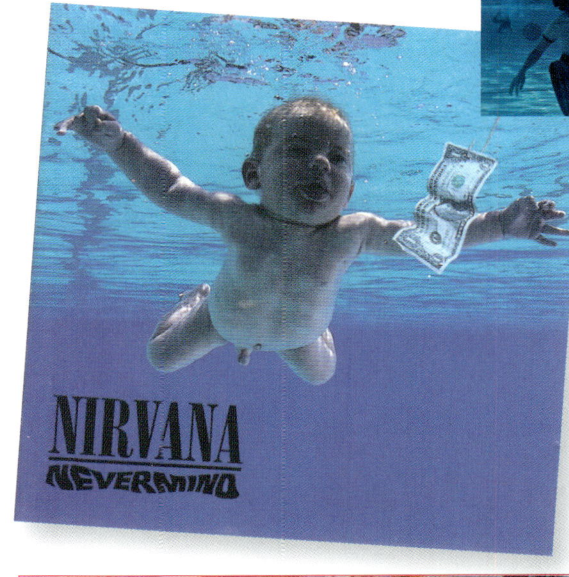

Artist : Weird Al Yankovic
Title : Smells Like Nirvana - Waffle King / 1992
Single / Scotti Bros.
Cover Photo : Kirk Weddle

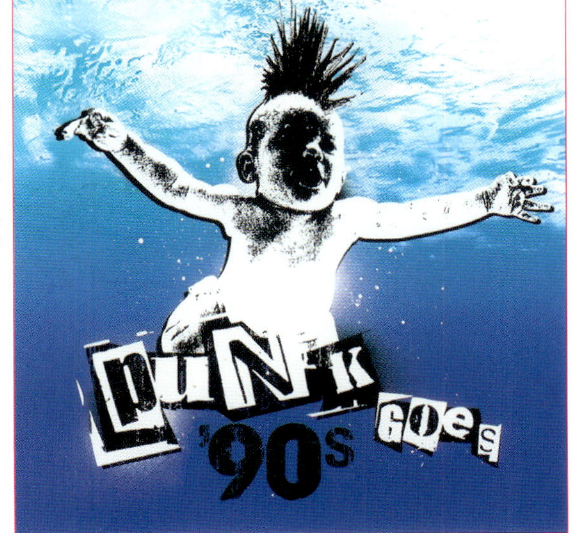

Artist : Various Artists
Title : Punk Goes 90's / 2006
Album / Fearless Records
Artwork : The Kuro Collective

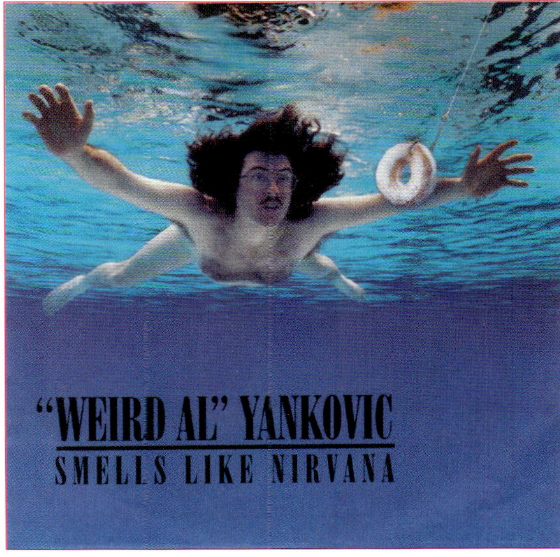

the right font), while the baby on the Gary's Place single (an Australian band who exist now only in myberspace) is after a container of nuclear waste. It's not exactly clear what the masked diver is chasing on Los Straitjacket's cover (page 94) (the single is split between two bands - Southern Culture On The Skids are on the flip), and the purple trunks aren't exactly teen rebel wear.

Unlike the guys who copied the Funkadelic sleeve (see page 59), The Mighty Bop managed to get a gatefold vinyl edition out of their record label when they did this facsimile of the Ohio PLayers' 1977 album Angel [Mercury. Artwork : Jim Ladwig / Ohio Players. Photo : Skrebneski]. The Players pushed the boundaries on a number of their covers but in a way which didn't come across as particularly gratuitous - certainly compared to a lot of Urban acts in recent years.

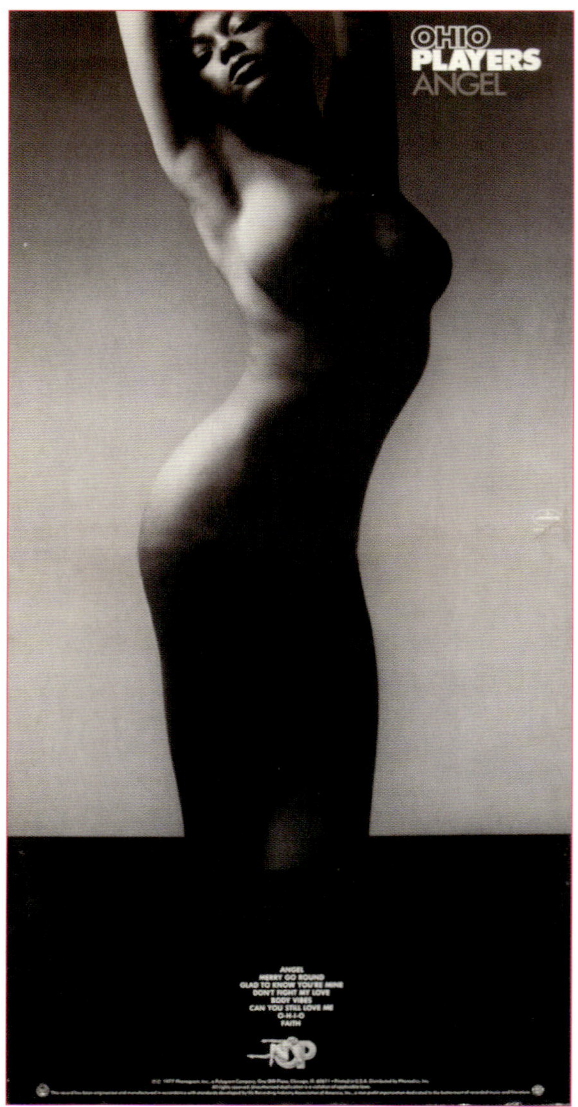

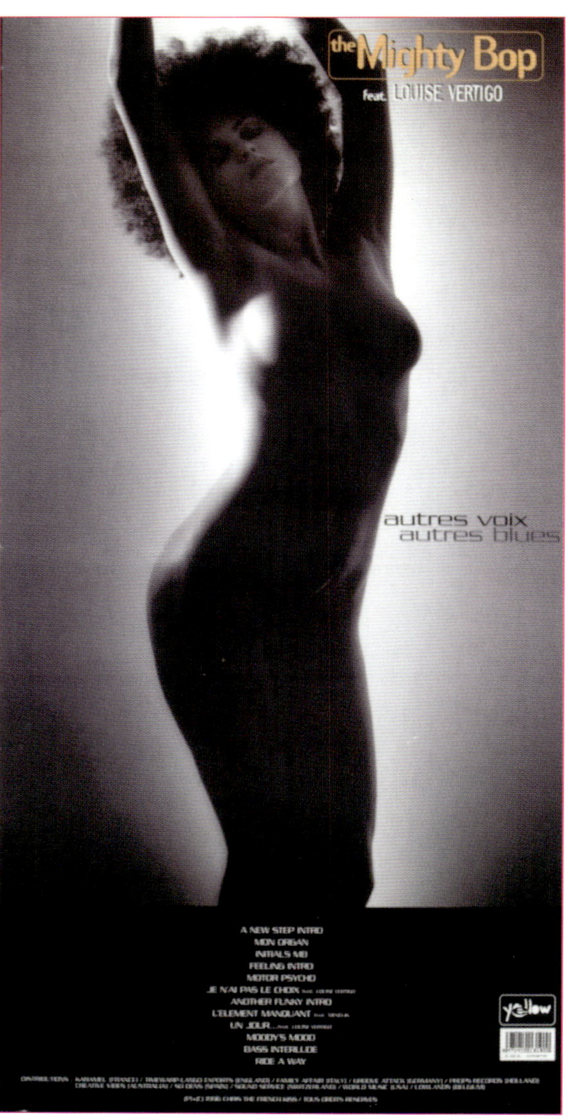

Artist : The Mighty Bop feat. Louise Vertigo
Title : Autres Voix Autres Blues / 1996
Album / Yellow
Artwork : Manetta Scott. Photo : Jean-Christophe Polien

clockwise from top right

Artist : Acen
Title : 75 Minutes
Anno : 1993
Album / Profile Records
Artwork : Rebecca Meek

Artist : Various
Artists
Title : All You Need
Is...Love
Anno : 2000
Album / GTV
Artwork : Indianapolis
Museum Of Art, James E.
Roberts Fund

Artist : Rage Against
The Machine
Title : Renegades
Anno : 2000
Album / Epic
Artwork : Rage Against
The Machine /
Rick Rubin /Aimée
Macauley

Artist : Oasis
Title : Little By
Little
Anno : 2002
Single / ?
Artwork : not credited

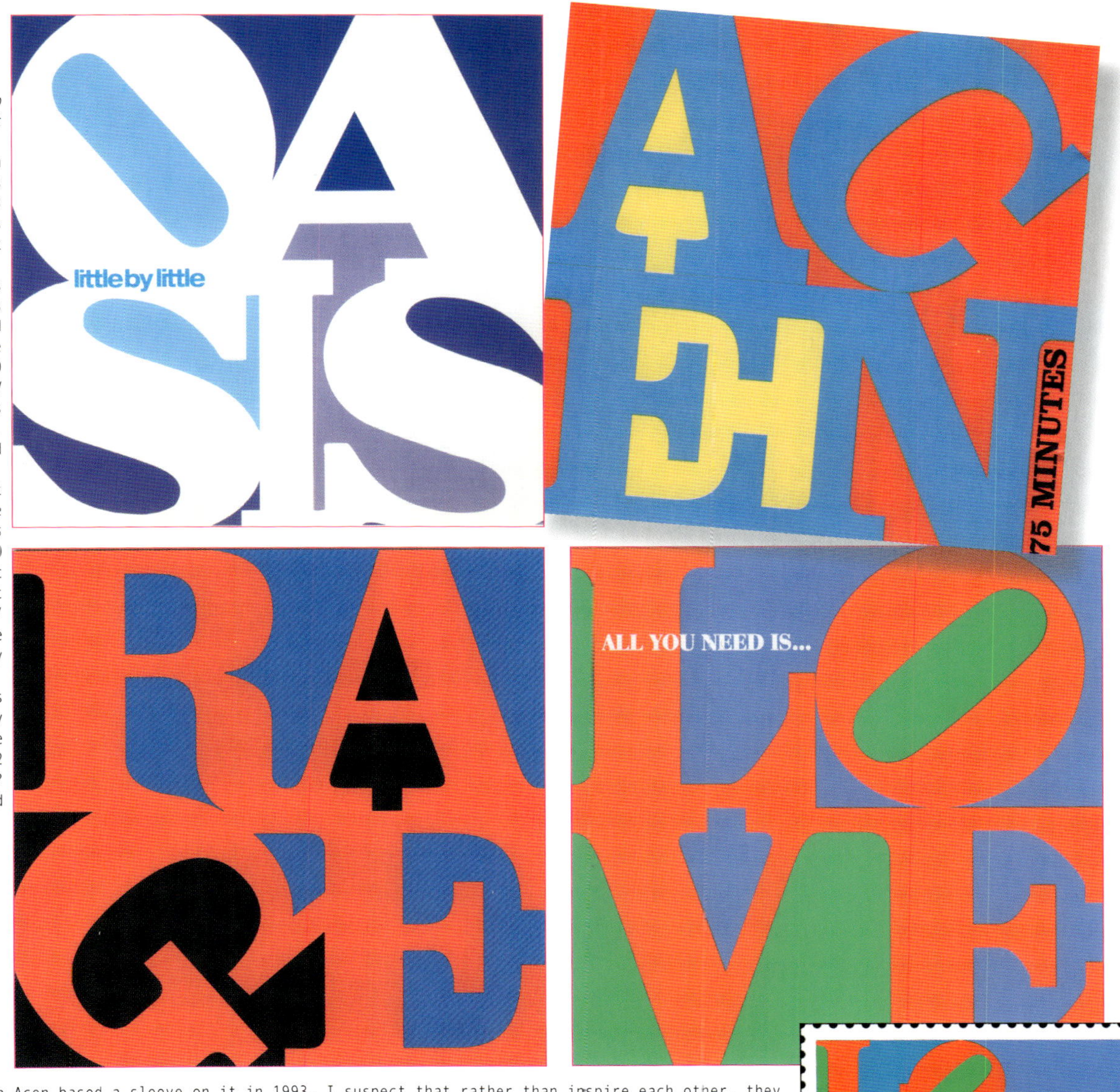

Although Acen based a sleeve on it in 1993, I suspect that rather than inspire each other, they and the rest all looked to the original Love design done by Robert Indiana for a Christmas card sold by the Museum Of Modern Art on America in 1964 (seen right on a postage stamp from 1973), a design which has been borrowed, copied (and worse) in hundreds of ways since (Google had Indiana do a variation for them on Valentines Day as recently as 2011). It wasn't until 2000 that the original design came to be used on an album cover. And no surprise that those arch borrowers Oasis should have got around to it a couple of years later either.

Even Floyd's 'enigmatic' Wish You Were Here from 1975 [Artwork : Hipgnosis, Peter Christopherson / Jeff Smith / Howard Bartrop / Richard Manning] has inspired a couple of covers (note how they both manage to get a rain grid to pose by).

Artist :
Govinda
Title : Wish
You Were India
/ 2002
Album / Nun
Entertainment
Artwork :
Paolo De
Francesco

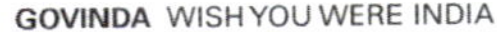

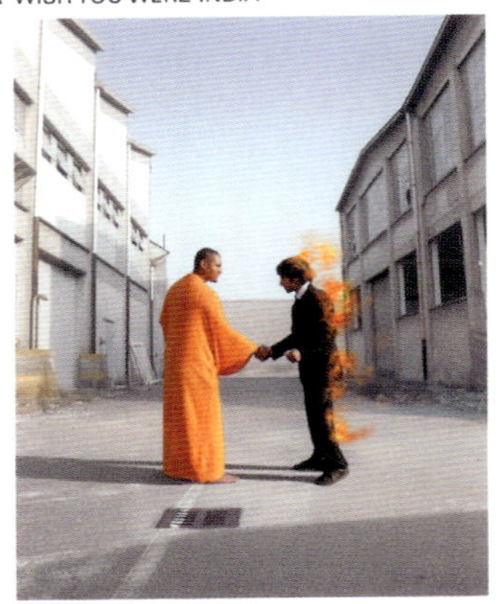

Artist :
Siniestro
Total
Title : Ojala
Estuvieras
Aqui / 1993
Album / Warner
Bros.
Artwork :
Diseno Dro
Photo : Javier
Sallas

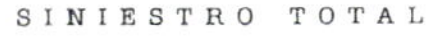

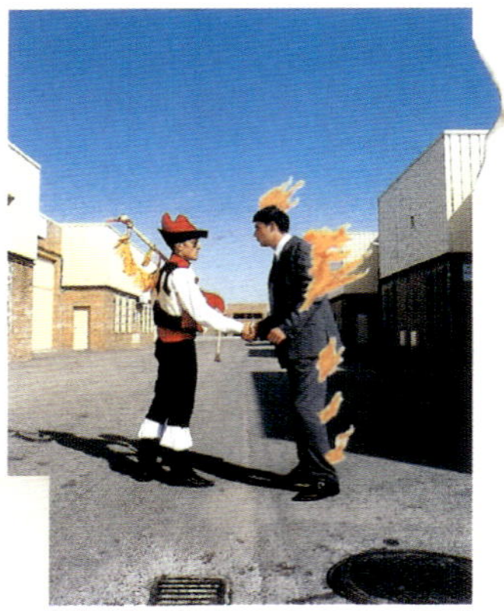

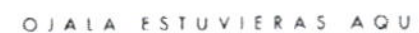

One of the most famous album covers - ever, I must admit Pink Floyd's Dark Side Of The Moon wouldn't make my desert island art sleeve gallery list (I much preferred the designs on the accompanying poster and sticker inside original copies of the LP). Still, this 1973 Harvest label design by Hipgnosis / George Hardie is one of the most imitated and parodied, with at least four dozen candidates for this book. Some were just a bit naff, we put to one side the umpteen musical tributes, and far too many (Americans) think the title Dork Side Of The Moon remains funny. We've chosen nine which worked for us on one level or another (especially A Capella which cleverly filters the prism through a mouth) but the message is clear, just because the original sold zillions, it doesn't follow that a copy will do the same. Perhaps the least appropriate has to be the attempt to update 1950s comedy radio recordings of The Goons with a strange parody of the Dark Side cover; what were EMI's art department thinking of?!

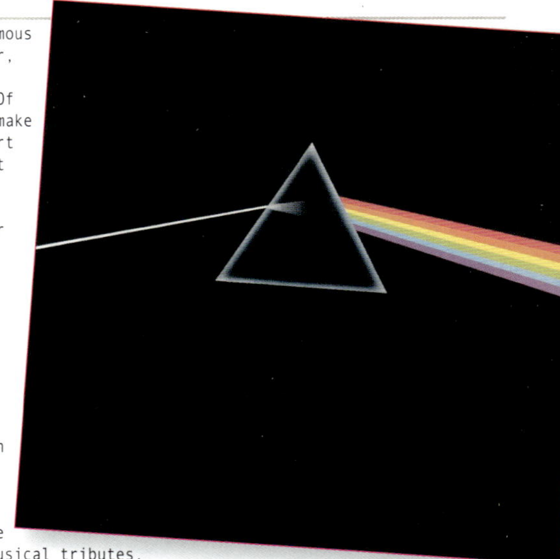

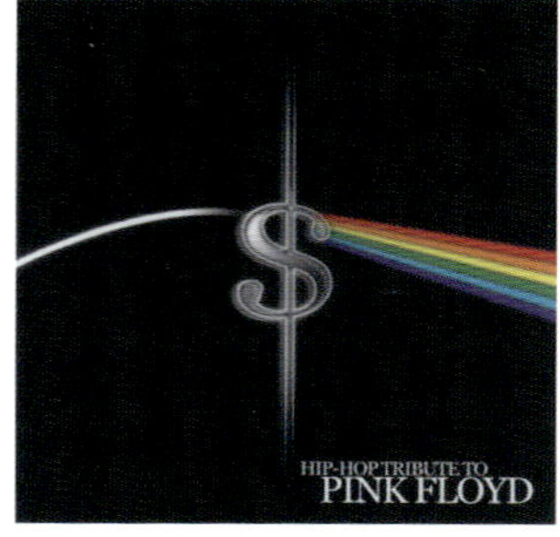

Page 99 L-R • Cab City Combo : Pork Side Of The Moon [1999 Artwork : Unknown] / Cheater Pint : Cheater Pint [2007 Artwork : Steve Reynolds / Mark Simon] / The Dan Orr Project : The Dork Side Of The Moon [1996 Artwork : The Funny Bone Comedy Club(Photo : Janoski] / Dave Warner And The Happy Hookers / The Dark Side Of The Scrum [1988 Artwork : Unknown] / Dark Side Of The Moon A Capella : Dark Side Of The Moon A Capella [2005 Artwork : Jenna Rounds] / The Goons : Dark Side Of The Goon [1980 Artwork : Feref] / Lazy : Floyd - A Chillout Experience [2006 Artwork : Highlights Photo : Faig] / Richard Cheese : Sunny Side Of The Moon [2006 Artwork : Jim Rasfeld / Mark Jonathan Davis] / The Squirrels : The Not So Bright Side Of The Moon [2000 Artwork : Salvador Disney /Eric Erickson Photo : Bill Larsen].
(*left*) Various Artists : Gatecrasher's Trance Anthems 1993-2009 [2009 Artwork : Ian Anderson / Sian Thomas] / (*right*) Various Artists : Hip-Hop Tribute To Pink Floyd [2007 Artwork : Bobby Czzowitz - Stereotype Multimedia]

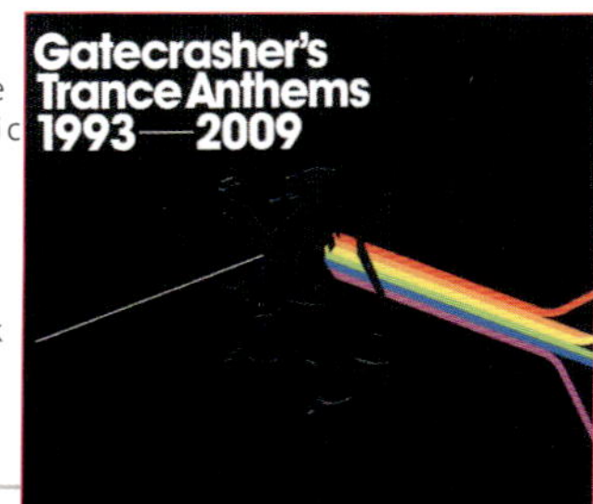

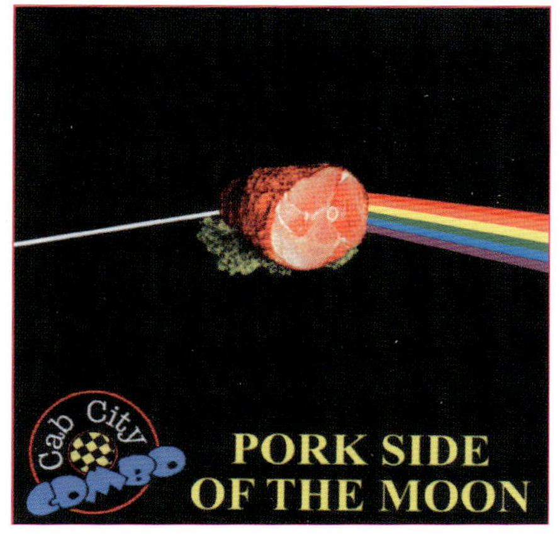
Cab City Combo
PORK SIDE OF THE MOON

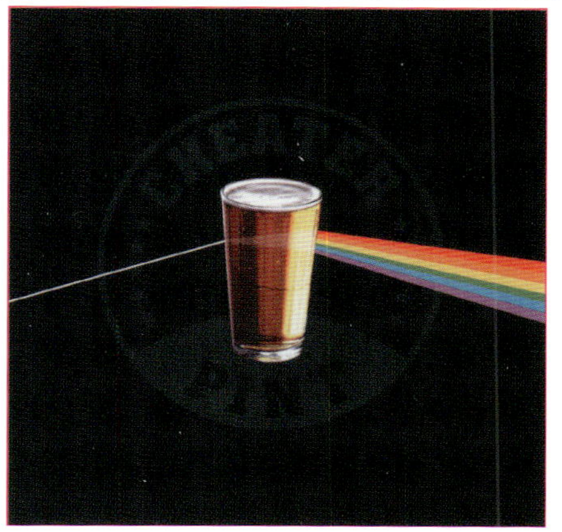

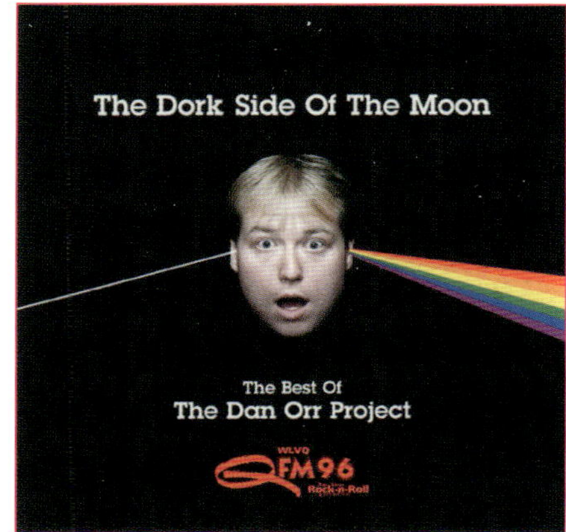
The Dork Side Of The Moon
The Best Of
The Dan Orr Project
WLVQ
QFM96
Rock-n-Roll

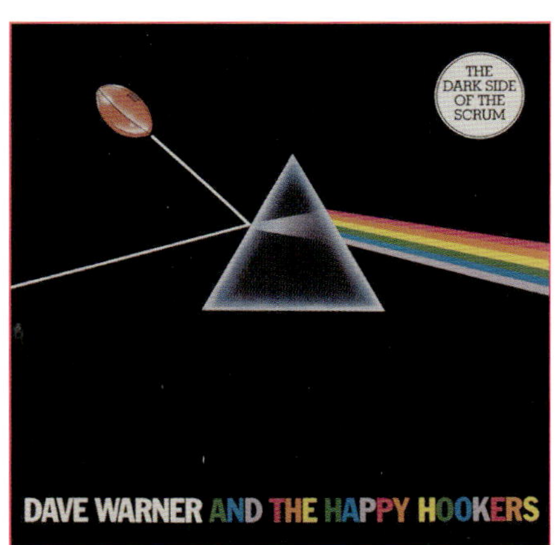
THE DARK SIDE OF THE SCRUM
DAVE WARNER AND THE HAPPY HOOKERS

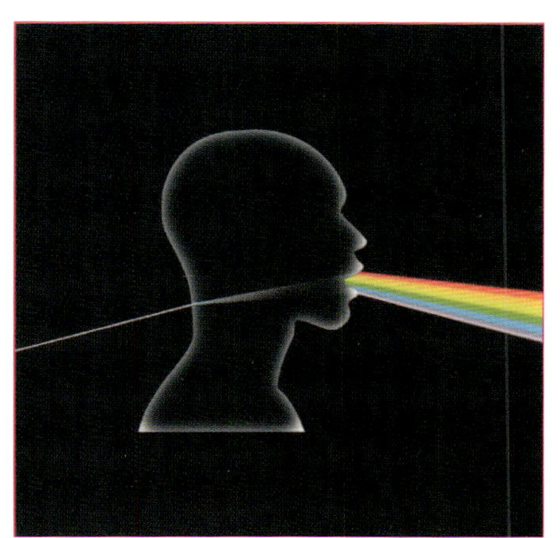

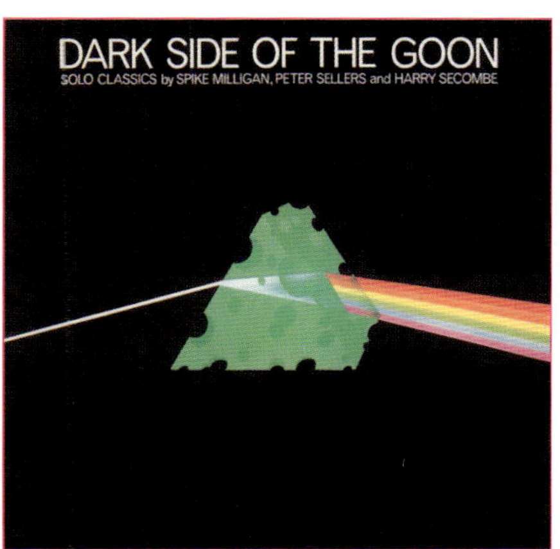
DARK SIDE OF THE GOON
SOLO CLASSICS by SPIKE MILLIGAN, PETER SELLERS and HARRY SECOMBE

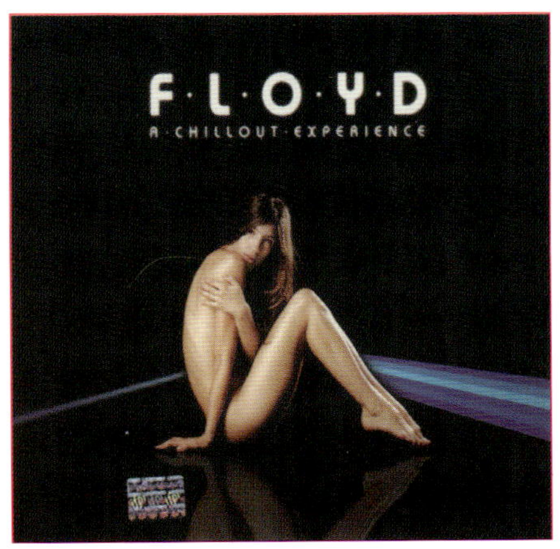
F·L·O·Y·D
A·CHILLOUT·EXPERIENCE

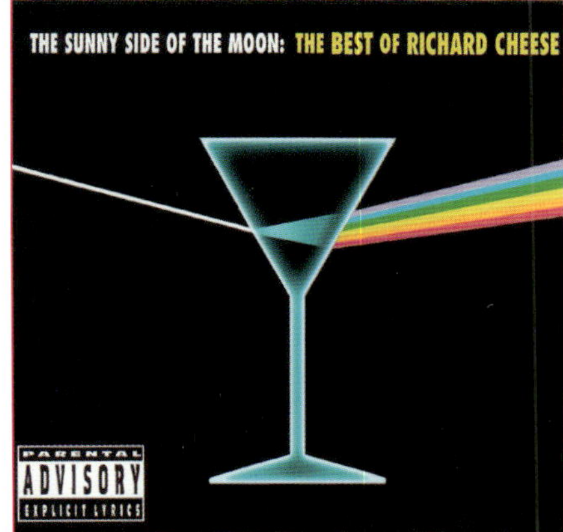
THE SUNNY SIDE OF THE MOON: THE BEST OF RICHARD CHEESE
PARENTAL
ADVISORY
EXPLICIT LYRICS

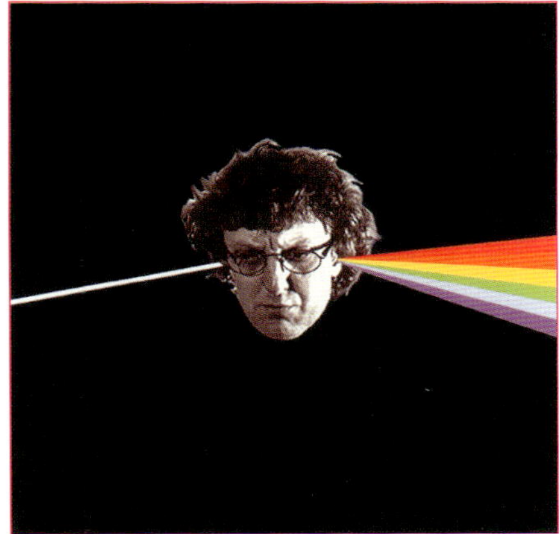

Even the early Pink Floyd album The Piper At The Gates Of Dawn [1967 : EMI] has been lifted, in particular Vic Singh's psychedelic multi-lens cover photo, the The Pickels having a fair bash at the type style as well. Southern Culture's version (with added sunglasses) is the second time this label makes the book, see their Nirvana variation (page 94).

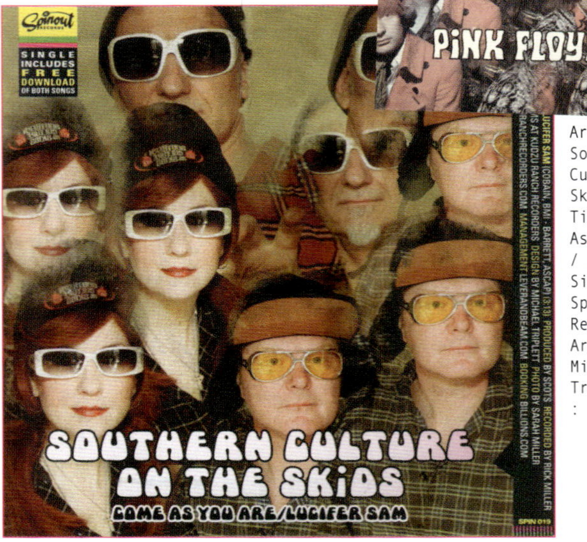

Artist : The Pickles
Title : Pardon Me, But Your Organ Is In My Back / 1996
Album / Teenage Kicks
Artwork : El Littbarski-Plödereder
Photo : Zattl

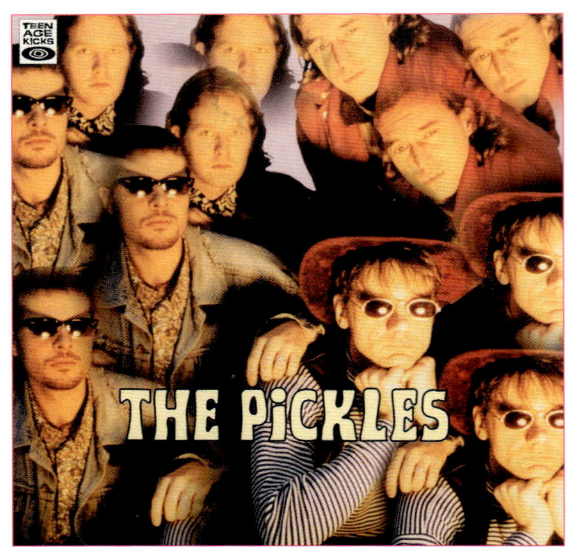

Artist : Southern Culture On The Skids + 1
Title : Come As You Are + 2 / 2009
Single / Spinout Records
Artwork : Michael Triplett Photo : Sarah Miller

Artist : Govinda
Title : Atom Heart Madras / 1997
Album / Dance Factory - EMI Italy
Artwork : Giuseppe Spada - Milk Studio

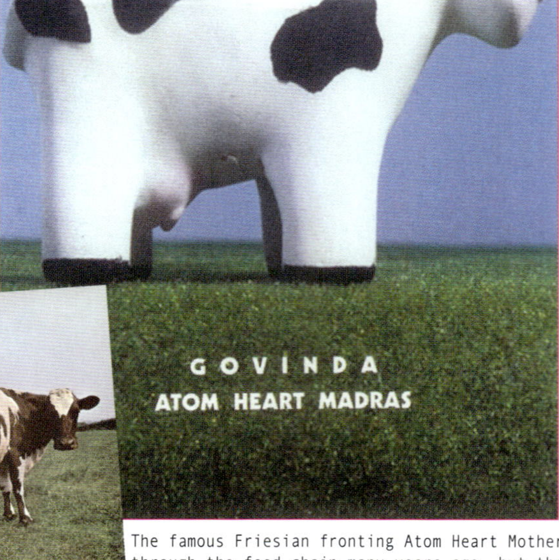

Artist : M Walking On The Water
Title : Pictures Of An Exhibitionist / 1993
Album / Polydor
Artwork : Markus Maria Jansen / Friedel Muders Fuego Ateliers
Photo : Rolf Giesen

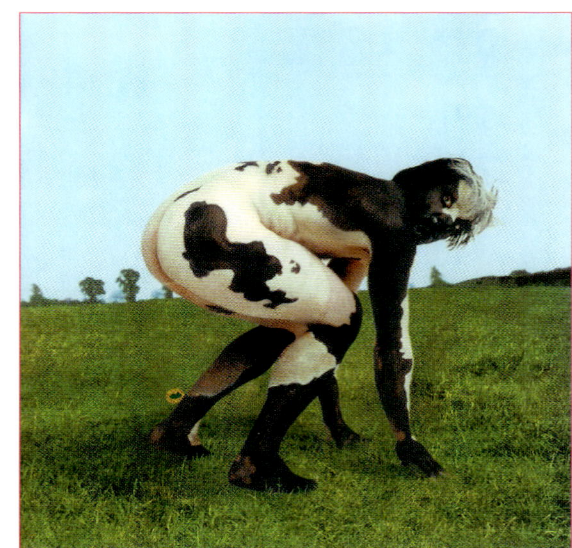

The famous Friesian fronting Atom Heart Mother [1970 : Harvest. Artwork : Hipgnosis] may well have passed through the food chain many years ago, but the sleeve continues to inspire, though many are poorly executed. Here are two interesting exceptions from Italy and Germany (guess which is the German one!).

Les Paul's The New Sound is very dated for 1960 (and on 10" vinyl too) but fun even so, and here borrowed by Slim Sandy. The real Slim Sandy we assume.

Artist : Slim Sandy
Title : Rough & Ready / 2006
Album / Sleaze Records
Artwork Photo : Tracey Nelson / Passia Pandora

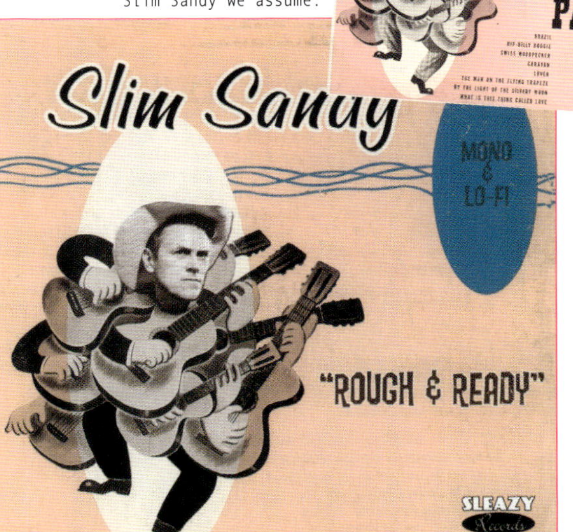

An example of a straight appropriation, the great retro look of Christmas With Patti Page [1955] just lifted outright to amuse buyers of a 10" compilation.

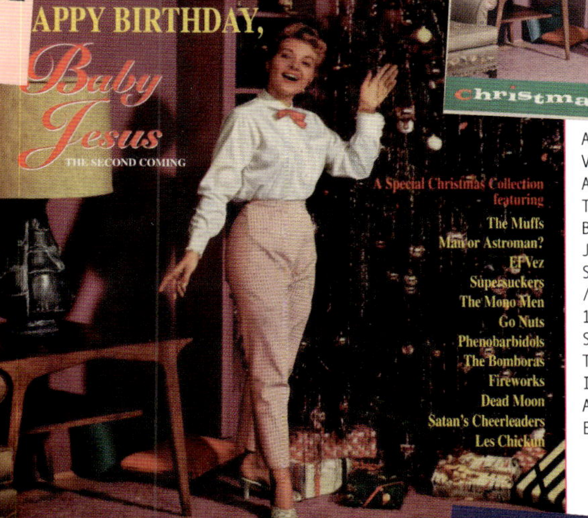

Artist : Various Artists
Title : Happy Birthday, Baby Jesus - The Second Coming / 1994
10" Album / Sympathy For The Record Industry
Artwork : Eddie Flowers

Artist : Various Artists
Title : He Put The Bomp In The Bomp / 2007
Album / Bomp Records
Artwork : David Allen / Art Trouble

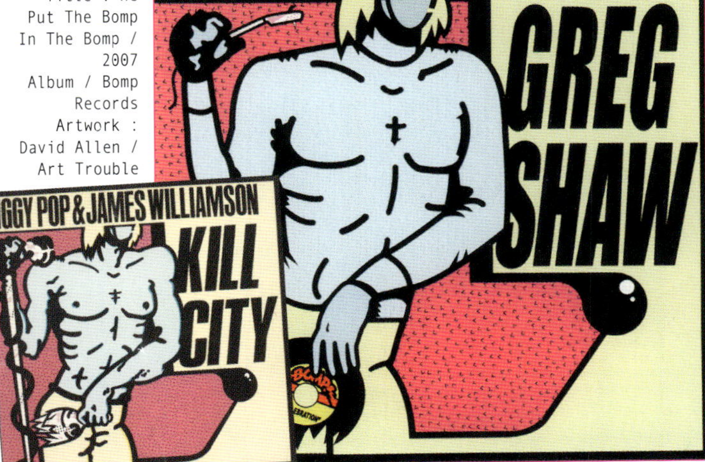

The illustration for Iggy Pop & James Williamson's Kill City [1977. Artwork : David Allen] is reprised by the original artist on a collection by the much revered US indie music magazine Bomp's editor who had issued the original on his own label when nobody else would.

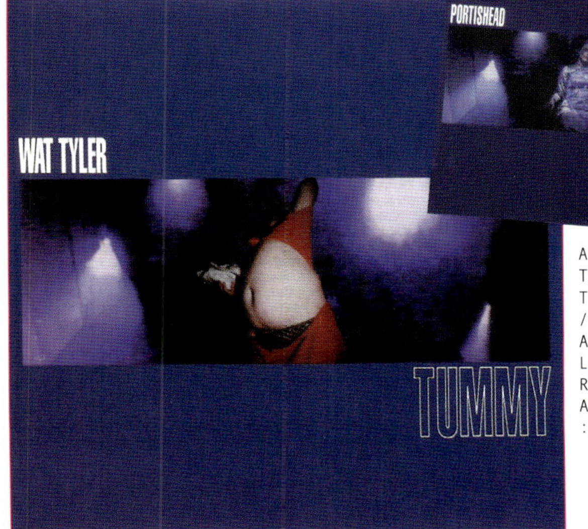

Artist : Wat Tyler
Title : Tummy / 1995
Album / Lookout Records
Artwork Photo : Kelly

Portishead's Dummy album [1994 : Go!Beat. Artwork : Unknown] is given a bit of a disturbing make-over by Wat Tyler here just a year later (he also had a go at The Prodigy on another of his CD covers).

Tribute act El Vez could fill a page on his own (if we let him), but this is a typical example of his catalogue, based on the original G.I. Blues cover from 1960.

Artist : El Vez
Title : G.I. Ay, Ay! Blues / 1996
Album / Semaphore
Artwork : Claudia Kefer / Tina Berning / El Vez. Photo : Randall Michelson

Artist : The New Lou Reeds
Title : Top Billin' / 2006
Album / Exit Stencil Recordings
Artwork : Stephe DK

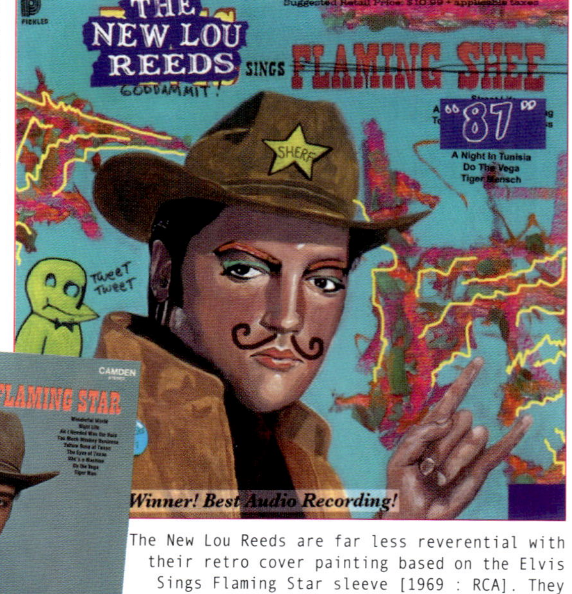

The New Lou Reeds are far less reverential with their retro cover painting based on the Elvis Sings Flaming Star sleeve [1969 : RCA]. They were in good company, Andy Warhol used stills from the film for his screenprints of Elvis.

After The Beatles, to Elvis Presley falls the honour of having more copies of his sleeves than any other artist. Good going really, considering many original Elvis covers were just studio photographs with little thought given over to design whatsover.

An exception is the superb 50,000 Elvis Fans sleeve, which used a brilliant studio shot repeated across the cover. Such was the lowly position of most designers back then [1960] that we don't even know who came up with the concept. Yet both the cover and title have proved hard to resist, albeit mostly in a self-deprecating way (brave indeed would be the act which tried to compare themselves; here only Rod Stewart seems not to have realised this). The Fall cover is one of the best (proof that a budget release doesn't have to look cheap), a fine contrast between the pringle jumpered Mark E. and the gold lamé original. Blumfeld just goes straight for a copy of the cover and slaps new heads on, while Sandra Weckert is not alone in reducing the number of her fans to a paltry 50 but wins out for having the band all dressed in cleaning outfits. Even the bootleggers have got in on the act, see Elvis Costello. The cover has also inspired a number of Christmassy themed variations.

L-R • Blumfeld : L'Etat Et Moi [1994 Artwork : Henjes / Blumfeld] / The Dino Martinis : 50,000,000 Santa Fans Can't Be Wrong [2001 Artwork : Lyle Grant Photo : Erin Kalin / SMTH Photography] / Elvis Costello & The Attractions : 50,000,000 Elvis Fans Can't Be Wrong (The Elvis Outtakes / The Elvis Live Show) [198- Pico Geek Studios] / The Fall : 50,000 Fall Fans Can't Be Wrong [2004 Artwork : Becky Stewart] / Lemmy, Slim Jim & Danny B. : Rock & Roll Forever [2000 Artwork : Unknown] / Rod Stewart : Body Wishes [1983 Artwork : Kosh / Ron Larson(Photo : Leon Lecash] / Sandra Weckert : 50 Sandra Weckert Fans Can't Be Wrong [2002 Artwork : Brigitte Redl Photos : Markus Brehm] / Soulwax (2 Many D.J.'s) : 50,000,000 Soulwax Fans Can't Be Wrong [2005 Artwork : Unknown]

(*right*) V/Artists : 50.000.000 Elves Fans Can't Be Wrong [2002 Artwork : John Soares] / (*above*) V/Artists : All Shook Up - A Reggae Tribute To The King [2005 Artwork : Mystery.co.uk]

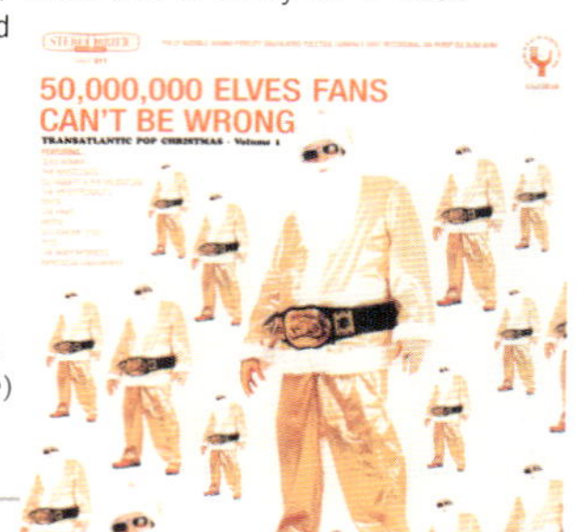

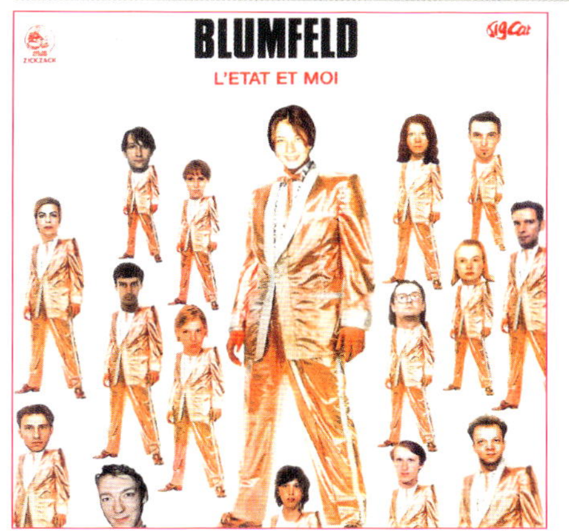
BLUMFELD
zickzack
fig Cat
L'ETAT ET MOI

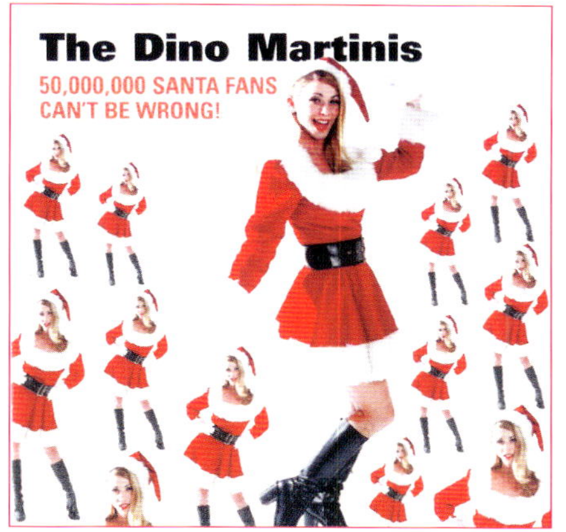
The Dino Martinis
50,000,000 SANTA FANS
CAN'T BE WRONG!

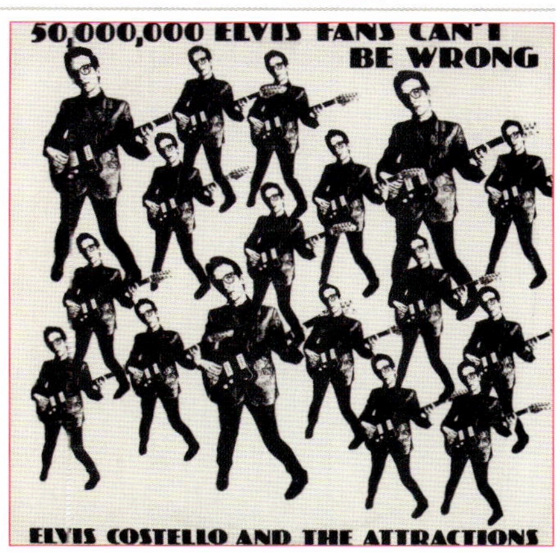
50,000,000 ELVIS FANS CAN'T
BE WRONG
ELVIS COSTELLO AND THE ATTRACTIONS

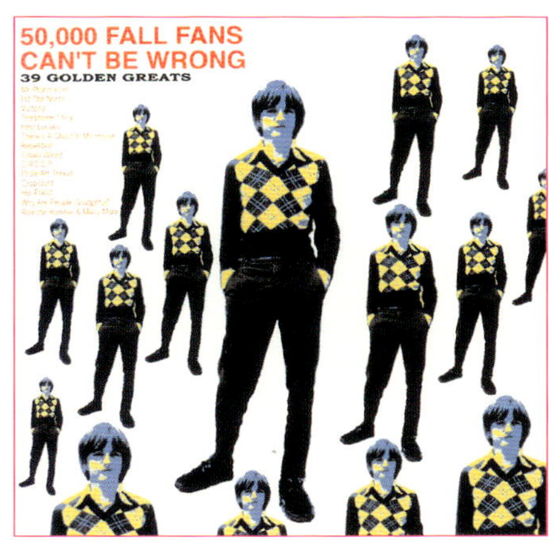
50,000 FALL FANS
CAN'T BE WRONG
39 GOLDEN GREATS

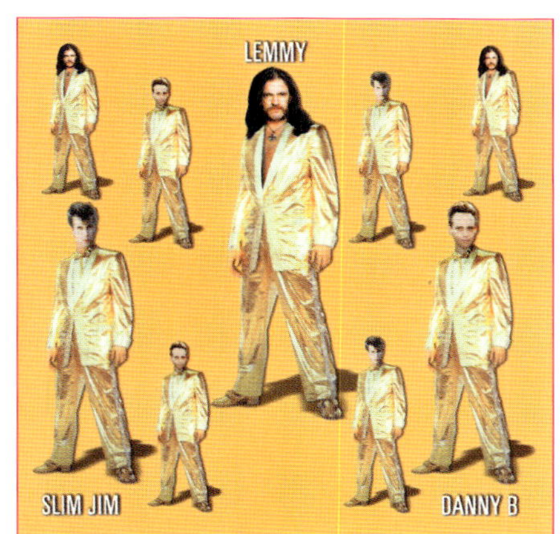
LEMMY
SLIM JIM
DANNY B

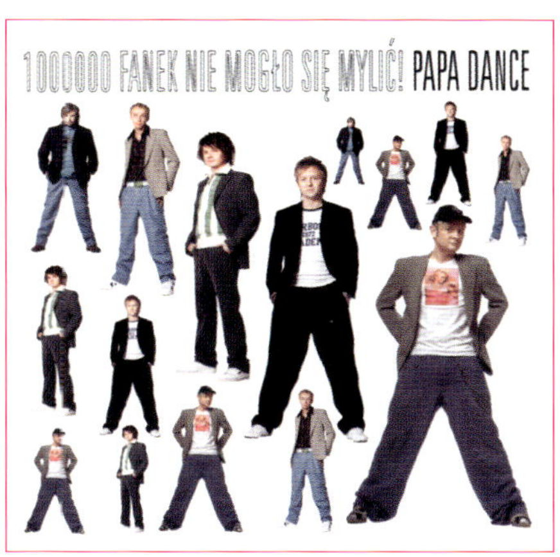
1 000000 FANEK NIE MOGŁO SIĘ MYLIĆ! PAPA DANCE

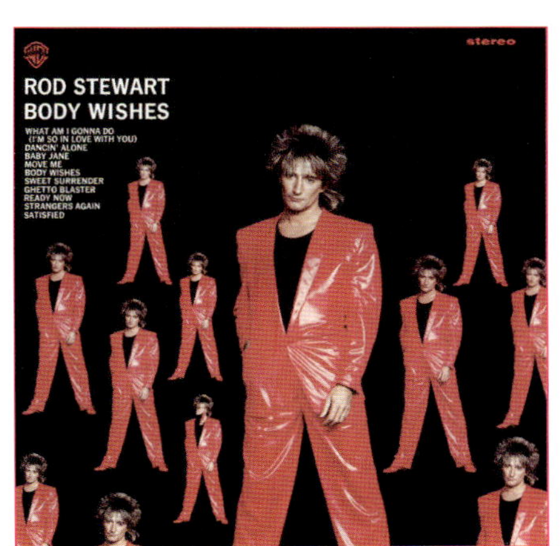
stereo
ROD STEWART
BODY WISHES
WHAT AM I GONNA DO
(I'M SO IN LOVE WITH YOU)
DANCIN' ALONE
BABY JANE
MOVE ME
BODY WISHES
SWEET SURRENDER
GHETTO BLASTER
READY NOW
STRANGERS AGAIN
SATISFIED

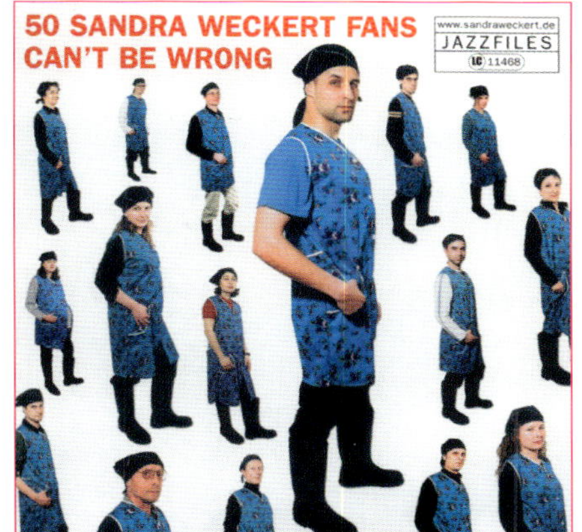
50 SANDRA WECKERT FANS
CAN'T BE WRONG
www.sandraweckert.de
JAZZFILES
LC 11468

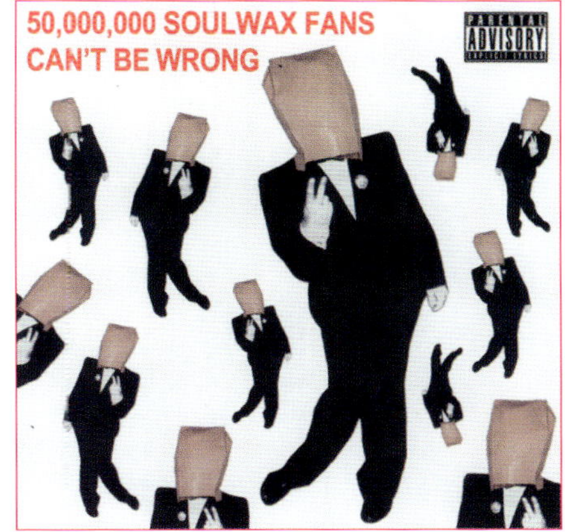
50,000,000 SOULWAX FANS
CAN'T BE WRONG
PARENTAL
ADVISORY
EXPLICIT LYRICS

Two bands take the michael out of Prince's Lovesexy cover [1988 : Paisley Park. Artwork / photo : Jean Baptiste Mondino] with Dangerous Toys going to a lot of trouble for a grim looking sleeve and Illinois punk outfit ("I saw their second drummer vomit right in the middle of a song and he never missed a beat." Midwest Punk website) Didjits Lovesicle doing a quick, lowbudget but funny knock off.

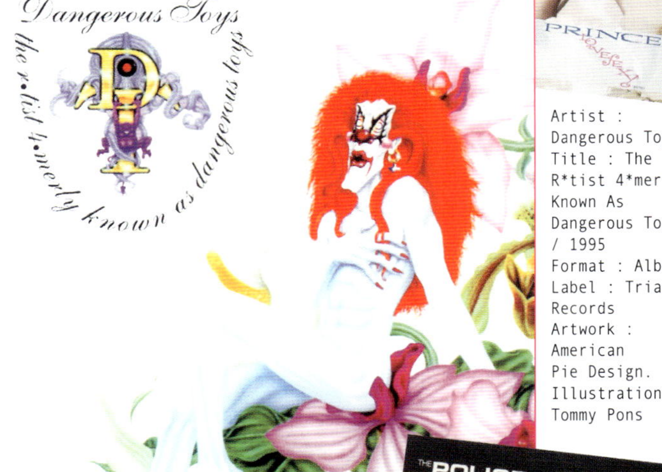

Artist :
Didjits
Lovesicle
Title :
Goodbye Mr.
Policeman + 1
[1989
Single / Touch
And Go Records
Artwork :
Unknown

Artist :
Dangerous Toys
Title : The
R*tist 4*merly
Known As
Dangerous Toys
/ 1995
Format : Album
Label : Triage
Records
Artwork :
American
Pie Design.
Illustration :
Tommy Pons

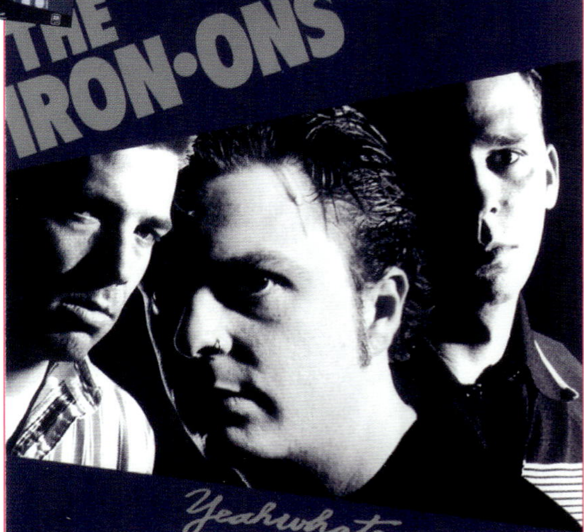

Artist : The
Iron-Ons
Title : Yeah
Whatever /
1998
Album / Vegas
Records
Artwork :
Sanford
Caswell. Photo
: Darkman /
Michael Munson
/ Ben Goetting
/ A.J. &
friends

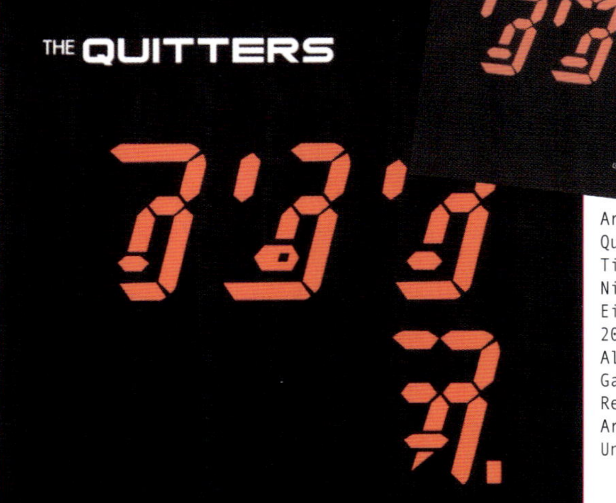

Artist : The
Quitters
Title :
Nineteen
Eighty-Two /
2006
Album /
Garage-Pop
Records
Artwork :
Unknown

Police sleeves were always well designed and executed, if a bit slick and lifeless at times, not unlike the group really. Few have bothered to copy them but Regatta De Blanc [1979 : A&M. Artwork : Michael Ross. Photo : James Wedge] and Ghost In The Machine [1981. Artwork : Jeffrey Kent Ayeroff / Mick Haggerty] have fans, though quite why anyone would want to copy the latter 25 years on I'm not sure (and should it not be Nineteen Eighty Two-oh?).

Using imagery akin to a range of supermarket own-brand products, the fifth album from Public Image Ltd. [Album. 1986 : Virgin. Artwork : Unknown] could have done with a touch of the Peter Saville's perhaps. The parody is great.

It's a different engraving and photo but S.L.A. have obviously been inspired by sixties Dutch band Q65's obscure debut LP Revolution [1966 : Decca. Artwork : Benno Petersson. Photo : Herman Baaren]

Artist : Various Artists
Title : Trousers In Action 2 / 1986
EP / Aberrant Records
Artwork : T.I.A.

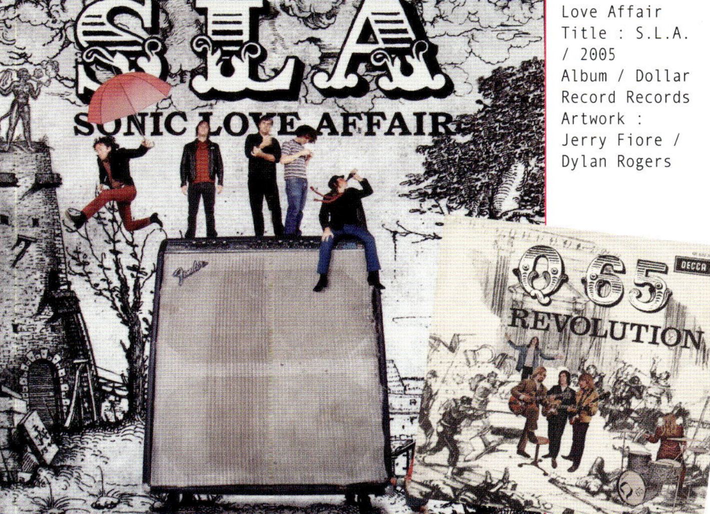

Artist : Sonic Love Affair
Title : S.L.A. / 2005
Album / Dollar Record Records
Artwork : Jerry Fiore / Dylan Rogers

Artist : Queers / Sinkhole (2 bands)
Title : Love Ain't Punk + 4 / 1995
5 track EP / Ringing Ear Records
Artwork : Unknown

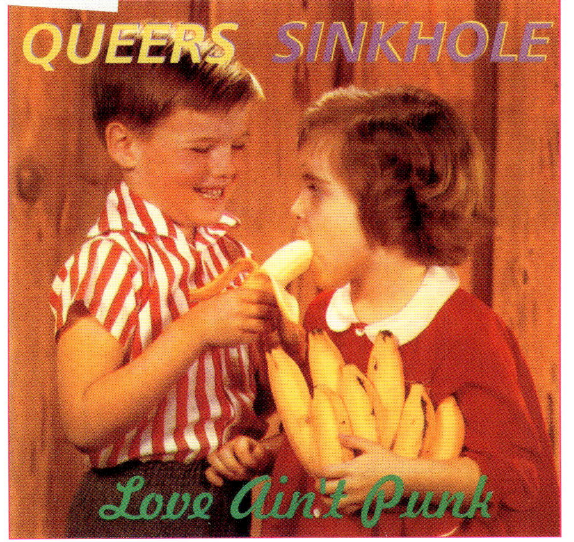

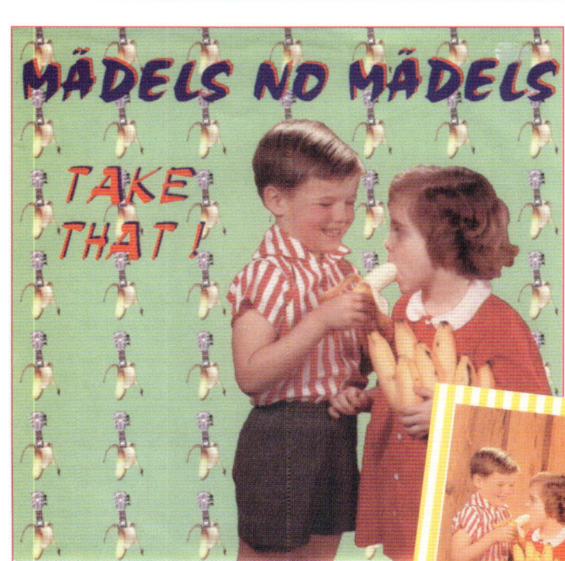

Artist : Mädels No Mädels
Title : Take That! / 1998
3 track EP / Incognito Records
Artwork : Johnny

You can see how this originally innocent image promoting your five-a-day could prove irresistable to some. The Persuaders went with it on their First Date 3P (sic) [right 1989 3 track EP. Artwork : The Persuading Sons], which has then been borrowed by two more bands

Queen's artwork hasn't been copied as much as you might expect for such a successful group, but arguably their covers weren't that great in the first place (a record label's worst nightmare, a band member who says he does design?). So we have some Japanese funsters mimicing Queen 2 (sorry II) from 1974 [EMI. Artwork : Mick Rock / Queen], Gerson's evil take on The Miracle [1989 : Parlophone. Artwork : Richard Gray

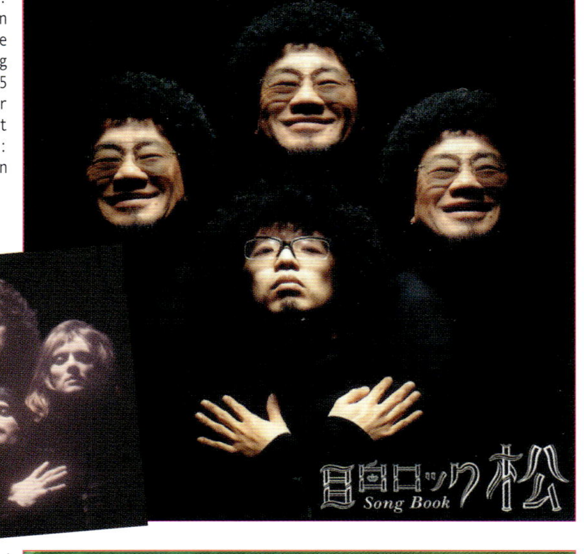

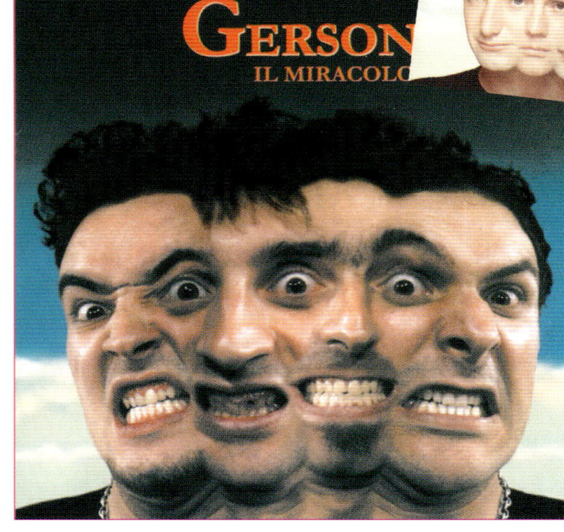

Artist :
Southern
Hurricane
Title : Song
Book / 2005
EP / Victor
Entertainment
Artwork :
Unknown

Artist :
Gerson
Title : Il
Miracolo /
2005
Album / Tube
Records
Artwork :
Unknown

Artist :
Engine
Title : Show
Me + 1 / 1998
Single / Damn
Entertainment
Artwork :
Chris Hosner

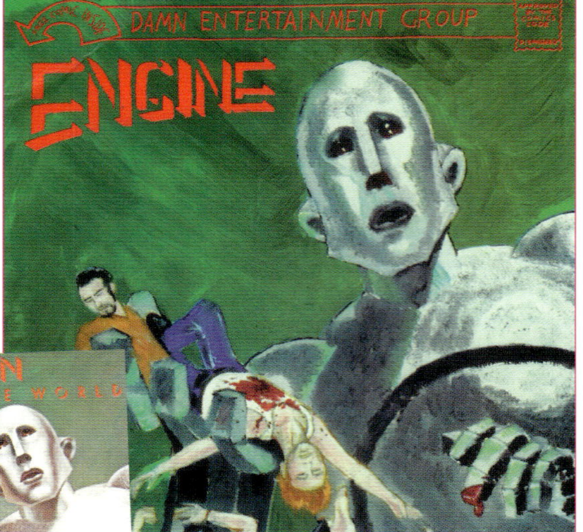

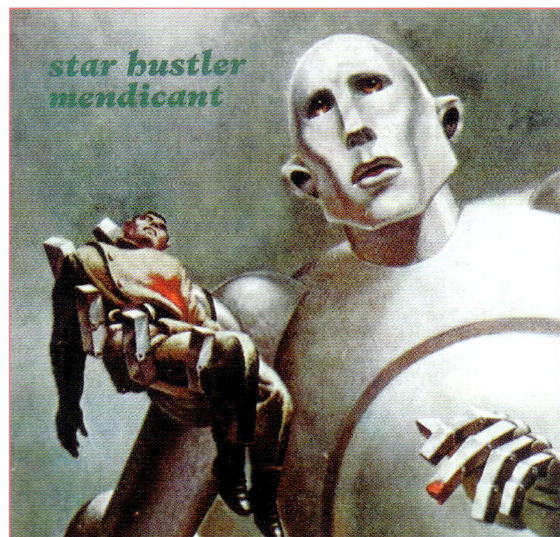

Artist : Star
Hustler
Title :
Mendicant /
1995
Album / Dirt
Records
Artwork :
Kelly Freas

/ ▼ Richard Baker. Photo : Simon Fowler] and interestingly indie rockers Star Hustler going back to the original vintage sci-fi illustration from Astounding Science Fiction (October 1953 issue) which Queen had asked artist Frank Kelly Freas to repaint for their News Of The World EMI LP in 1977.

The simple but memorable cover to Run D.M.C.'s 1985 album King Of Rock [Profile. Artwork : Andrea Klein. Photo : E.J. Camp] continues to be copied 25 years on, though few who have done so have risked obscuring quite so much of their faces.

Artist : D.J. D-Styles & D.J. Flare
Title : Pharaohs Of Funk / 1999
Album / Slit Wrist Recordings
Artwork : Unknown

Artist : Elevated Ruffians
Title : The Magnificent Soul LP / 2009
Album / Elevated Soul
Artwork : R. Alikpala

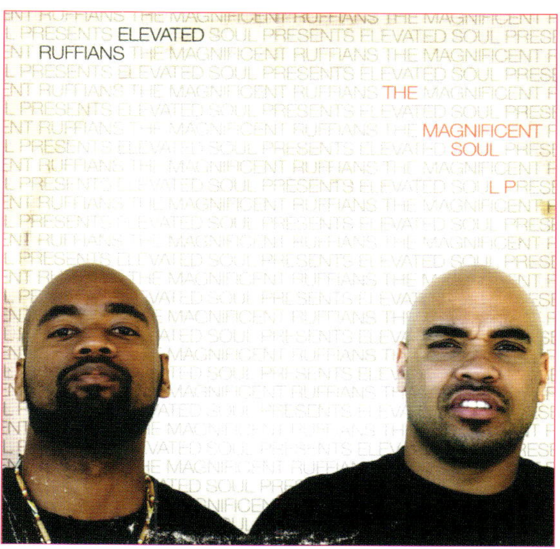

Artist : Bjørn Torske
Title : Nedi Myra
Anno : 1998
Format : Album
Label : Ferox Records
Artwork : Unknown

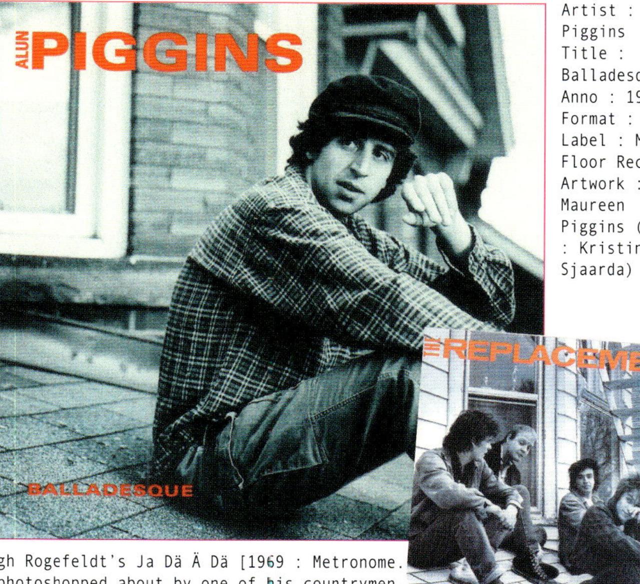

Artist : Alun Piggins
Title : Balladesque
Anno : 1999
Format : Album
Label : Moldy Floor Records
Artwork : Maureen Piggins (Photo : Kristin Sjaarda)

The obscure (to non-Scandinavians) Pugh Rogefeldt's Ja Dä Ä Dä [1969 : Metronome. Artwork : Stig Söderqvist. Photo : Lennart Wernström] album photoshopped about by one of his countrymen, while The Replacements' rooftop shot for Let It Be [1984 : Twintone / Restless Records. Artwork : Bruce C. Allen. Photo : Dan Corrigan] inspired vertigo-free Alun Piggins to do likewise.

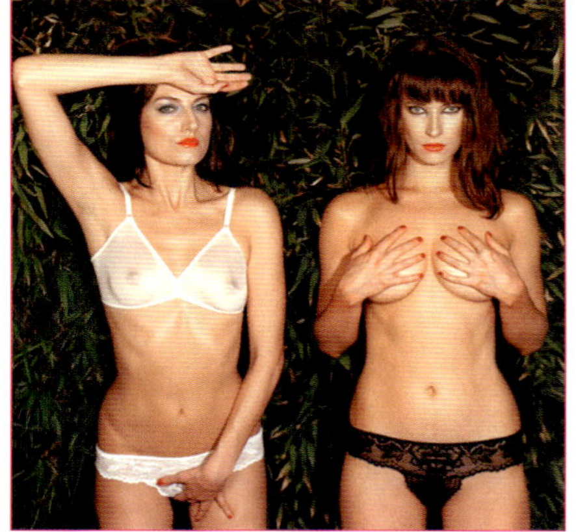

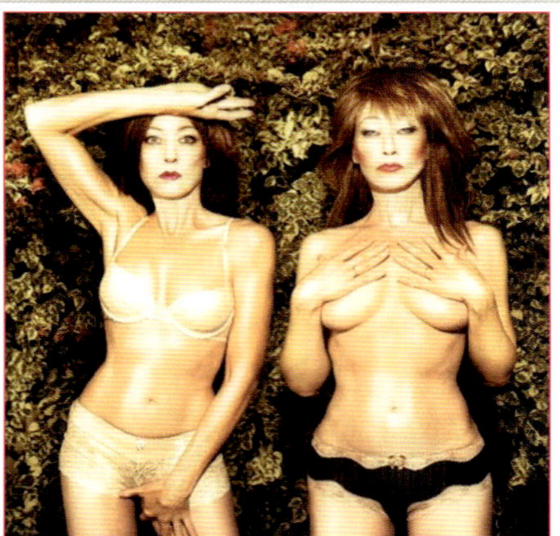

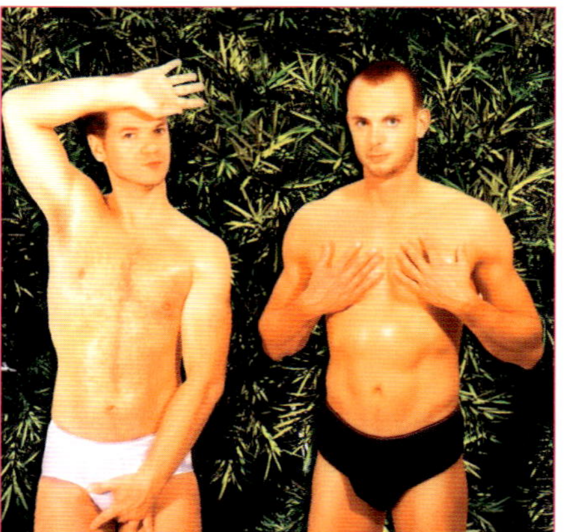

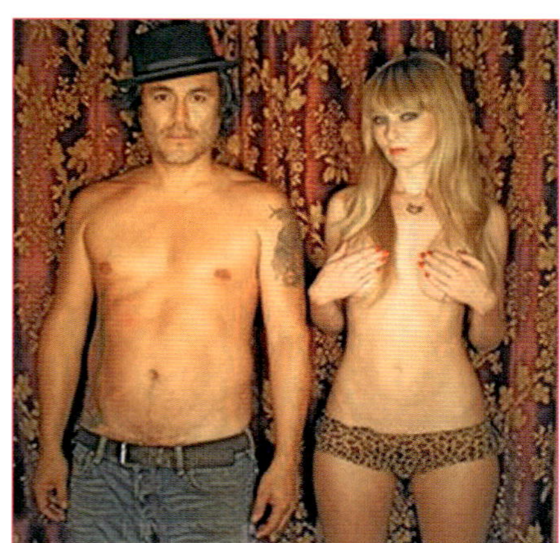

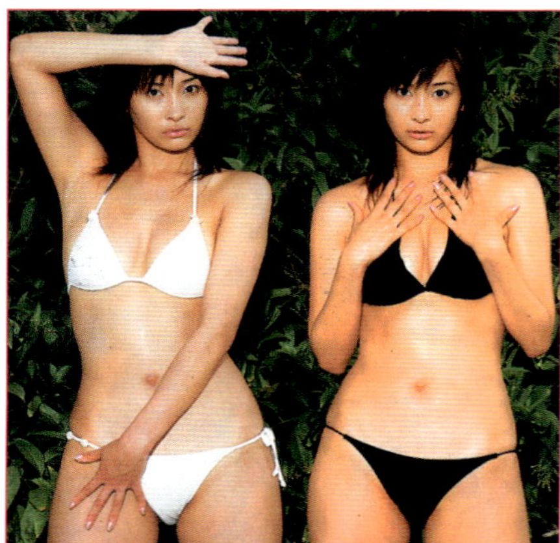

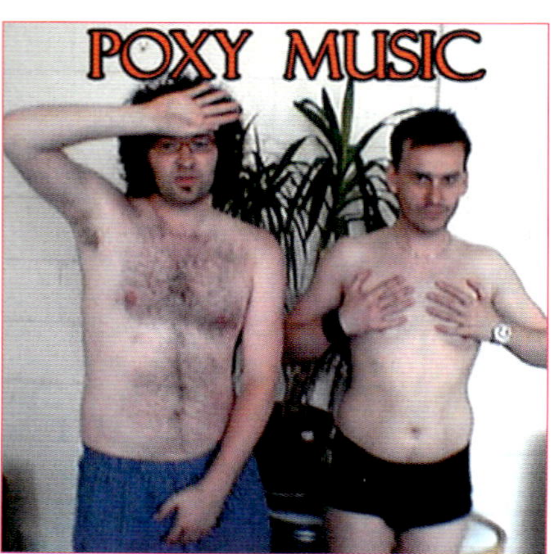

Brian Ferry reasoned pretty girls had been used to sell all other types of product, why not Roxy Music albums? The cover for their fourth (credited to Bryan Ferry and Nick DeVille, with photo by Eric Bowman), Country Life, was shot in Portugal where Ferry was working on lyrics. Country Life, a long established weekly magazine for the landed gentry, always featured a demure image of one of the daughters of the aristocracy, and Ferry liked the idea of subverting this using a more overtly soft-core image.

Cover models Eveline Grunwald and Constanze Karoli were spotted in a bar and the cover was shot in the garden at Eveline's parent's summer-house where they were staying. They hung around with Ferry and the guys for a few days, and helped translate one lyric into German for the album. Eveline went on to do cover designs for some other bands herself, including Holger Czukay.

As well as inspiring a number of sleeves, girls and boys have now begun doing their own versions of the cover shot, which are slightly off topic (but what the heck - seen here from top left). This idea originated in the art world, German artist Pia Dehne doing her version in 2008. Dehne has been interested in photographic recreations of album sleeves (Queen's Bicycle Girls, Hendrix's Electric Ladyland) and her Roxy project started out as a photographic copy of the sleeve, then developed into a series of camouflage paintings sparked by the disappearance of the cover models on the American edition of the sleeve (they first released the LP in green shrink-wrap, then used the back cover without the girls as the front). This was followed by another recreation by performance artist, musician, writer and actress Ann Magnuson (*top right*) who intended to use it for an album of 70s cover versions until she saw the Sweet Apple CD. When she posted her version on Friendface the owners of the social media site blocked access to it. The role reversal tribute shot (*left centre*) from 2005 is by German gay artist Harald Seiwert, featuring René and Rik posing, the background generated via a 3D computer modelling programme.

Hollywood-based electronic duo The Valentines (the third or fourth band with this name since the fifties) did a version (*right centre*) which they released as a promotional photograph. Then there are the amateurs; two Japanese girls making a brave effort albeit in bikinis for some reason. They're too young to have been born when the album first came out. The Poxy Music tribute was a submission to a Radio 6 Music competition for listeners to submit their own sleeve tributes.

American guitar-pop 'supergroup' Sweet Apple recreated a version for the cover of their cebut CD, while Canadian based Electro / Funk outfit Axxe issued their own tribute cover on an EP. Both came out in 2010. Unlike the original, both the Sweet Apple cover girls are topless, while on the Axxe cover they're both wearing lingerie.

Artist : Axxe
Title : Mainstream / 2010
Album / Mile End Records
Artwork : unknown

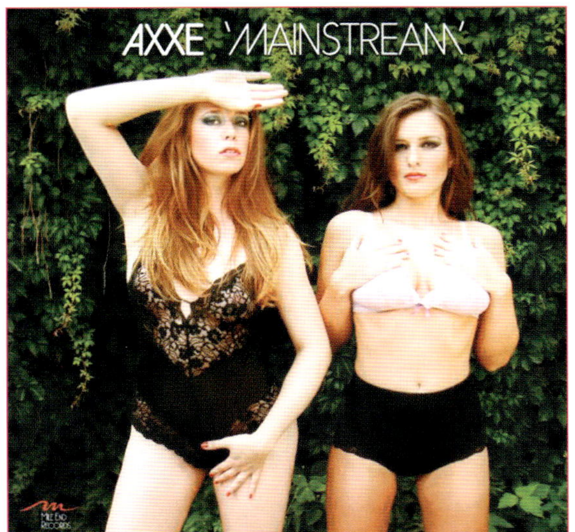

Artist : Robots In Disguice
Title : Boys / 2002
Single / Recall
Artwork : Julia East
(Photo : Sue Denim)

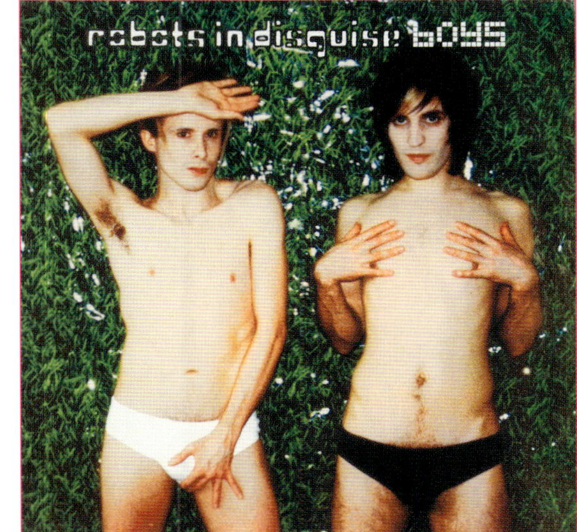

Artist : Sweet Apple
Title : Love & Desperation / 2010
Album / Tee Pee Records
Artwork : Seldon Hunt
(Photo : Jimmy Hubbard)

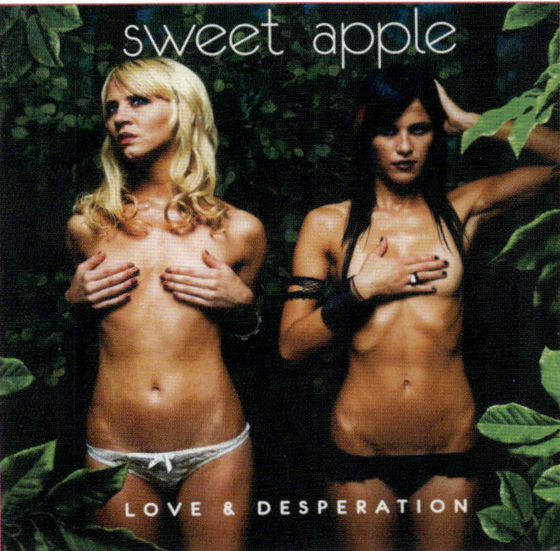

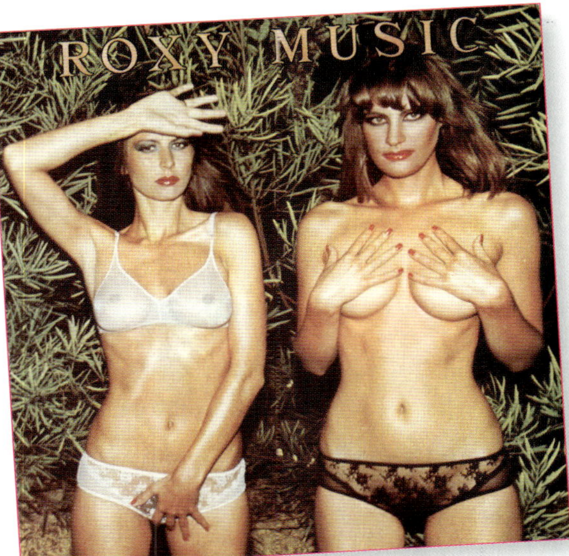

Lastly, Robots In Disguise (*top right*), a female "fashion-forward maverick electro-irdie-rock-dance duo" (according to their press release) change the cover gender. Chris Corner is wearing white, the guy on the right in black is Noel Fielding from The Mighty Boosh TV series. It was his girlfriend's band.

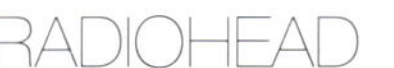

A bit of a Northern take on Radiohead's Kid A cover [2000 : EMI. Artwork : Stanley & Tchock], the dark satanic mills replacing the computer generated mountains of the original.

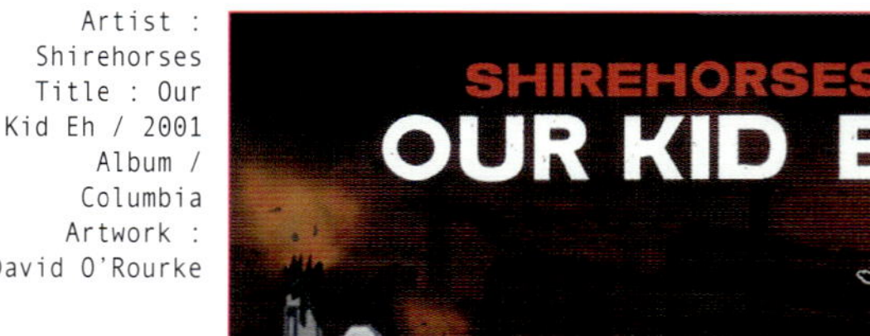

The design is very different, but the photo of Jayne Mansfield (and type off the back) has been liberated from this 1956 easy album Music For Bachelors [RCA Victor. Photo Barry Kramer].

Artist : Shirehorses
Title : Our Kid Eh / 2001
Album / Columbia
Artwork : David O'Rourke

Artist : The Insomniacs
Title : Wake Up! / 1994
Album / Estrus Superior Records
Artwork : Unknown

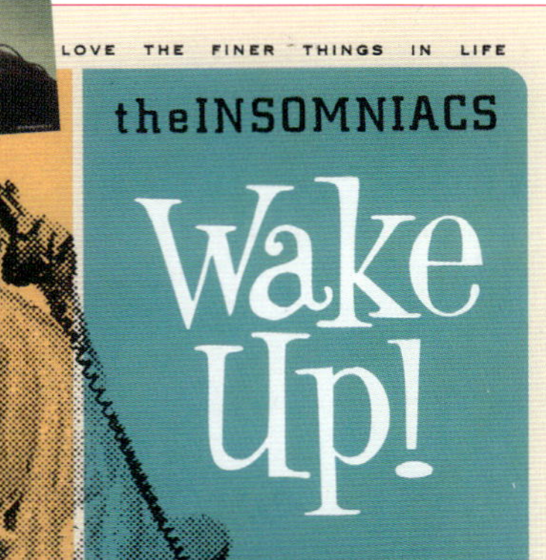

Artist : Acid Mothers Temple & The Melting Paraiso U.F.O.
Title : In C / 2002
Album / Squealer Music
Artwork : Sachiko @ Elf design Photo : Ishida Yoko

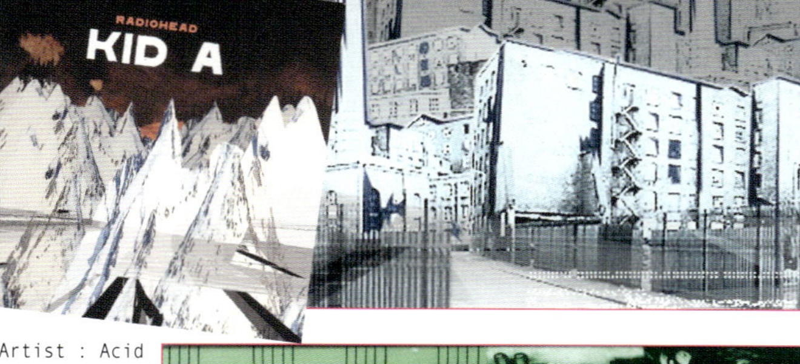

Artist : The A-Bones
Title : Here They Come! 1993
Single / Estrus Records
Artwork : Peter Ciccone Photo : Megan Dooley

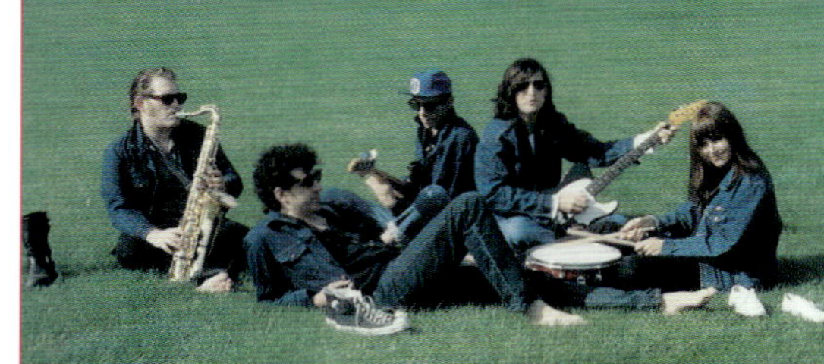

Quite a subtle bit of borrowing here, with just a section of Terry Riley's In C cover [1968 : CBS. Artwork : Unknown] sampled and rearranged by this Japanese group.

A fond tribute to one of their influences, Paul Revere & The Raiders, with the photo composition and type from Here They Come [1965 : Columbia. Photo : Frank Bez] both closely imitated.

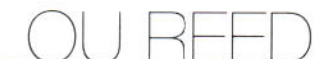

One strange piece of felt pen and ink cover art gets you another. Lou Reed's 1978 double live offering Take No Prisoners [RCA. Illustration : Brent Bailer] was never going to win any art prizes; my money would be on the Weird War tribute which is much more spirited (and a great title).

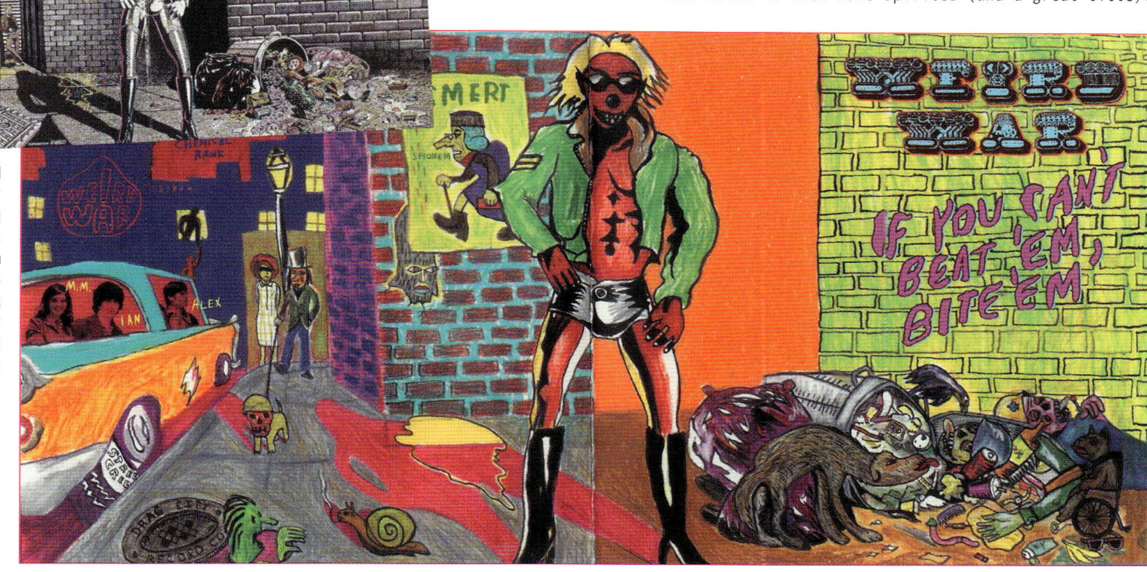

Artist : Weird War
Title : If You Can't Beat 'Em, Bite 'Em / 2004
Album / Drag City
Artwork : Name Names

Artist : Angel Corpus Christi
Title : Louie Louie / 2005
Album / Gulcher Records
Artwork : Unknown

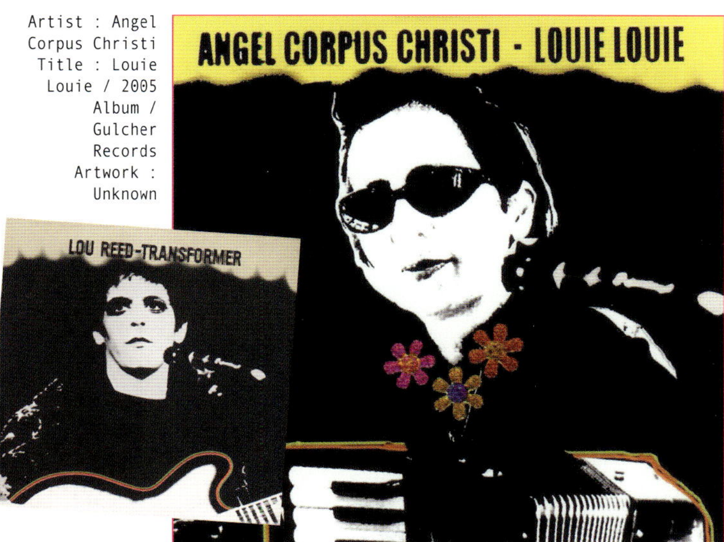

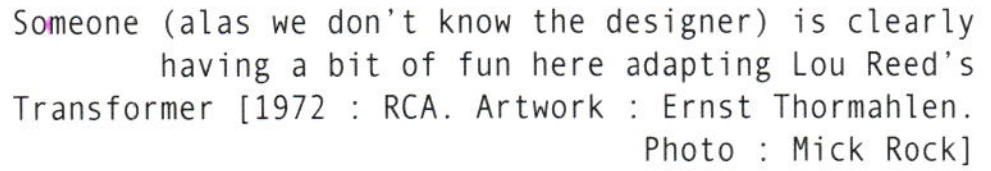

Someone (alas we don't know the designer) is clearly having a bit of fun here adapting Lou Reed's Transformer [1972 : RCA. Artwork : Ernst Thormahlen. Photo : Mick Rock]

Various Artists
Title : ...And Out Come The Teeth / 2001
Album / Fat Wreck Chords
Artwork : Unknown

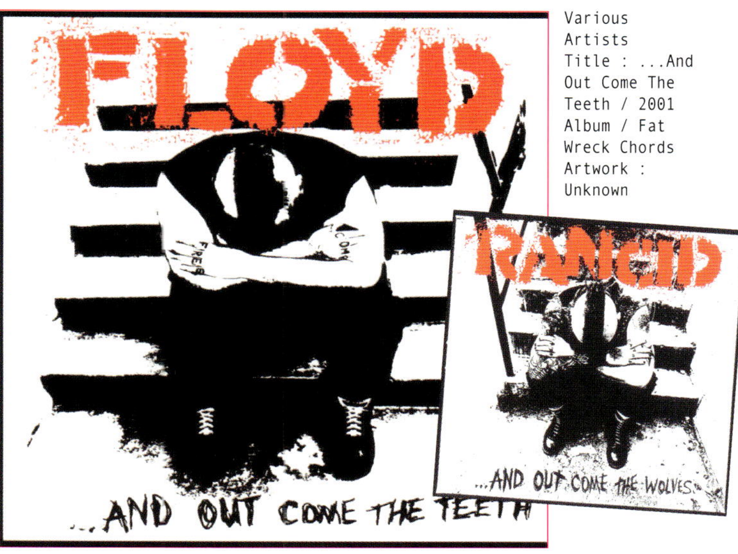

What we assume is an Oi type offering, based very closely on Rancid's And Out Come The Wolves' [1995 : Epitaph Records] mohican punk cover by Jesse Fischer.

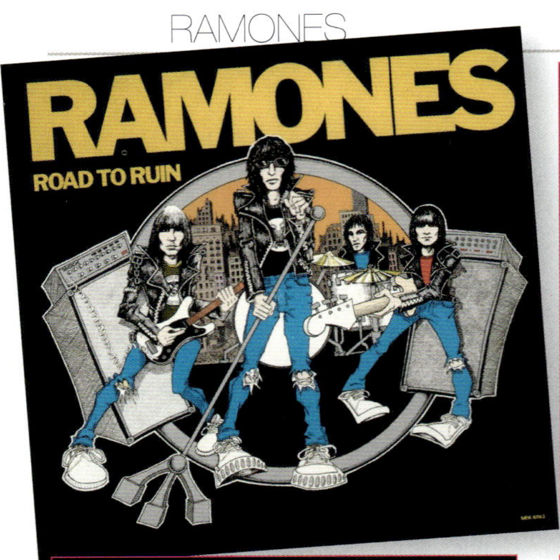
RAMONES
ROAD TO RUIN

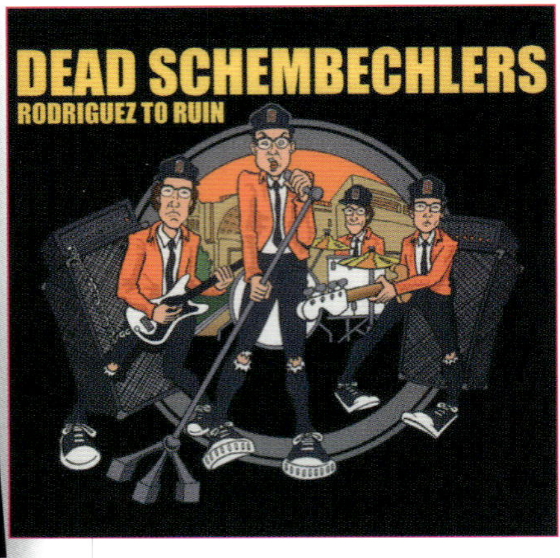
DEAD SCHEMBECHLERS
RODRIGUEZ TO RUIN

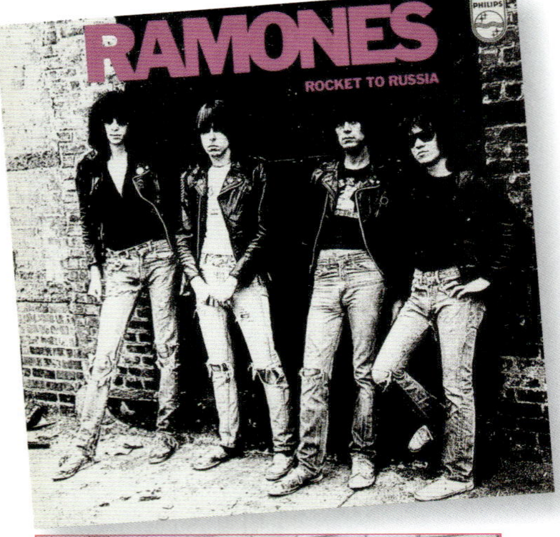
RAMONES
Rocket to Russia

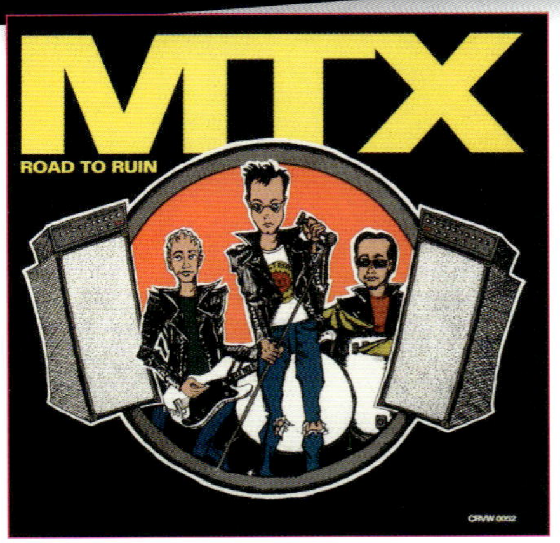
MTX
ROAD TO RUIN

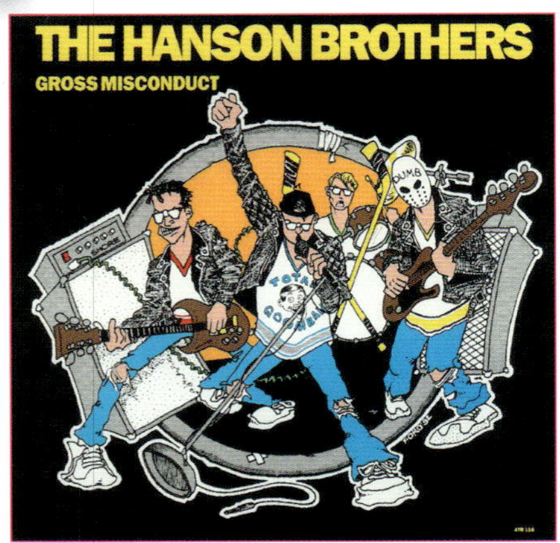
THE HANSON BROTHERS
GROSS MISCONDUCT

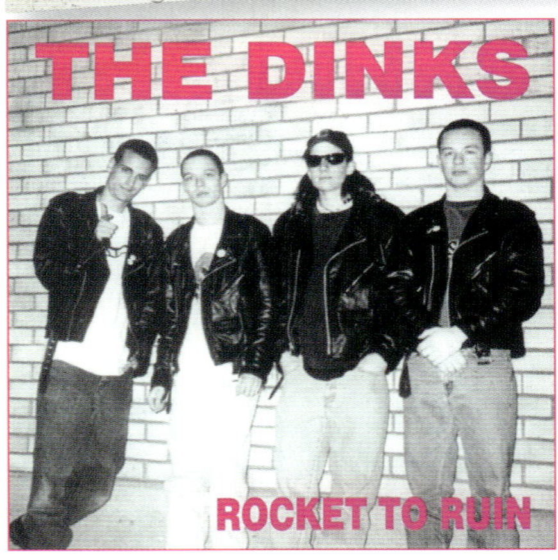
THE DINKS
ROCKET TO RUIN

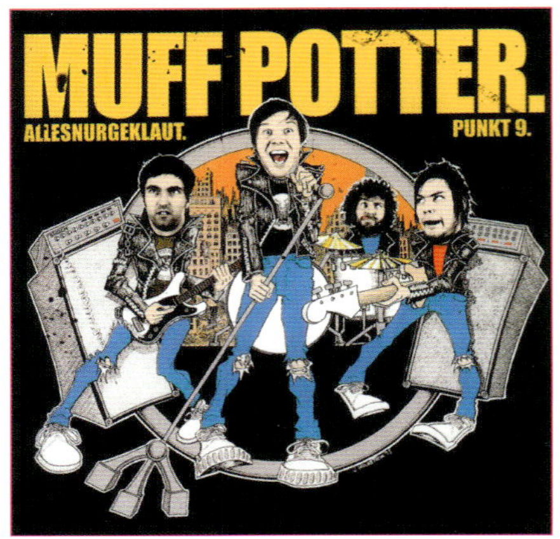
MUFF POTTER.
ALLESNURGEKLAUT.
PUNKT 9.

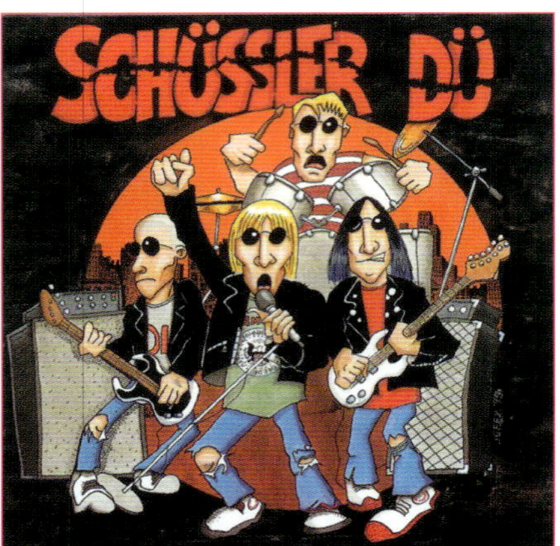
SCHÜSSLER DÜ

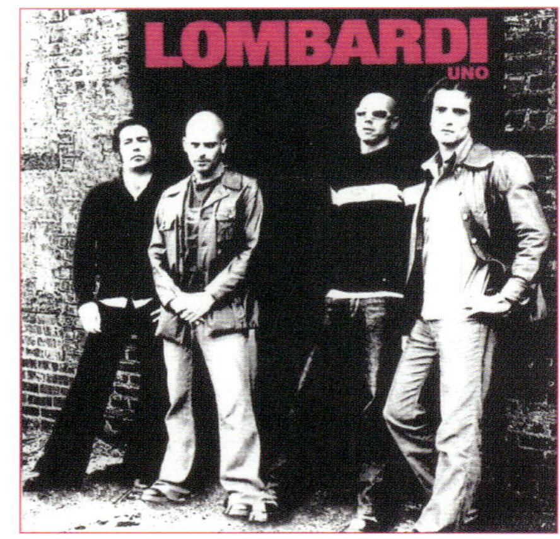
LOMBARDI
UNO

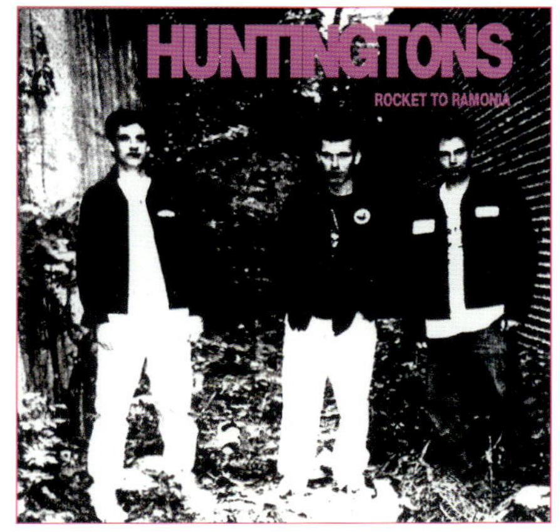

HUNTINGTONS
ROCKET TO RAMONIA

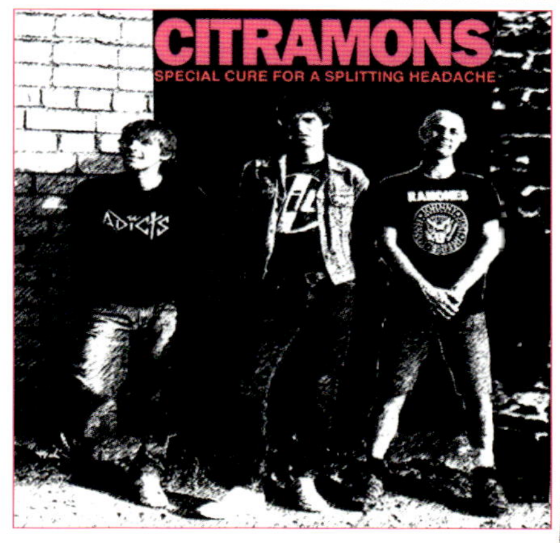

CITRAMONS
SPECIAL CURE FOR A SPLITTING HEADACHE

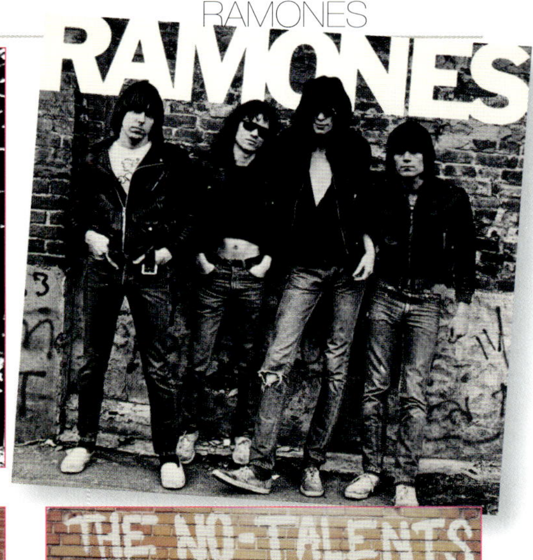

RAMONES

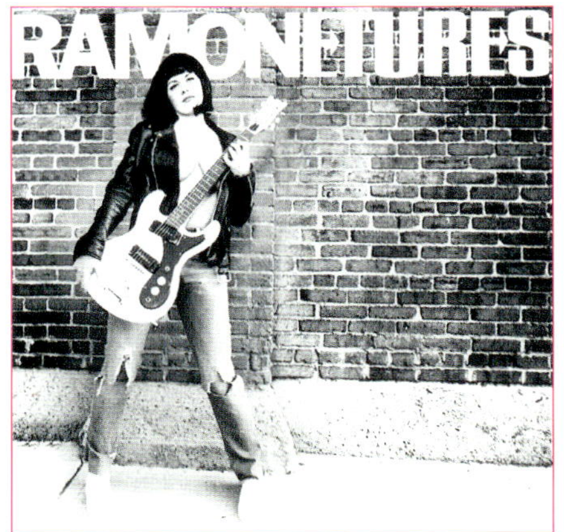

RAMONETURES

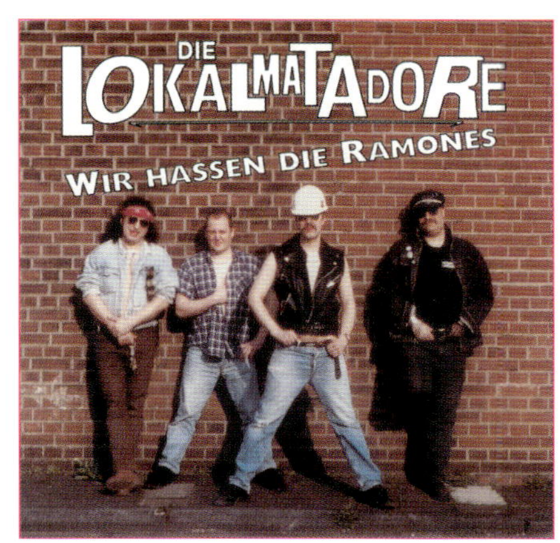

DIE LOKALMATADORE
WIR HASSEN DIE RAMONES

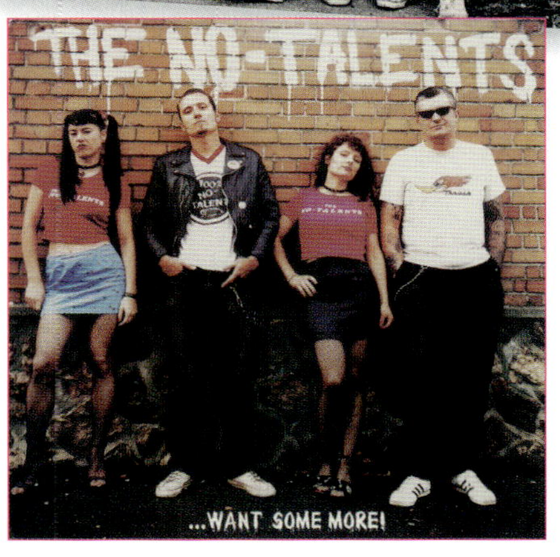

THE NO-TALENTS
...WANT SOME MORE!

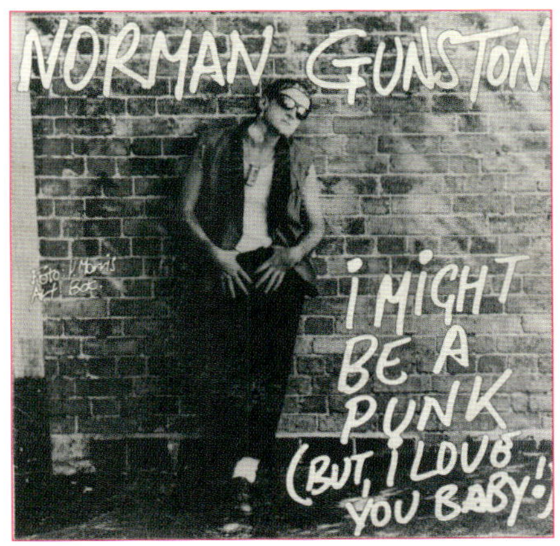

NORMAN GUNSTON
I MIGHT BE A PUNK (BUT I LOVE YOU BABY!)

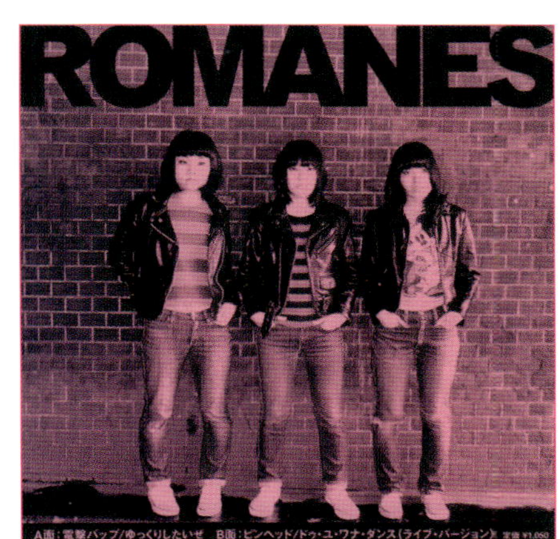

ROMANES
A面：電撃バップ／ゆっくりしたいぜ　B面：ピンヘッド／ドゥ・ユ・ワナ・ダンス（ライブ・バージョン）　定価￥1,050

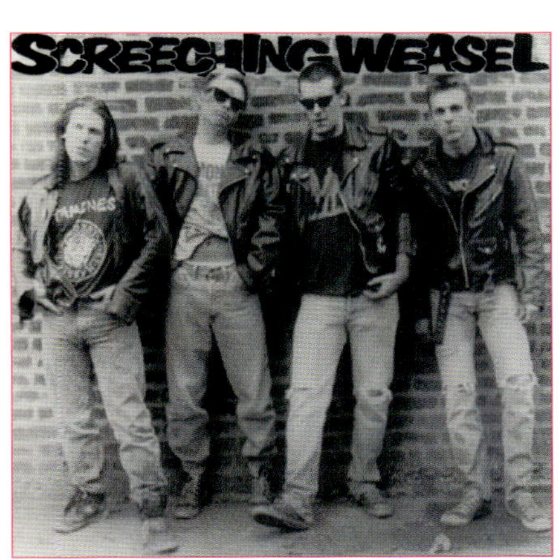

SCREECHING WEASEL

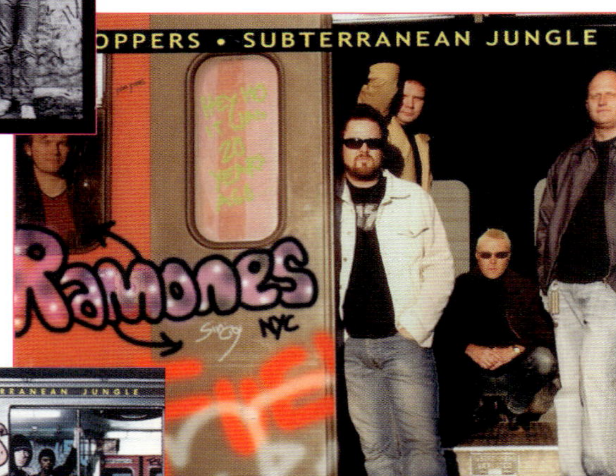

left • Various Artists : Coverones [2008. Artwork : Gakni. Photo : Roberta Bayley]

Artist : Tip Toppers
Title : Subterranean Jungle / 2004
Album / Stine
Artwork : Stine & UIF Bendiksen
Photo : Ole Kr. Trana

The Ramones' early albums influenced rock music out of all proportion to their commercial success and the band are widely credited as having launched punk music with their debut (even though regarded themselves as a rock band!), so it is no surprise their sleeves have been admired and imitated.

The high contrast image on their debut album [1976, page 113] was taken for the US music paper Punk by Roberta Bayley, and many bands have tried to recapture the look. Die Lokalmatadore rather miss the point, clad as they are in cheap fancy dress Village People outfits, the Ramonetures are clearly mixing punk with Ventures style instros and Joey would probably have towered over The Romanes!

After a colour portrait on their second album, the band returned to the bleak urban street look for their third, Rocket To Russia [1977. Artwork : John Gillespie Photo : Danny Fields, page 112 top right], inspiring The Huntingtons, who look like extras from Nosferatu (on the well known Lying Fart Records label), and Lombardi who get the pose right but the contrast button wrong.

You can see what the band were trying with the cartoon portrait which decorated the cover of the follow-up Road To Ruin [1978. Artwork : Spencer Drate / Gus MacDonald. Cartoon John Holmstrong, page 113 top left], it's just a shame they didn't get someone who was a better cartoonist. Even so, the blocky stylised drawing has again been much imitated and directly copied (by The Muff Potters).

Later less well-known albums have also proved popular, including the spray-can heavy Subterranean Jungle [1983. Artwork : Tony Wright Photo : George Du Bose, top right] which was so badly retouched (unlike the remake by The Tip Toppers) and the curiously bland cover for End Of The Century [1980. Artwork : John Gillespie / Spencer Drate Photo : Mick Rock, bottom right], aped by Boris The Sprinkler.

page 112 l-r • Dead Schembechlers : Rodriguez To Ruin [2008 Artwork : Alan MacBain / Chip Horaneck] / MTX Mr. T Experience : Road To Ruin [1998 Artwork : Bella / Gus MacDonald/ Christopher Appelgren] / The Hanson Brothers : Gross Misconduct [1992 Artwork : John Yates Illustration : Ford Pier] / The Dinks : Rocket To Ruin [1996 EP Artwork : Unknown] / Muff Potter : Allesnurgeklaut + 1 [2005 Single Artwork : Matthias Kampmann / Aku] / Schüssler Dü : Schüssler Dü [1996 Artwork : Unknown] / Lombardi : Uno (Inside) [2002 Artwork : Rafa Sañudo Photo : Jose Luis Santalla] /

page 113 l-r • Huntingtons : Rocket To Ramonia [1996 Artwork : Huntingtons Photo : Jolene Bianco] / Citramons (+ 1) : Special Cure For A Splitting Headache [2010 Single Artwork : Pat Fear] / Ramonetures : Ramonetures [2000 Artwork : Toby Tilley] / Die Lokalmatadore : Wir Hassen Die Ramones + 3 [2001 EP Artwork : Unknown] / The No-Talents : ...Want Some More [1999 Artwork : No-Talents Photo : Mad] / Norman Gunston : I Might Be A Punk + 1 [1977 Artwork : Bdc Photo : P. Morris] / Romanes : Romanes [2007 Artwork : Unknown] / Screeching Weasel : Ramones [1992 Artwork Photo : Kim Denk] /

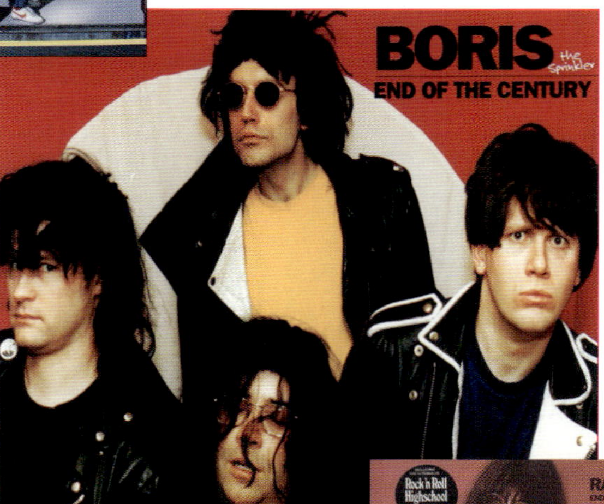

Artist : Boris The Sprinkler
Title : End Of The Century / 1996
Album / Clearview Records
Artwork : Unknown

Hard to remember (or realise - if you're younger) how much trouble Andy Warhcl stirred up with the cover shot of a bloke with a semi for The Rolling Stones' Sticky Fingers LP back in 1971 [Design : Craig Braun], a photograph which has been a template for a number of sleeves since (none of which managed to incorporate a working zip as the original had, which is just as well given how many copies it damaged).

Artist : Bracket
Title : Stinky Fingers / 1994
Single / Fat Wreck Records
Artwork : Tom Bejgrowicz
Photo : Troy Hahn

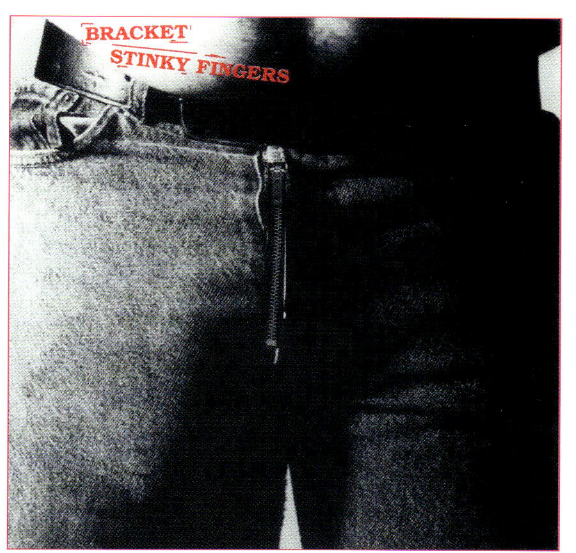

Artist : Brother To Brother
Title : Heart Of Stone / 1994
Album / Teichiku Records
Artwork : DeVarte Gaye ALCi Fantasia

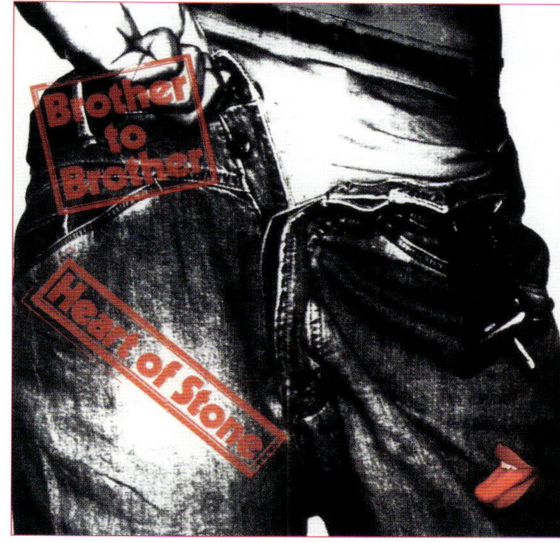

Artist : The Farel Gott
Title : Mess Tour Sessions / 2006
EP / Kokaina Project
Artwork : Kokaina Project / Serwin

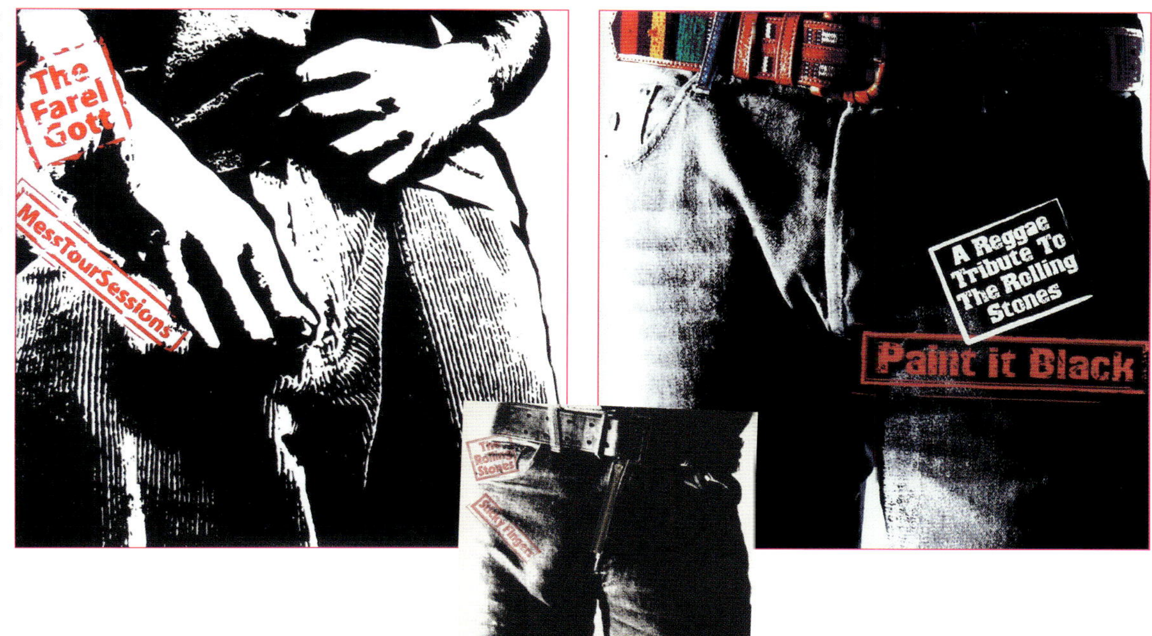

Artist : Various Artists
Title : Paint It Black - A Reggae Tribute To The Rolling Stones / 2002
Album / Eurotrend
Artwork : Unknown

The Rolling Stones' Some Girls cover [1978. Artwork : Peter Corriston] is a beaut, and has sparked some interesting variations (The League Bowlers is particularly clever), though none have the die-cut sleeve and pull out bag of the original I notice. The Bidochons are a French rock parody outfit (see also under Sex Pistols) who have copied loads of sleeves. They must be good, Yoko Ono sued them over a version of Hey Jude...

Artist : The League Bowlers
Title : Some Balls / 2003
Album / B Minus Records
Artwork : Unknown

Artist : Lyres
Title : Some Lyres / 1994
Album / Taang Records
Artwork : Curtis W. Casella

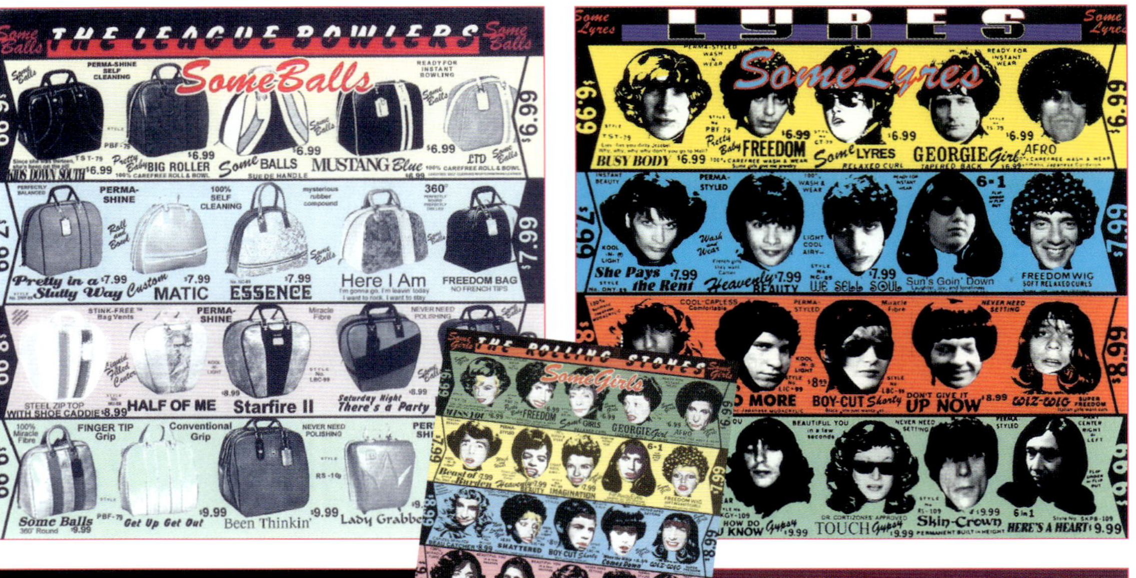

Artist : Rock City Morgue
Title : Some Ghouls / 2002
Format : Album Label : Antidote Records
Artwork : Sean Yseult (Photos : Christy Kane)

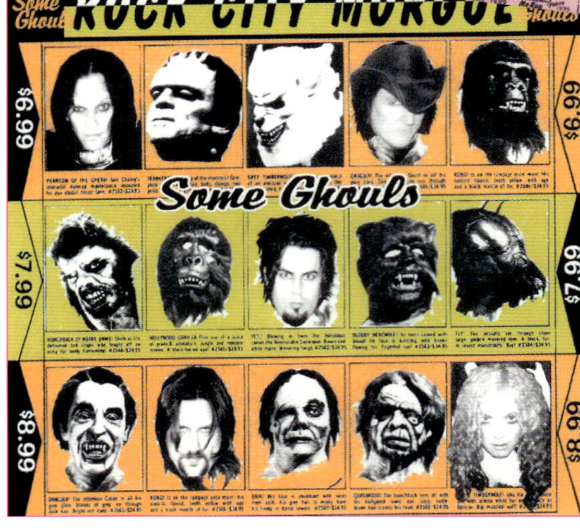

Artist : The Rolling Bidochons
Title : Sales Gueules / 1990
Album / Mantra Records
Artwork : Unknown [inset : Get Off Of St. Cloud, a single from LP]

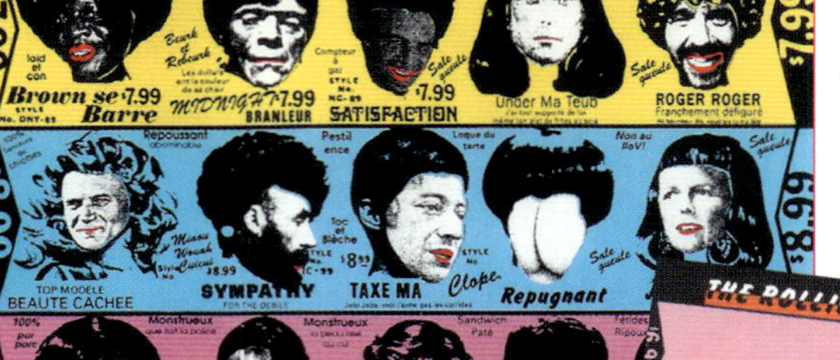

Exile On Main Street's vintage documentary image of novelty act promotiona. photographs is another of the band's best [1972 : Rolling Stones Records. Artwork : John Van Hamersveld / Norman Seeff. Photo : Robert Frank, 1950], helped by the punky handwritten titles. The photo has been copied and imitated on a number of covers. Jacknife and the V/Artists CD just copy it (albeit with a slight addition to the latter), while Urban Dogs and Pussy Galore have made their own montages up and the sleeves work better for it.

Artist : Jackknife
Title : San Francisco Beauty Queen / 1992
EP / Sympathy For The Record Industry
Artwork : Unknown

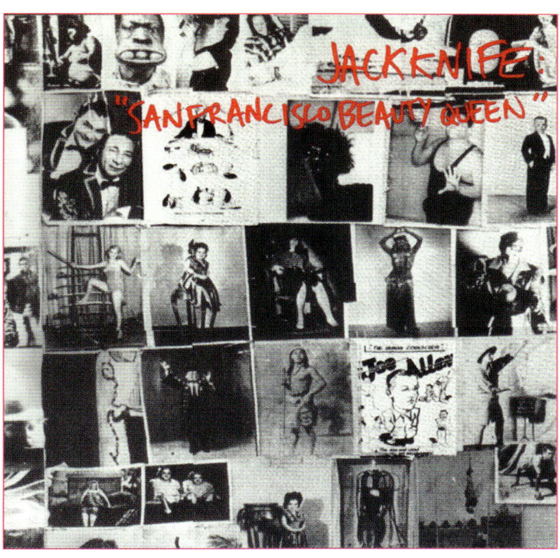

Artist : Various Artists
Title : Exile On Cameron Harper Street / 1996
Album / Ear Mouse Records
Artwork : R; Kent Steiner III

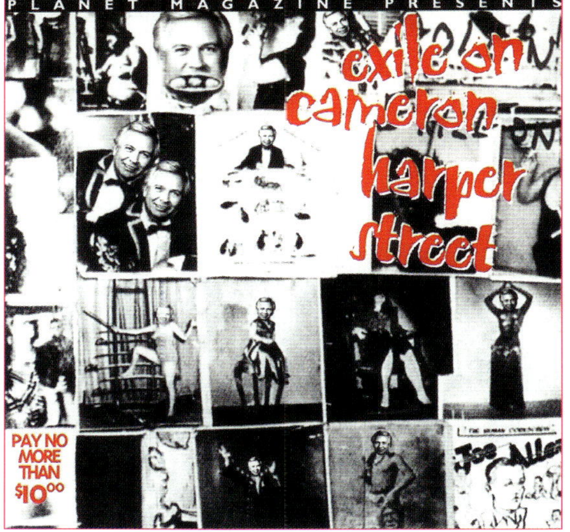

Artist : Pussy Galore
Title : Exile On Main St. / 1986
Album / Shore Records
Artwork : Rick Hall

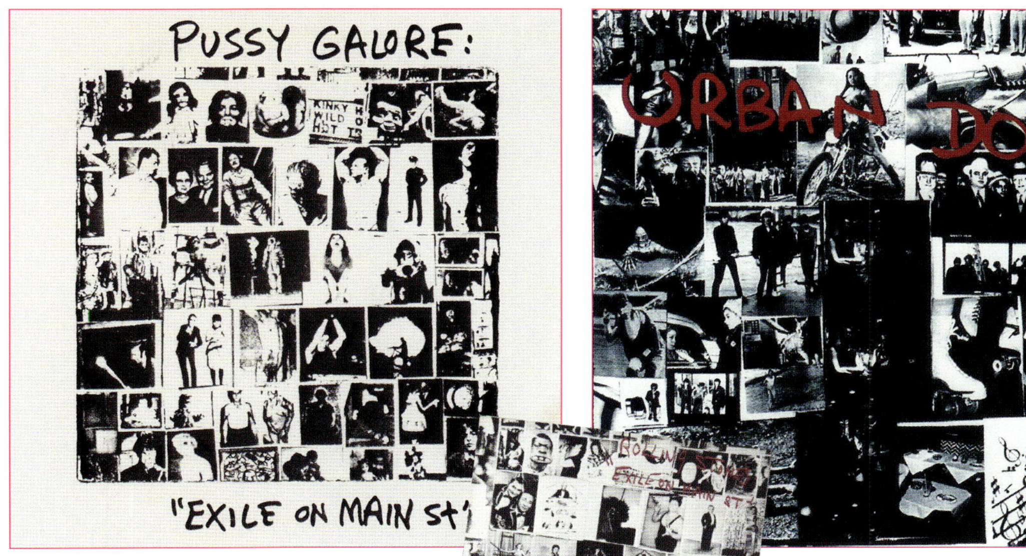

Artist : Urban Dogs
Title : Urban Dogs / 1993
Album / Cleopatra - Jungle Records
Artwork : Unknown

Posing in front of the stars & stripes was hardly a new idea (the Patton film poster?) but thanks as much to it being such a massive selling album as anything, Annie Leibovitz's shot for Bruce Springsteen's Born In The U.S.A. [1984. Artwork : Andrea Klein] has provided inspiration for a dozen or more covers; here are four of the 'best', from the alien on the v/a collection to the hairy backside of Herodes Falk.

Artist : Herodes Falk
Title : Born In Drammen
Anno : 1985
Format :
Album Label : Garbage
Artwork : Unknown

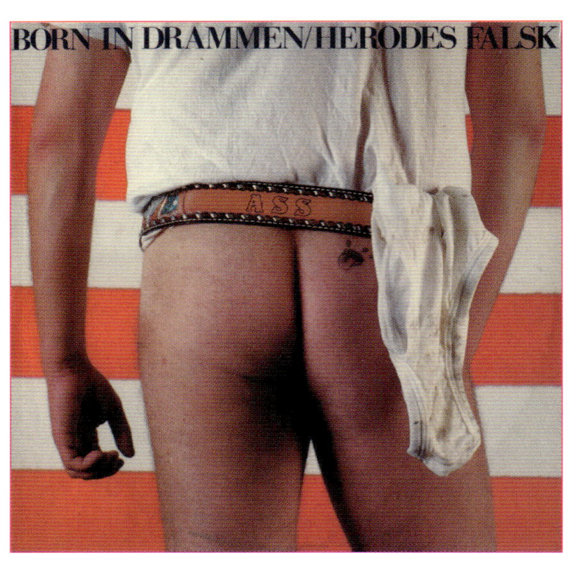

Artist : John Oswald
Title : Plunderphoinic Plexure / 1993
Album / Avant - Disc Union
Artwork : John Oswald / Lisa Wells

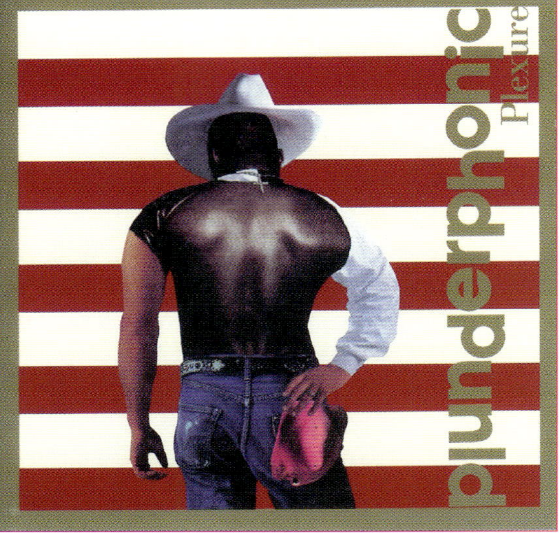

Artist : Sleepy Sleepers
Title : Born In The S.A.V.O.
Anno : 1985
Format : Album
Label : AMT Records
Artwork : Unknown

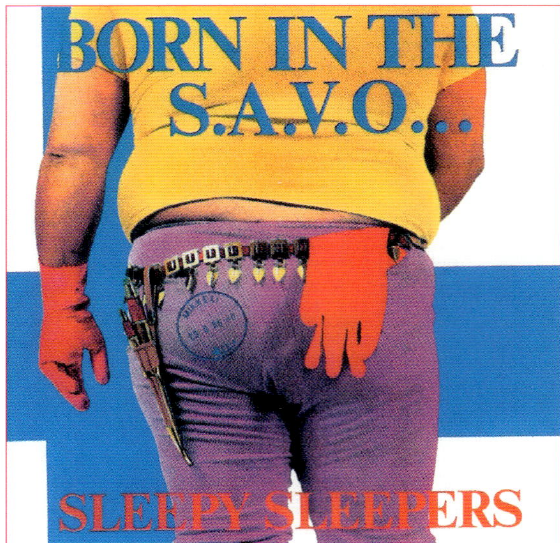

Artist : Various Artists
Title : Made In The U.S.A. - WEBN Album Project 9 / 1986
Album / Brute Force
Artwork : Tom Owens / David Montondo & Advergraphics (Photo : Trevor Hart)

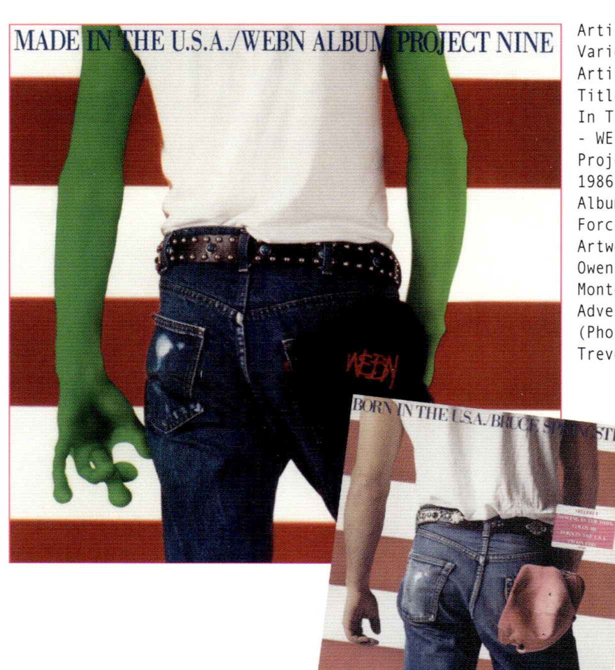

Artist : Bobby Valare
Title : Out To Lunch / 1982
Album / Tostada Records
Artwork : Richard Eissler Photography

Artist : Dion
Title : Rock 'N' Roll Christmas / 1993
Album / The Right Stuff
Artwork : Marlene Bergman Photo : Sandy Levy

Artist : Mai Kuraki
Title : Stand Up + 3 / 2001
EP / Giza
Artwork : Unknown

Artist : Sesame Street
Title : Born To Add / 1983
Album / Sesame Street
Photo : John E. Barrett

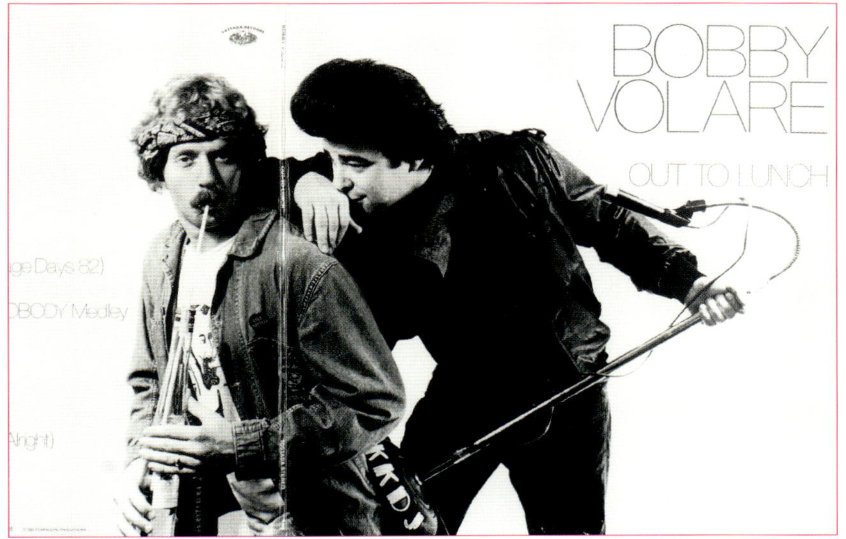

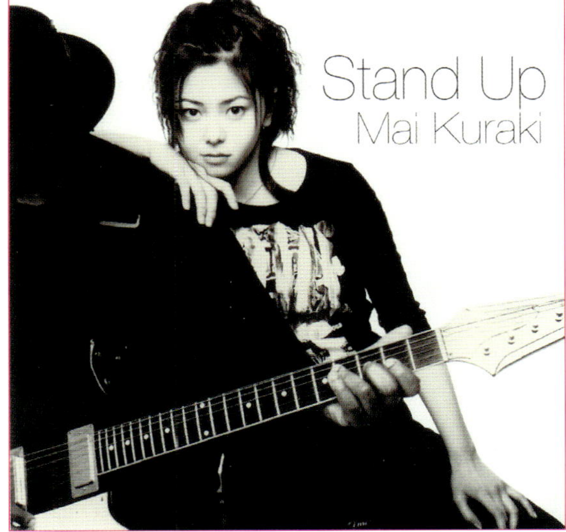

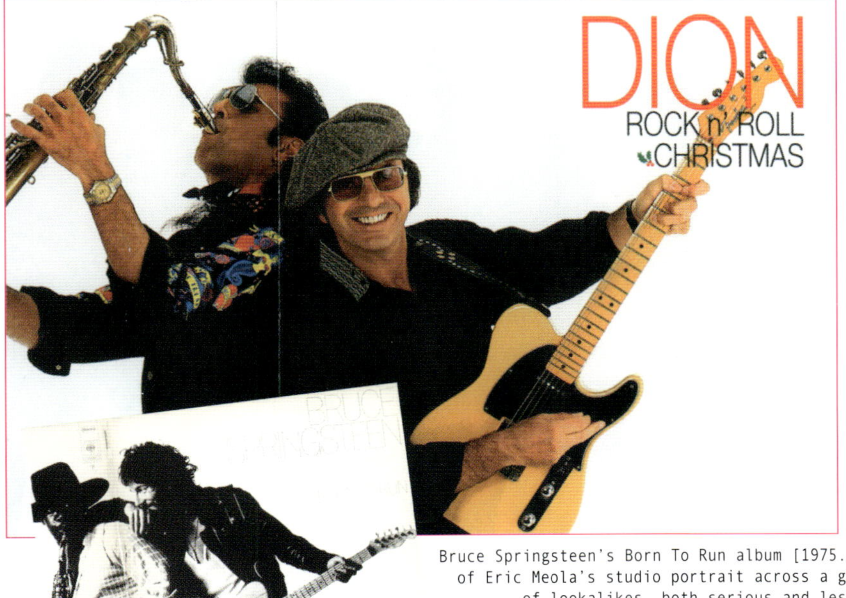

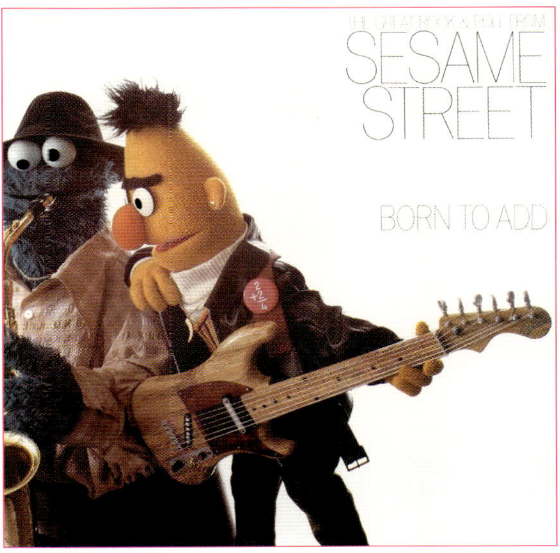

Bruce Springsteen's Born To Run album [1975. Artwork : John Berg / Andy Engel] makes great use of Eric Meola's studio portrait across a gatefold cover, an image which has spawned a number of lookalikes, both serious and less so, with a lucky few getting their own fold out.

The last two of the Springsteen imitators... Frank Turner having the same cover artist (the busy Mitch Clem) as his label mates Jr. Juggernaut on the right.

Cat Stevens himself drew the cover to his third LP Mona Bone Jakon [1970 : Island], the bin becoming a beer can on LA based alt-power-trio Jr. Juggernaut's version.

Artist : Cheap Trick
Title : Next Position Please / 1983
Album / Epic
Artwork : John Berg Photo : David Kennedy

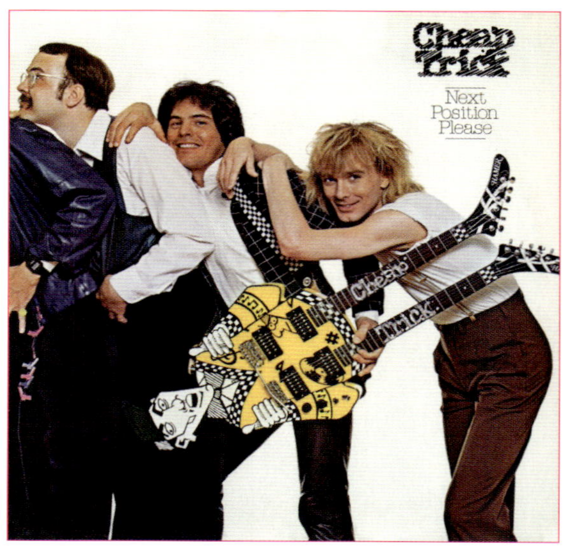

Artist : Jr. Juggernaut + 1
Title : Trouble + 1 / 2009
Single / Suburban Home Records
Artwork : Mitch Clem

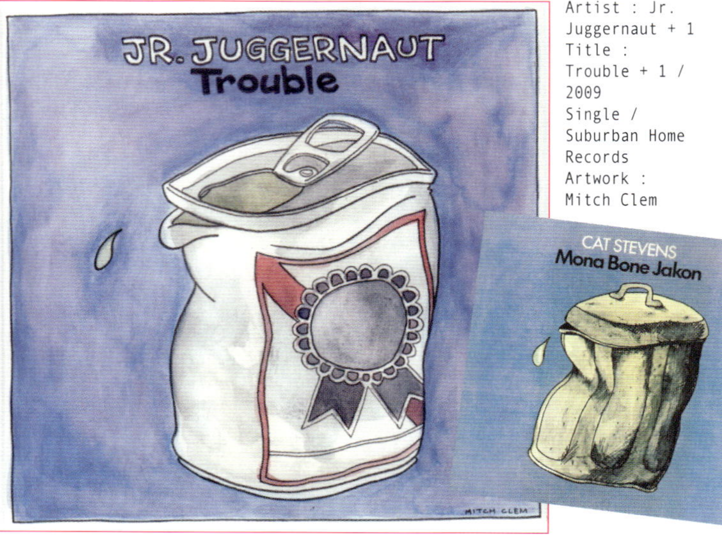

Artist : Frank Turner +1
Title : Thunder Road + 1 / 2008
Single / Suburban Home Records
Artwork : Mitch Clem

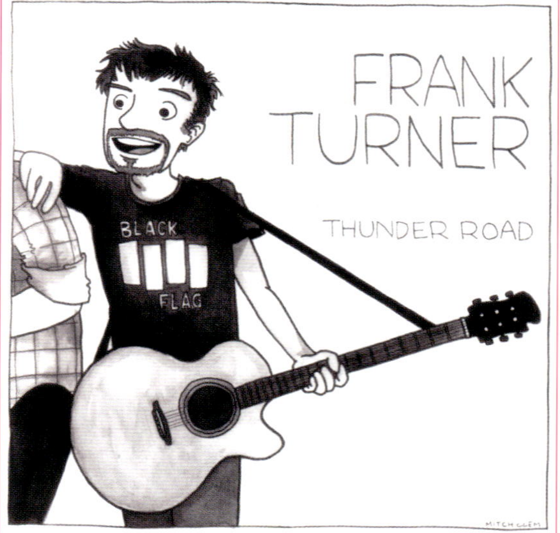

Artist : Terre Thaemlitz
Title : Replicas Rubato / 1999
Album / Mille Plateaux
Artwork : Terre Thaemlitz

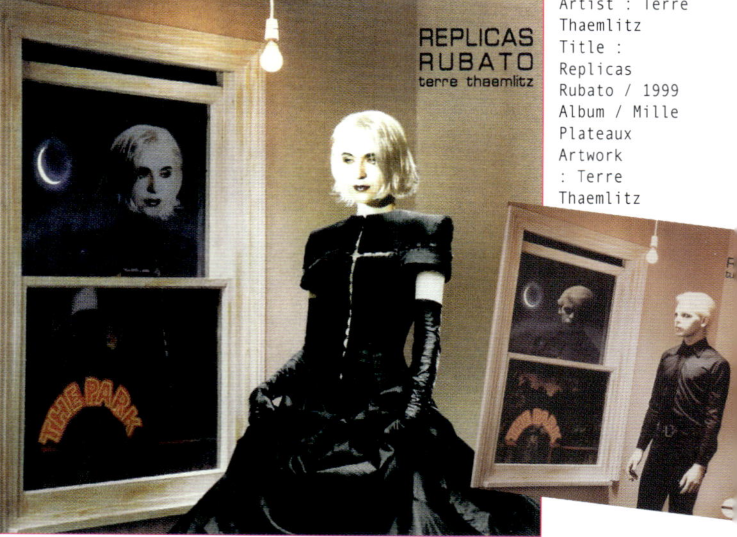

Terre Thaemlitz doesn't so much as copy Tubeway Army's Replicas LP [1979 : Beggars Banquet. Artwork : Malti Kidia. Photo : Geoff Howes] as simply photomontage a new cover model onto the original cover. The music is solo piano interpretations of the tracks.

Rod Stewart' early solo albums often had interesting sleeves, but as his audience changed so did the covers, with Blondes Have More Fun [1978. Artwork : John Cabalco / Rod Stewart. Photo : Claude Mougin. Lettering : Mike Manoogian] being typically obvious. It was nicely parodied by the female models turned singers Blonde On Blonde. Front and back!

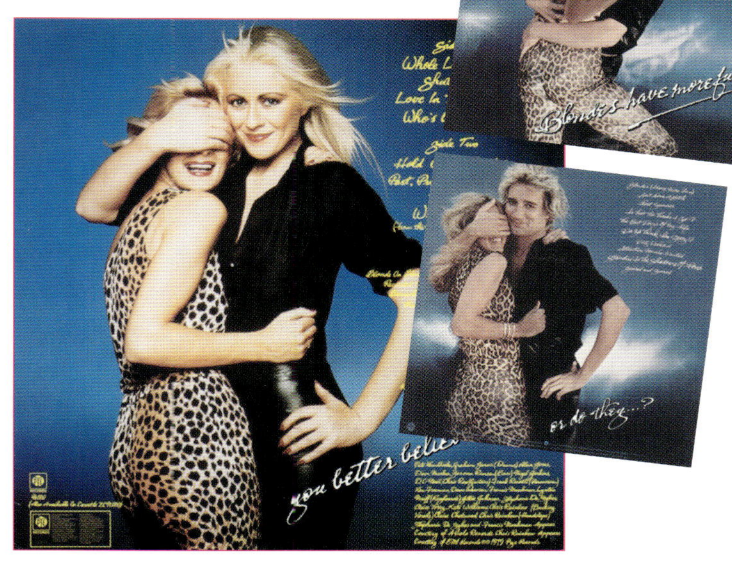

Artist : Blonde On Blonde
Title : And How! / 1979
Album / Pye Records
Artwork : Design Machine
(Photo : Brian Aris)

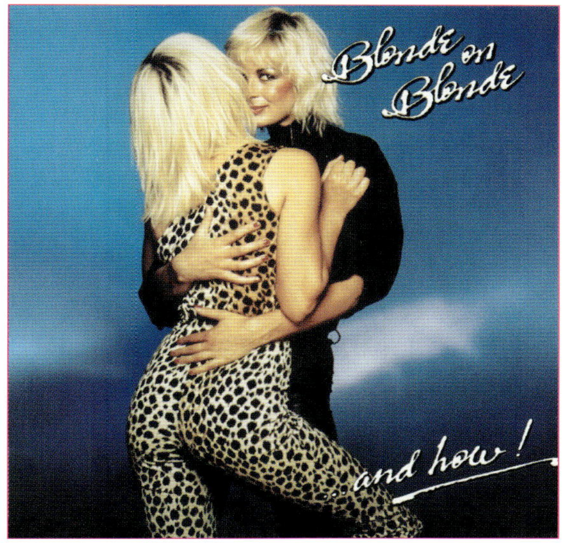

Artist : Claw Hammer
Title : Scuze The Excursion / 1996
Album / Sympathy For The Record Industry
Artwork : Unknown

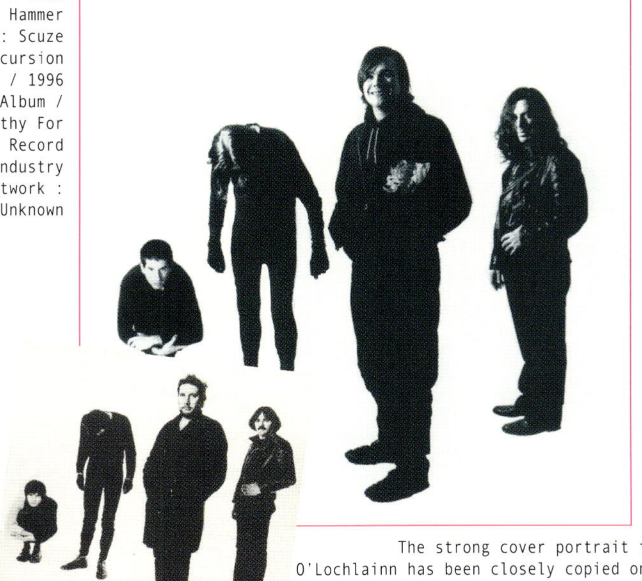

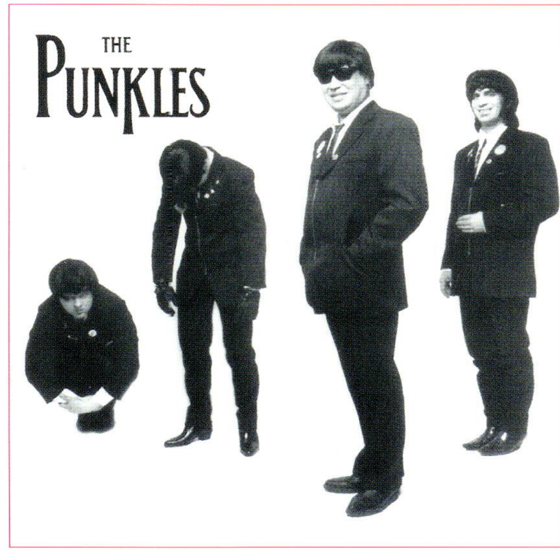

Artist : The Punkles
Title : The Punkles / 1998
Album / Wolverine Records
Artwork : Trash-Art International
(Photo : Zimmermann & Schoenrock)

The strong cover portrait for The Stranglers' Black And White album [1978 : EMI] by Ruan O'Lochlainn has been closely copied on a couple of sleeves, with The Funkles also seemingly tipping their hat at The Beatles logo as well - or was it The Rutles?

The illustration and lettering to Sonic Youth's Goo cover [1990 : DGC. Artwork : Kevin Reagan / Raymond Pettibon], their first for a major label, continues to resonate - three great versions here, and I saw it borrowed to extol the virtues of living in a local suburb on a t-shirt only a few months back. The original cover illustration was based on a photo of Moors Murders witnesses taken during the infamous trial.

Artist : Pechsaftha
Title : Dick In Frisco / 2007
CD / Tumble Weed Records
Artwork : Martin Büsser

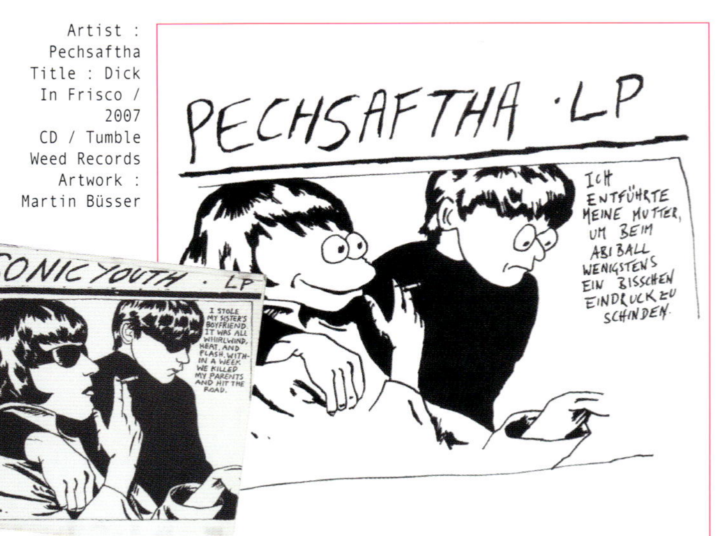

Artist : Prisonshake
Title : Spoo + 3 / 1991
EP / Estrus Records
Artwork : Unknown

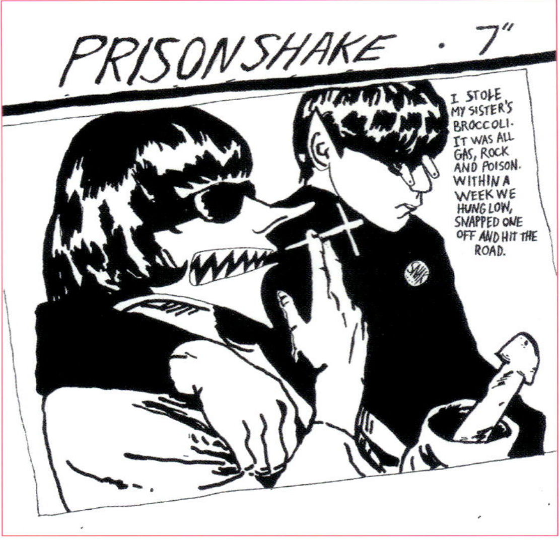

Artist : The Twilight Sad
Title : Killed My Parents And Hit The Road / 2008
Album / Fatcat Records
Artwork : Unknown

Artist : The Diff'rent Strokes
Title : This Isn't It / 2001
EP / Guided Missile Recordings
Artwork : Brian MacDougalll (Photo : Elly Tharby)

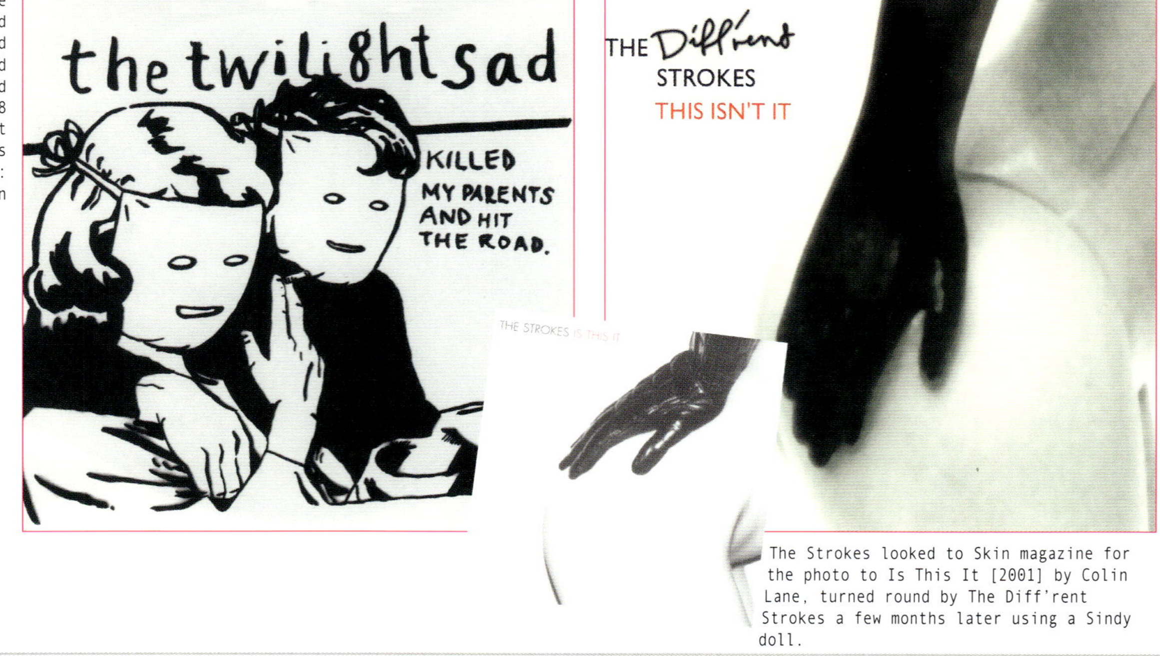

The Strokes looked to Skin magazine for the photo to Is This It [2001] by Colin Lane, turned round by The Diff'rent Strokes a few months later using a Sindy doll.

Frank Sinatra used a number of good illustrators for his fifties albums, but In The Wee Small Hours [1955 : Capitol] was one of the less convincing examples (it is thought to be by Alex Steinweiss of all people, the inventor of the album sleeve as we know it, but very unlike his regular graphic look). This hasn't stopped people copying the moody cover, with a lacklustre painting for Nilsson and a rather more sinister take from New Bomb Turks.

Artist : New Bomb Turks + 1
Title : In The Wee Small Hours : 1993
Single : Bag Of Hammers
Artwork : Unknown

Artist : Harry Nilsson
Title : A Touch More Of Schmilsson In The Night : 1988
Album : RCA
Artwork : Rob Burt (Painting : Steve Russell)

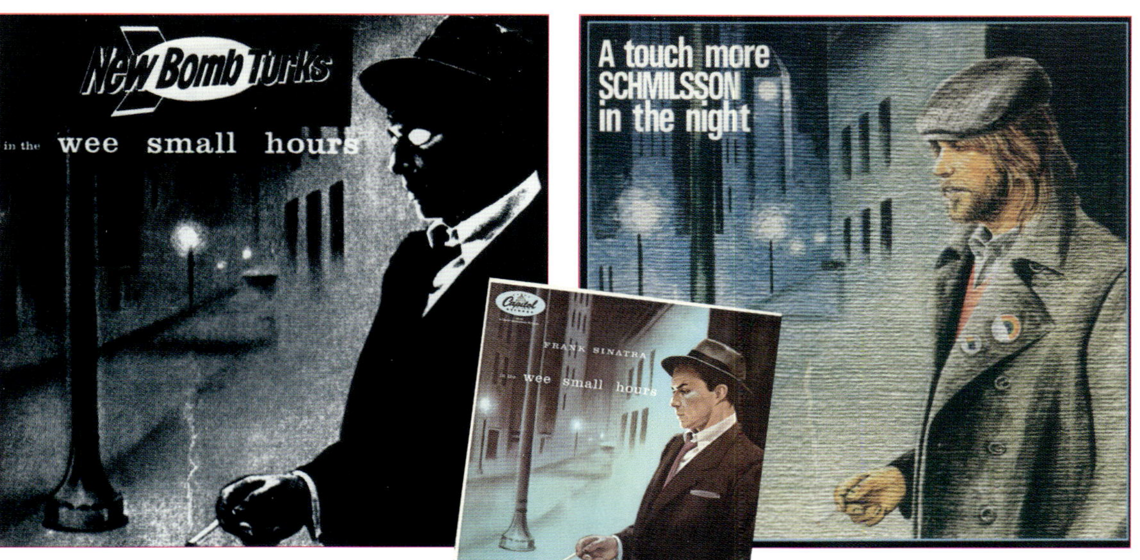

Artist : Die Lokalmatadore
Title : Ein Leben Für Die Ärmsten : 1990
Album : Teenage Rebel Records
Artwork : Dieter Gloede / Gerd Meißner

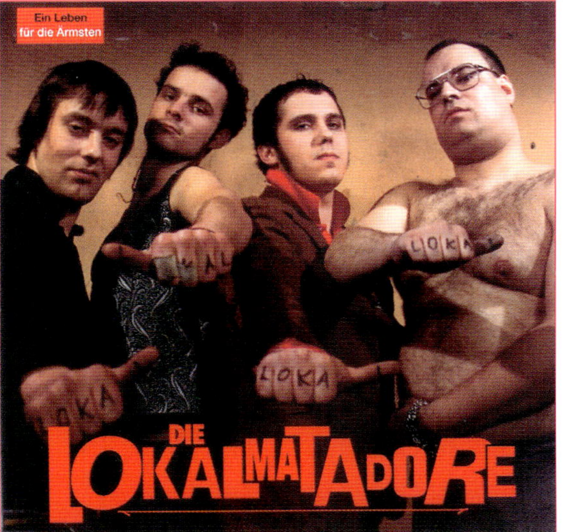

Artist : Armitage Shanks
Title : Urinal Heap: 2004
Album : Damaged Good Records
Artwork /

Photo : Alison Wonderland

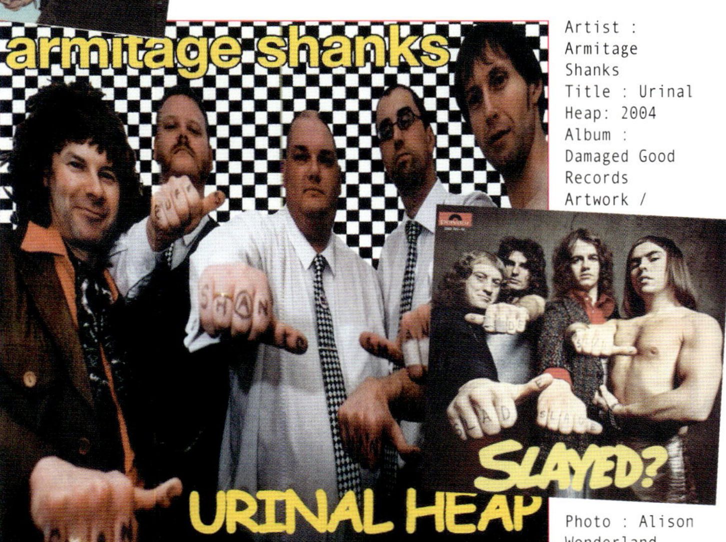

Slade's metamorphosis from skinheads to glam bovver boys was well captured by Gered Mankowitz on their 1972 Polydor LP Slayed? cover portrait which has inspired trouble makers since, including perhaps one of the worst title puns of all time from Armitage Shanks (the best thing about their cover being the name of the photographer!).

The striking cover for The Sensational Alex Harvey Band's 1973 opus Next [Vertigo. Artwork : Dave Field] provides a clear template for these two later sleeves. If either had a fraction of the live entertainment value of SAHB then they would have done well. Novelty "bubblegum-punk" Seattle band The Squirrels had an amazingly long career on stage and disc mashing up all sorts of covers long before the trend became popular.

Artist : The Squirrels
Title : What Gives ?
Anno : 1990
Format : Album
Label : Popllama Products
Artwork : Unknown

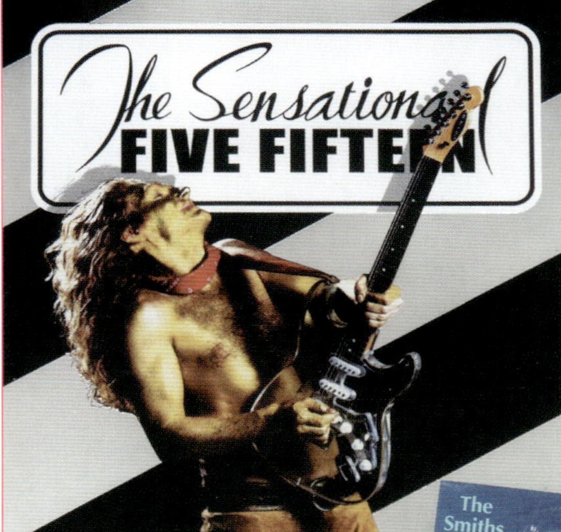

Artist : Five Fifteen
Title : The Sensational Five Fifteen
Anno : 2003
Format : Album
Label : Sweden Rock Records
Artwork : Wasel Arar (Photo : Mikael Kapplar)

Artist : The Pines
Title : Milk Bar / 2000 EP / Annika
Artwork : Unknown

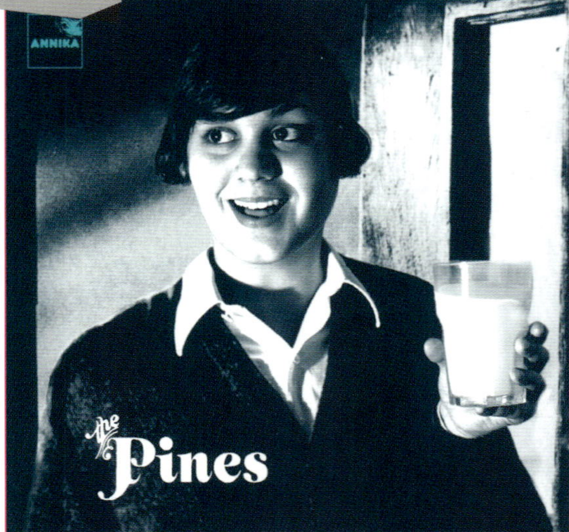

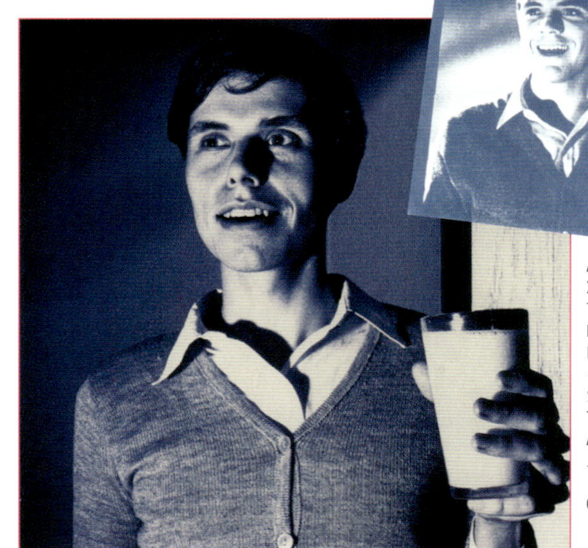

Artist : Xiu Xiu
Title : I Am Hated For Loving + 1 / ---- Single / Upset The Rhythm
Artwork : Jan Lankisch (Photo : Sarah Cass)

The Smiths' single What Difference Does It Make [1984 : Rough Trade] followed Morrissey's pattern of using a vintage post-war film still on the cover, and these photographs have in turn been copied by other bands; can't imagine the old Milk Marketing Board rushing to take advantage of either. Anthony Perkins impressionist Xiu Xiu is on one side of a two band single with the Parenthetical Girls.

Can't afford a Richard Avedon photographic print? The vintage vinyl racks are full of his top notch monochrome portraits, including this Simon & Garfunkel cover for Bookends [1968 : Columbia]. It has been a template for a number of acts. The New Americans could have done with spending more time in the darkroom, but the other two are worthy tributes, with Austrian remixers Kruder & Dorfmeister getting very close.

Artist : Jazzyfatnastees Title : The Tortoise & The Hare / 2002 Album / Cool Hunter - Rykodisc Artwork : Andrew Cunningham (Photo : Michael Schreiber)

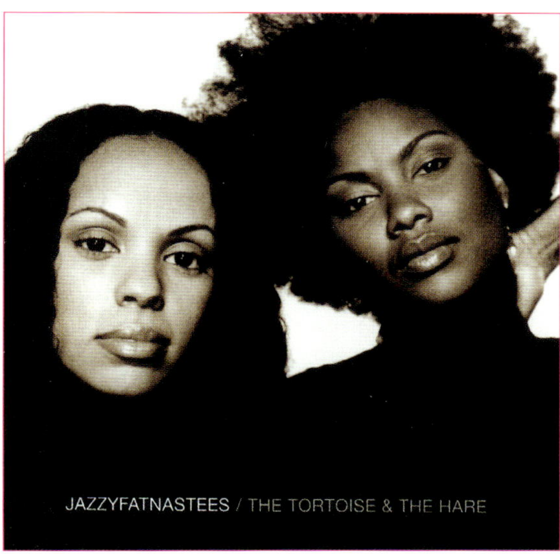

Artist : Kruder & Dorfmeister Title : G-Stoned / 1996 Album / G-Stone Recordings Artwork : Oka (Photo : Heller)

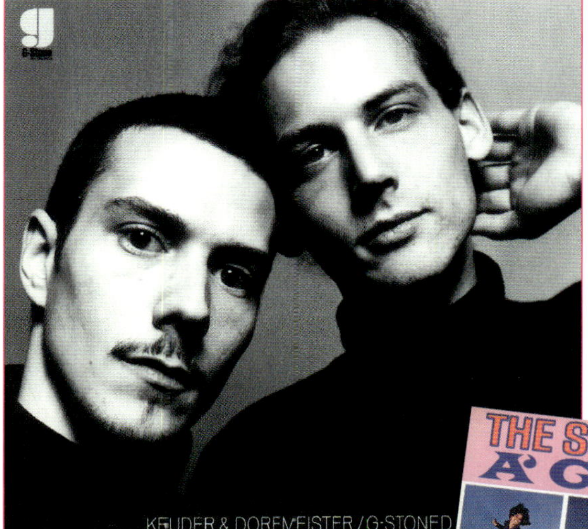

Artist : New Americans Title : New Americans / 2000 Album / David Fufkin Artwork : Mike Nicholson (Photo : Jill Kahn)

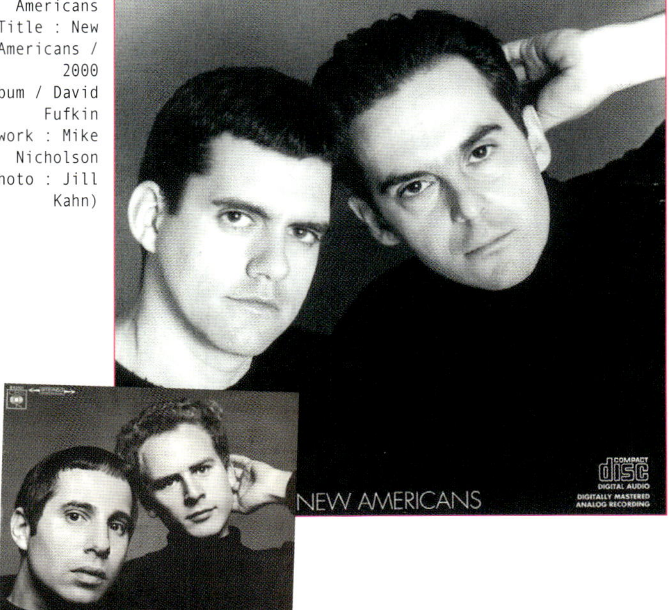

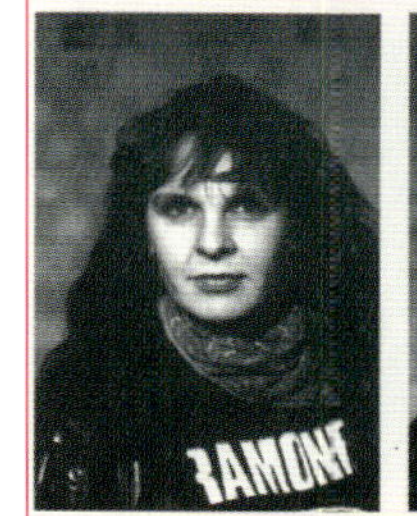

Artist : The Kissettes Title : A' Go-Go / 1993 4 track EP / That's Entertainment Records Artwork : Thelin & Bulldog

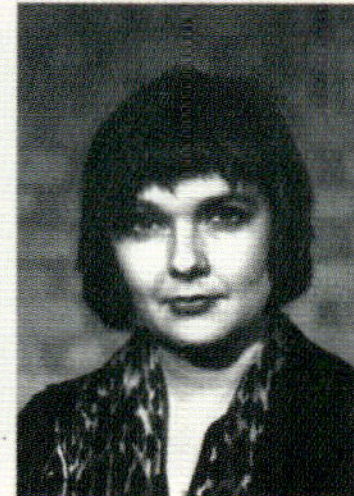

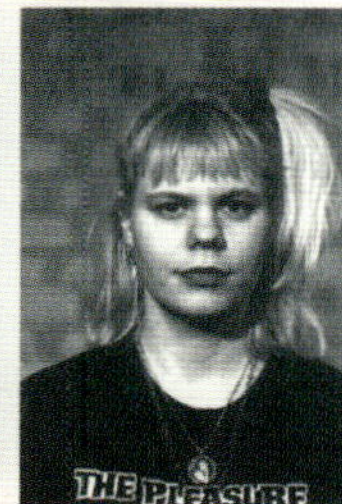

Norway based The Kissettes' tribute to The Supremes A Go-Go cover [1966. Artwork / Photo : Frank Dandridge] might have worked better had they not used what look like Police Wanted portraits...

Jamie Reid's shock and awe cover treatment of the monarch merged with the newsprint titles on God Save The Queen [1977 : Virgin] resulted in one of the most (in)famous sleeves of all time, a sleeve which proved hard to resist when it came to copying. Perhaps Die Lady Di comes closest in spirit (with a pun on the German), and the 'The Punk' tributes you can understand. The strange merging of the Pistols and Elvis does take a bit of getting to grips with, though it's a good cover.

Artist : The Star Club
Title : God Save The Punk Rock / 1987
Album Label : Invitation / Victor Musical Industries
Artwork : Toshimasa Matsuo

Artist : K.G.B. (Kongstreu Gottergeben & Blasiert)
Title : Die Lady D + 4 / 1997
EP / Entenschädel Productions
Artwork : Hannes Koerber / Volker Kahlig

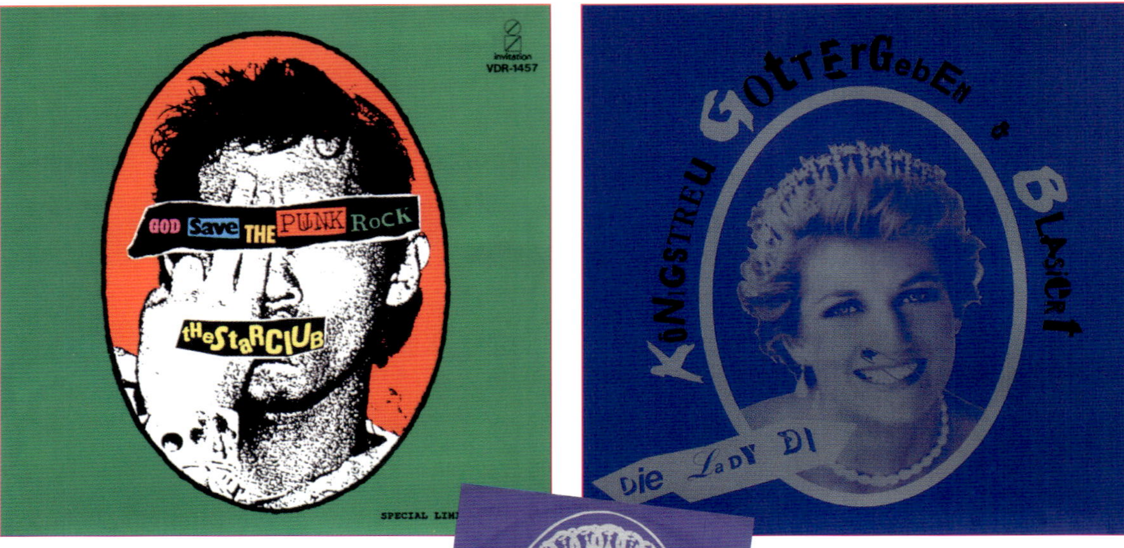

Artist : Various Artists
Title : God Save The King - A Tribute To Punk / 1998
Album / Home Sick Royal
Artwork : Unknown

Artist : The Sex Presleys
Title : God Save The King / 2009
Album / Raucous Records
Artwork : The Sex Presleys

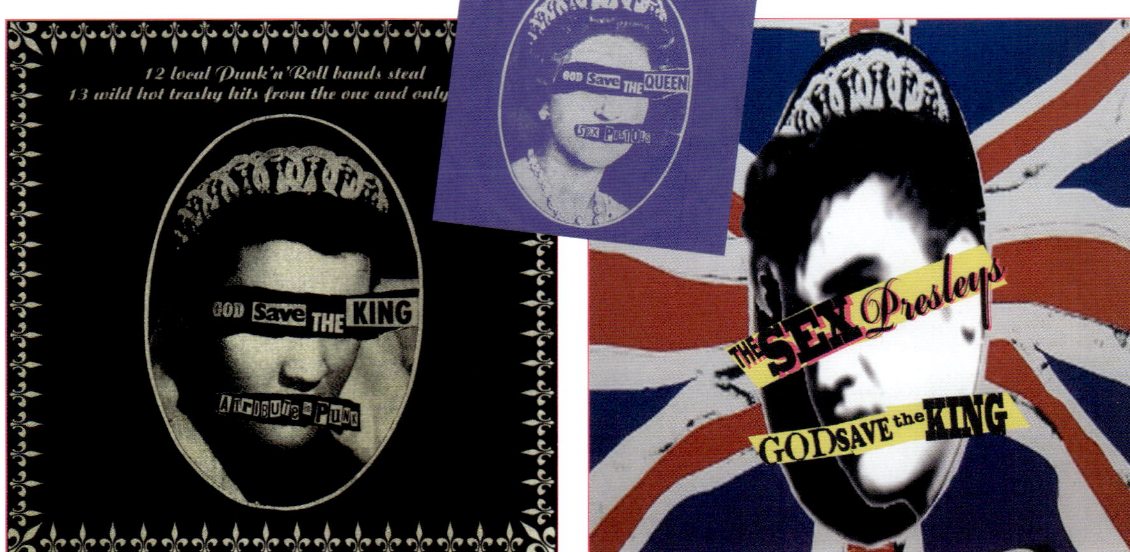

Two alt takes on the career of Britney Spears; her wholesome tanned Baby One More Time (U.S. version) album look from 1999 [Artwork : Jackie Murphy. Photo : Larry Busacca] is given an everyday twist by Junkyard.

Artist : Junkyard
Title : Tried And True / 2003
EP / Heat Slick Records - Smart Recordings
Artwork / Photo : Suzanne Allison

Artist : Happy Apple
Title : Youth Oriented / 2003
Album / Universal
Artwork : Nicolas Malherbe.
Cartoon : Bouco.

In contrast the slightly desperate pose from Britney [2001. Artwork : Fredrik Peterhoff / Jordana & Mark Archer-May] was quickly jumped on by Happy Apple, who added puppet strings to the grim cartoon.

Back to The Pistols and there are only a few album sleeves which actually deserve the overused word iconic. Jamie Reid's cut and paste graphic for the Sex Pistols' LP Never Mind The Bollocks Here's The Sex Pistols [1977 / Virgin] is one. Printed on matt card in day-glo inks, it remains one of the most memorable and recognisable covers of all time. Given this, and the importance of the band to the Punk movement, it's small wonder that dozens of bands have since borrowed the graphic. 18 covers are shown overleaf, with just about every type of tribute, pastiche or spoof (sometimes all three combined) imaginable. It's all too easy to imagine how dreadful The Wurzels offering was, but the Scottish Sex Pistols have got to be worth tracking down... (excuse Britney jumping in there, it was the only way to get pages 128/129 to work as a spread).

L-R • The Wurzels : Never Mind The Bullocks Ere's The Wurzels [2002 Artwork : Cruisin' Records Ltd.] / The Sex Presleys : Never Mind The Pollocks We're The Cod Army EP [2010 Artwork : Fleetwoodwebsites.co.uk] / The Bollock Brothers : Never Mind The Bollocks 1983 [1983 Artwork : The Raven Design Group] / Die Roten Rosen (Die Toten Hosen) : Never Mind The Hosen [1987 Artwork : Rip Off] / The Scottish Sex Pistols : Never Mind The Trossachs Here's The Scottish Sex Pistols [1993 Artwork : Unknown] / Sex Bidochons : On S'En Bat Les Couilles Voici Les Sex Bidochons [1983 Artwork : Unknown] / Dead Schembechlers : We Don't Give A Damn For The Whole State of Michigan [unknown] / The Pollocks (Matt Pollock) : Never Mind The Pollocks - Live At All Souls [2000 Artwork : Unknown] / Various Artists : Worse Than Alternative - It's Another Punk Comp [1999 Artwork : Millerworks] / Nid & Sansy : Never Mind The Bootlegs Here's Sex With Nid & Sansy [2003 Artwork : Unknown] / The Billionaires : Never Mind The Rabble [2001 Artwork : I.O. Yu Na Ting (James Levy) & Phil / T. Rich (Andrew Boyd) / Seymour Benjamins (Matthew Skomarovsky)] / Sore Throat : Never Mind The Napalm [1989 Artwork : Beano / Mutie Graphix] / Various Artists : Never Mind The Sex Pistols Here's The Tribute [2000 Artwork : Becky Tippenhauer] / Opium Jukebox : Never Mind The Bhangra Here's The Opium Jukebox - A Sex Pistols Tribute [2002 Artwork : John Bergin] / Sid Vicious : Never Mind The Reunion [1997 Artwork : Unknown] / United Nations : Never Mind The Bombings Here's Your Six Figures EP [2010 Artwork : Unknown] / Mimycen : Get Set Go 45 [2001 Artwork : Unknown] / Heebeegeebees : Never Mind The Originals [1981 Artwork : Cooke Key] / (left) Max Pashm : Never Mind The Balkans Here's Max Pashm [2008 Artwork : t(error)ist]

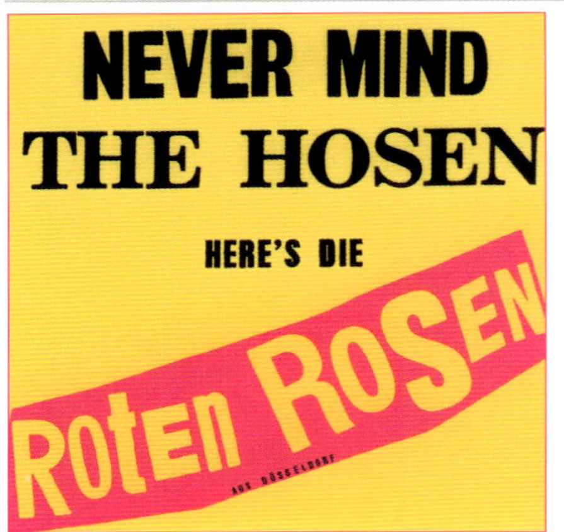
NEVER MIND
THE HOSEN
HERE'S DIE
RoTen RoSen
AUS DÜSSELDORF

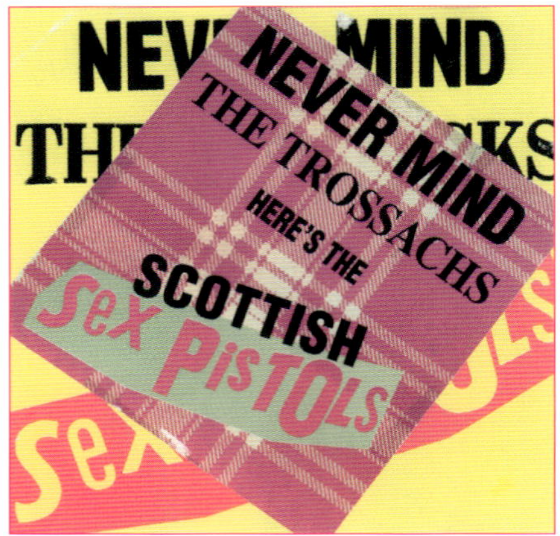
NEVER MIND
THE BOLLOCKS
NEVER MIND
THE TROSSACHS
HERE'S THE
SCOTTISH
SeX PiSToLS

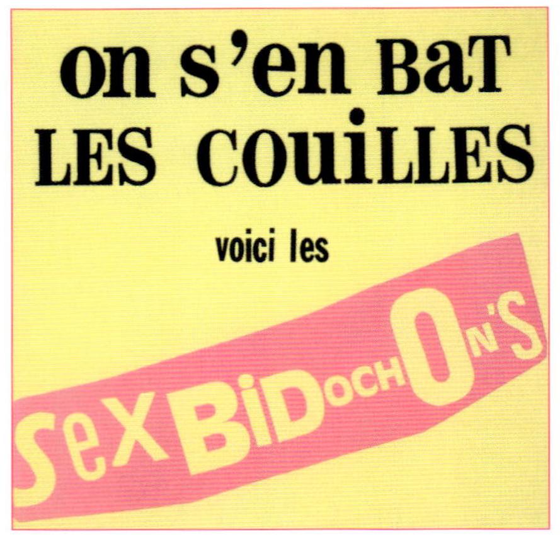
on s'en Bat
LES CoUiLLES
voici les
SeXBiDochOn'S

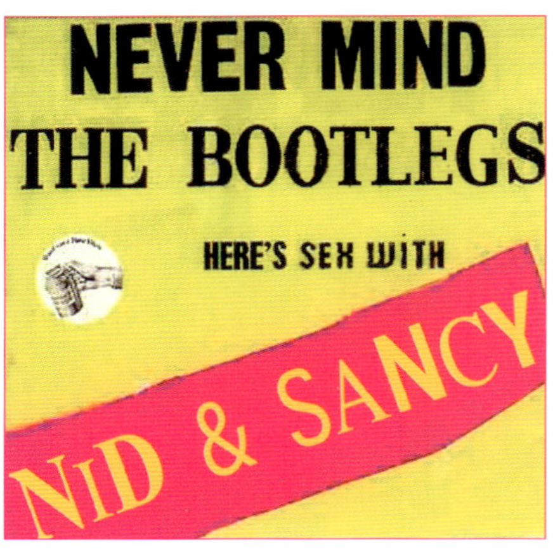
NEVER MIND
THE BOOTLEGS
HERE'S SEX WiTH
NiD & SANCY

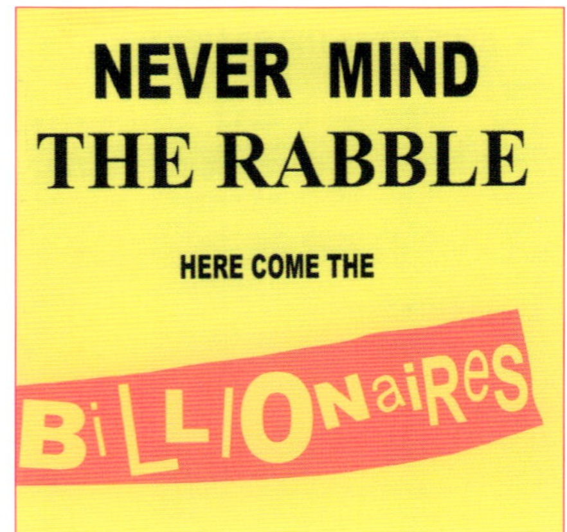
NEVER MIND
THE RABBLE
HERE COME THE
BiLL/ONaiReS

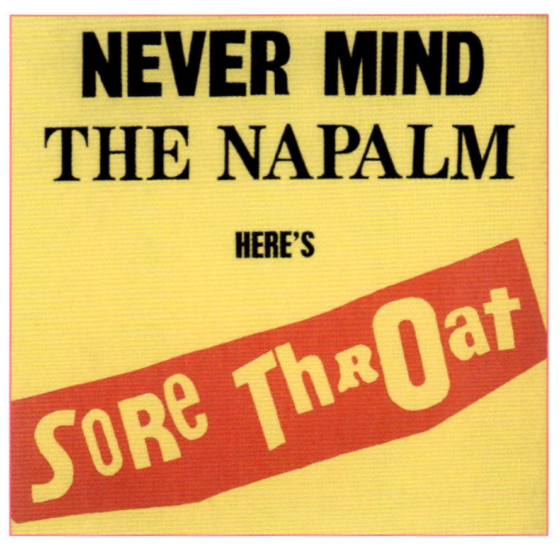
NEVER MIND
THE NAPALM
HERE'S
SoRe ThrOat

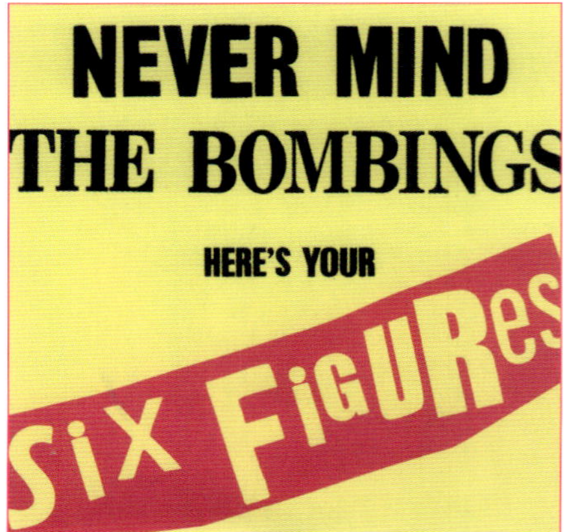
NEVER MIND
THE BOMBINGS
HERE'S YOUR
SiX FiGUReS

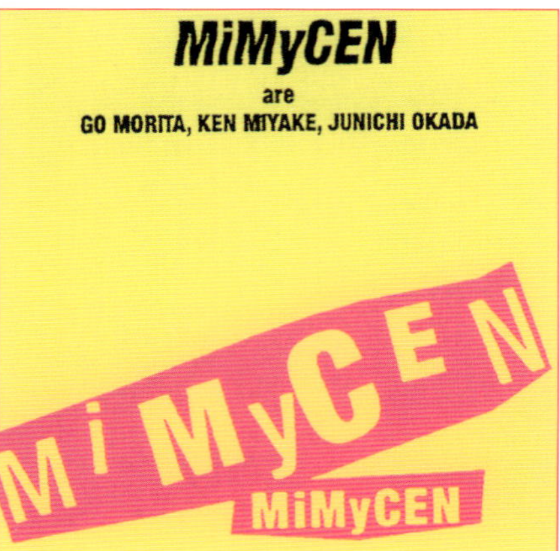
MiMyCEN
are
GO MORITA, KEN MIYAKE, JUNICHI OKADA
MiMyCEN
MiMyCEN

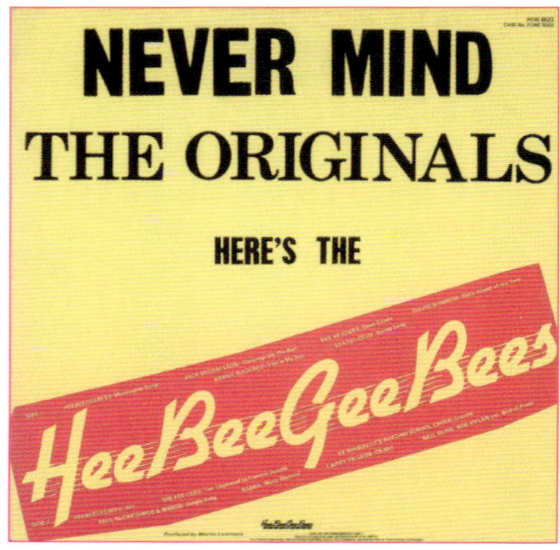
NEVER MIND
THE ORIGINALS
HERE'S THE
HeeBeeGeeBees

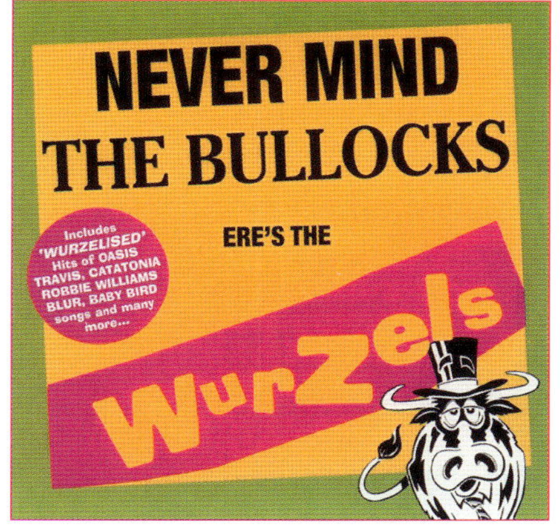
NEVER MIND
THE BULLOCKS
Includes 'WURZELISED' Hits of OASIS TRAVIS, CATATONIA ROBBIE WILLIAMS BLUR, BABY BIRD songs and many more...
ERE'S THE
WURZELS

NEVER MIND
THE POLLOCKS
MATT POLLOCK
LIVE AT ALL SOULS

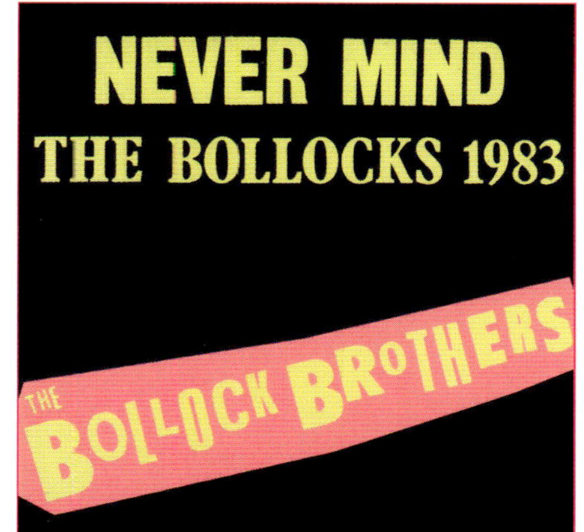
NEVER MIND
THE BOLLOCKS 1983
THE BOLLOCK BROTHERS

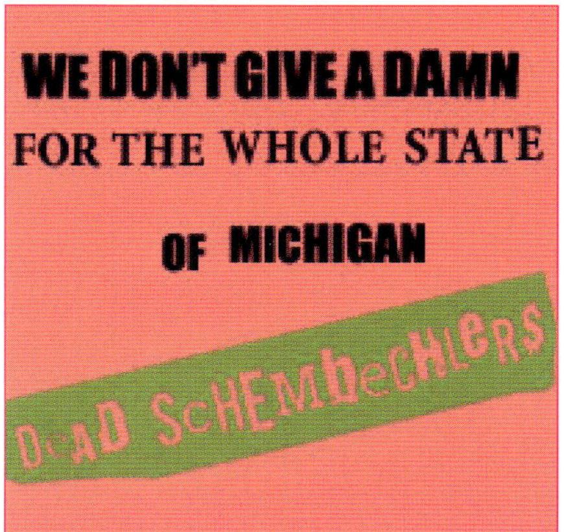
WE DON'T GIVE A DAMN
FOR THE WHOLE STATE
OF MICHIGAN
DEAD SCHEMBECHLERS

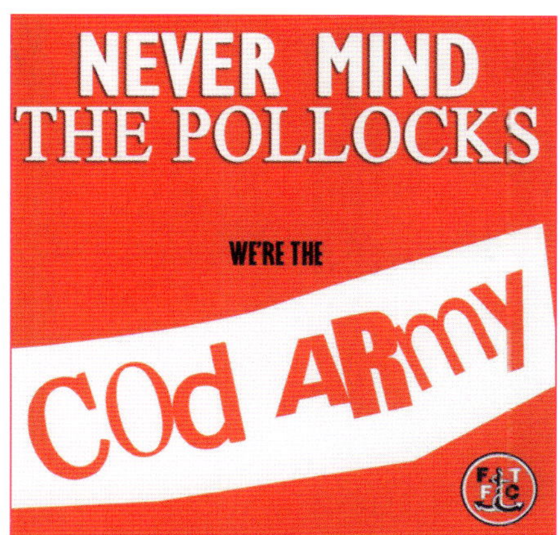
NEVER MIND
THE POLLOCKS
WE'RE THE
COd ARMy
FTFC

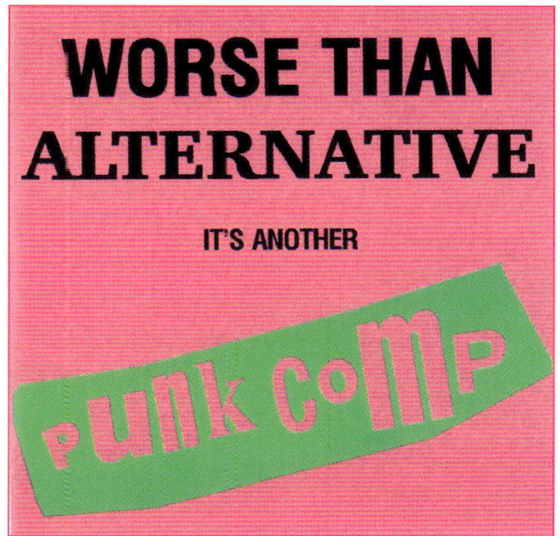
WORSE THAN
ALTERNATIVE
IT'S ANOTHER
PUNK COMP

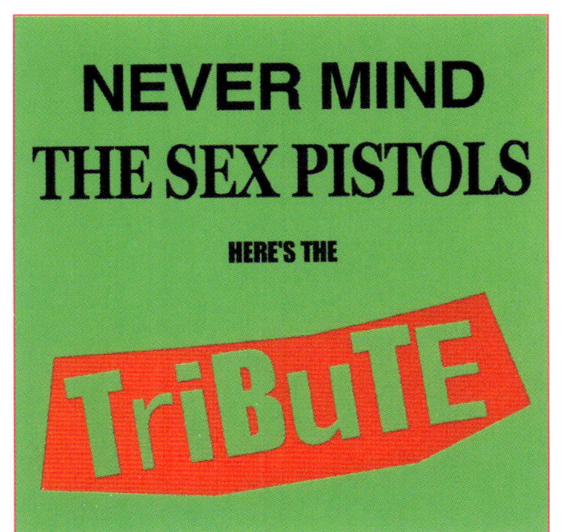
NEVER MIND
THE SEX PISTOLS
HERE'S THE
TRiBuTE

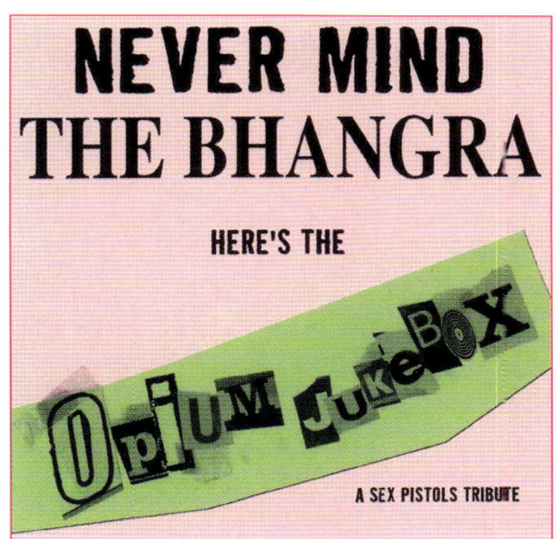
NEVER MIND
THE BHANGRA
HERE'S THE
OpiUM JukeBox
A SEX PISTOLS TRIBUTE

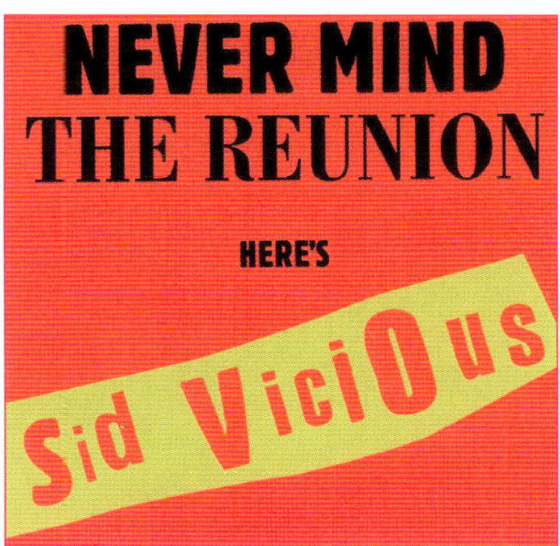
NEVER MIND
THE REUNION
HERE'S
Sid ViciOus

If only the designers of the Pulp Fiction publicity material had been brave enough to commission a genuine vintage paperback style illustration or at least choose some proper retro type. Even so, the soundtrack album looked and sounded good [1994 : RCA. Artwork : Donna Mercer / Tim Stedman] and has inspired several variations, including reissue labels looking to cash-in on their knowledge of garage classics sparked by the inspired use of same in the film.

Artist :
Various
Artists
Title : Punk
Fiction / 199-
Album / Wedge
Records
Artwork :
Winni at 3 AM.
Photo : Steve
Z.

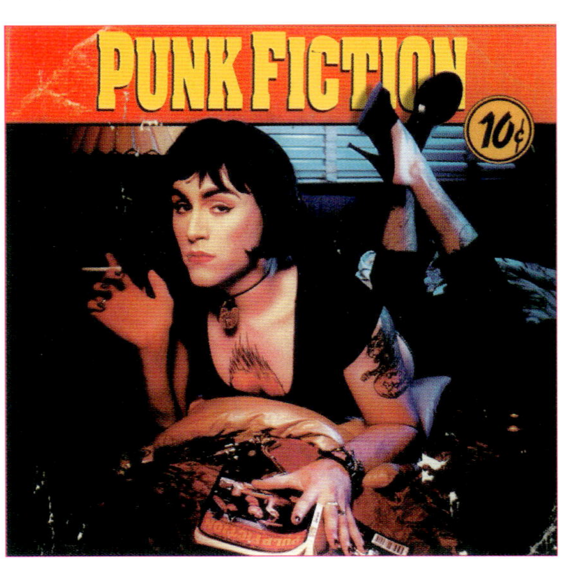

Artist :
Various
Artists
Title : Pulp
Surfin' / 1995
Album / Del-Fi
Records
Artwork :
Michael Rosen

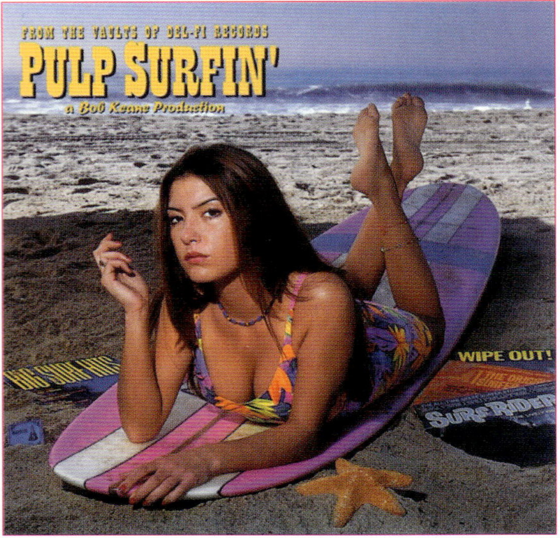

Artist :
Soundtrack
Title : Cyber
Punk Fiction
/ 1998
Album / Cargo
Music
Artwork :
Kevin Marburg

Artist : Pussy
Crush
Title : Punk
Friction /
1995
EP / Sympathy
For The Record
Industry
Artwork :
Unknown

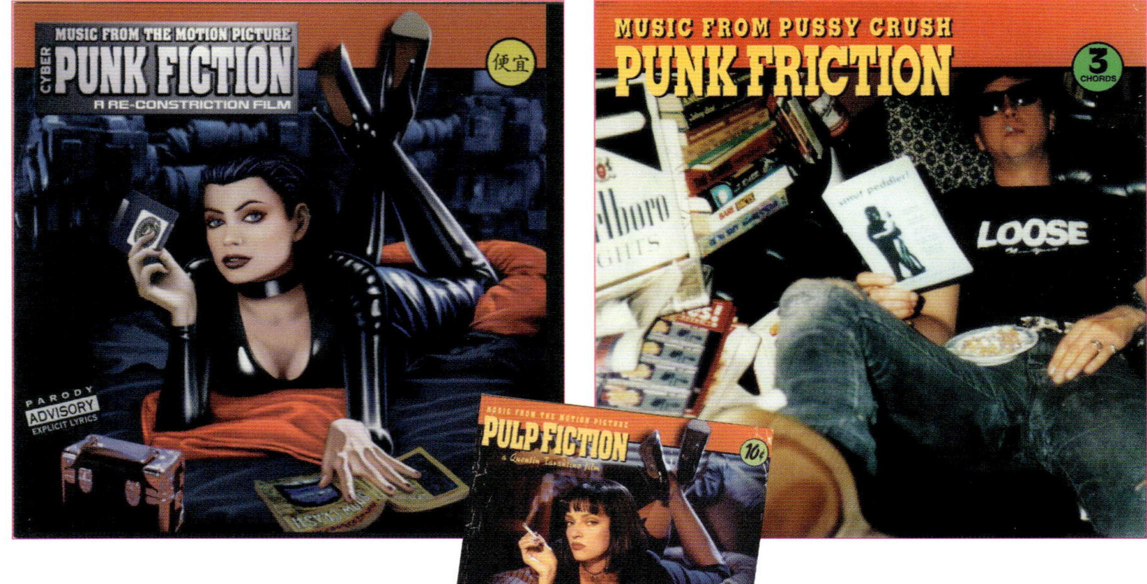

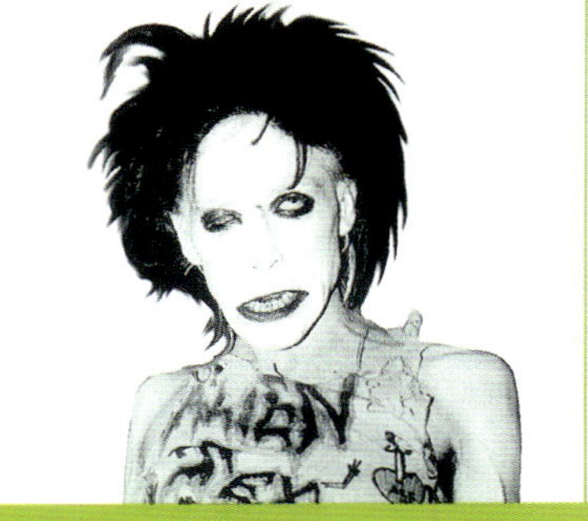

Easily one of the best film posters of the nineties, and another great soundtrack album (though the sleeve is not a patch on the poster graphics), Trainspotting [1996 : EMI Capitol. Artwork : Kave Quinn Photos : Brian Tufano] inspired no end of lookalikes in all types of media. Spotting goths and grooves we get, but camels? And why did it take five people to design that one?!

Artist :
Various
Artists
Title :
Gothspotting
/ 1998
Album /
Cleopatra
Records
Artwork :
Unknown

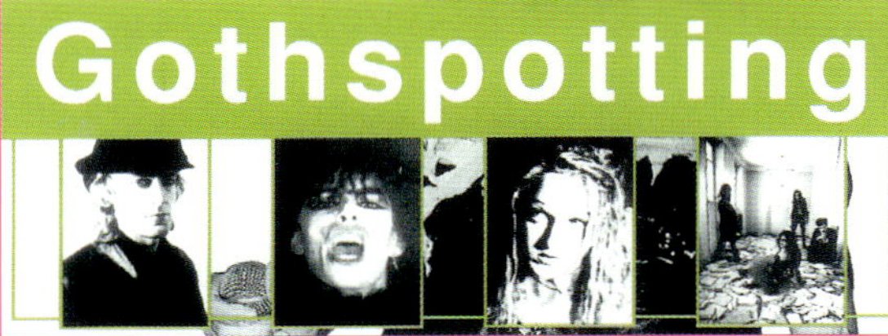

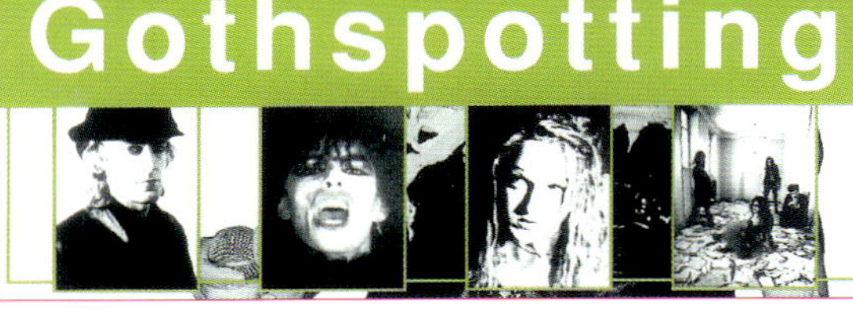

Artist :
Various
Artists
Title : Groove
Spotting /
1996
Album / XSV
Music
Artwork : Arco

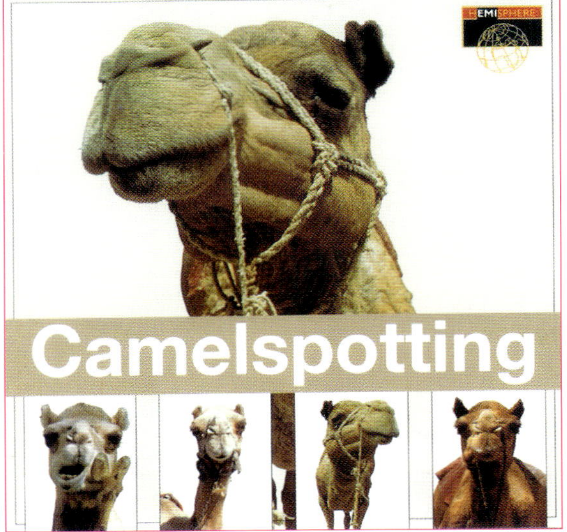

Artist :
Various
Artists
Title :
Camelspotting
/ 1999
Album / EMI
Artwork : Bill
Smith Studio /
Rob O'Connor /
Mike Harris /
Jeremy
Kimberlin
/ Andrew
Macdonald

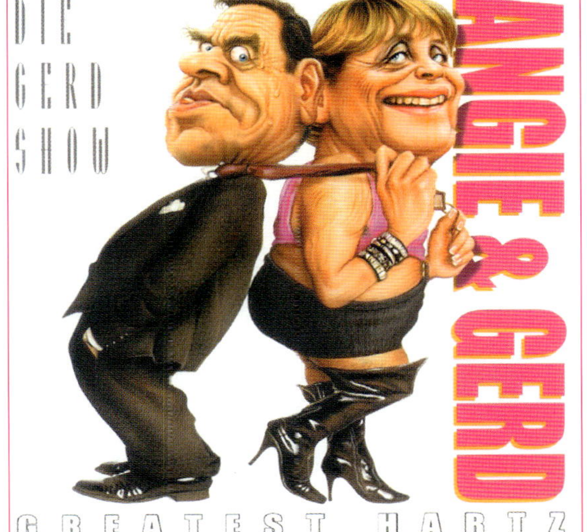

Artist : Die
Gerd Show -
Angie & Gerd
Title :
Greatest Hartz
/ 2005
Album / Polydor
Universal
Artwork : Mike
Schellenberger.
Illustration :
Bernhard Prinz

Pretty Woman in contrast... [1990 : EMI. Artwork : Unknown]. Die Gerd Show was a German political satirical radio programme by Elmar Brandt. We may not be familiar with it, but some of the show's songs were issued on CD and became massive selling platinum hits.

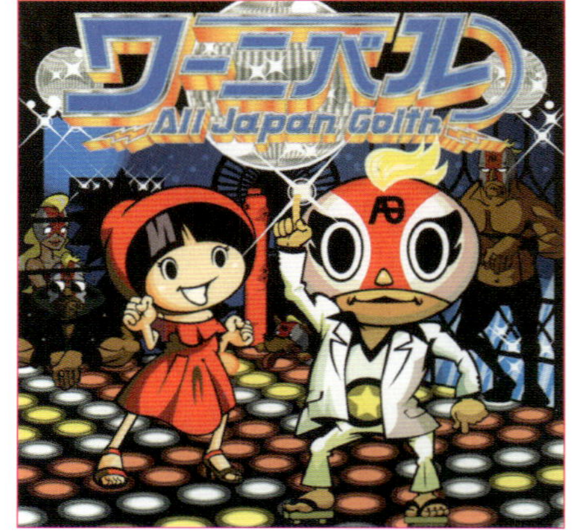
ワーニバル
All Japan Golth

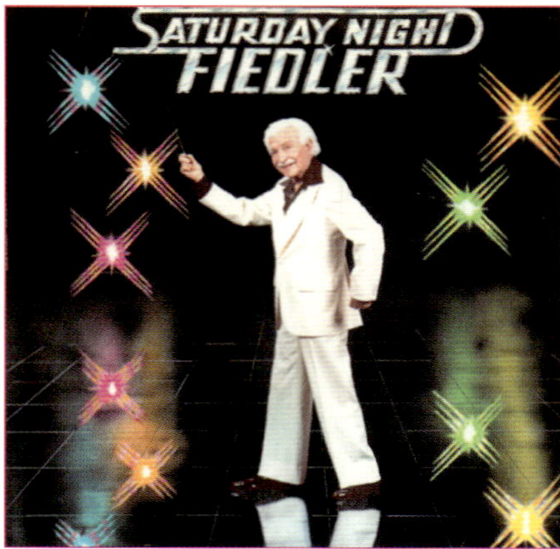
SATURDAY NIGHT
FIEDLER

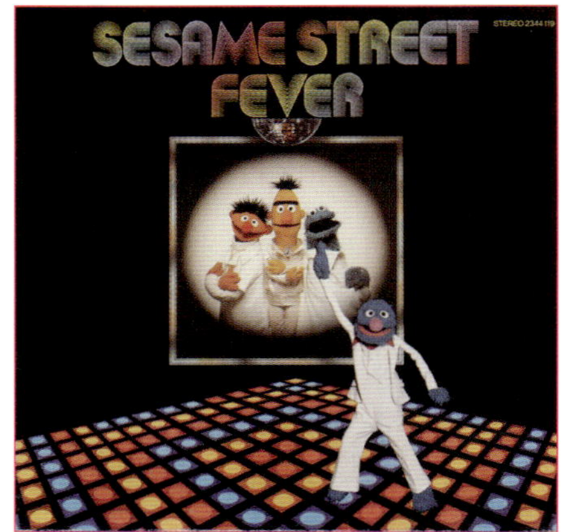
STEREO-2344.119
SESAME STREET
FEVER

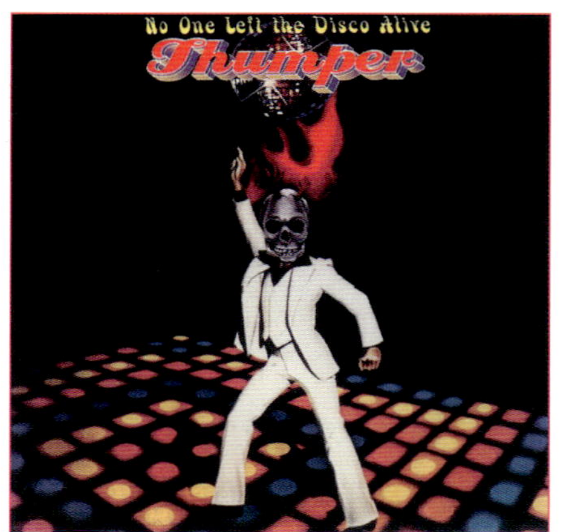
No One Left the Disco Alive
Thumper

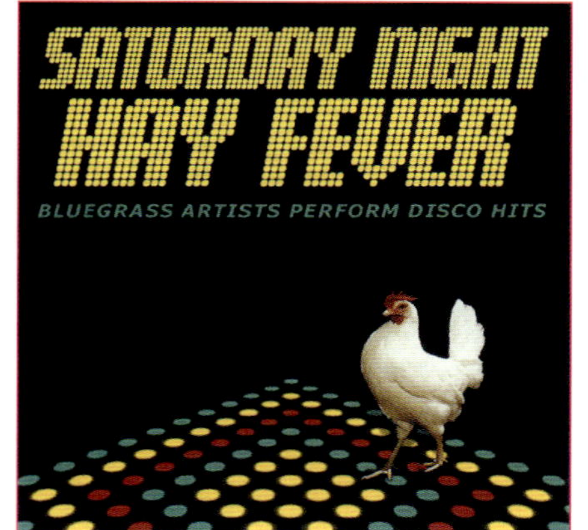
SATURDAY NIGHT
HAY FEVER
BLUEGRASS ARTISTS PERFORM DISCO HITS

2 LIVE JEWS
PRESENT:
DISCO JEWS

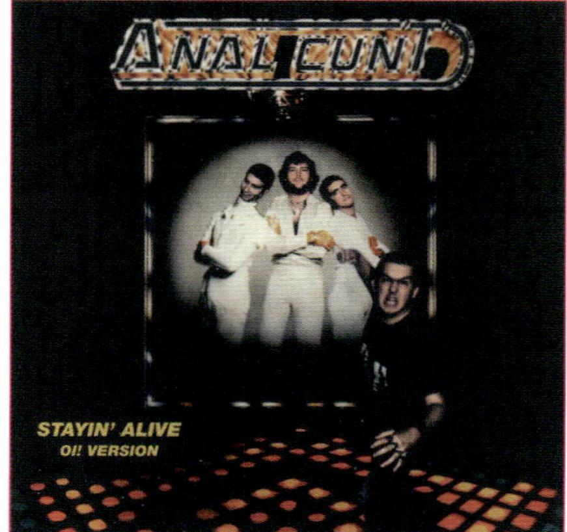
ANAL CUNT
STAYIN' ALIVE
OI! VERSION

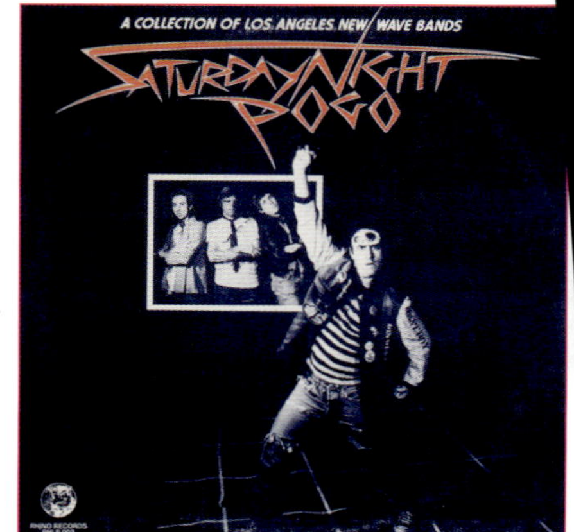
A COLLECTION OF L.O.S. ANGELES NEW WAVE BANDS
SATURDAY NIGHT
POGO
RHINO RECORDS
RNLP 303

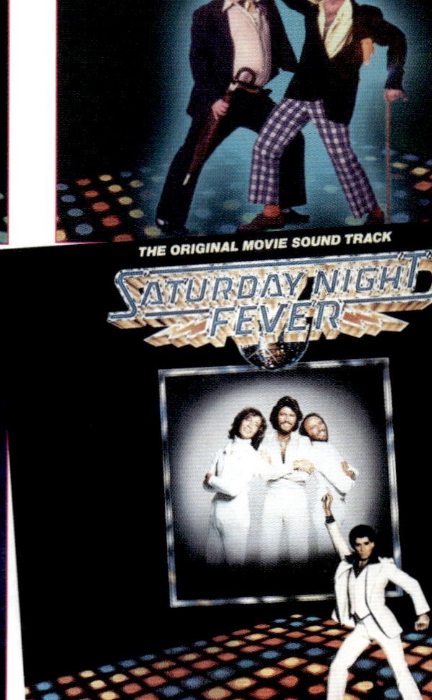
THE ORIGINAL MOVIE SOUND TRACK
2658 123
SATURDAY NIGHT
FEVER

Saturday Night Fever [1977. Artwork : Susan Herr / Tom Nikosey] is still providing material for comedians, advertisers and scriptwriters. There are over two dozen sleeves based on the original soundtrack cover. Many of the musical comedy names crop up again (Sesame Street and the Disco Jews), but best title has to be Saturday Night Hay Fever (no prizes for guessing the worst) and the fab low-budget looking offering from Arthur Fiedler is a gem (though no lesser name than Lynn Goldsmith took the original cover photograph).

(*page 132 l - r*) • All Japan Goith (sic) : All Japan Goith [2007 Artwork : Siro (Norishiro@ks)] / Boston Pops Orchestra With Arthur Fiedler : Saturday Night Fiedler [1979 Artwork : Hal Wilson. Illustration : Jim O'Connell. Photo : Lynn Goldsmith] / Sesame Street : Sesame Street Fever [1978 Artwork : Stigwood Group Ltd.] / Thumper : No One Left The Disco Alive [1995 Artwork : Adam Gillitt - Planet 23 Productions] / Various Artists : Saturday Night Hay Fever [2002 Artwork : One Acre Productions] / 2 Live Jews : Disco Jews [1994 Artwork : Ana Maria Restrepo] / Anal Cunt : Stayin' Alive + 3 [1994 Artwork : Unknown cretin] / Various Artists : Saturdaynight Pogo [1978 Artwork : Heather Harris]. above • Los Bidochons : Disco Bidochons [2004 Artwork : Fab Trovato. Illustration : Christian Binet].

The Sound Of Music [1965 : RCA. Cover painting : Howard Terpning], one of the biggest selling soundtrack albums ever (judging by the number of copies which still turn up in charity shops), hasn't actually inspired that many tributes, but ▼

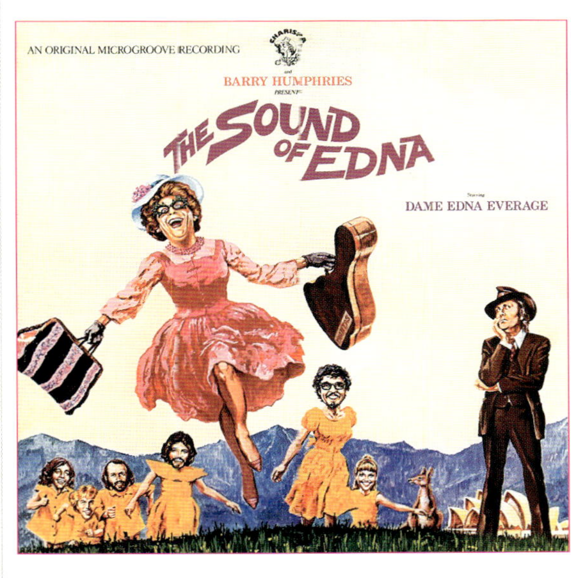

Artist : Barry Humphries (Dame Edna) Title : The Sound Of Edna / 1978 Album / Charisma Artwork : Shoot That Tiger. Illustration : Paul Cemmick

Artist : Jennifer Lopez Title : I'm Glad / 2003 Single / Epic Artwork : Unknown

A clear copy of the Flashdance cover pose here from young J-Lo, twenty years after the original [1983. Artwork : Mo Ström for Bob Heimall, Inc.]

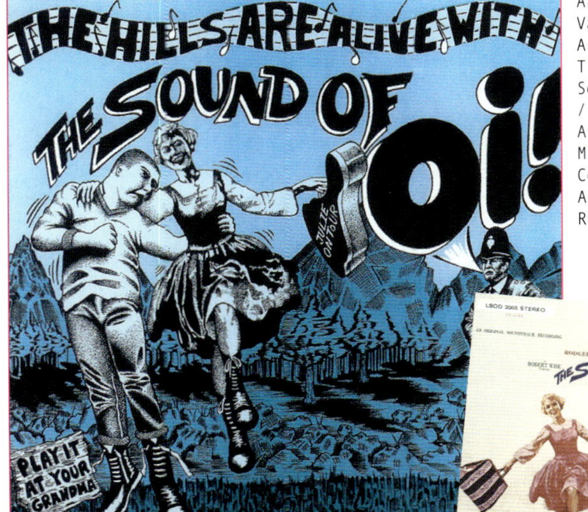

Artist : Various Artists Title : The Sound Of Oi! / 1987 Album / Harry May Record Company Artwork : Russell Walker

comedian Barry Humphries gets a really clever parody onto his sleeve. And if you can't remember (or never knew) what Oi 'music' was, think yourself lucky.

The very distinctive red and black imagery for the 1961 movie version of the musical West Side Story [1962 : U.A. Artwork : United Artists] is one of Saul Bass's most recognised designs (and picking up the album will set you back far less than the film poster would). Here it is adapted for a Punk stage version of the story and the amusingly titled West 12 To Wittering which was by occasional r'n'b group The Dirty Strangers featuring Keith and Ron Wood.

Artist :
The Dirty
Strangers
Title :
West 12 To
Wittering /
2009
Album / Track
Record
Artwork : Ra &
Paul Clayton

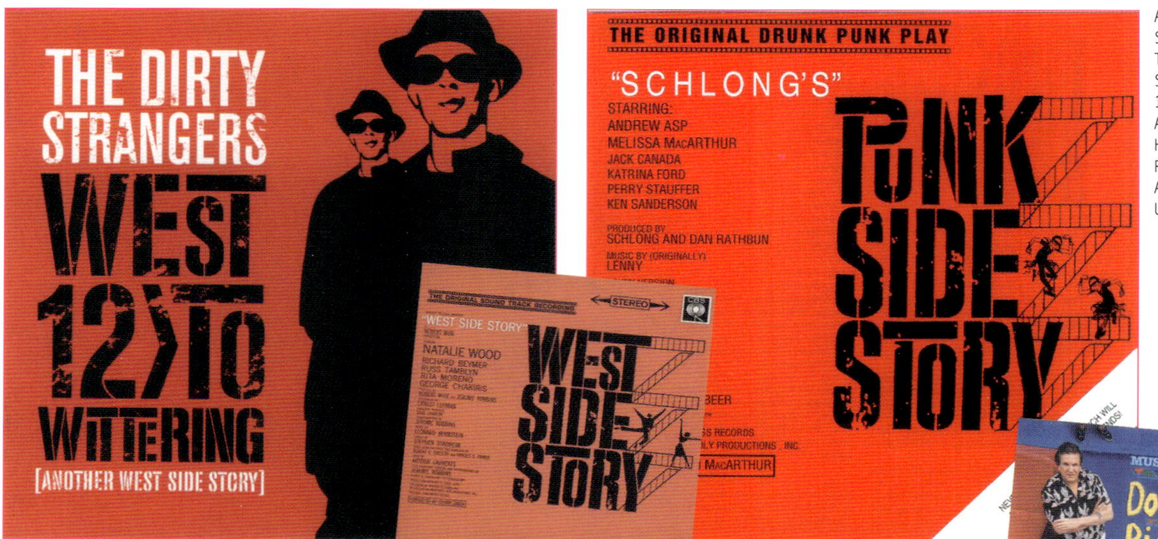

Artist :
Schlong
Title : Punk
Side Story /
1995
Album /
Hopeless
Records
Artwork :
Unknown

Artist :
The Sons Of
Hercules
Title : The
Sons Of
Hercules /
1994
Album /
Unclean
Records
Cover photo :
Joseph Tauber

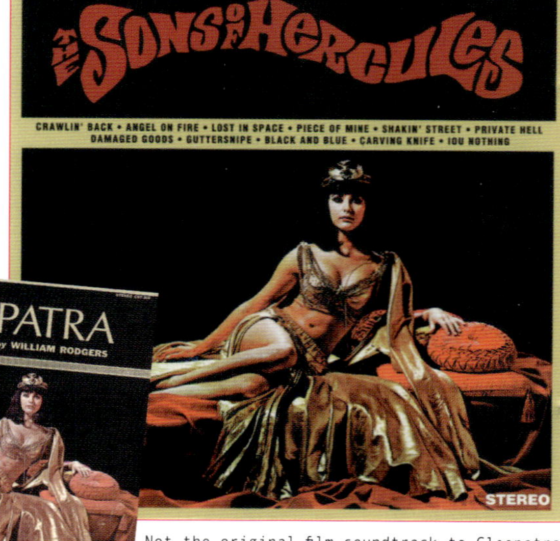

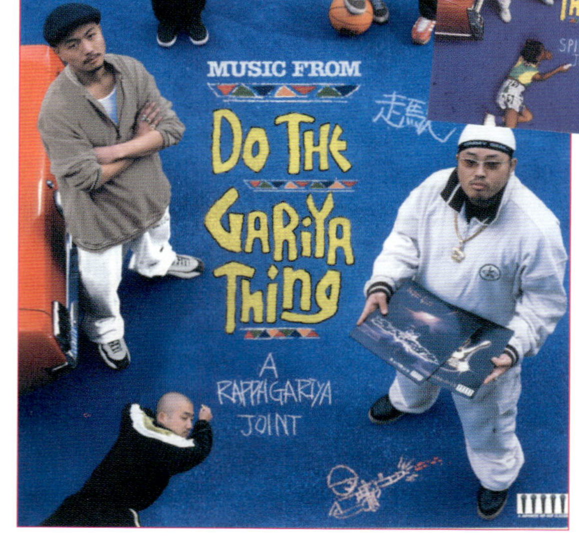

Artist :
Rappagariya
Title : Do The
Gariya Thing
/ 2000
Single / Happy
House
Artwork : Top
Graphickers /
Eiko Suzuki
(Victor Design
Center) (Photo
: Hiroshi
Nirei)

Not the original film soundtrack to Cleopatra, but a budget knock-off version with a model giving us the Elizabeth Taylor look [1964 : Crown Records. Artwork : Unknown], in turn copied by The Sons Of Hercules.

A Spike Lee film is always going to inspire, and the soundtrack sleeve for Do The Right Thing [1998 : Motown. Artwork : Ja / Georgopoulos / Imada] has here been carefully copied over in Japan.

It's hardly surprising that a powerful film franchise such as The Godfather [1972 : MCA. Artwork : Paramount] has brought a number of covers which borrow the soundtrack art, especially the lettering, particularly the extended G. The logo was designed by S. Neil Fujita in 1969 originally for the novel. Various urban crews have co-opted the imagery, fitting as it does into their often limited life-view, but there is also a bit of humour here from the Gagfactors.

Artist : The Gagfactors
Title : We Rock, You Suck, You Blow, We Fuck / 2007
Single / Rockin' Bones
Artwork : Unknown

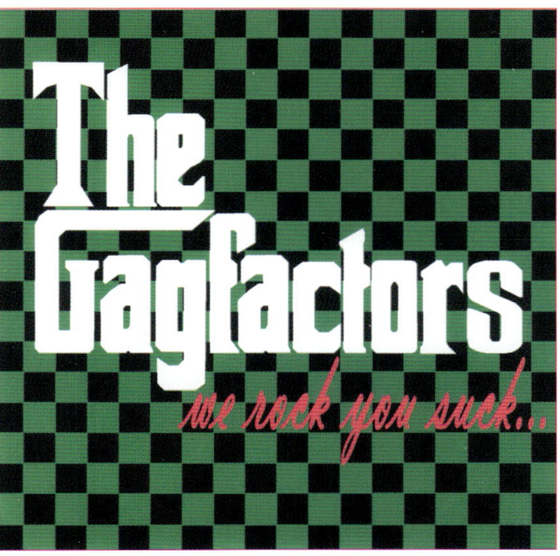

Artist :
Various
Artists
Title :
American
Gangstaz /
2008
Album / Street
Dance - Rams
Horn
Artwork :
Unknown

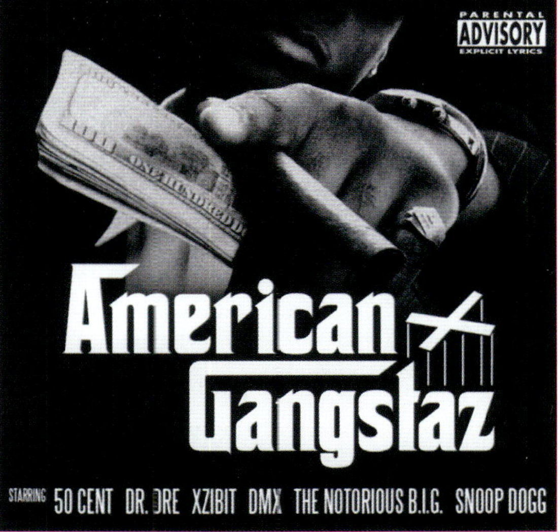

Artist : Los Planetas
Title : Dios Existe! / 1999
EP / RCA - BMG Spain
Artwork : Javier Aramburu

Artist :
Various
Artists
Title :
Godfathers
Of Hardstyle
- 2008
Album / Start
Stop Records
Artwork :
Alert BVBA

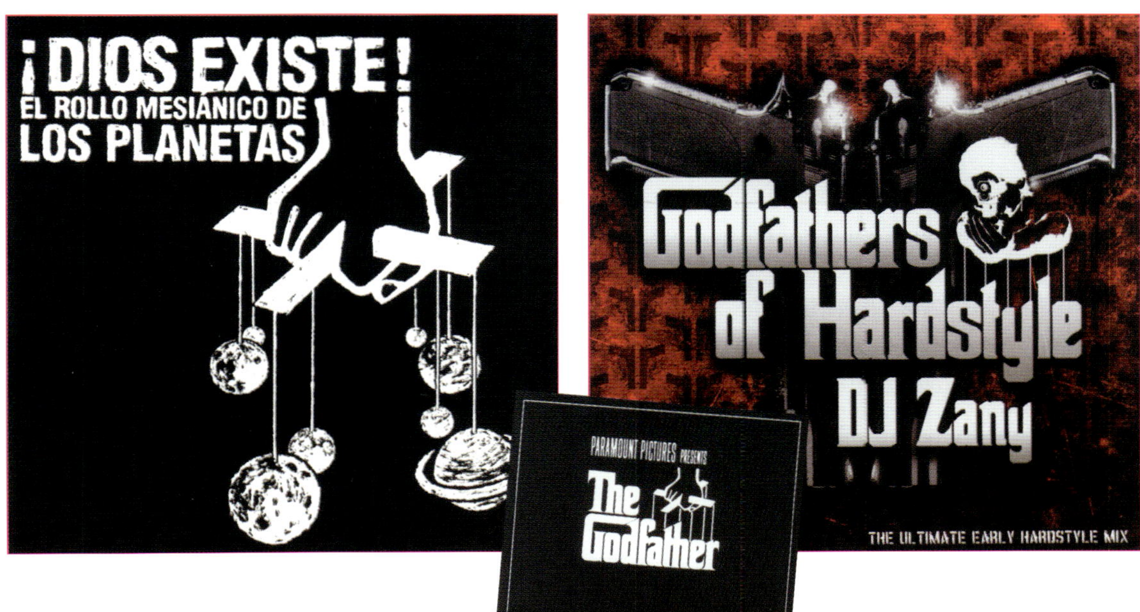

That Grease continues to be referenced on sleeves over three decades after release shows the power of this blockbuster teen movie from 1978 [R.S.O. Records. Artwork : Glenn Ross / Tim Bryant / George Corsillo - Gribbitt. Photo : Alan Pappe/ Lee Gross], and many of us can't wait for the rumoured Justin Bieber remake, but like many high-school centred films it mostly gets fun poked at it as this selection shows.

Artist : Patrick Topaloff & Sim
Title : Grise / 1978
Single / Trema
Artwork + photo : Jack Touroute

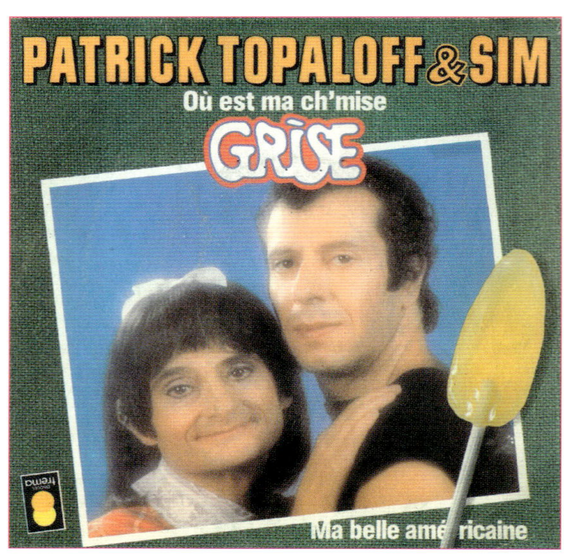

Artist : Slapping Suspenders
Title : Greece / 1995
Album / Count Orlok Music
Photo : Tom Holmlund

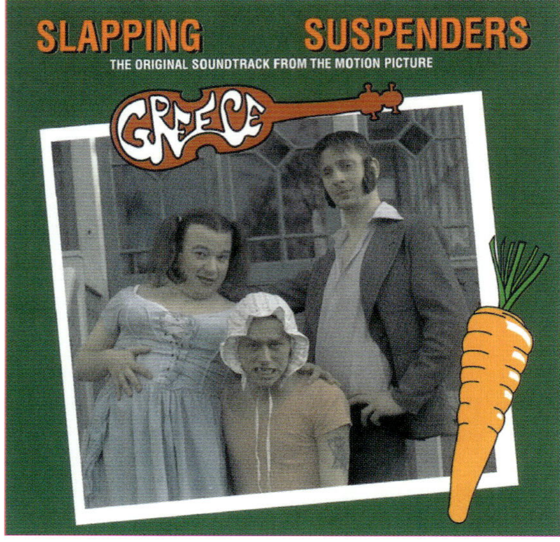

Artist : Various Artists
Title : Large Compilation # 17 / 2007
Album / Suburban Records
Artwork : Roel Smit / Mark A. Drillich

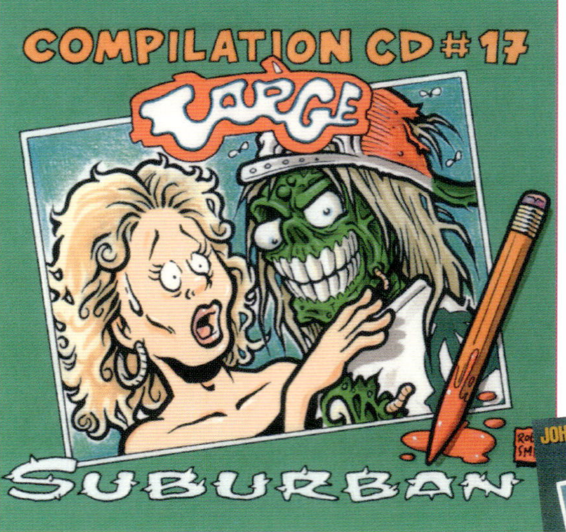

Artist : Various Artists
Title : Hopelessly Devoted To You / 1996
Album / Hopeless Records
Photo : Brian Archer

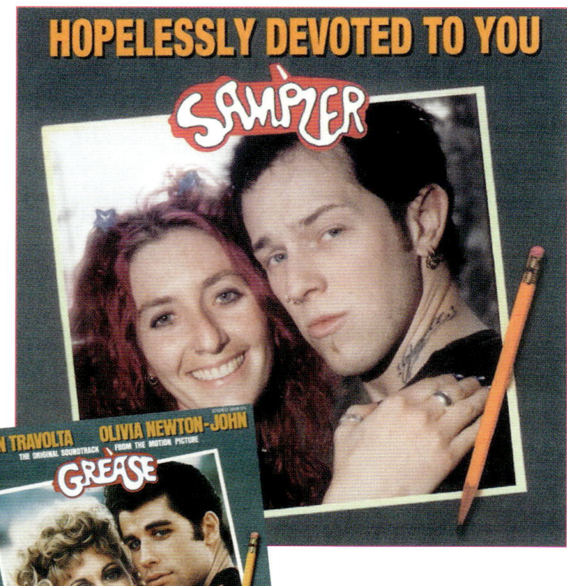

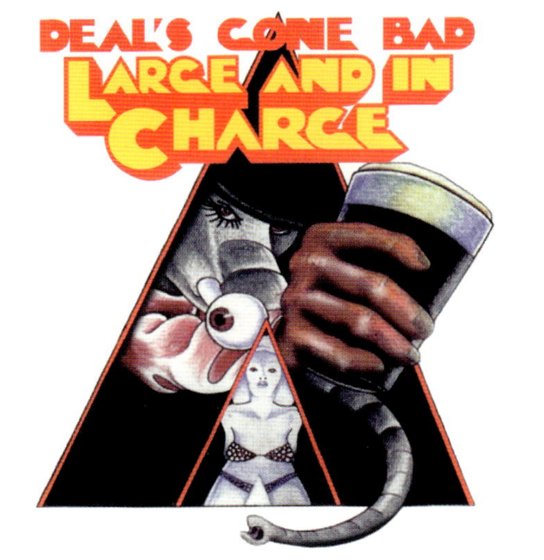

Kubrick's film version of Clockwork Orange [1972] caused a media reaction which ensured it cult status, and airbrush genius Philip Castle's art on the soundtrack (and other media, text and layout design by Bill Gold) has inspired a number of covers, which have their own strange take on the original. Here are a couple. Punk band Lowerclass Brats from Texas have used references to the film throughout their fifteen year long career.

Artist :
Deal's Gone
Bad
Title : Large
And In Charge
/ 1998
Album / Jump
Up
Artwork : Rob
Hostetter /
Judy Higgins

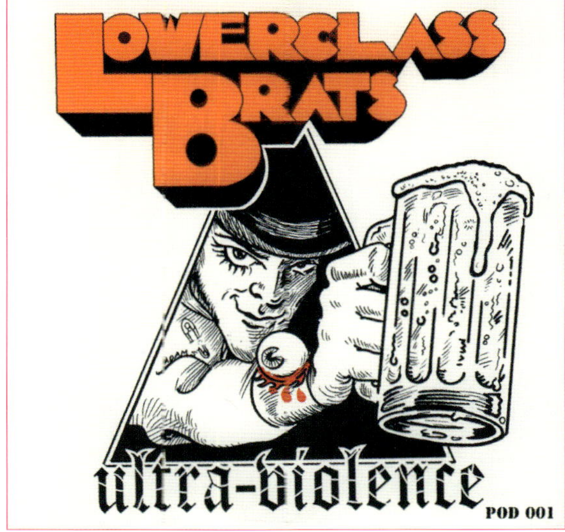

Artist : Lower
Class Brats
+ 1
Title : Ultra-
Violence + 3
/ 1996
EP / Pair-O-
Docs Records
Artwork :
Unknown

Artist : Color
Filter
Title :
Blueberry /
2007
Album / Long
Happiness
- Happiness
Records
Artwork :
Tomoyuki
Kuroda
Photo
: Maki
Ishii

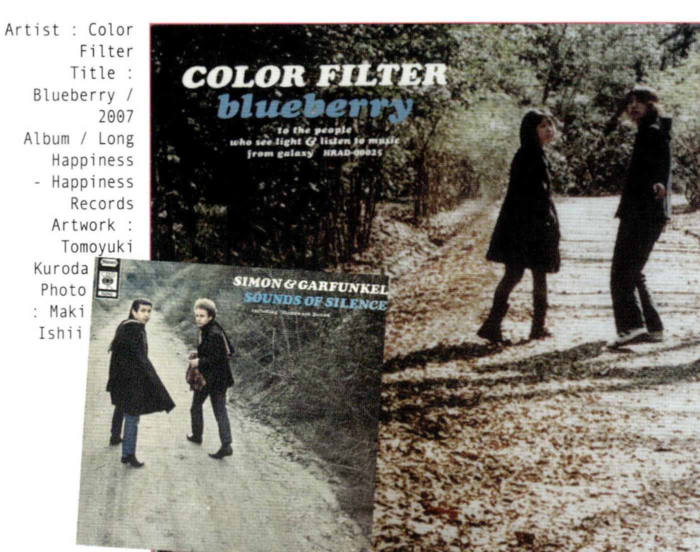

Another Japanese remake, this time of Simon & Garfunkel's Sounds Of Silence art [1966 : CBS. Photo : Guy Webster] taken on a dirt road on North Beverly Drive in Franklin County: ("I used to take a lot of rockers back there for shoots."), matching grainy cover image and type - Cooper italic.

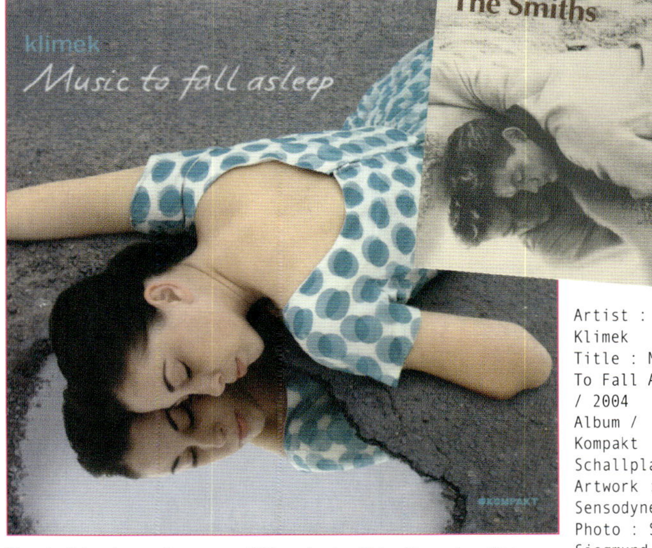

The Smiths (see also page 124) single This Charming Man [1983 : Rough Trade] used a still of actor Jean Marais (following a pattern of such images on Smiths covers), which was carefully reposed by German band Klimek.

Artist :
Klimek
Title : Music
To Fall Asleep
/ 2004
Album /
Kompakt
Schallplaten
Artwork :
Sensodyne
Photo : Sabine
Siegmund

Five people get credited with the photo for the Stray Cats debut [1981 : Arista] - Gavin Cochrane / Alain de la Mata / Toshi Yajima / Chalkie Davies / Chris Gabrin, not forgetting designer Malcolm Garrett. The neo-Hillbillys then ▼

Artist : Gigolo 13
Title : Please Baby Come Back To Me + 1 / 2001
Single / Blue Stone Records
Artwork : Ritsuko Ochi

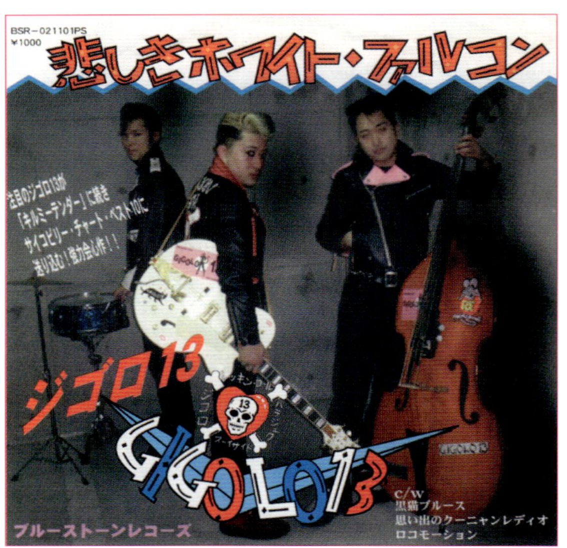

Another stunning Blue Note label offering for this Sonny Rollins album [1957. Artwork : Harold Feinstein, Photo : Francis Wolff], lifted in tribute by crooner Joe Jackson.

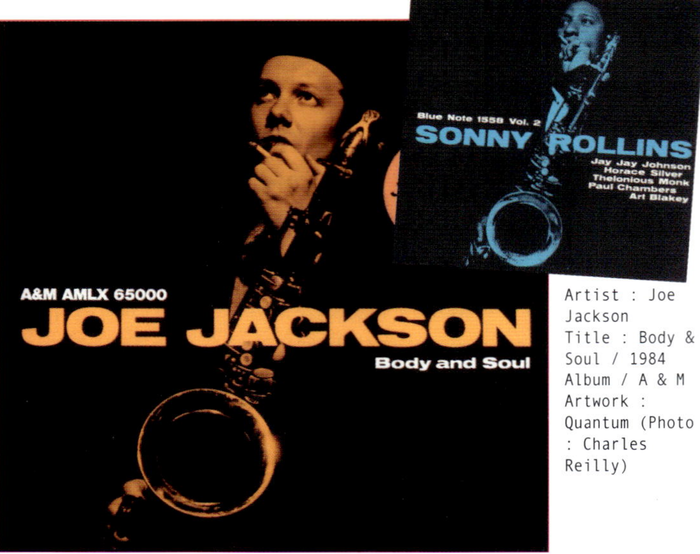

Artist : Joe Jackson
Title : Body & Soul / 1984
Album / A & M
Artwork : Quantum (Photo : Charles Reilly)

Artist : The Quakes
Title : The Quakes / 1988
Album / Nervous
Nick Garrard at Technimedia (Photo : Stewart Barker)

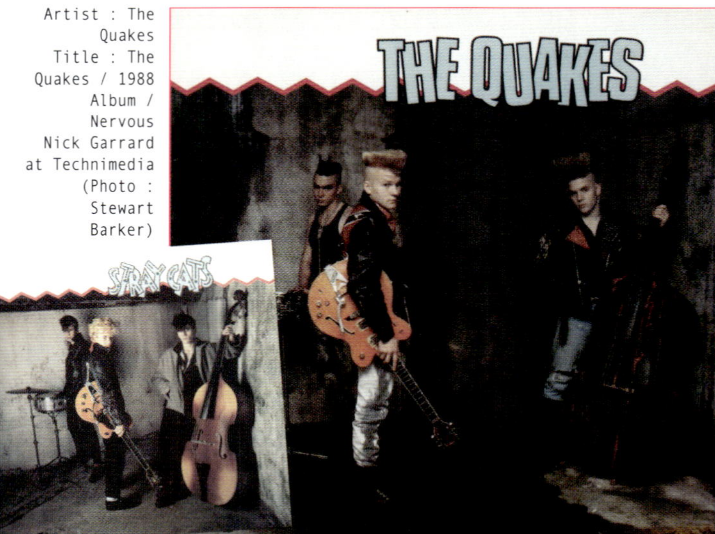

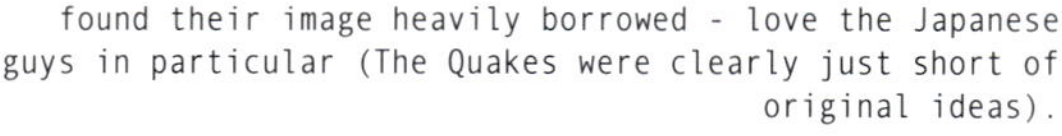

found their image heavily borrowed - love the Japanese guys in particular (The Quakes were clearly just short of original ideas).

Artist : Christian / Durand
Title : suggests Go West, Virginia / 1998
EP / Christian - Durand
Artwork : Tricia Watson

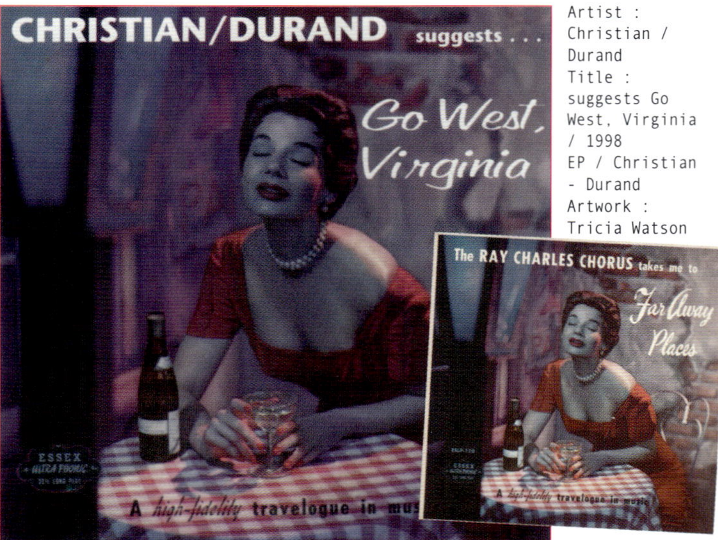

The fifties easy legacy mined again, this time The Ray Charles Chorus 10" album (takes me to) Far Away Places [1955 : Essex Records. Photo : Silver Studios, N.Y.C.] is carefully duplicated in its entirety, only the titles have changed.

The cover shot of Marc Bolan's The Slider album [1972] was taken by Ringo Starr and made a striking sleeve. As with Blonde On Blonde (pg 121) The Cynics' did their own version of both the front and back cover (check the anagram for their retoucher), while Kevin Seconds' designer (the same guy did the parody of Springsteen page 120) just went mad with the crayons (two bands shared the disc).

Artist : The Cynics
Title : Born To Lose + 1 / 19--
Single / Get Hip Recordings
Artwork Photo : Michelle Cercone
(Retouching : Ognir Rrats)

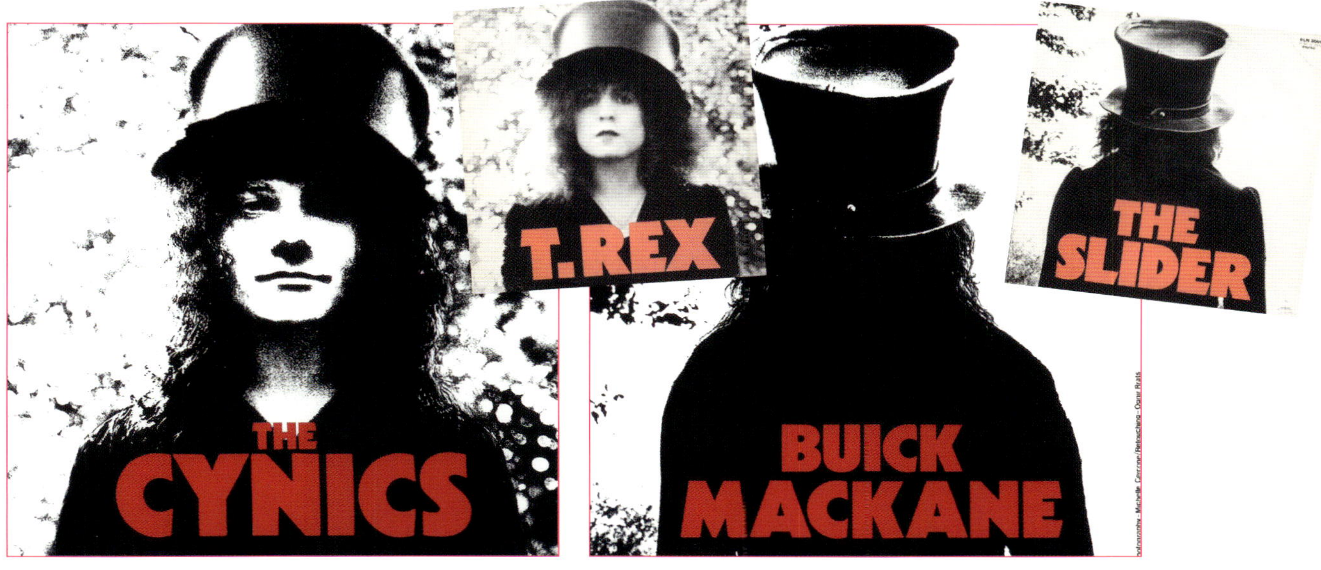

Artist : Kevin Seconds + 1
Title : Hot Love + 1 / 2009
Single / Suburban Home Records
Artwork : Mitch Clem

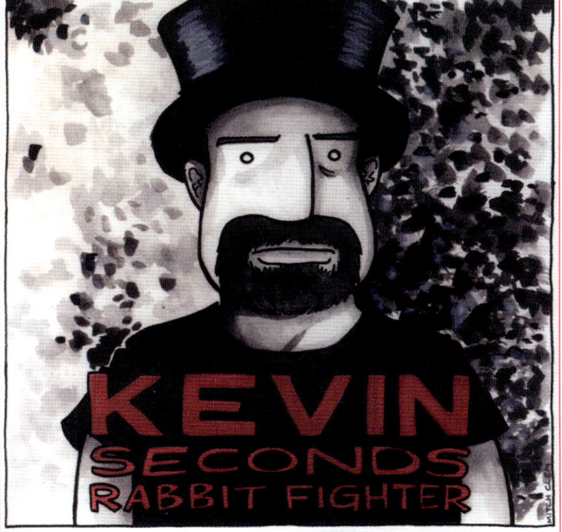

Name : Bidophone
Title : Cache Ton Machin / 1996
Album / Mantra - Arcade Music
Artwork / Photo : Christophe Mourthé

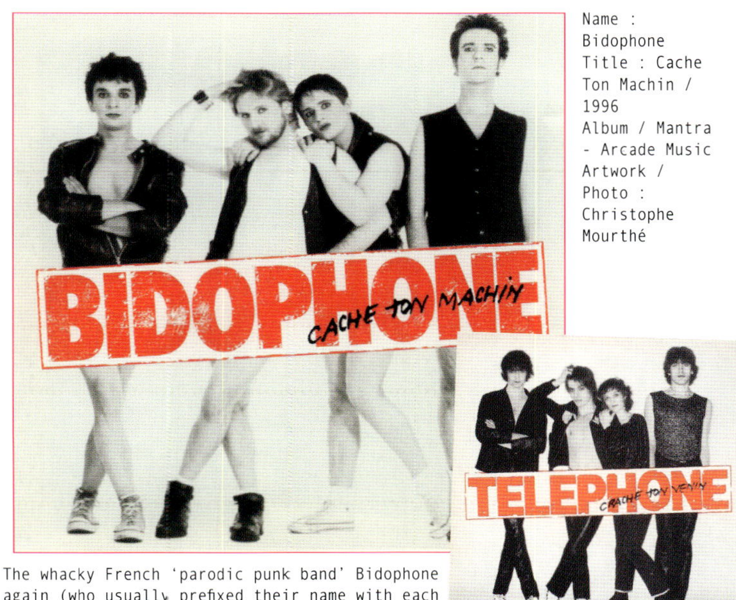

The whacky French 'parodic punk band' Bidophone again (who usually prefixed their name with each release according whoever they were parodying), this time lifting the title, sleeve pose and typography from Telephone's 1979 LP Crache Ton Venin [Artwork : Studio de l'air].

All coming from an art school background, Talking Heads had some impressive sleeves (and a couple of turkeys - Naked anyone?). More Songs About Building And Food [1978 : Sire. Artwork : Jimmy DeSana / David Byrne] inspired two more Polaroid print mosaic covers (and perhaps David Hockney as well). End Of A Year even covered the Talking Heads track Wild Wild Life on their EP. The original concept for More Songs called for no type on the cover at all, the label weren't so sure.

Artist : End Of A Year
Title : More Songs About Transportation And Intercourse / 2009
3 track EP / Hex Records
Artwork : Hex

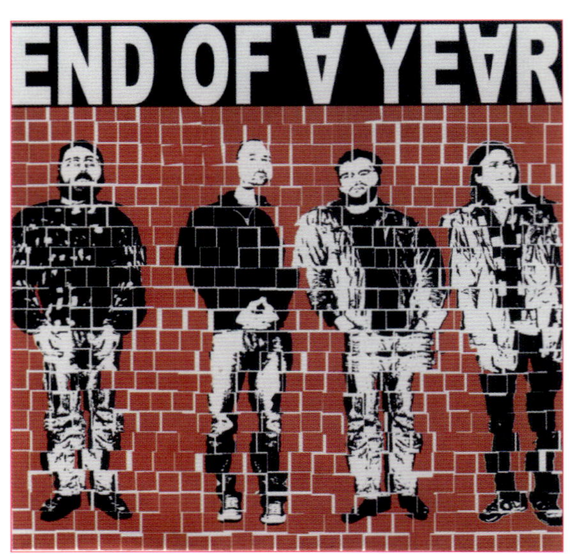

Artist : Ren Takada
Title : RT / 2004
Album / Nowgomix Records
Artwork : 333 design

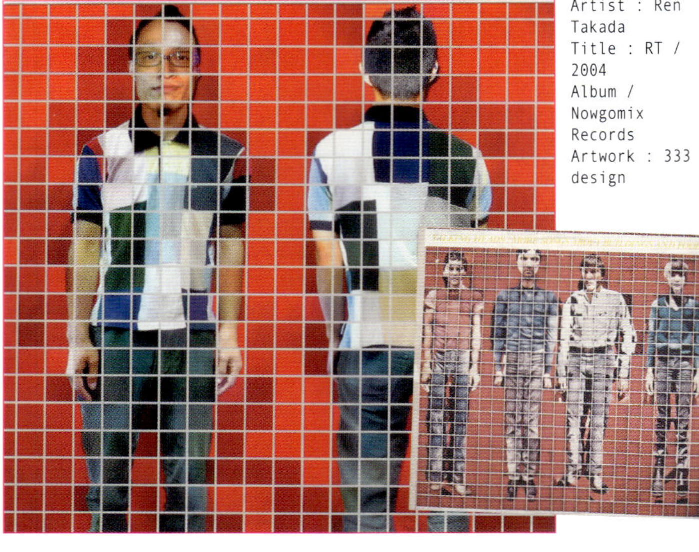

Artist : Hank McCoy & The Dead Ringers
Title : Still Feeling Blue / 1991
Album / Okra - Normal Records
Artwork / Photo : Reneé Velkoff

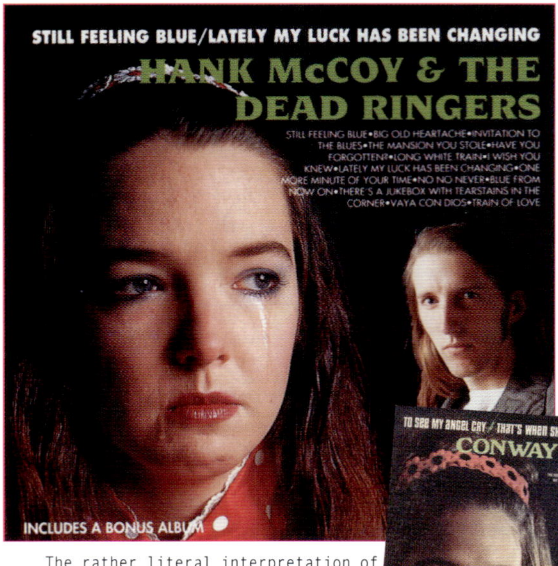

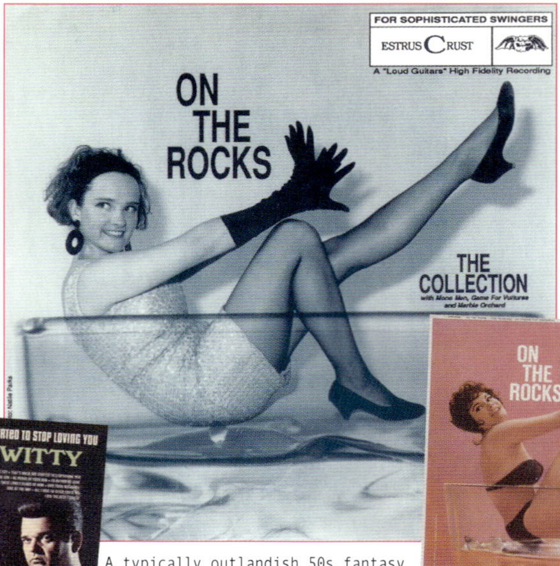

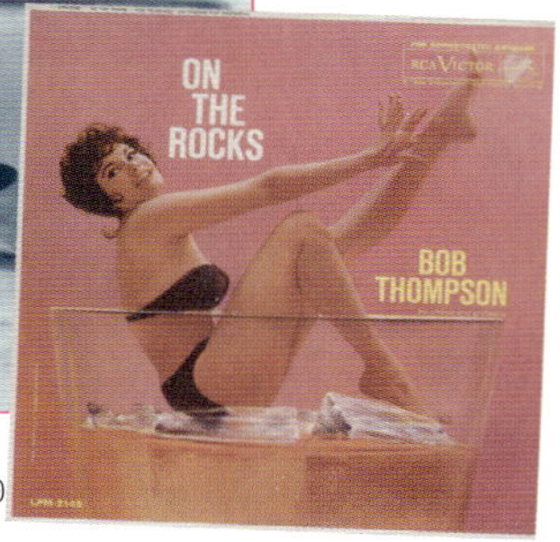

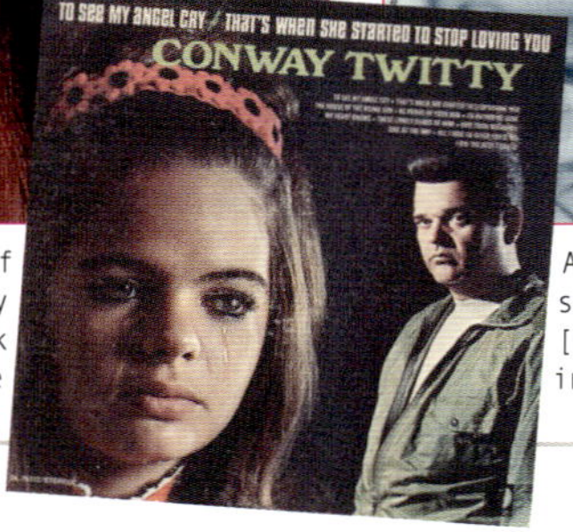

The rather literal interpretation of Conway Twitty's 1970 album To See My Angel Cry is closely copied by Hank McCoy, the designer even giving the original a concept credit.

Artist : Mono Men + 2
Title : On The Rocks/ 1991
3 track EP / Estrus Records
Artwork : Natile Parks (Cover Photo)

A typically outlandish 50s fantasy studio shot for Bob Thompson in 1960 [Photo : Ken Whitmore] is given an ironic make over by Estrus for this 3 band EP.

 CONWAY TWITTY   BOB THOMPSON

I couldn't work out why there were so many covers styling themselves after an obscure and fairly bland Various Artists Hootenanny Collection sleeve from 1963 [Crestview / Elektra. Artwork : Unknown], but it turns out respected alt-rock pioneers The Replacements nicked the idea in 1983, and others have borrowed the cover idea from them. Including '23 Australian Bands Playing Tribute To The Genius of The Replacements'. As you do.

Artist : The Replacements
Title : Hootenanny / 1983
Album / Twin Tone
Artwork : Fake Name Graphx

Artist : Various Artists
Title : I'm In Love ... With That Song / 1999
Album / Tomboy Records - Shock Records
Artwork : Ian Underwood, Popart Digital Media

Artist : Hellnation
Title : At War With Emo / 1997
CDEP / Slap A Ham Records
Artwork : Unknown

Artist : The Perverts
Title : You Drive Me Wild + 3 / 1995
EP / Demolition Derby
Artwork : Arie Egmond / Snoesje / Melzz

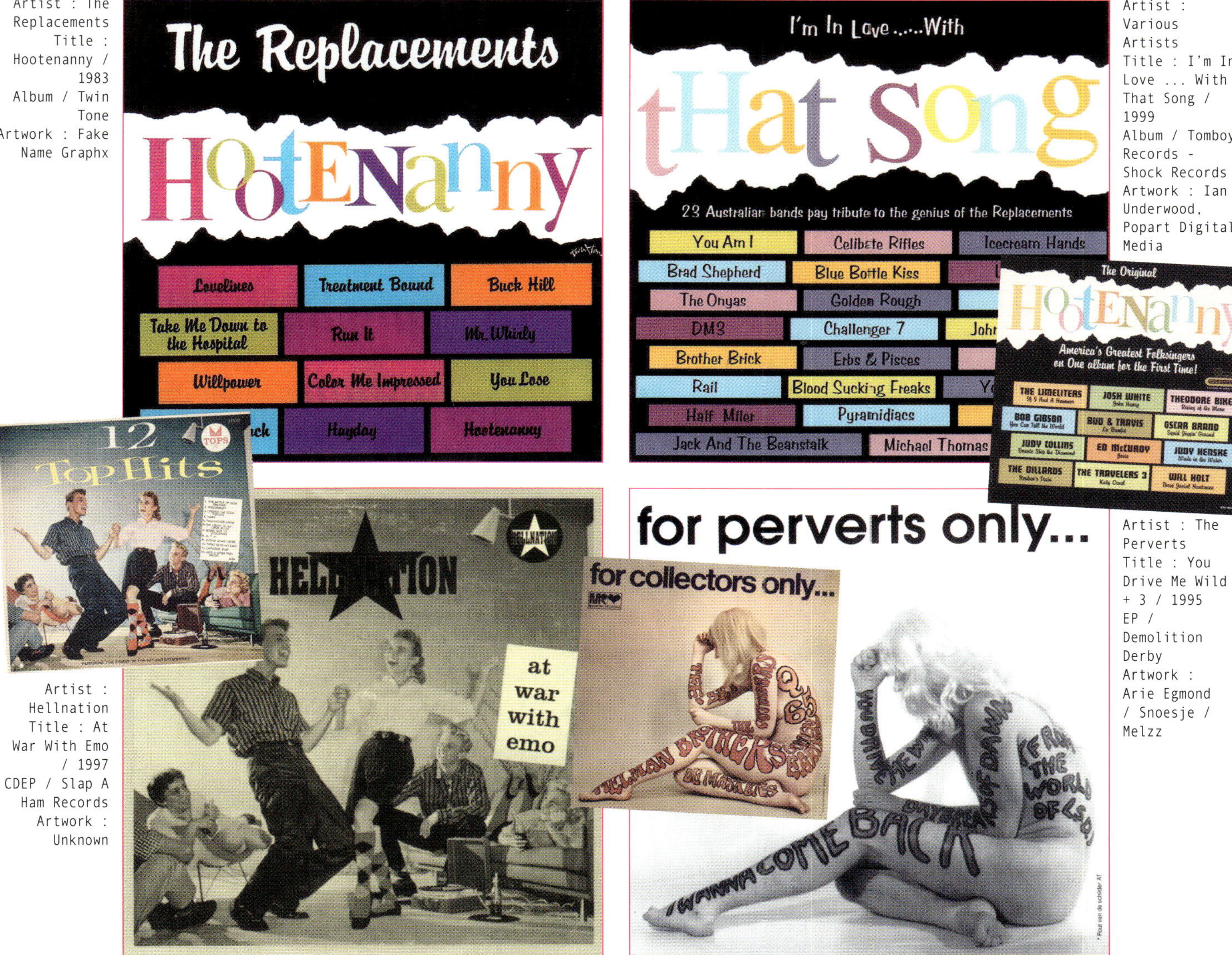

12 Top Hits is not only a great American V/Artists hits selection from 1957 [Hi-fi Tops. Artwork : Unknown] but a source of graphics to plunder for the excellently titled At War With Emo CDEP.

For Collectors Only... was a Dutch V/Artists pop album from 1967 [Modern Records. Artwork : Unknown], with the old psych lettering on a female nude style cover inspiring a remake by The Perverts for a three track EP.

Jack Good's Oh Boy was a pioneering UK TV pop entertainment show, and this 1957 tie-in album on Parlophone captures all the glitz and glamour. Wreckless manages to pay a nice tribute right down to the pastel coloured outfits.

The original BBC Sound Effects albums ran to several volumes, but the budget didn't, so they just changed the colourway each time. Vol 8 in 1972 was pink. The design is still much admired and collected, and copied. First quite▼

Artist : Wreckless Eric
Title : The Wonderful World Of Wreckless Eric / 1978
Album / Stiff Records
Artwork + Photo : Chris Gabrin

Artist : The Jam
Title : Sound Affects / 1980
Album / Polydor
Artwork : Bill Smith / The Jam (Photos : Martyn Goddard / Andrew Rosen)

Artist : Monster Magnet
Title : Dead Christmas / 1995
EP / A & M
Unknown

Artist : Various Artists
Title : 20 Original Mod Classics / 2010
Album / Spectrum Music
Artwork : Unknown

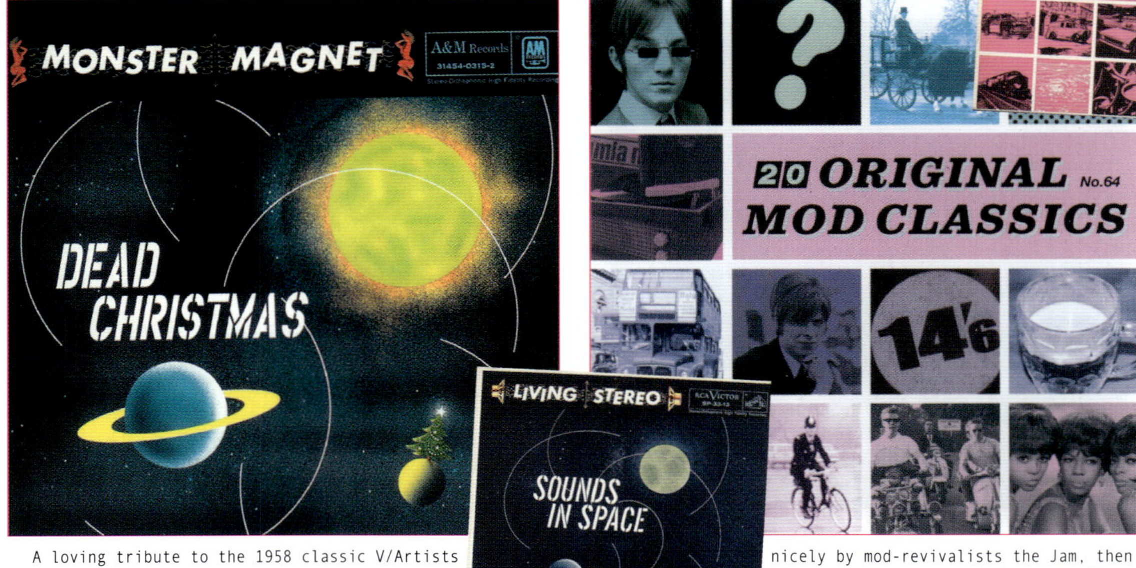

A loving tribute to the 1958 classic V/Artists Sounds In Space cover, down to replicating the vintage RCA Victor Living Stereo logo, one of the great vinyl graphics of all time, with just the addition of a solitary christmas tree.

nicely by mod-revivalists the Jam, then 20 years later very cheaply for a 60s mod collection courtesy of Polydor's petrol forecourt budget label Spectrum.

US political right-wing satirist Paul Shanklin clearly using Vanilla Ice's 1990 rapathon To The Extreme [Artwork : Janet Perr. Photo : Michael Lavine] as the basis for this cartoon parody a decade on.

Indie singer-songwriter Mike Doughty doing a geeky variation on Suzanne Vega's Nine Objects Of Desire CD from 1996 [Artwork : Emily Philpott. Photo : Jim Wright], with an anaemic looking apple!

Artist : Paul Shanklin
Title : Vice Vice Baby / 2000
Album / Narodniki Records
Artwork : Michael P. Ramirez / John Sanders

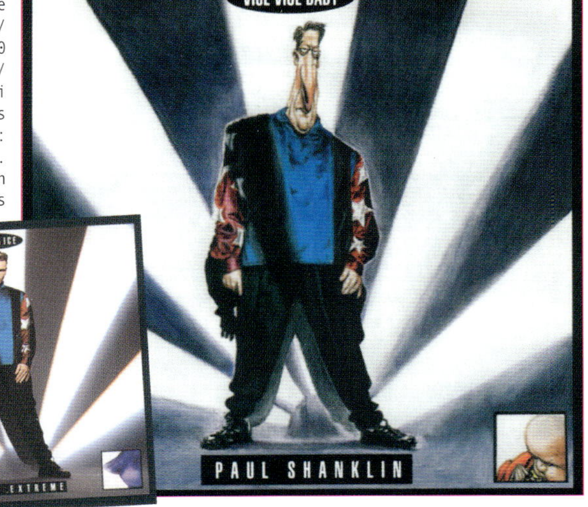

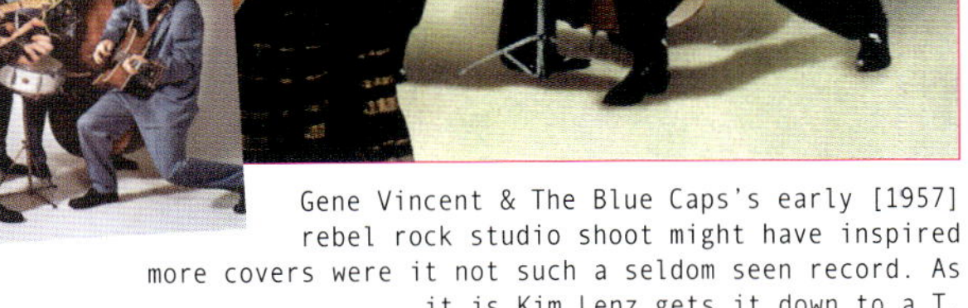

Mike Doughty
Title : Golden Delicious / 2008
Album / Ato Records
Artwork : Emily Philpott
(Photo : Jim Wright)

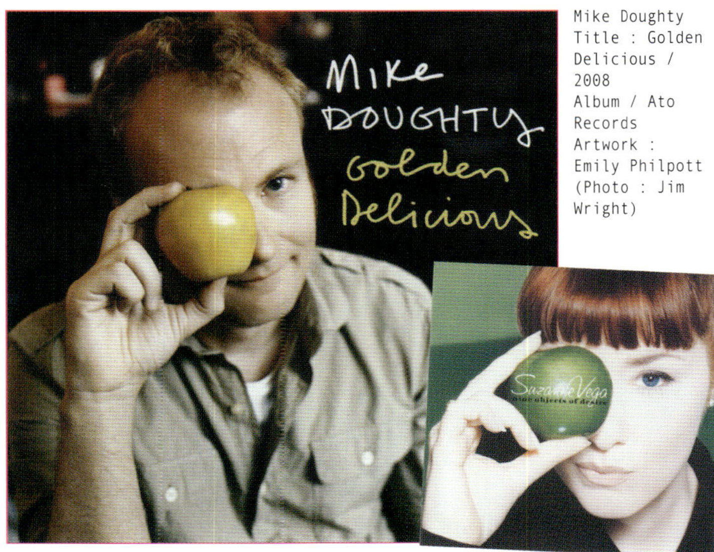

Artist : Kim Lenz & Her Jaguars
Title : Kim Lenz & Her Jaguars / 1998
Album / HMG – Hightone Records
Artwork : Frank Laudo
(Photo : Jean Phillipe Studios)

Andy Warhol's cover illustration for The Velvet Underground & Nico [1967 with Acy R. Lehman] is real record-sleeve-as-art territory, with the artist's name replacing the band's. With that and the influential music inside, the cover has been widely copied.
Overleaf are eight of the best examples.

L-R : Band Zonder Banaan : 'k Mag Niet Klagen [1999 Artwork : Unknown] / The Dead Milkmen : Smokin' Banana Peels [1988 Artwork : Photo : George Moore] / Gossip : Love Long Distance [2009 Artwork : Unknown] / Mama Rosin : Brule Lentement [2009 Artwork : Seriously Delicious Graphics] / Marijke Boon : Een Lange Groene Komkommer [2000 Artwork : Marijke Boon / Diederik Hummelinck] / Papa Wortelman & Jah Stonehenge & The Dreadbangers : Vlieg Tiepotsken Vlieg + 1 [45 year + artwork : Unknown] / Pooch : Surfin' Kill City + 3 [1988 12" Single Artwork : Al] / White Flag + 1 : Special Cure For A Splitting Headache [2010 Artwork : Pat Fear Photo : Coco Hadley / Gordon Moore]. Left : Various Artists : Die Goldenen Zitronen - A Tribute To... [2008 Artwork : Lars Nagler].

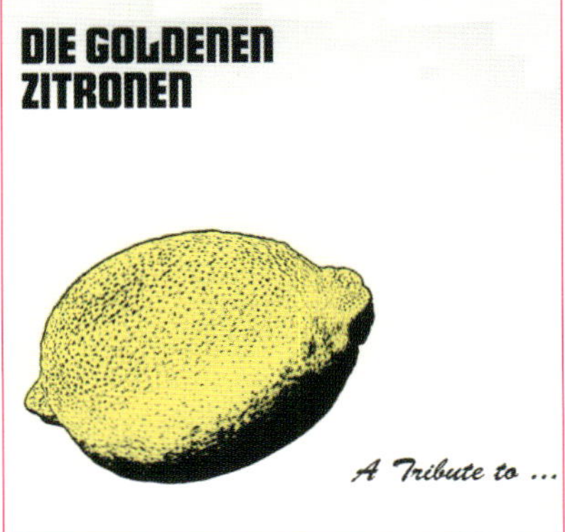

Gene Vincent & The Blue Caps's early [1957] rebel rock studio shoot might have inspired more covers were it not such a seldom seen record. As it is Kim Lenz gets it down to a T.

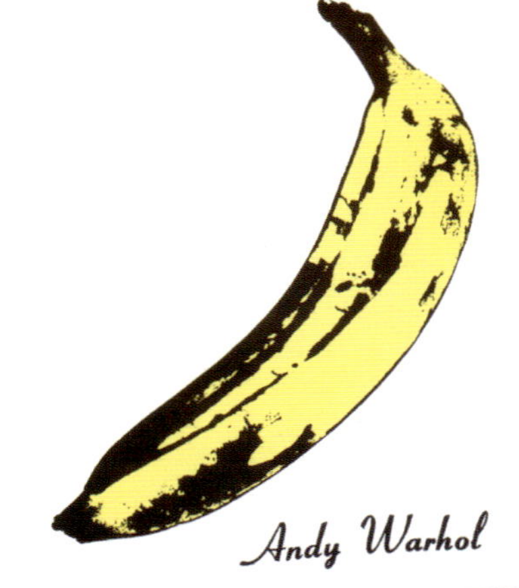
Andy Warhol

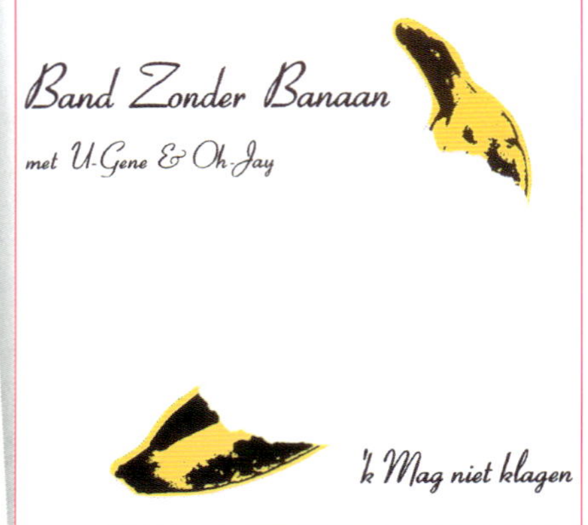
Band Zonder Banaan
met U-Gene & Oh-Jay
'k Mag niet klagen

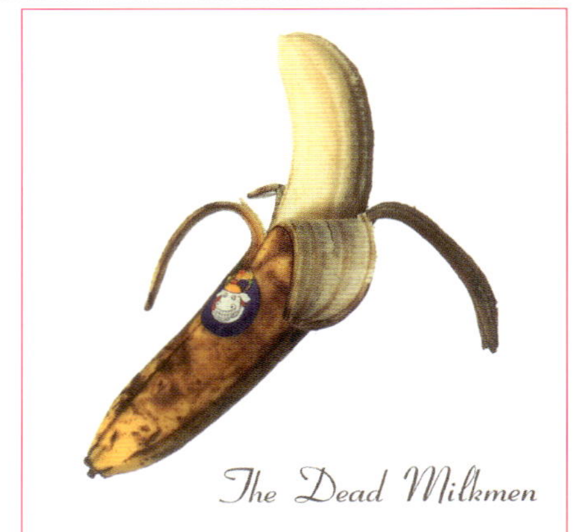
The Dead Milkmen

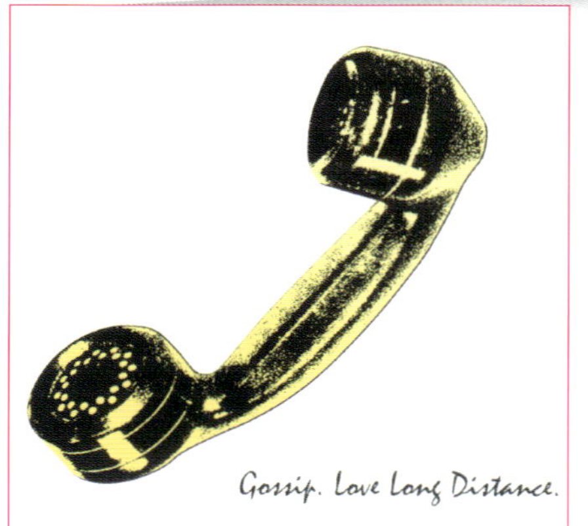
Gossip. Love Long Distance.

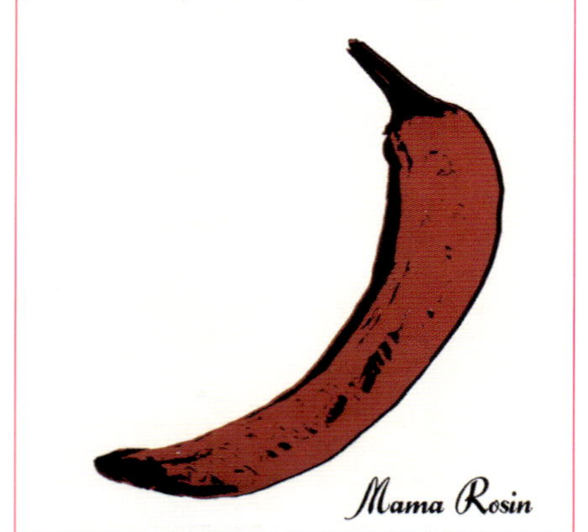
Mama Rosin

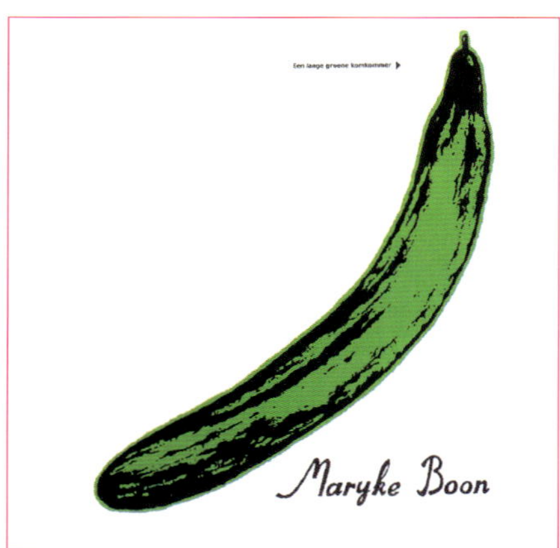
een laage groene komkommer
Maryke Boon

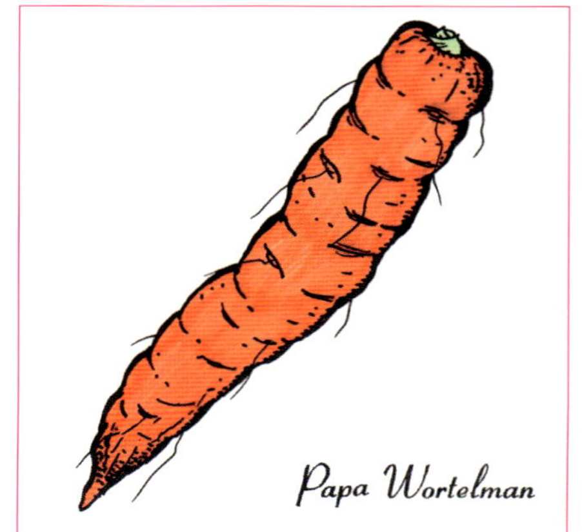
Papa Wortelman

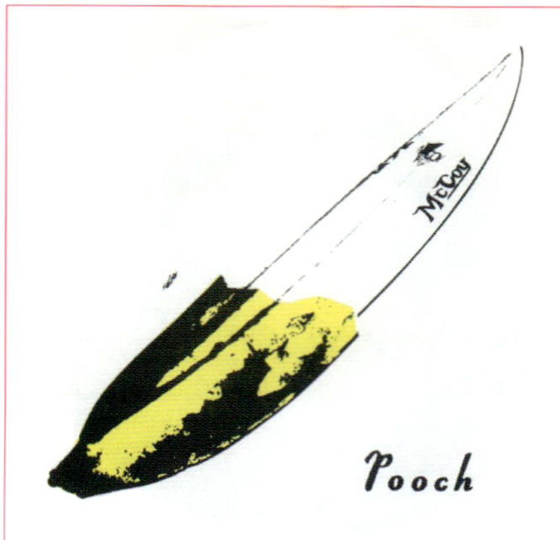
McCoy
Pooch

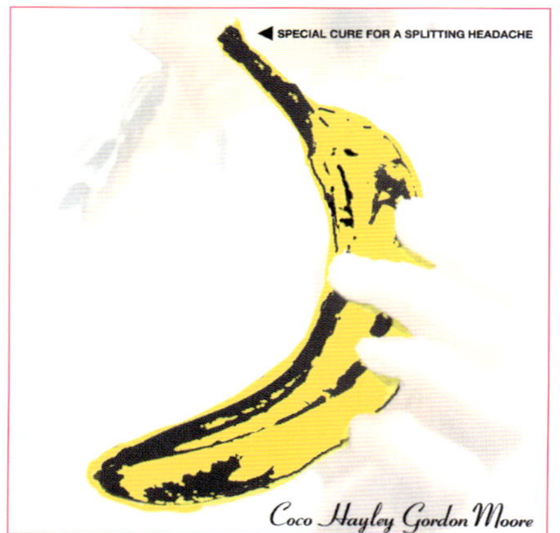
SPECIAL CURE FOR A SPLITTING HEADACHE
Coco Hayley Gordon Moore

An album endorsed by John Wayne, Pat Boone AND Walt Disrey? Up With People! [1965 : Pace Publications. Artwork : Unknown] is parodied here with those original messages of support left in situ.

The Japanese again, this time hijacking Tom Waits' Swordfishtrombones [1983 : Island. Artwork : Michael Russ / Tom Waits / Frank Mulvey Illustration : Michael Russ] down to the yellow and pink colourway.

Artist :
Lambchop
Title : Up
With People /
Up With People
(remix) / Miss
Prissy
Anno : 2000
Format : EP
Label : City
Slang
Artwork :
Unknown

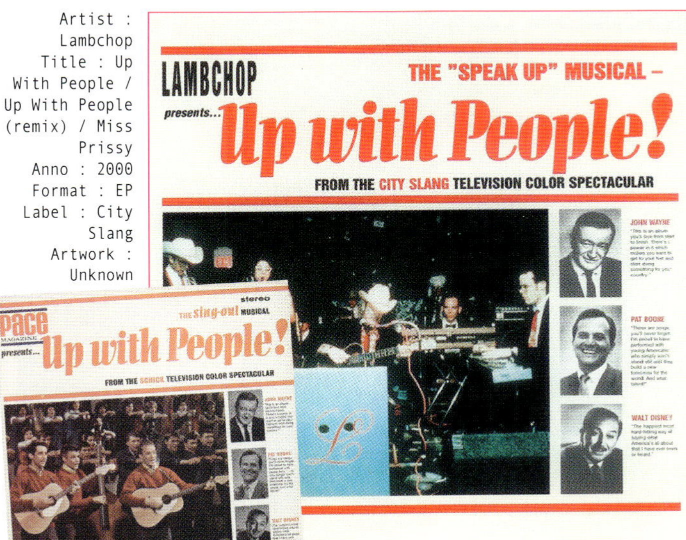

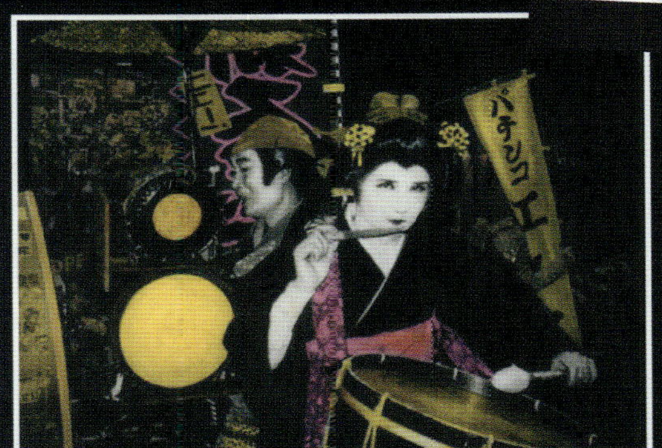

Artist :
Katteni-
Shiyagare
Title :
Swinishtown
2002
Album / Grande
Papa Records
Artwork :
Syohei Muto
/ Shinobu
Fukushima.
Illustration
: Takehiro
Yoshizawa
Photo : Harumi
Ohno

Artist :
Various
Artists
Title : Happy
Birthday, Baby
Jesus / 1993
Album /
Sympathy For
The Record
Industry
Artwork :
Eddie Flowers

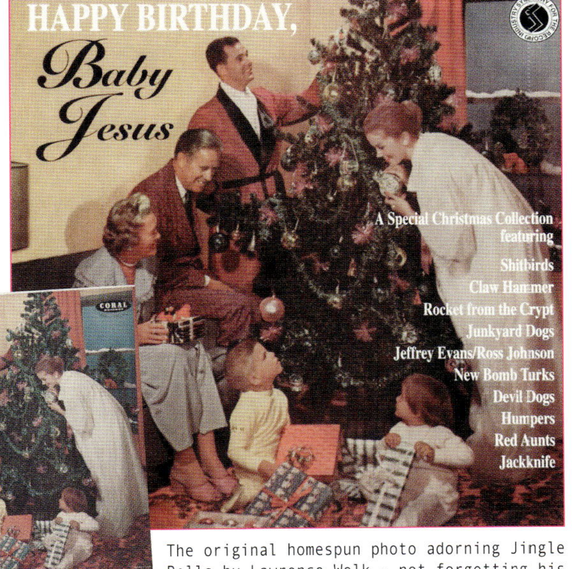

Artist :
Shisho
Title : Get
Behind Me
Santa / 2005
Single Artwork
: Unknown

The original homespun photo adorning Jingle Bells by Lawrence Welk - not forgetting his Champagne Music [1957 : Coral Records. Artwork : Unknown] is put to a new use on this V/Artists CD!

Another Christmasy effort based - only months after the original came out - on the The White Stripes photo from the cover of Get Behind Me Satan [2005 : XL Recordings. Artwork : The Third Man / Artnole Photo : Ewen Spencer].

Here The Nomads recreate Porter Wagoner's 1967 RCA LP cover The Cold Hard Facts Of Life - featuring what we assume is a chap returning to his hotel room to find his partner cheating on him - in close detail.

The Wailers' The Fabulous Wailers album [1959. Artwork : Pete Ciccone] is clearly the inspiration for this strange single sleeve, albeit with the natty white suits replaced by bandages.

Artist : The Nomads
Title : The Cold Hard Facts Of Life / 1995
Album / Lance Rock Records
Artwork : Neko Case - Shane Sparks [Urban Studios] Photo : Paul Clarke

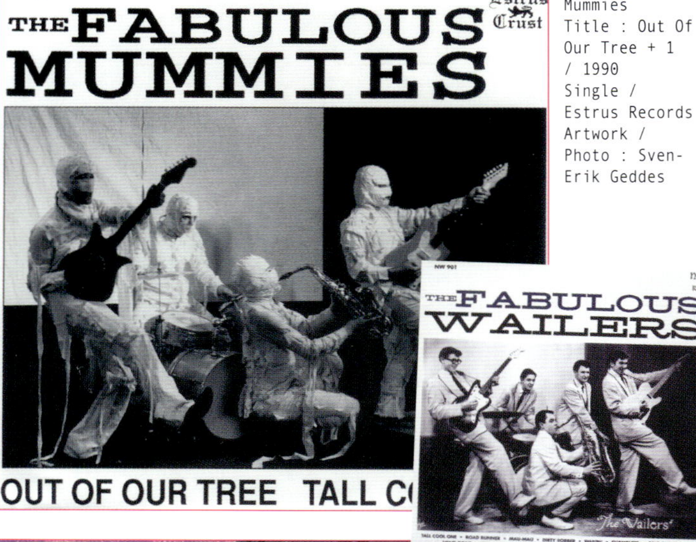

Artist : The Mummies
Title : Out Of Our Tree + 1 / 1990
Single / Estrus Records
Artwork / Photo : Sven-Erik Geddes

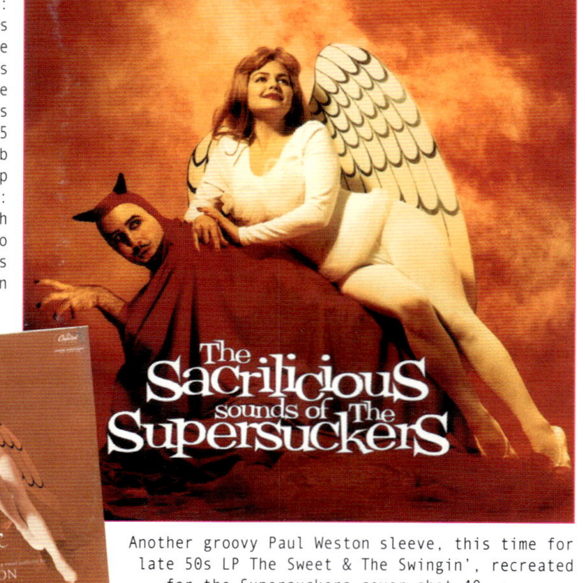

Artist : Supersuckers
Title : The Sacrilicious Sounds Of The Supersuckers / 1995
Album / Sub Pop
Artwork : Kenneth Sherwood Photo : Charles Peterson

Another groovy Paul Weston sleeve, this time for late 50s LP The Sweet & The Swingin', recreated for the Supersuckers cover shot 40 years on.

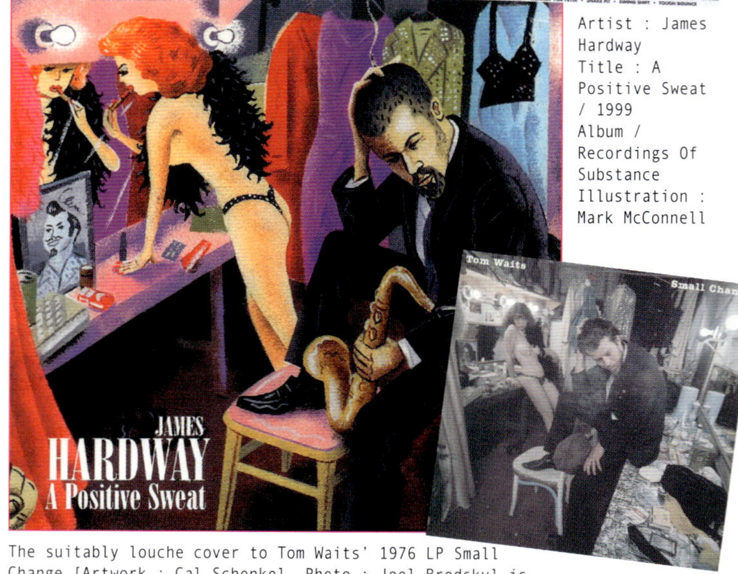

Artist : James Hardway
Title : A Positive Sweat / 1999
Album / Recordings Of Substance
Illustration : Mark McConnell

The suitably louche cover to Tom Waits' 1976 LP Small Change [Artwork : Cal Schenkel. Photo : Joel Brodsky] is the basis for the painting on the James Hardway cover.

Nice to know I wasn't the only one to be transfixed by the cover to The Who Sell Out when I first saw it. Issued in 1967 [Artwork : David King / Roger Law. Photos : David Montgomery], here are two bands who were up for bathing in cold baked beans to replicate the original; US punk indie rockers on the left, Petra Haden's a cappella version of the originals - recorded on a cassette studio - on the right. Pete Townshend is a big fan of this.

Artist : The Fast
Title : The Fast For Sale / 1980
Album / Recca
Artwork : Bob Coogan (Photos : David Rice)

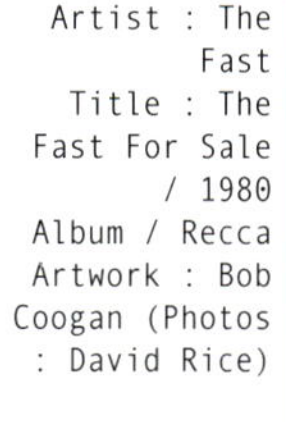

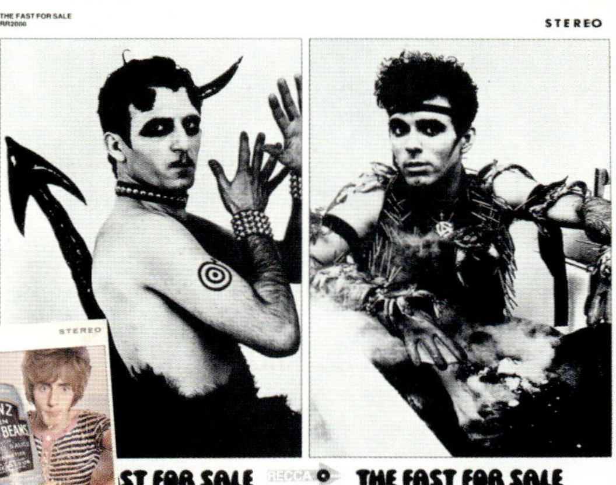

Artist : Petra Haden
Title : Sings The Who Sell Out / 2005
Album / Bar - None
Artwork : David Richman
Photos : Alicia J. Rose

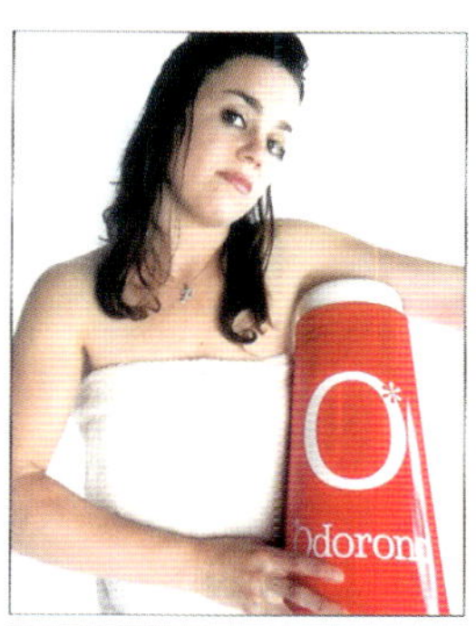
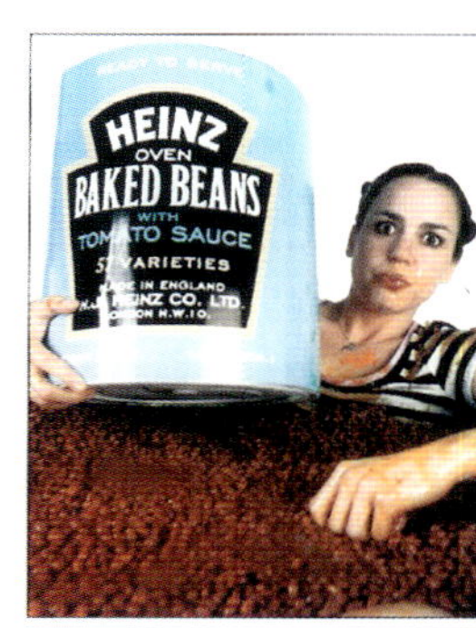

Artist : Cinnamon
Title : The Many Moods Of Cinnamon / 1999
EP / March Records
Artwork : Designlab

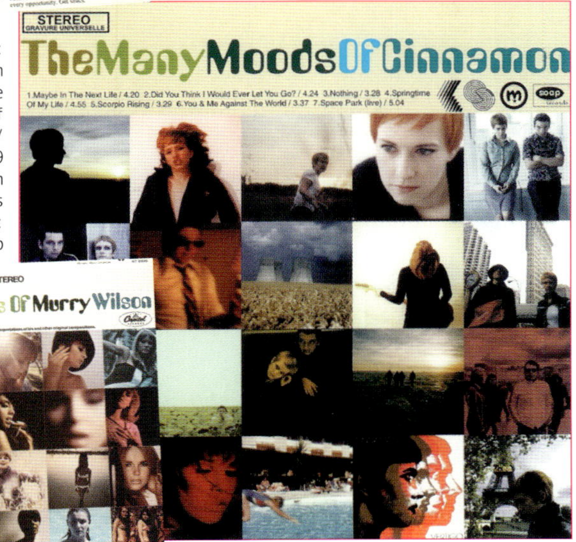

Artist : Boris With Merzbow
Title : Walrus & Groon / 2007
EP / Hydra Head Records
Artwork : Fangs Anal Latan

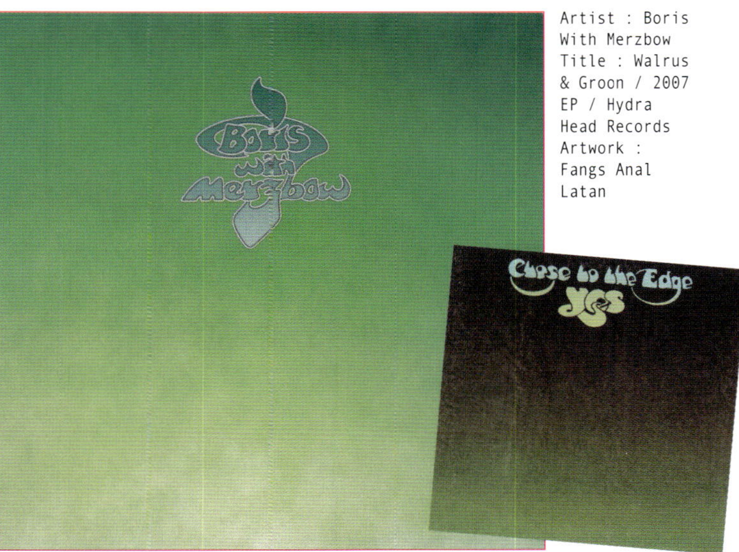

The Many Moods Of Murry Wilson (The Wilson Beach Bcys' father cashing in) is a very classy 1967 sleeve from Capitol Records, and is carefully replicated by the Cinnamon EP cover.

Roger Dean's artwork was inspirational enough to spawn any number of sci-fi fantasy sleeve illustrators but he is still the one who set the standard. This is a nice tribute to the 1972 Yes classic Close To The Edge by the Japanese band Boris (who clearly enjoy doing this, see also page 51).

THE
WHO
LIVE AT
LEEDS

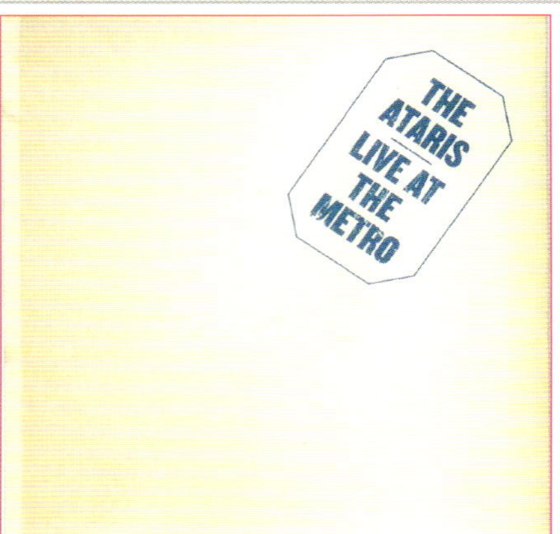
THE
ATARIS
LIVE AT
THE
METRO

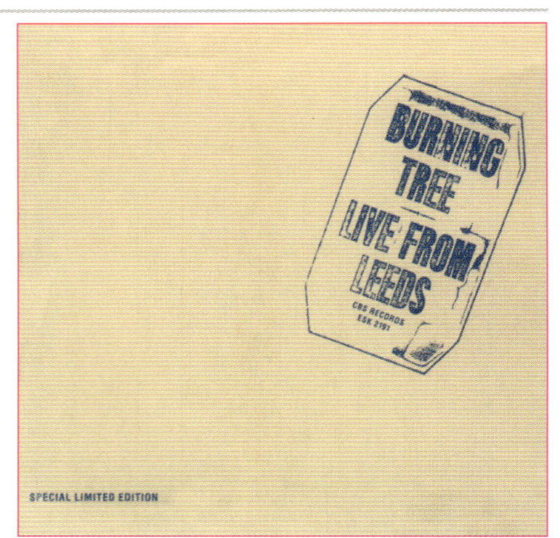
BURNING
TREE
LIVE FROM
LEEDS
CBS RECORDS
ESK 2791
SPECIAL LIMITED EDITION

HER-
ESY
LIVE AT
LEEDS

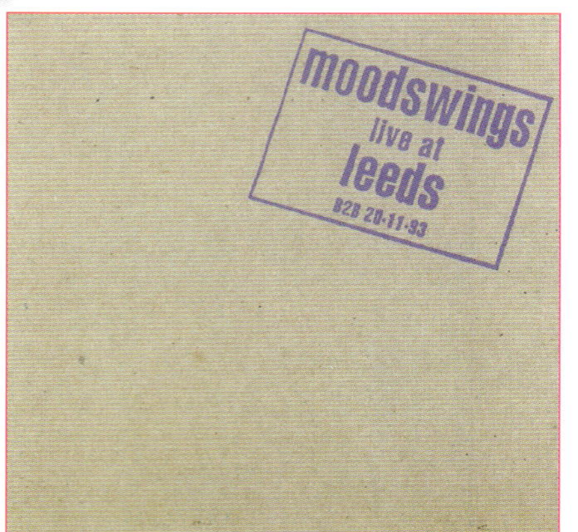
moodswings
live at
leeds
02B 20·11·93

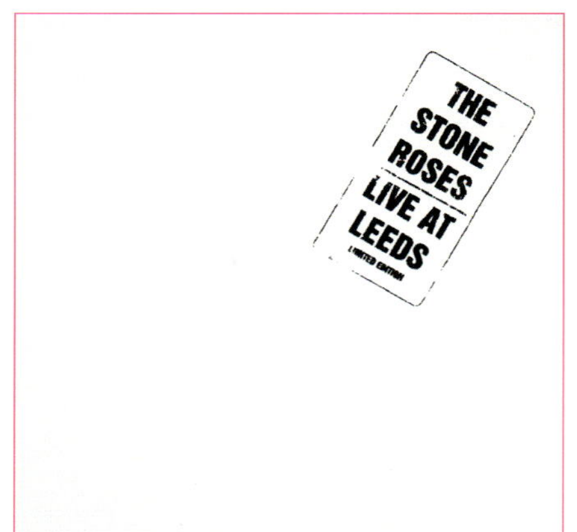
THE
STONE
ROSES
LIVE AT
LEEDS
LIMITED EDITION

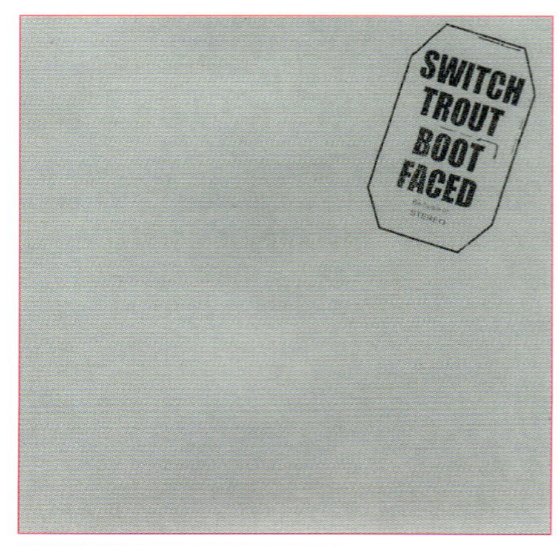
SWITCH
TROUT
BOOT
FACED
STEREO

TRAILER
TRASH
LIVE AT
LEE'S
0154-2

FULL
TILT
LIVE FROM
CALI
SPECIAL EDITION

X-Ray Specs' 1978 album Germ Free Adolescents got the full EMI art budget treatment [Falcon Stuart / Cooke Key. Photos : Trevor Key] which was a tad ironic, given it was lyrically an anti-consumerist tirade. EMI may have tried to market the band in a way which went against their punk beginnings, but it has inspired a couple of groups to copy the idea for singles (remember those?)..

Artist : Popdefect
Title : Every Day Is Brenda Day - I Am Poseur / 1996 Single / Scooch Pooch Records Artwork - photo : Barbara Radlein

Artist : Girls Aloud
Title : Biology / 2005 EP / Polydor Artwork : Form (Photos : Sean McMenomy)

The Who Live At Leeds (*previous page*) took inspiration from the newly emerging bootleg albums which started to appear in late 1969. It was designed by Polydor stalwarts Graphreaks (who did some great covers for the label), and if fans were a little disappointed by the sparse nature of the cover, it was more than compensated for by the goodies enclosed with the original pressing. It was also one of the first live rock albums, a format which arguably reached a peak with Deep Purple's Made In Japan two years later. Wanting to have some of the Live At Leeds glory rub off on them means this impressive Northern city must have generated more live albums than anywhere else in the UK (except perhaps London). Page 148 carries the following tribute covers:

The Ataris : Live At The Metro [2004 : No Label : Artwork Unknown] / Burning Tree : Live From Leeds [1990 EP : CBS : Artwork Unknown] / Full Tilt : Live From Cali [1992 : Artwork Unknown] / Heresy : Live At Leeds [1990 Single : Open Records Artwork : Unknown] / Moodswings : Live At Leeds [1994 : Arista Artwork : Cooke & Wright] / The Stone Roses : Live At Leeds : STR Recordings Artwork : Unknown] / Switch Trout : Bootfaced [2000 : K.O.G.A. Records Artwork : Yasuko Sato] / Trailer Trash : Live At Lee's [1997 : Lee's Liquor Records Artwork : Strees Lab].

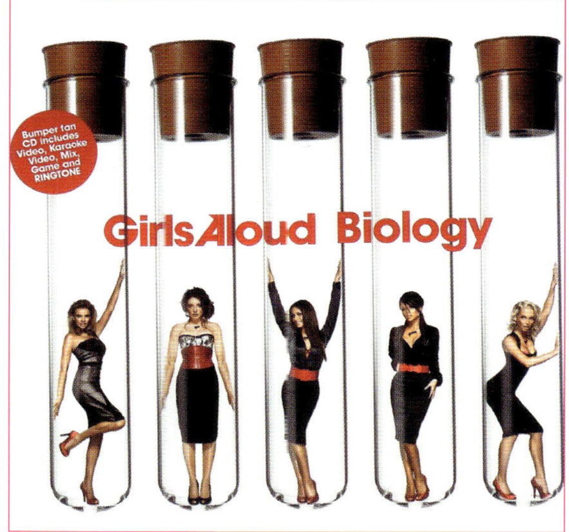

Artist : Kid Dynamite
Title : Cheap Shots , Youth Anthems / 2003 Album / Jade Tree Artwork : JD @ Comfortable Lead (Photo : Shane McCauley)

The Who's Odds & Sods 1974 album sported a great cover, partly designed by singer Roger Daltrey with Graham Hughes (who also took the photo). It's not one you'd immediately try and copy, but Kid Dynamite not only had a go in 2003 but arguably did it even better.

The interesting solarisation effect on Neil Young's 1970 LP After The Goldrush [Reprise], taken by Joel Bernstein is ignored by Japanese band Art School, but the composition of the people, and the railings, are a clear reference back to the original design.

Young hippies Hard Lessons are less overt than some in where their sleeve comes from, but once you see Neil Young's eponymous 1969 LP cover it's fairly clear [Reprise Records. Artwork : Ed Thrasher. Portrait : Roland Diehl]. The title's a bit of a giveaway too.

Artist : Art School
Title : Requiem For Innocence
Anno : 2002
Format :
Album Label : Toshiba / EMI
Artwork : Central 67
(Photo : Taeko Yamamoto)
(Illustration : Jun Ohyama)

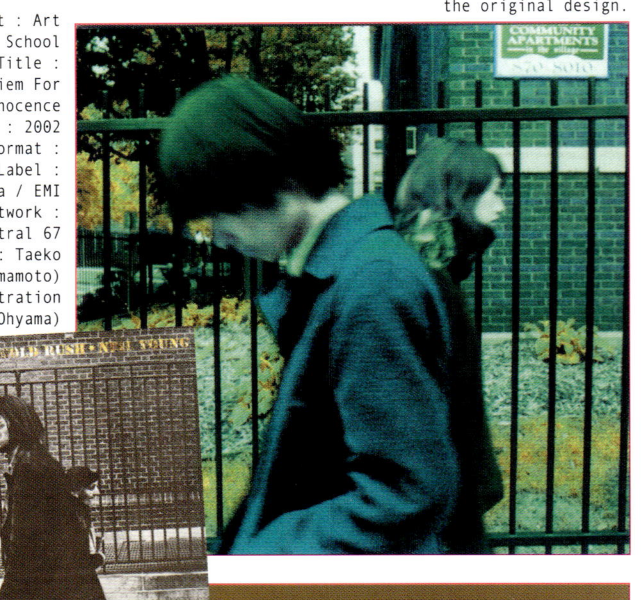

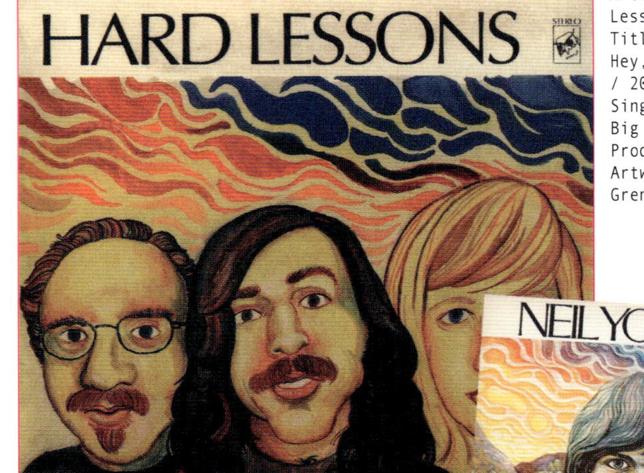

Artist : Hard Lessons
Title : Hey Hey, My My + 1 / 2007
Single / Big Gig Productions
Artwork : Eric Grenier

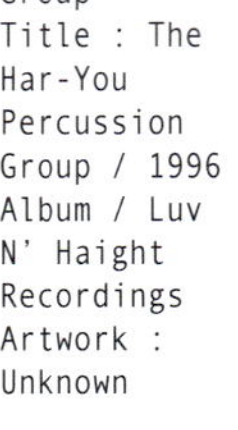

Artist : Trevor Rabin
Title : 90124 / 2003
Album / Voiceprint
Artwork : Unknown

Artist : The Har-You Percussion Group
Title : The Har-You Percussion Group / 1996
Album / Luv N' Haight Recordings
Artwork : Unknown

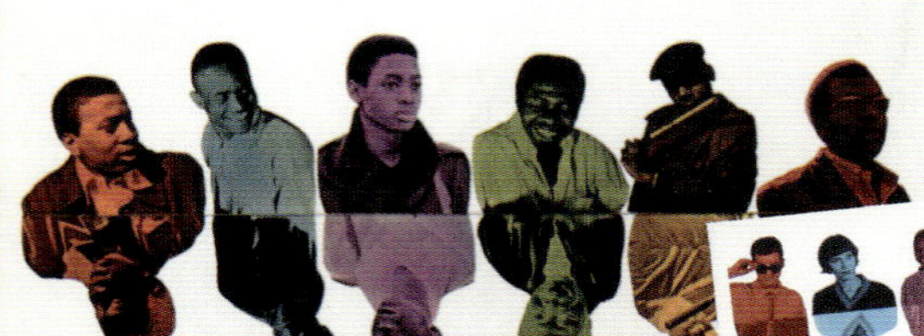

Not often you see artists referencing their own back-catalogue, but Yes man Trevor Rabin clearly felt copying one of his old Yes era sleeves [1983 : Atco. Artwork : Garry Mouat] would suit his post-Yes CD of demos done for the group.

Swifty often gets a fairly easy ride, but this is one of his best covers, done for Young Disciples Get Yourself Together 12" single in 1991. It was closely copied just five years on.

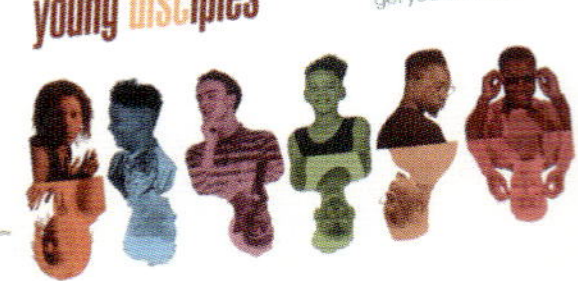

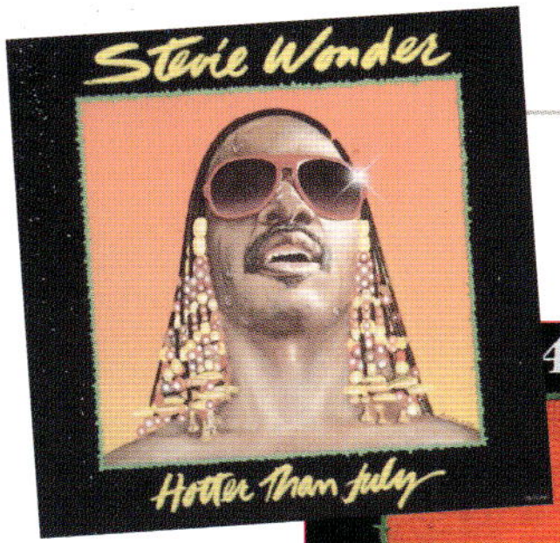

Stevie Wonder's 1980 LP Hotter Than July [Motown. Artwork : Al Harper / Stephanie Andrews] is a clear role model for this Japanese sleeve for Yuzo Hayashi, but as to why that should be...

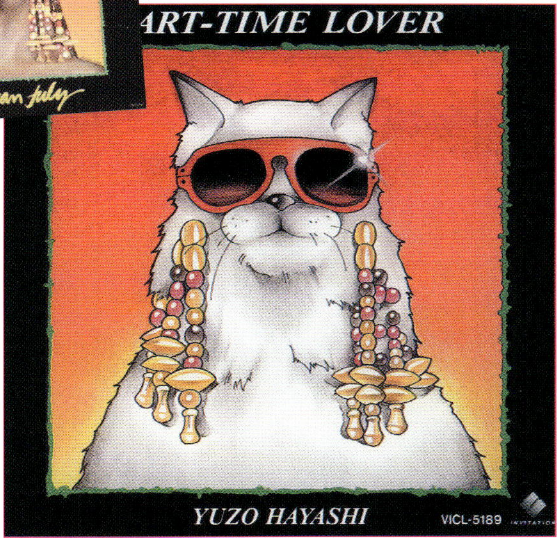

Stevie Wonder's early Tamla Motown album I Was Made To Love Her [1967] was designed by Frank Dandridge, who would probably have been amazed to see The Dirtbombs copy it over 30 years on.

Artist : Yuzo Hayashi
Title : Part-Time Lover / 1993
Album / Invitation - Victor Musical Industries
Illustration : Yoshitaka Tamaki

Artist : The Dirtbombs
Title : Ultraglide In Black / 2001
Album / In The Red
Artwork : Jimmy Hole (Photo : Danny Hole)

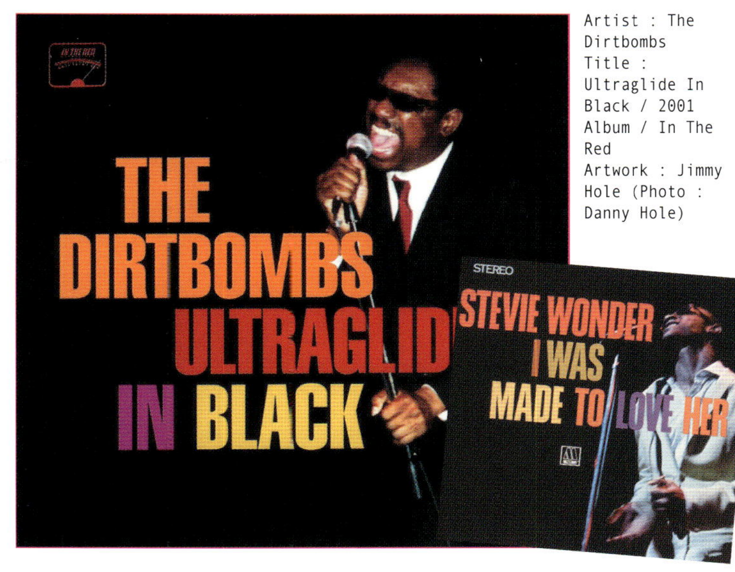

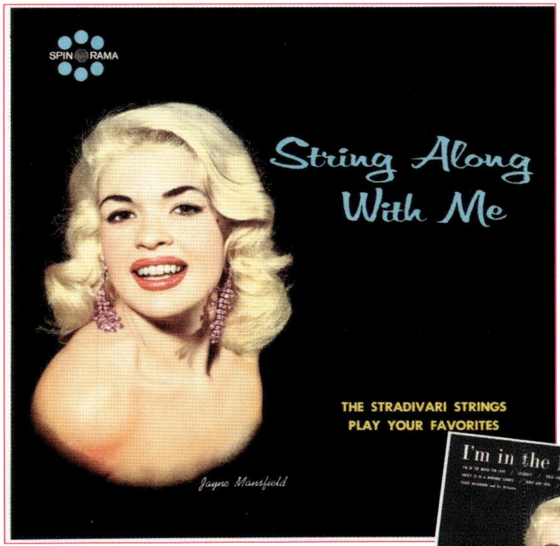

Artist : The Stradivari Strings
Title : String Along With Me
Anno : 1964
Format : Album
Label : Spinorama Records
Artwork : Unknown

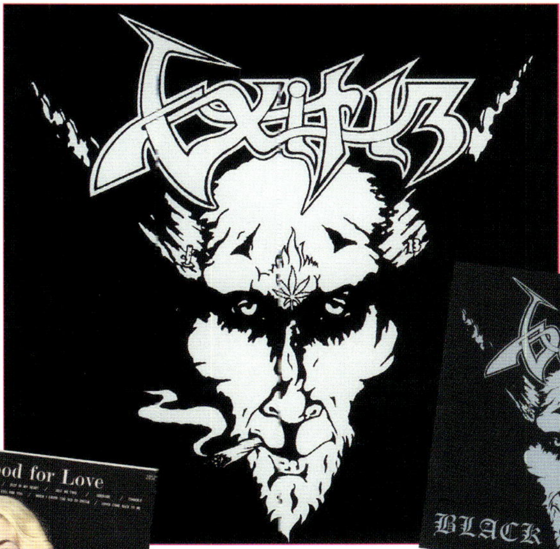

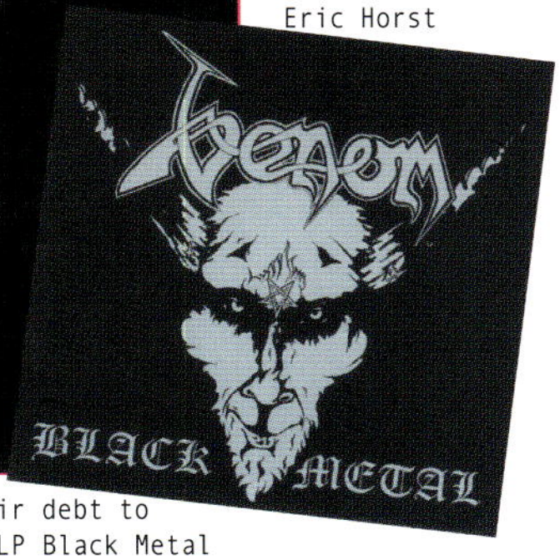

Artist : Exit 13
Title : ... Just A Few More Hits
Anno : 1995
Format : EP
Label : Relapse Records
Artwork : Wes Benscoter / Eric Horst

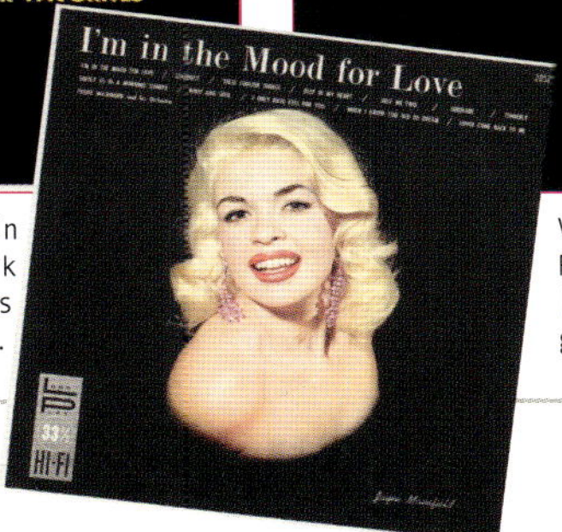

Frank Washburn & Orchestra's 1957 LP I'm In The Mood For Love [Promenade Records. Artwork : Unknown] finds their cover shot of actress Jayne Mansfield lifted just a few years on.

Venom (whose logo owed a fair debt to Roger Dean) fnd their 1982 LP Black Metal [Combat. Artwork : Venom / Hugh Gilmour] given a stoner make-over.

We don't know who designed The Yardbirds' 1965 album For Your Love [Epic], it may well have been a humble in-house staffer, but such is the reverence for the borderline Mod-band amongst the Freak Beat brigade that even a basic (albeit smart) grid format has been almost reverentially copied ever since, even down to pastiches of the vintage label logos. Stroll on...

Artist : The A-Bones
Title : Music Minus Five / 1993
Album / Norton Records
Artwork : Pete Ciccone (Photos : Megan Dooley)

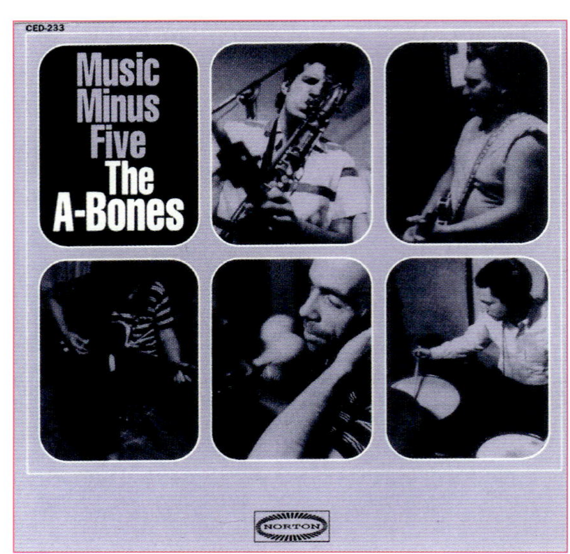

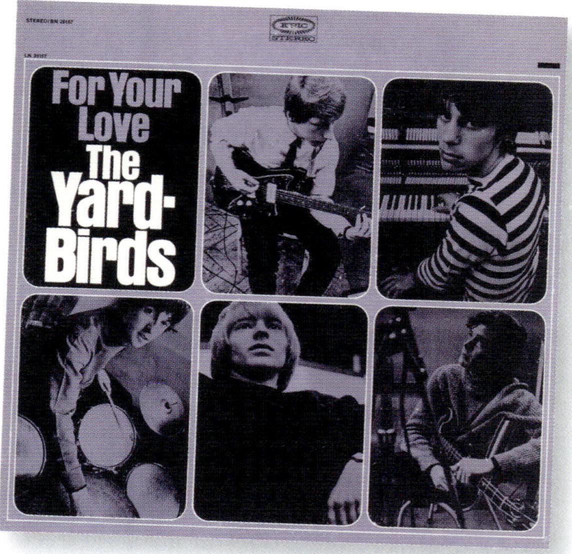

Artist : Les Black Carnations
Title : These Were ... / 1985
Album / Twang Records
Artwork : Uwe Friedrich / Curt Crescendo (Photos : Uwe Friedrich / Mike Korbik

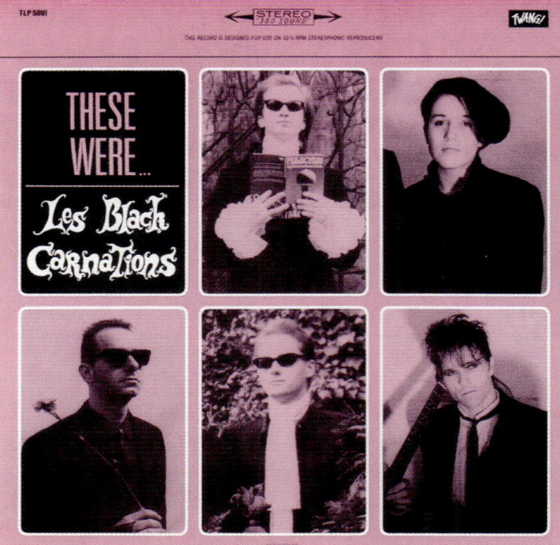

Artist : Switch Trout
Title : Thrill With Maximum / 2000
Album / K.O.G.A. Records
Artwork : Yasuko Sato (Photos : Miki.N / Rie.F)

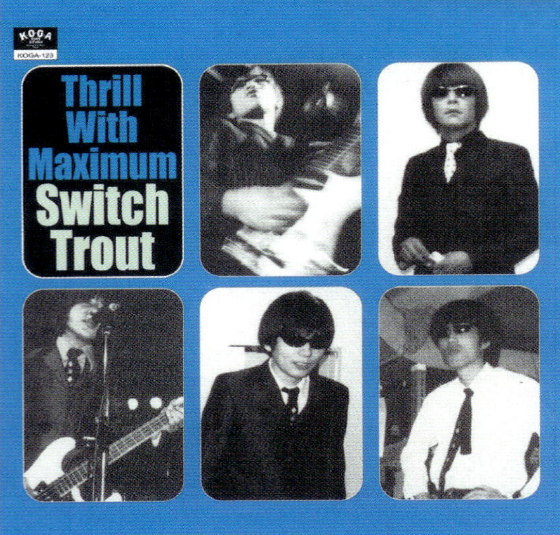

Neil Young's album Zuma from 1976 featured what might politely be called a naive pen sketch by Mazzeo, such as would normally be given as a brief to an illustrator. It was copied and reworked by National Heroes.

Zappa's LP covers were at least as adventurous as his music. Hot Rats [1969] was put together by his regular designer Cal Schenkel. The copy isn't slavish (a hot tub does for the pool) but has enough references for those in the know to pick up on. The name seals it.

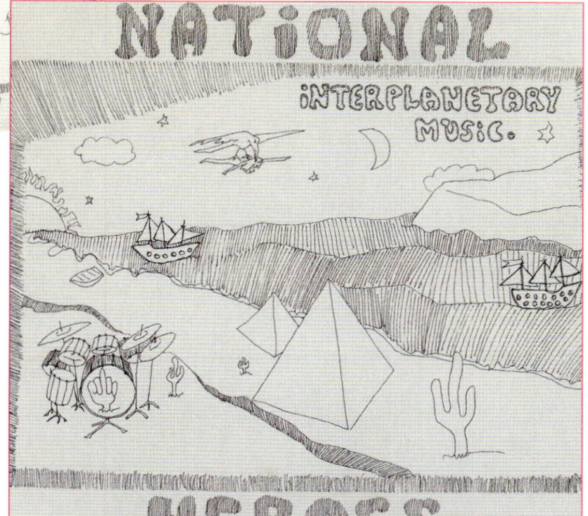

Artist :
National
Heroes
Title :
Interplanetary
Music / 1995
Album / Theme
Park
Artwork :
Russell Hill
/ Catie
Macnamara /
Spike

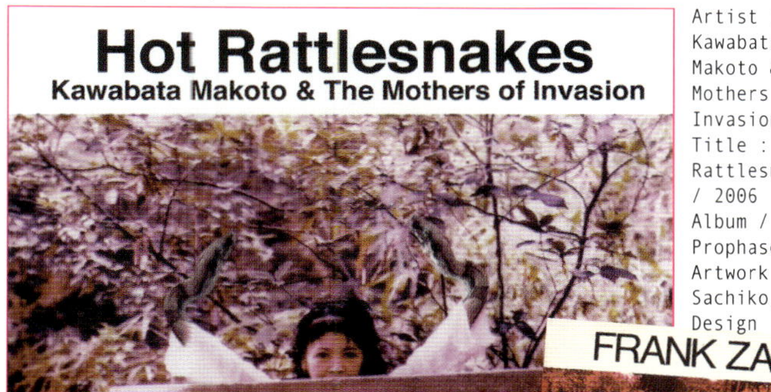

Artist :
Kawabata
Makoto & The
Mothers Of
Invasion
Title : Hot
Rattlesnakes
/ 2006
Album /
Prophase Music
Artwork :
Sachiko, ELF
Design

Artist : Eddie
Meduza
Title :
Garagetaper /
1980
Album / CBS
Artwork :
Anders Bühlund
(Photo :
Labe Allwin
/ Lennart
Dannstedt)

Zappa moved to more 'traditional' covers later, but even these he would often subvert as on Joe's Garage Act 1 in 1979 [Artwork : John Williams. Photo Norm Seeff). Eddie Meduza just replicates.

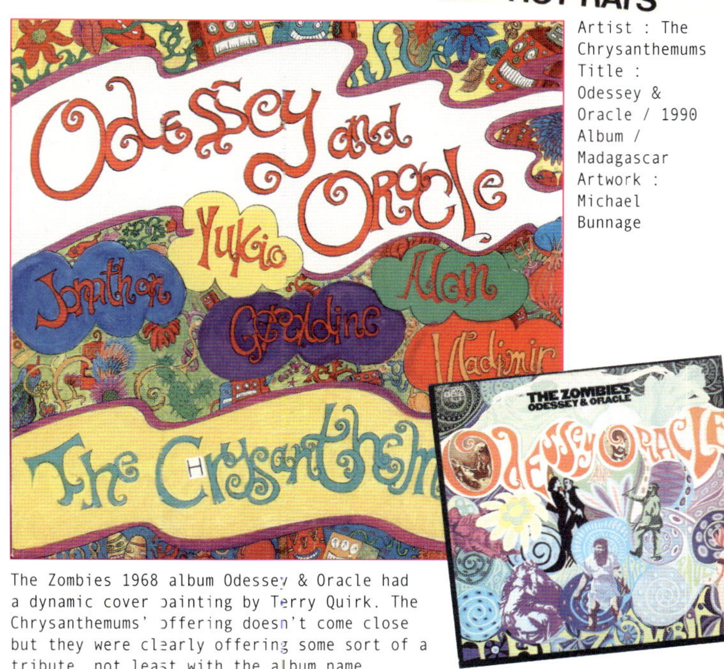

Artist : The
Chrysanthemums
Title :
Odessey &
Oracle / 1990
Album /
Madagascar
Artwork :
Michael
Bunnage

The Zombies 1968 album Odessey & Oracle had a dynamic cover painting by Terry Quirk. The Chrysanthemums' offering doesn't come close but they were clearly offering some sort of a tribute, not least with the album name.

INDEX

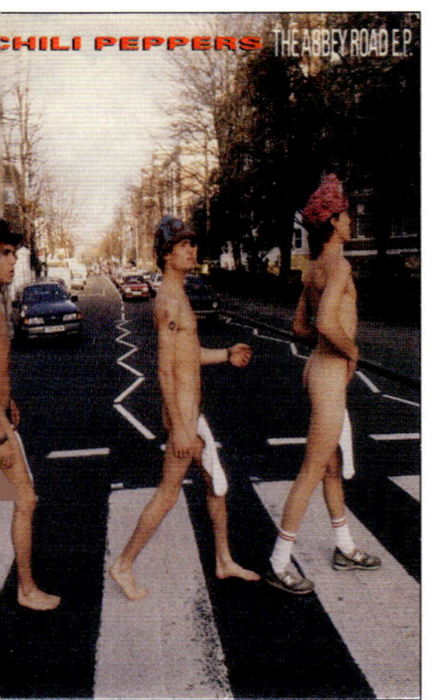

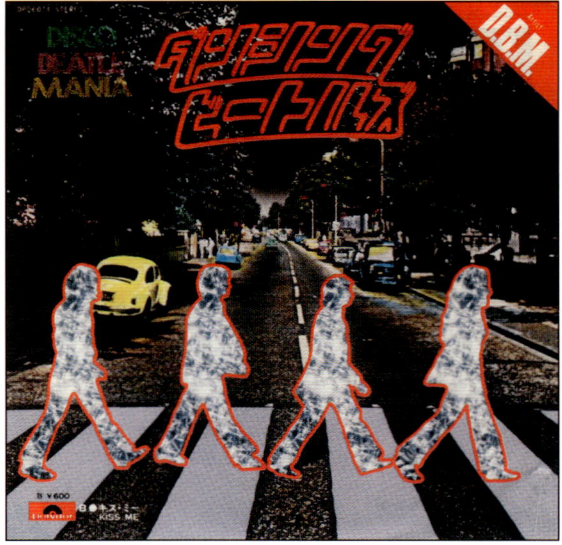

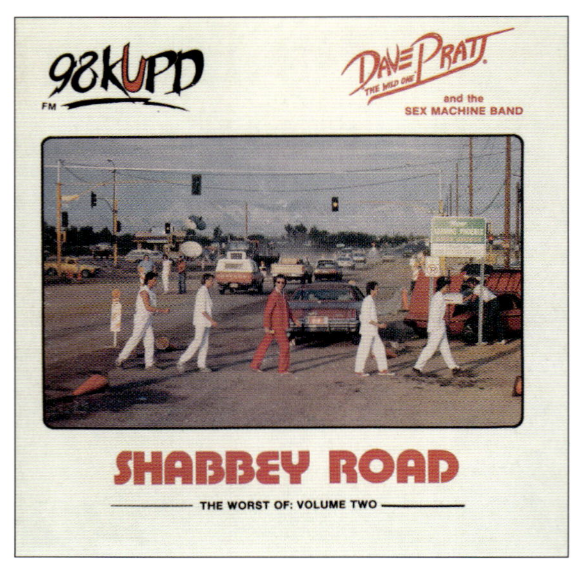

This page : D.B.M. : Disco Beatle Mania 45 [1977, Polydor. Artwork : Unknown] / Dave Pratt & The Sex Machine Band : Shabbey Road [1985, 98 KUPD Records. Artwork, photo : Mick Paladin] /

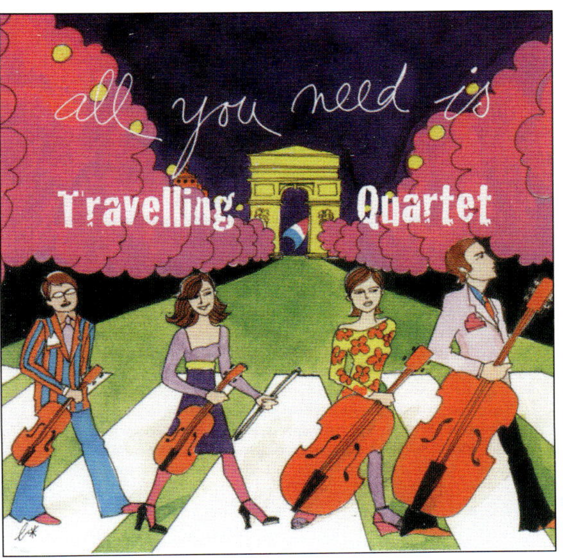

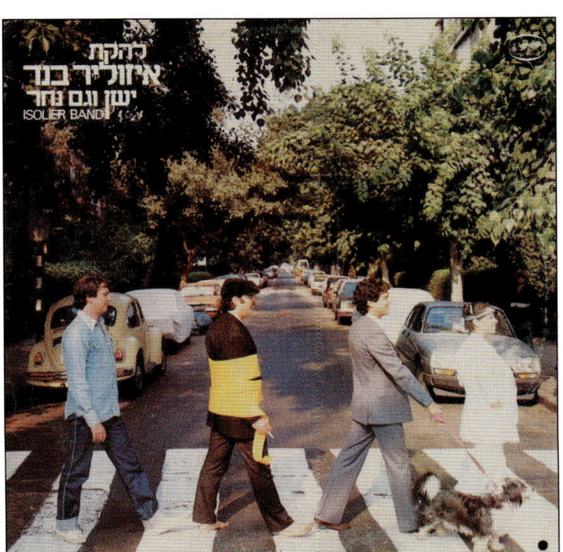

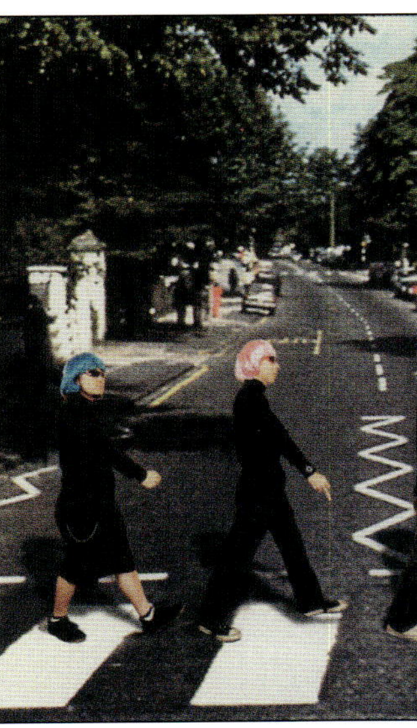

This page : Travelling Quartet : All You Need Is [2010, Integral Distribution.
Artwork : Blonde-fauchee] / Isolier Band : Isolier Band [1982, Israel Record.
Artwork : Unknown] / Nicotine : Hey Dude! We Love The Beatles [2005, Sky Records.
Artwork : Akio Hikasa, photo : Shigeo Kikuchi]

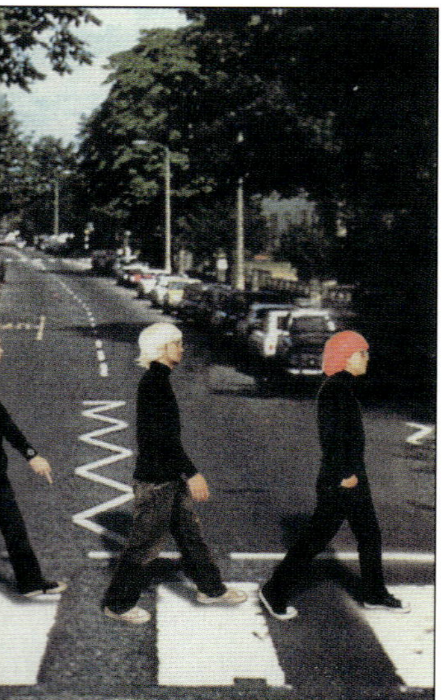

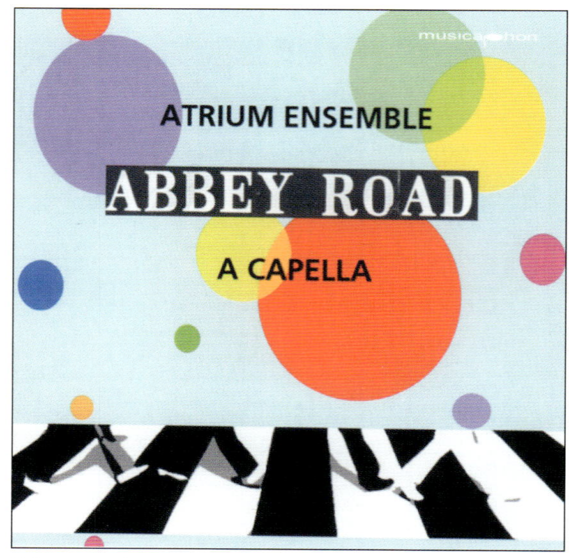

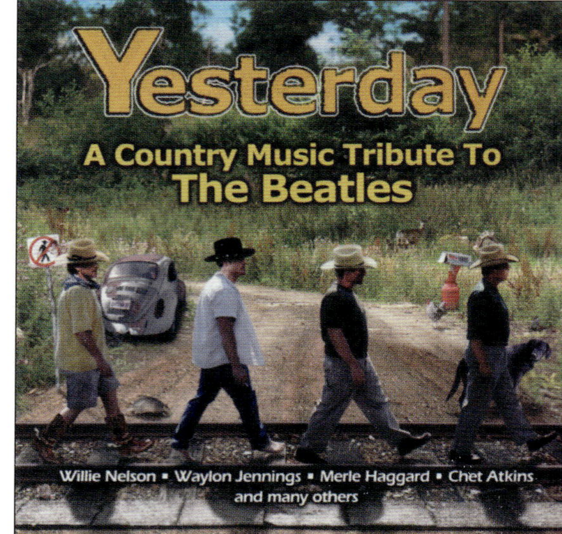

This page : Atrium Ensemble : Abbey Road - A Capella [2008, Musicaphon. Artwork : Irene Suhr] / Various Artists : Yesterday - A Country Music Tribute To The Beatles [2005, Sterling - Sony. Artwork : MMV Sterling Entertainment Group]

www.S‾33.wordpress.com

is devoted to the art of the record sleeve

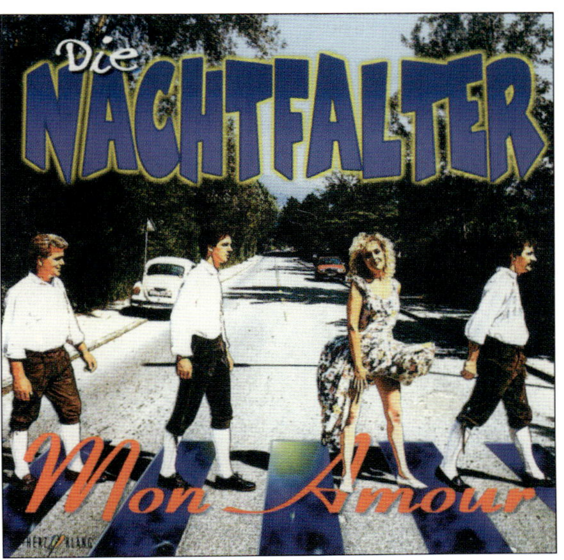
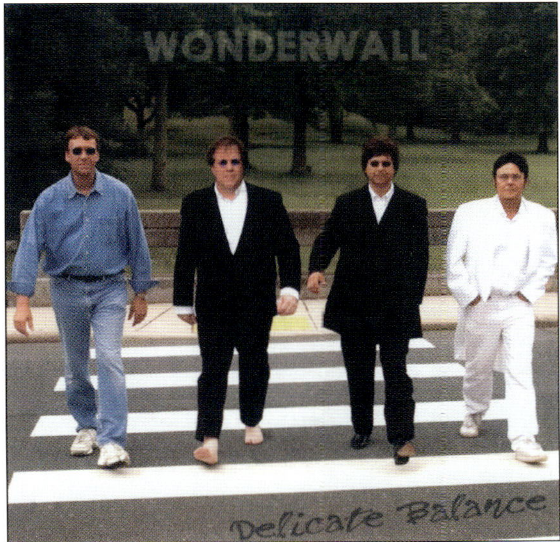

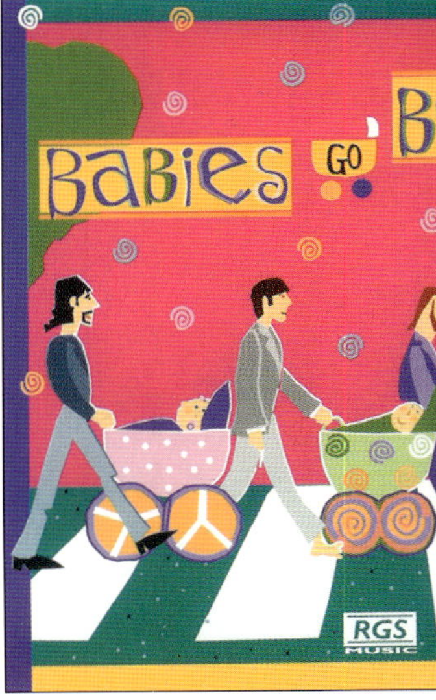

This page : Die Nachtfalter : Mon Amour [1995, Herz Klang - Sony. Artwork : Alfred F. Bina. Photo : Adolf Bereuter] / Wonderwall : Delicate Balance [2007, Neon Pie Records. Artwork : Marc Diffendal, Ronald Tucker. Photo : Mike Hill] / Babies Go Beatles : Babies Go Beatles [2002, RGS Music. Artwork : Sergio Eisen, Leticia Sordo]

FORTHCOMING EASY BOOKS

The titles below are in preparation, in matching size and format to this volume. More details and up to date information on these and other titles can be found at www.easyontheeyebooks.wordpress.com. There are also special posters and associated material available. Electronic editions are also planned. We are always interested in hearing from other collectors who may have ideas for future titles, please contact us via the website.
We would much prefer customers to order from their local bookshop and help support them. Our website has distribution details for shops. In case of difficulty we have our own online store. Please be aware that the big online retailers demand massive discounts of publishers which are especially damaging to small independent publishers, bookshops and specialist retailers.

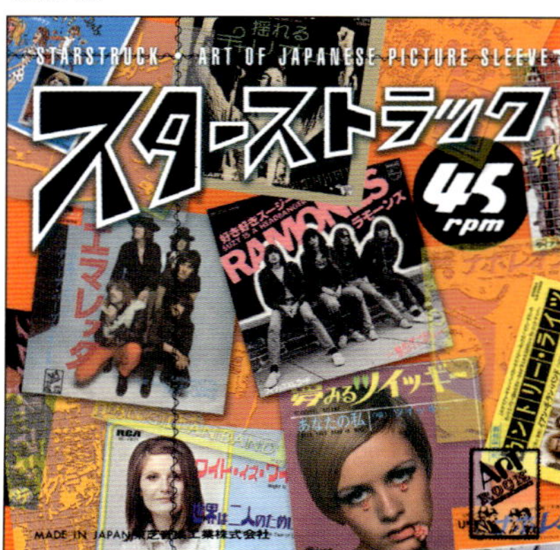

STARSTRUCK
Art of Japanese Single Sleeve : Volume 1

ISBN: 978-0-9561439-0-7

Japan was one of the first countries to issue vinyl singles in special sleeves, so when licensing Western pop and rock they were free to do their own covers. The resulting blend of Western images and exotic Japanese typography and design was visually unique. When these unique Japanese sleeves finally came to the attention of music fans outside the country, their exclusivity, the rare pictures and the unlikely coupling of tracks not issued on single elsewhere saw them become very collectable. This book presents a visually stunning selection of 7" covers from the sixties to the eighties which will interest collectors, music fans and designers, with close on a thousand sleeves in full colour and is the first survey of Japanese sleeves outside the country.
While many of the biggest European, British and American bands are included, numerous cult and downright obscure acts are also featured; the emphasis being squarely on the visual look of the single. A comprehensive written introduction to the book gives the background to the Japanese singles industry, the way the designs developed, and other details. There is a full index of all the artists featured.

WHEN COVER GIRLS RULED THE CHARTS
The Story of the Top Of The Pops Albums

ISBN: 978-0-9561439-1-4

Anyone who went to a disco or party in the seventies will remember the Top Of The Pops albums, budget priced monthly collections of chart hits with a difference - these were all cover versions! With their cheap but memorable typography, and colourful sleeves featuring sexy models (all illustrated inside), the albums were affordable for one good reason - they were cut by session musicians, chosen for their ability to get as close to the real thing as possible.
Major record labels didn't want to cheapen their big acts by selling the rights to reissue hits of the day, and cover versions were a way forward. Hallmark quickly set the standards with their Top Of The Pops collections.
They went on to sell hundreds of thousands of albums, and became so successful that industry bigwigs had them banned from the charts!
This is the first book to tell the story of how the albums came about, the singers who cut their teeth on them, and looks at the heroic efforts of the session players. Twenty years after the final volume, the colourful and kitschy sleeves have made these albums very collectable (mail-order only special edition also planned).

GO HOME ON A POSTCARD
The Story of Walking Pictures

ISBN: 978-0-9561439-5-2

This book looks at the now largely vanished trade of Walking Pictures, informal street portraits of people taken around Britain's coastal resorts between 1920 and 1960. Unlike formal studio photographs, or even our own snaps, these images are unique - capturing people in everyday life, largely unaware that they were going to be snapped. Having taken the photo, the cameraman would hand over a ticket, and the resulting postcard portrait would be ready to collect later in the day. The core of the book, the first to look at this undocumented area of portrait photography in detail, is a fascinating selection of previously unpublished images of the British public spanning four decades. The changing fashions of the time and the mass of incidental detail in the photographs add to the interest, documenting differences in class and social standing. The images are supported by detailed captions, a history of Walking Pictures and details some of the firms who took them.
This book has already prompted a lot of interest. There has been an exhibition in Bridlington, BBC Radio 4 have featured the project on Making History, and numerous magazines have run pieces on the subject.

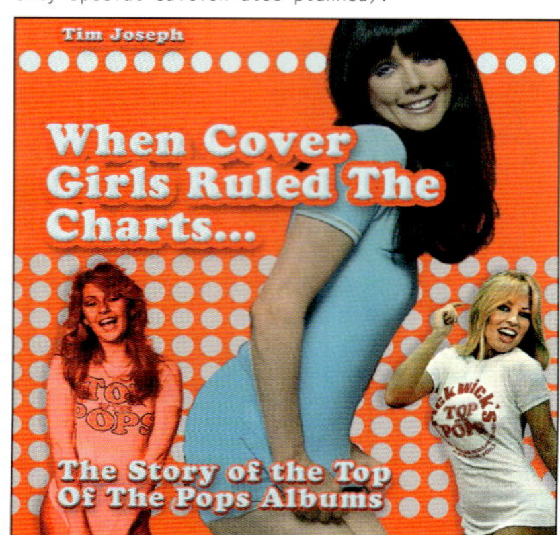

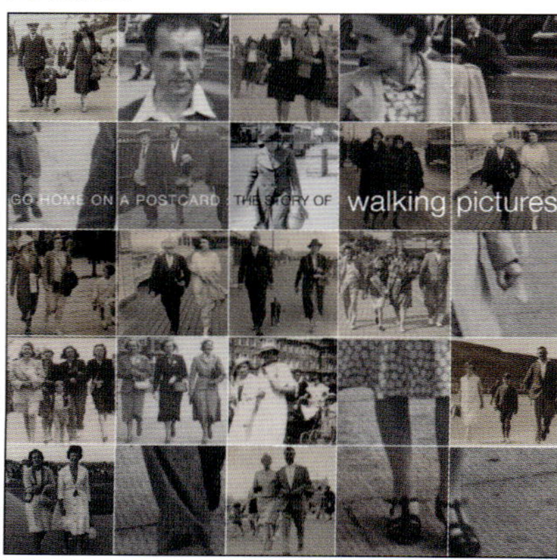

COMPILER PROFILE

JAN BELLEKENS / Compiled the collection + annotated the sleeves

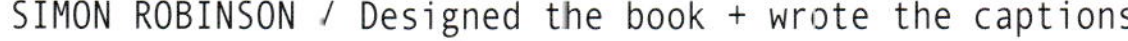

Jan Bellekens purchased his first record at the age of 10 - and hasn't stopped since. His first steps in the media business were in the eighties as a presenter for free radio station FM Bruxel (an alternative / new-wave / punk / rock station).

Later Jan became a music-producer for Belgian national radio (BRT/VRT) as well as for Studio Brussel, Radio Donna and RVI (Radio Vlaanderen Internationaal) radio stations.

For several years he also worked as a roadie/lighting-engineer for Belgium's famous Flemish-rock band De Kreuners and was also involved in the production of a number of Belgian TV-programs: Hitquiz, De Drie Wijzen, Het Swingpaleis, De Muziekquiz, Nonkel Pop (a local version of Never Mind The Buzzcocks).

Jan has since done projects for several independent production TV houses including Tubbax TV and IDTV, where he worked closely with Zaki (father of the famous Dewaele Brothers/2 Many DJ's/Soulwax). More recently he worked for the Belgian multimedia chain/record store Extrazone, until they closed in 2010. *Photo : Janie Bellekens.*

SIMON ROBINSON / Designed the book + wrote the captions

Simon Robinson began working in the print industry after studying at Manchester College of Graphic Design, at a time when local punk and new wave bands were sneaking in to put together their own sleeves. He began freelancing on a variety of design work. After early commissions for 4AD (their second ever single release), Harvest and local labels he has since designed hundreds of CD packages, many for the much admired reissue label RPM, who pioneered the use of large fold out CD inlays - several releases being awarded CD of the month status in Record Collector magazine and elsewhere.

More recently Simon has run a reactivated Purple Records as well as working on packaging designs for EMI, Sanctuary, Westside, Connoisseur, Warners, VAP and other labels. His packaging for the anniversary edition of the Deep Purple album Burn was voted 'best reissue of 2004' in Classic Rock magazine, and a 6CD box set he designed was a close runner up to 'best box set of the year' in Record Collector and Mojo Magazine in 2003.

DIRK THEYS / Photographed the majority of the sleeves.

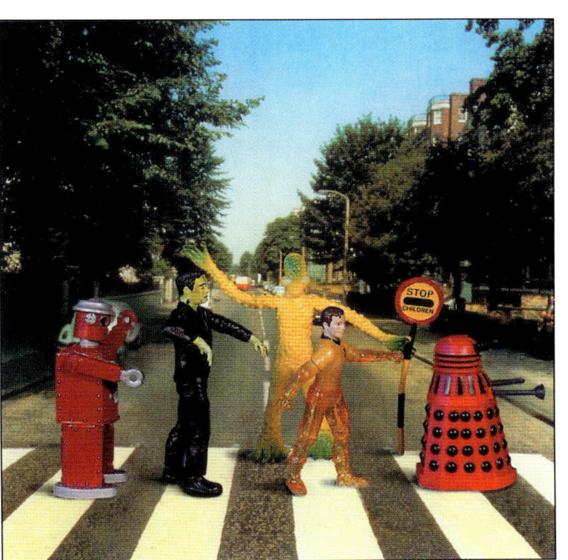

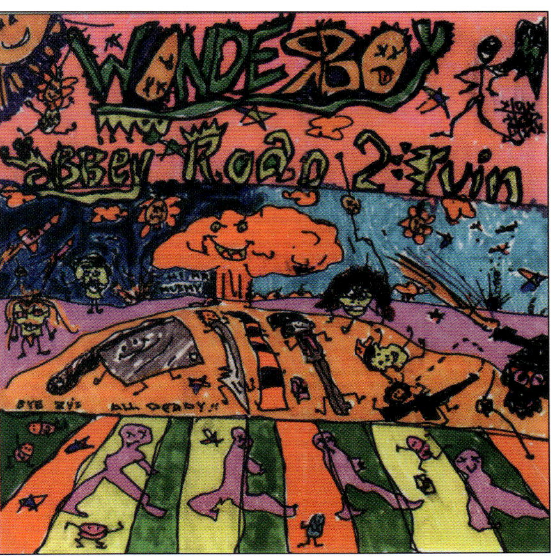

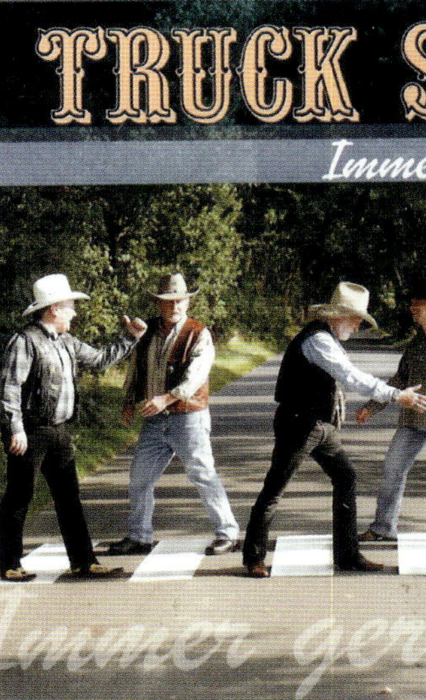

This page : Various Artists : The Exotic Beatles [1999, Exotica Records. Artwork : Jim Phelan. Photo : Victor Napolski] / Wonderboy : Abbey Road To Ruin [1994, Racer Records. Artwork : Bart Flynn, Kristi Wachter] / Truck Stop : Immer Geradeaus [2006, Sony Music. Artwork : Sony. Photo : Redpoint Image Factory]

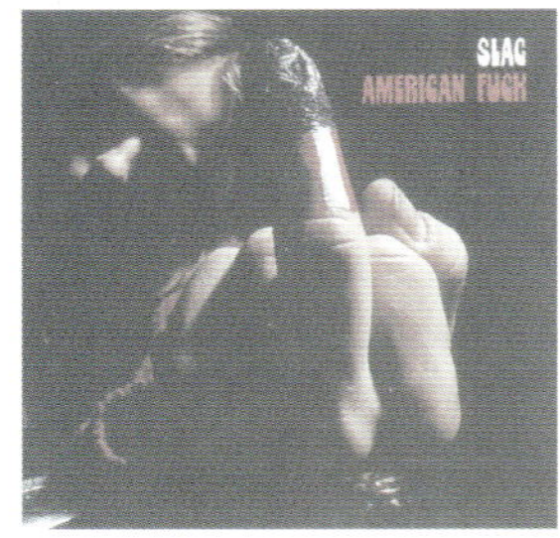

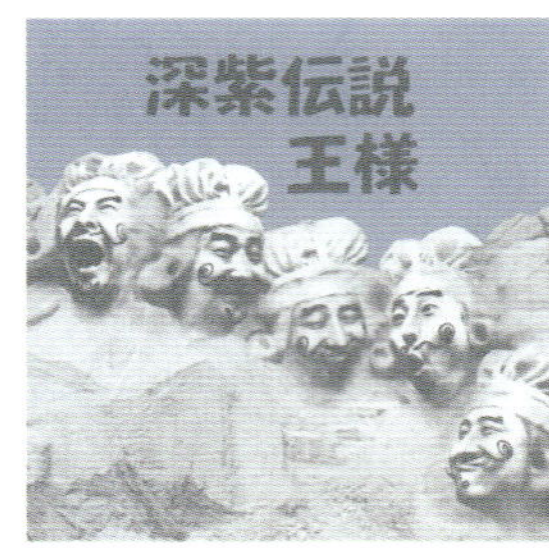

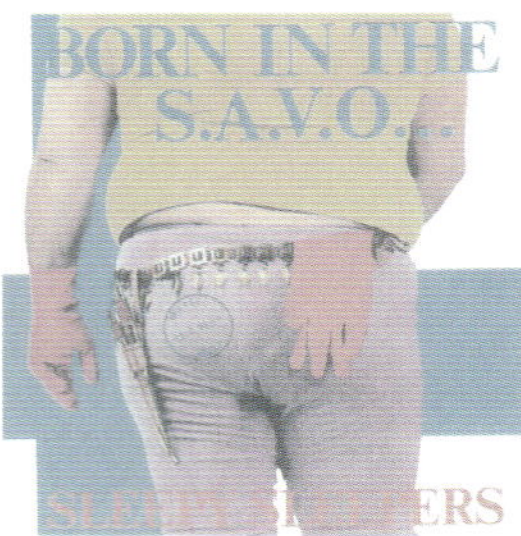

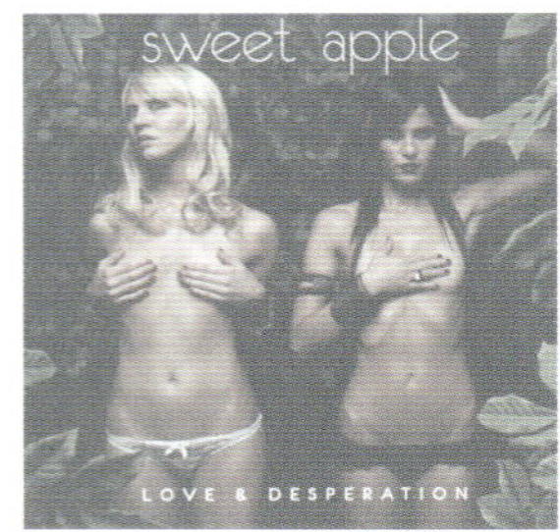

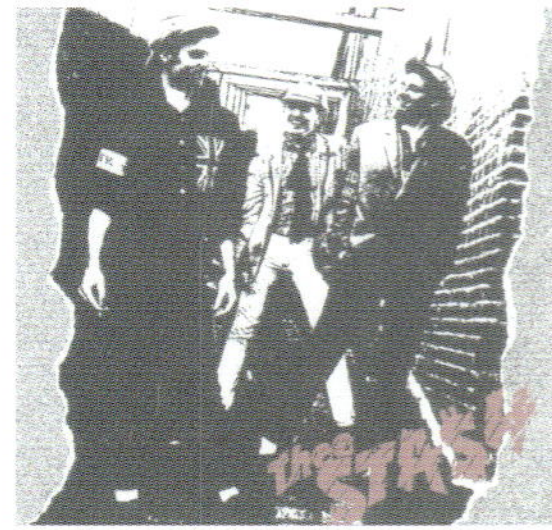

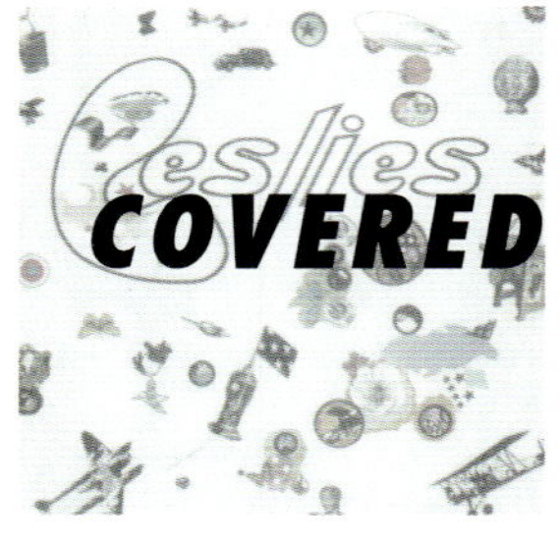

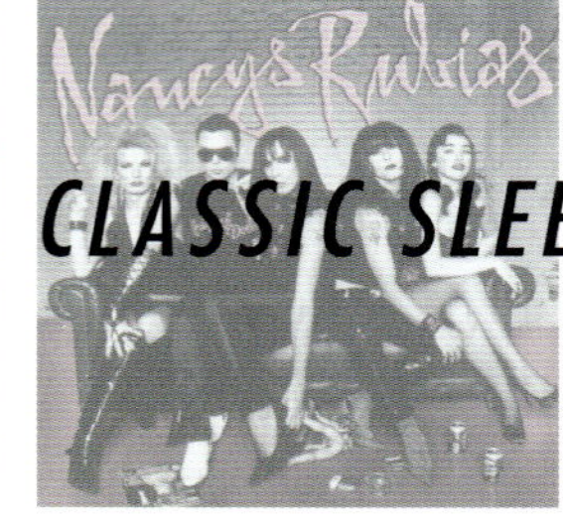

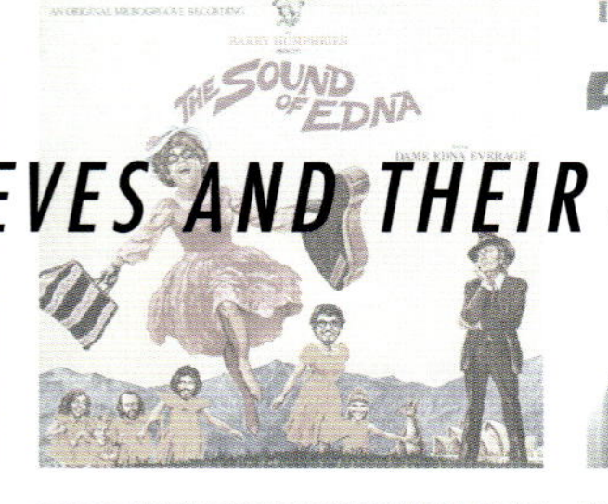

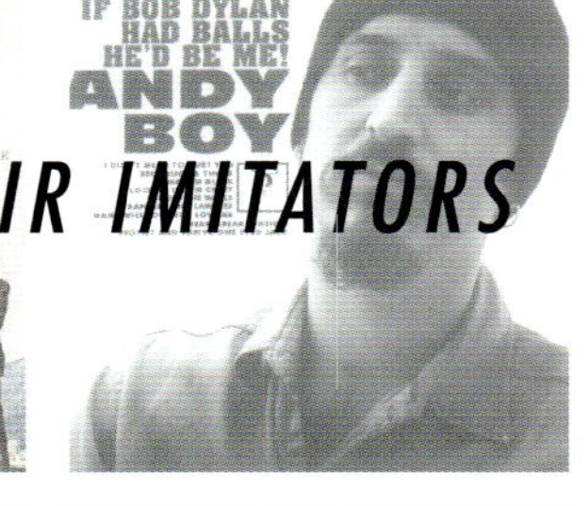

COVERED *CLASSIC SLEEVES AND THEIR IMITATORS*

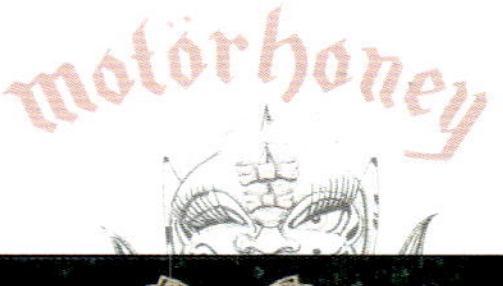

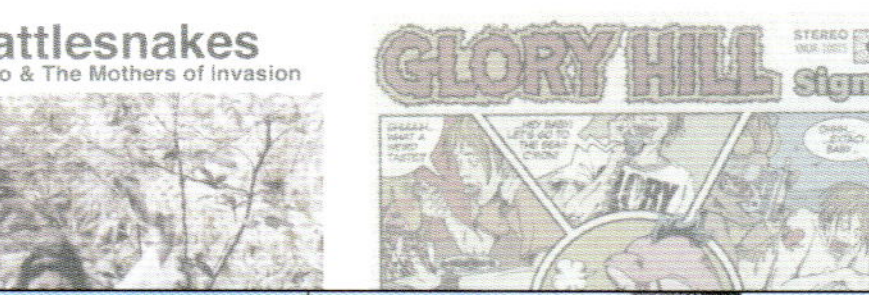

GLORY HILL

AUTOMATICS
GO BANANAS!

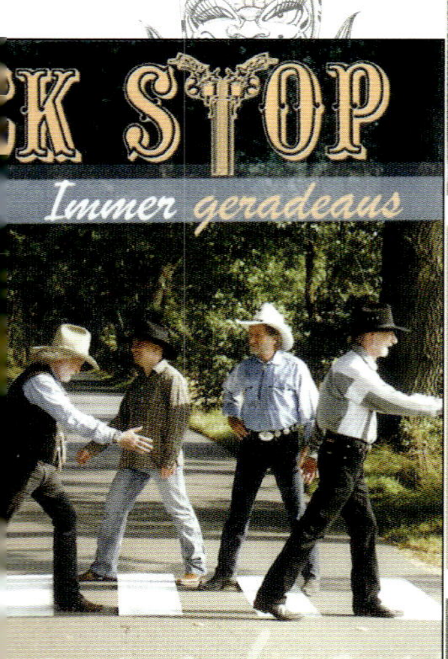

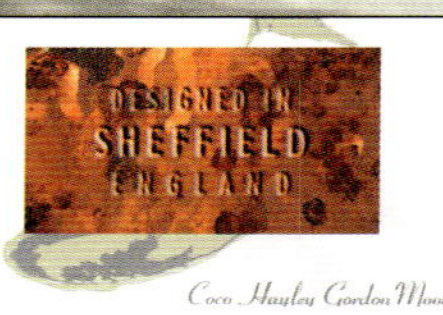

Coco Hayley Gordon Moore

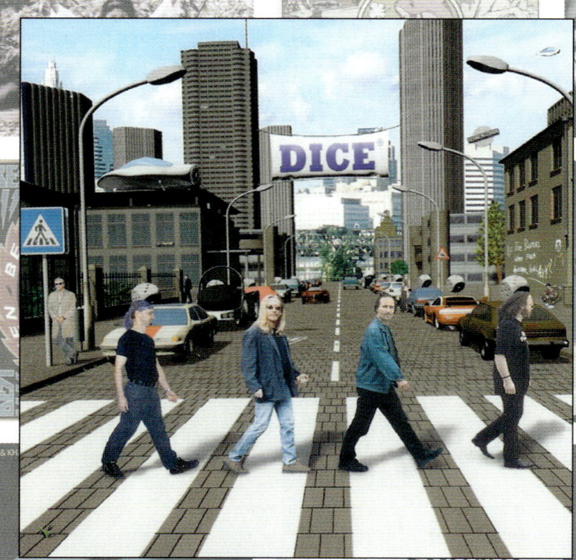

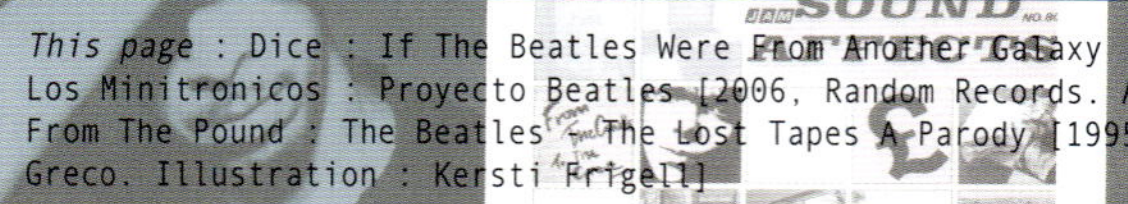

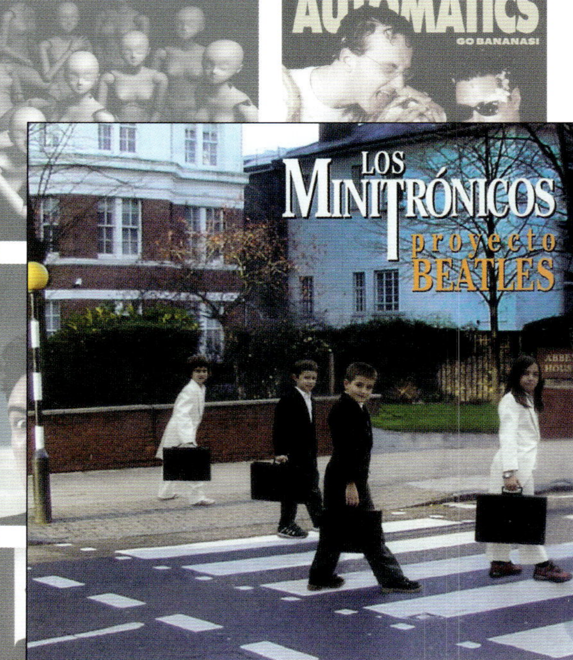

This page : Dice : If The Beatles Were From Another Galaxy [2004, Scene Records. Artwork : Mr. Tif] / Los Minitronicos : Proyecto Beatles [2006, Random Records. Artwork : Artico. Photo : Alfredo] / Live From The Pound : The Beatles – The Lost Tapes A Parody [1995, Dove Records. Artwork : Susie Dotan, Tony Greco. Illustration : Kersti Frigell]